Ronald Taylor is Professor of German in the University of Sussex. He has been Visiting Professor at the University of Chicago, at Northwestern University and at the University of British Columbia, and has lectured widely on literary and musical topics at universities in Britain, Germany, the United States and Canada. Among his previous books are *Richard Wagner: His Life, Art and Thought*, *The Romantic Tradition in Germany* and *The Art of the Minnesinger*. He has contributed articles on music to various cultural journals, is a well-known translator of German literature, and has played piano music on BBC and German radio.

By the same author

E. T. A. Hoffmann
The Art of the Minnesinger
The Romantic Tradition in Germany
The Intellectual Tradition of Modern Germany
Richard Wagner: His Life, Art and Thought
Literature and Society in Germany 1918–1945

RONALD TAYLOR

Robert Schumann

His Life and Work

PANTHER
Granada Publishing

Panther Books
Granada Publishing Ltd
8 Grafton Street, London W1X 3LA

Published by Panther Books 1985

First published in Great Britain by
Granada Publishing 1982

Copyright © Ronald Taylor 1982

ISBN 0-586-05883-4

Printed and bound in Great Britain by
Collins, Glasgow

Set in Times

Contents

List of Plates		9
Preface		11
1	The Security of Youth	17
2	Reluctant Student	41
3	The World of Butterflies	62
4	Literature and Music	89
5	Masks and Realities	108
6	Clara	132
7	'Hail wedded love, mysterious law . . .'	161
8	'Liederjahr'	184
9	The Classic and the Romantic	201
10	Uncertain Intermezzo	234
11	Disintegration and Death	281
Postscript		329
A Note on Sources		335
Bibliography		340
Index		347

For Mark and Diana

List of Plates

1 Zwickau: a mid-19th-century engraving. *Robert Schumann Haus, Zwickau.*

2 Dresden: a contempory print. *RSH, Zwickau.*

3 Schumann's earliest extant letter. *RSH, Zwickau.*

4 Clara Wieck, aged 15. *RSH, Zwickau.*

5 Schumann: portrait by Kriehuber. *RSH, Zwickau.*

6 Robert and Clara Schumann. *Stadtarchiv Bonn.*

7 Schumann's original score for 'The Merry Peasant'. *RSH, Zwickau.*

8 The Leipzig Gewandhaus. *RSH, Zwickau.*

9 Schumann, from a daguerrotype. *RSH, Zwickau.*

10 Carl Jäger's portrait of Schumann. *Mansell Collection.*

11 Schumann's children. *Stadtarchiv Düsseldorf.*

12 Inselstrasse No. 15, Leipzig. *RSH, Zwickau.*

13 Bilker Strasse, Düsseldorf. *Stadtarchiv Düsseldorf.*

14 Drawing of Schumann by Jean-Joseph-Bonaventure Laurens, 1853, *Musée de Carpentras, France.*

15 Chorale ('When my hour of parting comes'). *RSH, Zwickau.*

16 The asylum in Endenich. *Stadtarchiv Bonn.*

Preface

So unforgettable are the crucial moments in Robert Schumann's sad life, so familiar the works that have given him his inimitable place in the musical affections of the world, that one is tempted to take the relationship between his life and his art for granted, to leave the unity of his psychological and creative worlds unexamined and unchallenged. Successive biographies have tended to repeat, and re-repeat, often with scant reference to original sources and little fresh analysis of the evidence, the story told by their predecessors. His works have been described and analysed, re-described and re-analysed, subservient to the law of diminishing returns. But it is some while since a fresh attempt was made to integrate his intellectual and musical activity into the framework of his material and psychological life as a whole, an attempt to blend a 'life and times' drawn mainly from contemporary sources with a characterization of the way his art emerged from that life and related to those times.

In these pages I have tried to do something of this kind. For the biographical narrative I have gone back to Schumann's and Clara's diaries and letters, the testimony of those who knew him, both the famous and the forgotten, and the chronicles of contemporary events. I have also sought to trace early articles in journals which have become less easy to find since the end of the Second World War. Many of these, like the primary material in Schumann's and Clara's hands, especially from the early and middle years of his life, are stored in the archive of the Robert-

Schumann-Haus in Zwickau. For his last years the city of Düsseldorf, above all its Stadtmuseum and Heinrich-Heine-Institut, holds a large number of personalia, including letters and music manuscripts.

With a pedantic tidy-mindedness that surprises many whose vision of him is that of the impulsive, unpredictable 'romantic', Schumann recorded in his 'Briefbuch' the receipt of 4770 items of correspondence and the despatch of 2446 of his own. The fate of many of these is unknown: not even all those extant have been published, and so scattered are they that a complete edition is hardly conceivable. And while those published by F. Gustav Jansen (*Briefe. Neue Folge*, Leipzig, 1886) are impeccably reproduced, the selected *Jugendbriefe* released by Clara Schumann in 1885 are edited with an arbitrariness which, uncorrected, would leave a very imperfect image of their subject. His conductor's notebooks, relating to his work in Dresden and Düsseldorf, also await publication. Of the planned three-volume edition of his various diaries undertaken by the Robert-Schumann-Haus in Zwickau only Volume I, covering the years 1827 to 1838, has appeared (1971), while Volume II, spanning seventeen years of his so-called 'Haushaltsbücher', is announced for 1982. Clara's diaries for her married years have disappeared and are generally assumed to have been destroyed by her daughters after her death, so that we can only call upon the excerpts quoted in Berthold Litzmann's biography of her.

In one sense the record is thus very imperfect. In another, one might suppose that there is sufficient material, published and unpublished, taken together with the evidence of others and the implications of circumstance, for us to form a rounded picture of his private and creative personality, acceptably complete in scope, acceptably accurate in detail, and above all acceptably true in spirit.

But in practice it proves disconcertingly otherwise. For one thing the personal evidence from Schumann's own hand – in contrast to Wagner, for example – is disappointingly flat and non-committal: places visited, people seen, money spent, books read and music heard, lists of compositions planned, started or completed – such things cannot reveal the heart of the man. Nor can his scattered effusions on his musical ideals or his public activities. Only in his early letters to his mother and to Clara, written in his twenties, does he allow us to glimpse his intimate world of thought and feeling, and even these glimpses tend to be of the anxieties of the moment – professional, practical, emotional.

Above all, however, the problem lies in the personality of the man himself, a complex personality that yields no simple, harmonious pattern of development either in its psychology or in its creativity. The disharmonies are part of the pattern – one could even say they dominate it – and the biographer cannot but record what he finds. At the same time one is bound to seek an encompassing context, or series of contexts, for events and achievements, a framework within which to demonstrate at least a measure of cause and effect in order to come closer to the heart of the subject.

Thus in relating the story of Schumann's life I have sought both to uncover the psychology of his creative processes and to portray the nineteenth-century scene which sets the context for his work. Schumann was a creature of the romantic age, in many ways an epitome of the associations of the word Romanticism. He grew up under the spell of German romantic authors like Jean Paul and E.T.A. Hoffmann, inherited the world of romantic idealism, lived through the liberal romantic revolution of 1848 and composed a multitude of beautiful Lieder to the texts of German romantic poets. Indeed – to turn the subject round – one could make him, as one can make Richard Wagner, or Henrich Heine, or Caspar David Friedrich, a case-study in German romanticism, its essence and its implications.

Each biographer is bound to make his own use of the evidence he finds, and earlier writers on Schumann, the man and the composer, have set the emphases where they considered they belonged, just as I have. However, I have not wished to cross swords with my predecessors at every point where my views differed from theirs, and I have avoided personalizing such differences. Indeed, I would rather record my indebtedness to the earlier writers whose works I have read, irrespective of whether my judgements agree with theirs or not.

Since it is Schumann as man and creative artist who stands in the centre of the picture, my concern with his musical works has been with their significance as events in his spiritual biography rather than as objects for historico-musical analysis. In trying to uncover the personal and artistic impulses that determined the pattern of his creative life, I have found a greater relevance, for example, in the changes of title a work might undergo in the course of its composition, or in the psychology of his leaps from one poet to another in his search for texts to set, than in thematic character, key relationship, the influence of other composers and similar immanent musical details. This too has widened the context of the book in its own way.

Mutatis mutandis I have confined purely musical analysis to the aim of showing how Schumann's thoughts developed at a particular moment, and it is with this in mind that I must ask for the indulgence of those who feel that I should have mentioned each and every work he composed and subjected it to an inner-musical critique. But I did not set out to write a book of this kind. Indeed, I could have done little more in this direction than has already been done by the contributors to the symposia edited by Gerald Abraham and Alan Walker, by Eric Sams in his book on Schumann's songs, by Wolfgang Bötticher and other scholars.

Inevitably, however, I have found myself moving towards an interpretation of the nature and tendency of Schumann's music as such, an interpretation that has emerged from the total picture that I have tried to give of the man, his mind and his world. This picture amounts in essence to the dichotomy in Schumann between the principles of classicism and romanticism, a polarity in terms of which so much nineteenth-century art, and especially, perhaps, music, can be defined, or at least adumbrated.

Not that I have wanted just to 'use' Schumann's music as an excuse for a general discussion on such abstract matters. But these issues have arisen involuntarily from the central figure in the story. He poses them himself – sometimes explicitly, always implicitly – in his writings as in his music. I hope that my readers will accept the legitimacy of the wider framework of discussion that this approach brings with it.

Equally insistent in any Schumann biography is the question of the relationship between the deterioration of his mental condition and the quality of his music. Whereas many nineteenth-century observers, from men as different as Eduard Hanslick and Tchaikovsky onwards, found a striking decline in his compositions from the time he left Leipzig for Dresden, and unhesitatingly linked this decline with the onset of the disintegration of his mind, a more recent school of thought has maintained that there is no such link, and has tried to rescue these later works from what they regard as a prejudiced oblivion.

It has been neither my purpose nor my desire to take specific issue with writers of either the one or the other persuasion, or to add my own glosses to their opinions. But again, in laying out the narrative and musical evidence, I have found the argument pointing in a particular direction, a direction which, having reached that point, I could hardly refuse to follow. Although many – especially, I suspect, critics and others in the music industry – may well challenge my interpretations and approach, and dispute my judgements, I have tried to present such judgements as the linear consequence of the events and considerations I describe, not just as blunt, unsubstantiated, even prejudiced conclusions.

For the rest, it is my hope that this attempt at a full biography, part domestic, part intellectual, will present a coherent picture of this profoundly unhappy but profoundly significant genius of nineteenth-century German culture. Schumann commands attention for a number of different reasons and from people of differing interests. If I have held most of my readers' attention for most of the time, I shall be content.

It is my pleasure to thank the British Academy for offering me a grant to study material at the Robert-Schumann-Haus in Zwickau, the Deutsche Staatsbibliothek, Berlin, and the Heinrich-Heine-Institut in Düsseldorf. In the same connection I should like to record my gratitude to the Robert-Schumann-Haus itself, in particular to Dr Gerd Nauhaus, for giving me access to their archives and for allowing me to photograph pictures, manuscripts and documents in their possession. The staff of the Music Library of the University of London were also very helpful to me. My sincere thanks are due to Miss Jenny Vowles for helping me to read the proofs and for making critical suggestions from which the text has greatly profited, while to Mrs Elisabeth Lord, Frau Doris Brock and Mrs Rita Goldman, who shared the typing of my manuscript, I owe a special debt of gratitude.

Finally a warm thank-you to Richard Johnson of Granada Publishing for his help in steering the book through production.

R.T.
Berlin

CHAPTER ONE

The Security of Youth

It was a comfortable home into which Schumann was born, a cultured family where aesthetic values and pursuits of the mind had their established place. True, neither of his parents had the gifts to guide his first practical steps in music as Johann Ambrosius Bach, Leopold Mozart and Franz Theodor Schubert gave their famous sons their earliest musical instruction. Nor was music the art that meant most to the family, as it was in Chopin's home, or in Mendelssohn's.

But it was a zealously literary household, a household of books and scholarship – an old house on the corner of the market square in Zwickau in Saxony. Here on 8 June 1810 Schumann was born. In the lofty Gothic Marienkirche, with its superb vaulting and its famous retable by Dürer's teacher Michael Wohlgemuth, he received the names Robert Alexander at the ornate Renaissance font that still stands there today. His mother appears on the baptism certificate simply as 'Christiane Schumann *née* Schnabel', his father as 'Herr August Schumann, bookseller and worthy burgher of this town'. Already in the family were Emilie, rising fourteen, and three boys – Eduard, aged eleven, Karl, aged nine, and Julius, five. A sixth child, a girl christened Laura, had been stillborn the previous year. August Schumann was thirty-seven, his wife in her early forties (the exact date of her birth is unknown) when Robert was born.

The mother of the family, Johanna Christiane Schumann, was the eldest daughter of Abraham Gottlieb Schnabel, chief surgeon

(Ratschirurg) to the municipal authorities of Zeitz, a town some forty miles south of Leipzig. 'A straightforward and unassuming person,' as she described herself, 'with no desire to appear other than she is', Christiane enjoyed a happy marriage and the relaxed affection of her children. With her husband's help she used to practise operatic arias, and it was at her instigation, she later recalled with pride, that the seven-year-old Robert had his first piano lessons. Her education may have been, in her words, 'of a highly moral nature and of no great cultural standard', and she played only a subsidiary role in the development of his gifts, but her letters reveal an earnest affection and a lively imagination which passed into the personality of her youngest son.

His father August, by contrast, dominated the intellectual and cultural life of the family from the beginning. Far from being remembered only as the father of a famous son, he has his own fame as author and publisher and earned his personal entry in the *Universal-Lexicon aller Wissenschaften und Künste*, the most comprehensive German encyclopedia of cultural and scientific knowledge in the nineteenth century. Son of a Protestant pastor in the village of Endschütz, near Gera, he received a reasonable school education by eighteenth-century standards and was apprenticed at the age of fifteen to a merchant in the little Saxon town of Ronneburg. Even at school he had started to write poetry, and as his interest in literature grew, so also did his dissatisfaction with the life of a shop assistant.

In 1791, when he was eighteen, he wrote a drama of country life called *Die Familie Thalheim* and sent it to a publisher, who said he would print it if the author turned it into a short story. This August immediately did, which earned him his first literary fee. With this and some other money he had scraped together he gave up his job and enrolled as a student of philosophy at the University of Leipzig. But his funds quickly ran out and he was forced to leave. He had just finished a new novel, a piece of 'Gothic' romanticism called *Rittersszenen und Mönchsmärchen (Scenes of Chivalry and Monkish Tales)*, which he sent to a writer in Zeitz called Heinse, inviting his criticism. Heinse was about to open a bookstore in the town, and though disparaging in his comments about the novel, offered its young author a job as clerk in the new bookstore.

This launched August Schumann's career in its decisive direction. Within eighteen months he wrote seven more novels and various other works which together earned him a total of almost 1,000 thalers.* In 1795, at the age of twenty-two, he married Christiane Schnabel, whom he had met in Zeitz, went back with her to Ronneburg and four years later opened his own publishing and bookselling business there. He now turned to the compilation of reference books – a geographical survey of German trades and industries, a trade directory, and aids to the study of foreign languages, among them a French-German dictionary and a *Repertorio della letteratura Italiana*. In 1808, seeking a larger market for his business, he moved with his wife and four children to Zwickau, two years before Robert was born. Here, in partnership with his brother Friedrich, he established the *Verlagsbuchhandlung* of the 'Gebrüder Schumann', living first on the market square, Am Markt No. 5, then at Amtsgasse No. 2, the house in which Robert spent the greater part of his youth. The firm survived under its original name until 1940, well after the family association with it had passed.

In Zwickau, where he spent the rest of his life in comfortable and secure financial circumstances, August Schumann concentrated his energy as a writer on two areas of activity – the translation of modern European classics and the investigation of the history and geography of his native Saxony. He translated Sir Walter Scott, Byron and Bulwer Lytton, founded two periodicals devoted to regional Saxon interests and embarked in 1814 on a massive encyclopedia of information on Saxony called *Vollständiges Staats-, Post- und Zeitungslexikon von Sachsen*. This he left unfinished at his death in 1826, and it was eventually completed in eighteen volumes in 1833. All these works he published and sold through his own firm, which made a particular

---

*More realistic than trying to put a modern equivalent on such a sum is to assess its purchasing power at the time. 800 thalers, for example, was considered a good salary for a civil servant; a fair-sized family apartment could be rented for 12 thalers per month, and two furnished rooms for 4 thalers per month. Schiller said that an unmarried man of his class could live in Jena on 270 thalers a month, and in Dresden on 400 thalers a month. 1 thaler = 24 groschen.

name for itself with an attractively produced pocket edition of European classics – Scott, Byron, Alfieri, Calderon, Cervantes and others – together with Goethe, Schiller, Lessing and other German authors. A collection of these little volumes is on display in the rebuilt family house, Schumann's birthplace, which today houses a Schumann museum and an archive of valuable material.

Serious and reserved, a man to whom work mattered more than all else and who drove himself hard, August Schumann had the talent both of a creative writer and of an enlightened manager. At his death he left an impressive estate of 60,000 thalers, a sum which represented sixty times Robert's annual income at the time he married Clara Wieck. Emil Flechsig, a school friend of Robert's, who saw the family circumstances for himself, recalled later: 'I never saw him do anything but work. From 1817 onwards he became prosperous through the novels of Walter Scott, which he translated with great speed and circulated in thousands of copies'.

A writer of poetic imagination and a critic of acumen; a man with the urge both to raise the standards of art and broaden the base of its reception, and with the practical ability to mould his vision into reality: such characteristics, central to Robert Schumann's creative personality, had already manifested themselves in his father.

In the early 1800s, before the modern coal industry stamped its grimy personality on the landscape, Zwickau was a quiet little town of 900 houses and some 5,000 inhabitants. A Slav settlement in origin, it grew dramatically in the late fifteenth century with the discovery of silver in the nearby Schneeberg, and its finest buildings – the Marienkirche, designated a cathedral in 1932, the Katharinenkirche, the Gewandhaus (Clothmakers' Hall), turned into a theatre in 1823 and still used as such – date from the period. From 1520 to 1522 the Protestant reformer Thomas Münzer, spiritual leader of the Peasants' Revolt in 1525 and the first man in Germany to preach from the pulpit in the vernacular instead of in Latin, was pastor at the Katharinenkirche, where he helped to found the radical sect of the Anabaptists. The celebrated actress Caroline Neuber spent her youth in the town, and with the rise of Leipzig to a position of intellectual and cultural supremacy in Germany during the eighteenth century, the cultural life of the smaller towns in the Saxon kingdom, Zwickau among them, also became livelier. With its wealth of manufacturing industry and its trading interests, Protestant Saxony boasted over two hundred towns at this time, compared with a mere forty or so in her Catholic neighbour Bavaria, which had a population of a similar size.

As to Zwickau in the early nineteenth century, August Schumann describes it almost ecstatically in his *Saxon Encyclopedia*:

The town, together with its outlying areas, nestles in one of the most beautiful and romantic corners of Saxony, on the left bank of the River Mulde, among gardens, meadows and fertile fields. To the east, on the right bank of the river, there rises a gentle eminence known as the Brückenberg, from which one can see far out across the charming countryside, particularly attractive being the view over the town and beyond. To the west stands the Windberg, far bigger and higher, its upper slopes covered with woods and fields. Indeed, so rich in natural beauty is the whole area that one could fairly call it a park. The vegetation has everywhere a luxuriance that few other parts of Germany can surpass.

The political development of Saxony in the latter half of the eighteenth century under the respected rule of King Friedrich August had induced a phlegmatic tranquillity in the population at large. 'The composure with which they let you scold them is inconceivable', wrote Squire Morritt of Rokeby, a friend of Sir Walter Scott. 'If you were to spit in a man's face here, he would just wipe it off'. The people's general satisfaction with the *status quo* – a natural concomitant of rising prosperity – had as one of its significant social consequences that, of the larger German states, none was so little affected as Saxony by the French Revolution. This stability also induced the cultural atmosphere that led Dr Burney to write from Dresden, the Saxon capital, in 1772: 'This city has been regarded by the rest of Europe as the Athens of modern times'.

Yet the inhabitants of Zwickau in the early nineteenth century hardly found life the idyllic, undisturbed semi-paradise that August Schumann's description made it sound. Germany was in the grip of the Napoleonic wars. The coming and going of cavalry and men on foot, of baggage trains and artillery, became commonplace, and even areas many miles from the battlefront could not escape the rumbling passage of reinforcements, the shuffling columns of prisoners and the convoys of wounded. 'Most of the prisoners', wrote Dr Emil Herzog in his *Chronik der Kreisstadt Zwickau* of 1839, 'were in a lamentable state, starving, their clothes in tatters, many without shirts, shoes or stockings'. When Prince Jerome Bonaparte, one of Napoleon's younger brothers, was quartered in Zwickau shortly before Schumann's birth, over 16,000 troops flooded the town – more than three times the entire civilian population.

Besides the casualties of war there were the attendant miseries of disease, together with the social tensions created by martial law, especially the billeting of soldiers in private houses. The bodies of men and animals killed on the battlefield were thrown into the lakes and rivers; water supplies became polluted and epidemics of typhoid fever, bubonic plague and smallpox broke out. The police force also had to be strengthened, according to Herzog's *Chronicle*, 'in order to deal with the begging and with the general threat to safety in a situation which was almost out of control'.

Things were at their worst in 1813 as the first battered survivors of the once glorious Grande Armée trudged back into the town after the disastrous Russian campaign, followed by the king of Saxony and what was left of his contingent. Then came the Prussians, and after them a detachment of Cossacks. 'However', wrote Herzog in his *Chronicle*, 'all these men behaved themselves admirably. But they did have enormous appetites, and were especially eager for beer and brandy, which soon became quite unobtainable. Among other commodities herrings in particular rose in price, because the Russians, who were fasting and would not eat meat, demanded fish'.

As the year went on, the situation deteriorated still further:

Piles of severed arms and legs lay stacked up in front of the houses being used as hospitals, and it was not long before a virulent epidemic of typhus broke out in these dreadful places, spreading to the whole town and claiming the lives, among others, of two surgeons and three officials. The total number of civilian victims reached 376 (the previous year it had been only 183), and 380 soldiers died. The epidemic was at its worst in November and December, when not a single house or a single family escaped its clutches. And all the while endless columns of troops marched through the town.

Cultural life had to struggle to survive in times like these, and music, like all public arts of performance, particularly so. Church music, both vocal and instrumental, was at a low ebb. In the secular sphere much depended on the initiative of the *Stadtmusikus*, a municipal functionary with the responsibility inherited from the medieval musicians' guild, for the musical life of the town. Bach's father held such a post in the town of Eisenach. The duties of the *Stadtmusikus* included arranging for the training of young musicians, providing music for balls, weddings, birthday celebrations, processions and other public events and generally gaining the town a reputation for the quality of its musical life. Where the particular interests and abilities of the *Stadtmusikus* lay, there he would concentrate his efforts. In Zwickau, in the tradition of mining communities, his forte was the coaching of brass band players, and performances there by woodwind and brass ensembles had a reputation for miles around. But until peace and stability returned to Germany after the Congress of Vienna in 1815, when, as part of the punishment inflicted on the defeated, over half the kingdom of Saxony was annexed by Prussia, the arts had little chance to assert themselves.

Such was the world of confusion and agitation, of residual feudalism and a nascent political consciousness, an age when paternalism was giving way to individualism, rationalism to idealist romanticism, in which August and Christiane Schumann began to bring up their youngest child. Family life in the house on the market square was settled enough, although publishing and bookselling suffered more during the war than many other businesses. The intellectual drive in the household came from August, whose health, never strong, suffered further under the weight of work with which he insisted on burdening himself, while his wife was left to provide for the everyday needs of her five children in difficult and sometimes dangerous conditions.

Looking back on his earliest years, Schumann wrote at the age of fifteen:

I have only a hazy recollection of my childhood. Up to three I was a child like any other. Then my mother caught typhoid, and for fear lest I too should catch the infection, I was put into the care of Frau Ruppius, wife of the present *Bürgermeister*, in the first place for six weeks. These weeks passed quickly, and to the credit of this good woman I must say that she knew a great deal about bringing up children. I grew very fond of her; she became a second mother to me, and in the end I stayed in her care for two and a half years.

But when he finally returned home, the old love for his own mother soon came back. He was her favourite, her 'pretty child', as she called him. Maybe she spoilt him. Maybe she unwittingly nurtured the inflexibility, the sometimes heedless determination to get his own way, whether by wheedling and coaxing or by sullen obstinacy, that became a feature of his character. But his affection outlived his years of dependence on her, survived her reluctance to allow him to make music his career, and ended only with her death. On his twenty-fifth birthday she recalled the happiness his childhood had brought her, and wrote to him in the somewhat flowery style to which she tended:

Twenty-five years ago to the day, my dear son, you came into the world. With tears of joy I pressed you to my heart, knowing that there were hard times ahead. God created you a healthy child, thus giving you a passport to a wonderful future, and from the very beginning dear little Robert enjoyed the love of us all. You looked so happy, and we, your parents, watched with joy as your body grew. Your mother, I may say, was not without a certain sense of vanity!

At six and a half Robert was sent to a new private school in Zwickau run by a Protestant clergyman, Archidiaconus Hermann Döhner, where he stayed for three years. At seven he learned Latin, at eight, Greek and French. In confident self-assessment he declared later: 'I was a good, well-mannered child and diligent in my studies'.

During his second year at the school, in 1817, the family moved from Am Markt No. 5 to Amtsgasse (now Burgstrasse) No. 2, a larger house just off the opposite side of the square, which August Schumann had bought to accommodate his expanding business (the house was destroyed in an air raid in the spring of 1945). Here Robert lived until the moment in 1828 when he left for the university. This same year, 1817, he had his first piano lessons at the hands of Johann Gottfried Kuntzsch, the forty-two-year-old organist and choirmaster of the Marienkirche, who as organizer and conductor made strenuous efforts to raise the standard of musical life in Zwickau in the early years of the century. 'He was a good teacher who liked me', Schumann remembered, 'though he was only a mediocre pianist himself'. His mother later claimed the credit for arranging these lessons. Schumann himself thought 'it was probably the great deal of singing I did which made my parents aware of my gifts'.

What Kuntzsch actually taught his pupil during the years he had him in his charge we do not know. Probably not a great deal in measurable terms. But what a pupil learns from a teacher – a true teacher, that is, an inspirer, an instigator, one who, in the literal sense, educates, 'draws out' – cannot be quantified by volume or weight. It can only be absorbed through a kind of osmosis, sometimes known, sometimes unrecognized, whose unpredictable effects may show themselves, transfigured, in the passage of time. One need not exaggerate Kuntzsch's abilities. But nor need one welcome the supercilious comment of the elderly Clara Schumann over thirty years after her husband's death: 'He was certainly not distinguished enough to be my husband's teacher, for the pupil outstripped the master'. Schumann himself made no secret of his admiration for his first teacher. 'You were the only one', he wrote to Kuntzsch in 1832, the year of *Papillons* and his other earliest published pieces, 'to recognize the musical gifts that dominated my nature, and to set me at an early age on the path along which my guardian angel was sooner or later bound to lead me.' Indeed, Schumann's own reference in an autobiographical sketch to his first compositions as a child – a group of dances for the piano – belongs to the earliest years of his study under Kuntzsch. Many years later, in 1845, he recalled his debt by dedicating to him his Studies for Pedal Piano Op. 56, and as late as 1852, his fame long established, he wrote a charming letter of gratitude to mark Kuntzsch's silver jubilee as a music teacher.

In the spring of 1820, after three years at Döhner's preparatory school, his father sent him to the *Lyceum*, or grammar school, in Zwickau. The school had some two hundred pupils, and Schumann was to spend eight years there. Classes in the basic subjects at the *Lyceum* ran every morning except Sunday, from 7 till 10, and in the afternoon, except on Wednesdays and Saturdays, from 1 till 4. Optional subjects were taken between ten and twelve, among them French and English. The most important optional subject, however – though not necessarily the most popular – was singing, since the choir of the Marienkirche was drawn from the boys of the school, and the cantors of the Marien-kirche and the Katharinenkirche were both members of the school staff.

To present-day eyes the curriculum makes strange reading. Of the thirty hours teaching a week, no fewer than twenty were devoted to Latin and Greek; in the top class, the *Prima*, only Latin was spoken in Latin lessons, and when Greek had to be translated, then not into German but into Latin. History, Geo-graphy and Divinity each received two hours a week throughout the school; so also did German, which consisted of exercises in rhetoric and essays, the only contact with classical German authors – Goethe, Schiller, Wieland, Herder, Lessing and earlier writers – being through a few excerpts read in the *Prima*. The junior grades had Arithmetic, but Mathematics was only just being introduced into the curriculum when Schumann joined the school, while Physics, a new-fangled subject which the authorities suspected to be important but were unsure how to present, slowly took its place in Zwickau and other Saxon towns in the course of the 1820s.

Between 4 and 8 in the evening pupils were expected to be busy with their homework, and the duties of the school prefects, called *Inspektoren* – Schumann became one in the *Prima* – included visiting the homes of junior boys during these hours to check that they were doing what they had been told. The *Inspektoren* then reported to a staff meeting held each Saturday morning.

Inspektor Schumann needed nobody to check him. He did all

that was required of him and, without displaying any particular brilliance, moved from one grade to the next with no apparent difficulty, though he confessed to a sense of strain under the rigidity of the routine. 'My life began to become more restless', he later wrote; 'I was not as diligent as I should have been, though I by no means lacked ability. If one has not done one's preparation properly, one gets worried, and everything seems distasteful – in fact, the supremely happy years of my childhood started to become irksome. I liked best of all to go for walks by myself and pour out my heart to nature'.

One of the more interesting personalities at the *Lyceum* was the deputy headmaster, Carl Ernst Richter. Author of a monograph on August Schumann which is our main source of information about Schumann's father, Richter was a man of radical political views who edited a weekly periodical called *Die Biene (The Bee)*, which was banned in 1833. Some of his liberal attitudes left their influence on Schumann *père* and *fils*. In the hall of the family house there hung a portrait of Ludwig Sand, the revolutionary student who assassinated the poet and suspected Russian spy Kotzebue in 1819, and when he was seventeen Schumann had on his wall a picture of Johann Gottfried Seume, the much-travelled social critic and supporter of political independence movements in various parts of the world.

The earliest extant document in Schumann's handwriting, dated 3 July 1817, is a letter that could have been written by any well-brought-up child of seven. More original, dating from his first year at the *Lyceum*, is a note inscribed in the house-book of a schoolfriend, which reads in a remarkably self-assured manner for a boy not yet eleven:

> Everything can be bought with money,
> Except friends and happiness.
>
> Zwickau,
> 14 May, 1821
>
> When you read these lines,
> think of your true friend
>
> Robert Schumann

In retrospect these school years take their place as a far from unproductive period in his life, and in a *curriculum vitae* written when he was thirty he was able to say with satisfaction: 'I enjoyed a most scrupulous and sympathetic education'. The self-confidence he already showed impressed itself on his fellow-pupils, as his friend Flechsig noted:

At school he was an average student, somewhat dreamy and inattentive. But what very soon struck me about him was his unshakeable conviction that he would become a famous man. The question of 'famous for what' still remained open, but famous he knew he would be, whatever the circumstances.

More important than the acquisition of book knowledge, however, or a proficiency in academic disciplines was the stirring of his talent in the two realms which over many years vied for his affection and his commitment – literature and music.

Already at such an early moment in his life this rivalry – it amounts virtually to a dichotomy – reveals a fundamental trait in the character of both Schumann the man and Schumann the artist. The history of the arts is not poor in examples of men who have practised, even excelled, in more than one medium – the troubadours as poets and musicians, Nietzsche as poet-philosopher and composer, William Blake as poet and graphic artist, E.T.A. Hoffmann as novelist and composer, Ernst Barlach as sculptor and dramatist. In the hands of a giant like Michel-angelo – painter, sculptor, architect, poet – everything may turn to gold. The *Last Judgement*, the Florentine *Pièta*, the final design of St Peter's in Rome, the Sonnets: such universality of genius lies beyond what the ordinary mind can grasp.

But save in this heavenly sphere, the painter who also writes poetry or the novelist who also composes music will, as it were by nature, find his true originality, and hence the soil for the cultivation of his deepest thoughts, in one particular art of those in which he expresses himself. At the same time the other arts will feed this main art, sometimes along the path of demonstrable motifs and techniques, sometimes through mysterious processes of osmosis or symbiosis. E.T.A. Hoffmann, author of the famous *Tales*, long believed that fate had intended him to live in the mind of posterity as a composer. But although his music is today almost forgotten, and posterity remembers him mainly for his extraordinary stories of the supernatural and the psychologically disturbed, his fiction would not have been what it is without the informing insights of Hoffmann the musician. Equally, though no one today heeds the songs and choral music of Nietzsche, his whole literary *ouevre* could be described, in a phrase borrowed from the title of his first book, as having been 'born from the spirit of music'. Nor is it an accident that between the names of Hoffmann and Nietzsche lies the century of German romanticism, of philosophical idealism, a century when the values of music prevailed in the arts as in life, a century in the middle of which, moulding and being moulded by its spiritual and aesthetic ethos, stands the figure of Robert Schumann.

Schumann's twin loyalties of literature and music – they were not divided loyalties, for they issued from a common emotional and intellectual source – already declared themselves in his early years at the Zwickau *Lyceum*. A new grand piano, a Streicher, arrived from Vienna, and with a new schoolfriend called Friedrich Piltzing, son of the principal oboist in a regimental band stationed at Zwickau, he set about playing piano duets, among them arrangements of Haydn and Mozart symphonies. From 1821 he performed regularly at the school concerts – piano pieces (some for duet, some solo) by Pleyel, Cramer and various now forgotten names, but also, in 1824, Weber's *Invitation to the Dance*, no mean technical achievement for a boy of fourteen. The previous year he had written some songs and a choral setting of the 150th Psalm, which he performed in the privacy of his home with a small group of singers and players. He also arranged and conducted what he called 'Musical Evening Entertainments', with adapted orchestral works, operatic arias and choruses, concertos and items of chamber music. As in the programmes of the school concerts, the composers range from Mozart and Weber through minor figures like Boïeldieu and Cramer to names – Grosheim, Lecour, Eichner and many others – that survive today only in reference books, and sometimes not even there.

He set about such performances with great enthusiasm. Rummaging one day among the books and papers in the store-room of his father's bookshop, he came across the orchestral parts of the overture to Righini's opera *Tigrane*. It was something of a mystery how they came to be there but he immediately decided to perform the piece, got together a motley band of instrumentalists – two violins, two flutes, a clarinet and two horns were all he could muster – and, having handed out the parts, proceeded to conduct the performance from the keyboard, where he filled in the brass and the missing harmony. It would probably be kinder not to try to imagine the result. His enterprise did, however, win from his father, always concerned to do what he could for his son's education, the gift of a set of music stands for use on future occasions.

Still in his thirteenth year, this time airing his literary pretensions, he assembled a mammoth work with the opulent title *Blätter und Blümchen aus der goldnen Aue, gesammelt und zusammengebunden von Robert Schumann, genannt Skuländer (Leaves and Blossoms from Golden Pastures, picked and tied into a bunch by Robert Schumann, known as Skuländer)*. With the name Skuländer – the first of the fanciful, sometimes cryptic pseudonyms that he gave himself – Schumann seems to affect a blend of 'school inmate' with mythological overtones of Skuld, the Norn of the Future. The work itself is an idiosyncratic anthology of bits and pieces from a bewildering variety of sources – epigrams and gobbets from Greek and Roman authors, excerpts from Christian Friedrich Daniel Schubart's *Ideen zu einer Asthetik der Tonkunst*, poems and anecdotes about composers, a scene from a pretentious five-act tragedy of his own called *Der Geist (The Spirit)*, and two poems by his mother. A volume of his own poems followed two years later under the title *Allerley aus der Feder Roberts an der Mulde (A Miscellany from the Pen of Robert of the Mulde* – the river Mulde flows through Zwickau).

August Schumann's confidence in the intelligence and literary ability of his fourteen-year-old son showed itself when he invited him to help in writing the text for a volume of portraits of famous men that he was preparing for publication, and a few years later Robert's brothers Karl and Julius, who had followed their father independently into the world of publishing, paid him to help read the proofs of the famous Latin lexicon of Egidio Forcellino which they were producing.

At the *Lyceum* his growing enthusiasm for literature led him to become co-founder in 1825 of a school literary society designed to stimulate interest in that sphere in which he felt the official curriculum to be shamefully inadequate, viz. German literature. The society held regular weekly meetings and had its official rules of procedure. On each occasion a major work or group of works was read out loud – Schiller ranked among the most popular authors, though many minor figures were also of the company – together with an account of the life of some famous national figure and the recitation of original poems written by members of the society. These latter were discussed by the assembled students, then formally entered into a book as a record of the proceedings.

The inspiration for these meetings came in the first instance from the fraternity of rapturous young poets who had come together in the 1770s to create the romantic poetic circle known as the 'Göttinger Hainbund'. The idealism of the early nineteenth century offered fertile soil for the growth of such societies, some of them real communities, others utopian visions, most a romantic synthesis of the two. Of practical disposition, for instance, was the 'Harmonischer Verein' in Berlin, founded by Meyerbeer, Carl Maria von Weber and other musicians in 1810, while in his 'Serapion Brotherhood' E.T.A. Hoffmann translated a real-life situation into a literary fiction. Schumann's own schoolboy society was to find its mature successor in his 'Davidsbund' a few years later.

Schumann's enthusiasm for literature amounted at this time to an obsession, both with the great figures of literary history – 'I was familiar with the most important writers of more or less every country', he blithely claimed – and with his own poetry, dramas and novels. The earliest work to which he was later prepared to confess – his literary Opus 1, so to speak – was a whimsical, semi-autobiographical love story called *Juniusabende und Julitage (Nights in June and Days in July)*, written at sixteen. 'A kind of idyllic vision,' he described it, 'of what four happy people once dreamed'.

Many years later Flechsig filled in a few more colourful details about Schumann the young literary lion:

He addressed love poems to real and un-real damsels, began to write tragedies and indulged himself with particular delight in reciting poetic works. In fact he was almost the death of me and Röller [another schoolfriend] with his endless recitations, all delivered with passionate zeal. But this much I must say to his credit: he was not only the most ambitious man I have ever known but also the most hardworking and energetic.

This indefatigable determination to succeed remained Flechsig's dominant impression of the young Schumann, the schoolboy wrestling with the daemons of literature and music that fought for his allegiance:

Apart from short visits to a tavern in the evening, he used to spend the whole day from the crack of dawn working on whatever occupied his mind. I am almost inclined to agree with Röller that he has become a great composer less by virtue of his genius than through an iron strength of will. This, however, I leave to the judgement of the experts.

His mother, in the most patent of wish-fulfilments, visualized him as a lawyer who would play the piano for his private enjoyment. Flechsig thought he would become a writer – 'but we both guessed wrong'.

Though they did not have the ability to sing or play in the amateur *soirées* that their son arranged in the house, August and Christiane Schumann had an earnest concern to do what they could for his musical education, and he remained ever grateful to them for it. But closer to his inner artistic world were members of the gifted Carus family, at their head Carl Erdmann Carus, an executive in the chemicals firm of Devrient and Co, who kept open house in Zwickau for musicians, actors and all other artists. On Carl Carus' death in 1842 Schumann recalled with admiration: 'In his house Haydn, Mozart and Beethoven were among the names eagerly discussed every day, and it was here that I first came to know the rarer works of these masters, especially the quartets, which were scarcely ever heard in small towns. Sometimes I was even allowed to join in on the piano . . .'

Above all it was for Agnes Carus, the young wife of Carl Carus' nephew Ernst August, that Schumann conceived an adolescent hero-worship. Through her he gained his first insight into the world of Lieder, especially those of Schubert, and he played Schubert's pianoforte duets with her. His devotion earned him the name Fridolin, after the enamoured young servant in Schiller's ballad 'Der Gang nach dem Eisenhammer'.

Agnes' eldest son, Julius Victor Carus, who became a doctor, later inherited some of the scientific products that issued from the medical research carried out by the man who made the name of this Saxon family famous to the world at large – Carl Gustav Carus. Philosopher, literary critic, painter, and above all medical scientist, Carus was a protagonist of the inseparability of mind and body, and a pioneer in the treatment of pathological conditions via the psychology of the patient rather than through the clinical symptoms of his malady.

Robert's elder brothers had by this time followed their father into the world of publishing – Karl, independently, in the old silver-mining town of Schneeberg ten miles or so from Zwickau, Eduard and Julius in the family firm itself. All three of them were to die before him. But Robert's earliest loss came with the death in 1825 of his sister Emilie at the age of twenty-nine, under unhappy circumstances still not fully understood. From childhood she had suffered from a persistent skin infection. Eventually it spread over her whole body, driving her to distraction and producing what Richter, in his biography of August Schumann, called 'an incurable mental condition which at times took the form of a quiet madness'.

But what finally caused Emilie's death we do not know. The often-repeated story that she drowned herself lacks documentary evidence and does not tally with her mother's account. Similarly, the once-current notion, encouraged by the circumstances of Schumann's own derangement in his final years, that her mental sickness was congenital and that insanity ran in the family, is a piece of lurid fiction. As described by her mother a few years later, the poor girl's condition suggests some kind of infectious disease:

Twelve sleepless nights, weeping constantly in my suffering, I spent quite alone in the chamber where my dear Emilie passed away. This loneliness made her loss a double agony, for there was no loving hand to bring me cool refreshment or even give me a cup of coffee before five o'clock the next morning. A daughter is such a source of happiness for a mother, and her loss irreplaceable.

Nowhere, it seems, does Schumann mention Emilie's name in diaries or letters, nor do we know how close he was to her. But the loss of his father less than a year later struck deep. 'My wonderful father', he called him in his diary. 'Is it not terrible to be deprived of such a man, so delightful a writer, so keen a judge of human nature, so hardworking in his business?' Over the last few years August Schumann, determined to fight off the ailments that plagued him, especially gout, had paid the price for his unremitting industry, holding his firm together through the war and constantly bringing out new books of his own. The death of his beloved Emilie, who had helped to look after him, and whose own deterioration he had watched day by day, also took its toll of his resistance. But those around him had grown used to seeing him in poor health and did not suspect in August 1826 that anything especially serious was amiss. Had Christiane done so, she would hardly have left for a rest cure in Carlsbad at the time. When she returned to Zwickau a few weeks later, she found her husband already dead from a heart attack. Her letters to Robert over the following years show how fondly she thought back on her life with August, and how deeply the loss, first of her daughter, then of her husband, affected her. August bequeathed to Robert the substantial sum of 10,000 thalers, which was held in trust for him by Gottlob Rudel, a family friend appointed to act as his guardian for the remaining years of his minority.

One of August Schumann's last services to his youngest son was to write to Carl Maria von Weber in Dresden asking whether he would be willing to take over Robert's musical education. The letter arrived as Weber, himself a sick man, was preparing to leave for London to conduct the first performance of his opera *Oberon* at Covent Garden. His reply, if he sent one, has not survived. A few months later, still in London, he too died. His principles concerning standards and his proposals for the reform of musical taste later had their influence on Schumann's own attitudes to these matters, while as a composer Schumann, with Wagner and many other Germans of their generation, owed Weber a fundamental debt.

Into the mood of sadness that settled on Schumann after his father's death there suddenly penetrated a new experience – the feeling of being in love. He already cherished an idealized devotion to the twenty-three-year-old Agnes Carus. Now, in the pages of his earliest diaries and in letters to his schoolfriend Emil Flechsig, he effuses about two young Zwickau girls, Nanni Petsch and Liddy Hempel, who have turned his head. 'It was the most wonderful time of my life', he wrote in his diary for January 1827, 'the most blissful hour of truth, when, last spring, I loved and was loved in return'. That he was 'loved in return' by either of them was the purest fantasy, for he loved in silence, secretly, romanticizing his emotion and not daring to let his beloved see what he felt.

That winter he danced with Liddy at a ball. 'If only she were to love me!' he wrote excitedly in his diary the next day. 'How heavenly a thought! – I can scarcely grasp it! She pressed my hand – we did not say a word. I can write no more. It was divine'. A few days later he joined a party of friends on a sleigh ride through the mountains: 'She arrived later. I did not speak to her – she did not seem to notice me . . . In the evening there was a dance. I was in a terrible mood. Yet I still dare to hope. She pressed my hand – words cannot express what I felt . . .'

These emotions were not without their sensual content. One day during another winter excursion into the mountains, he watched Liddy riding on a sleigh in front of him and envisaged her as his own. Then he shrank from his temerity: 'When the pleasures of the senses become too prominent, man becomes an animal – and that is what I was'. And he added, almost afraid of what might follow: 'But enough of this. It makes me feel ashamed of myself'. In a letter to Flechsig he later affected a deprecating attitude towards such episodes: 'Liddy was a small-minded creature, a simple little lass from utopia, incapable of grasping noble ideas . . . I never concealed from you or anyone else that I liked her – I think I even loved her – but it was external appearances which, as is usually the case, led my youthful imagination to draw conclusions about her inner nature'. But at the time his infatuation was real enough.

To the same outgoing world of social pleasure and personal gratification belongs a penchant of Schumann's, trivial yet in its way revealing, that showed itself in his adolescence and never changed – his love of champagne. Insignificant in itself and, one might think, worth at most a passing reference, like Wagner's predilection for silk dressing-gowns, it became for him a kind of touchstone of well-being, like his later taste for expensive cigars. His diaries abound in undisguised phrases like 'Utterly and completely drunk' and 'Terrible hangover', with champagne more often than not the elicitating agent. 'To climb to the many springs on sunny Pindus', he wrote to Flechsig, 'one needs a friend, a sweetheart – and a glass of champagne'. Were it not so trite, one might conclude that the young Schumann's values seemed at times to be enshrined in the holy trinity of wine, women and song.

The literary style of his early diaries, and even more markedly of his formal written work such as school essays, already shows the florid, self-conscious characteristics that fill page after page of his musical articles ten and fifteen years later. As in his journalism he played with words in the same spirit of fantasy that dances its way through *Papillons, Carnaval, Kreisleriana* and numerous other piano works, so as a schoolboy, with the often uncritical self-indulgence to which youth is entitled, he feels himself moved by the romantic genius of the poetic imagination to seek his true relationship to the world and his true position within it. At sixteen, the year before he left school, he wrote in his diary a remarkably keen self-characterization:

What I really am, I do not yet know for certain myself. I have imagination, I think – nobody will deny me this. Profound thinker I certainly am not – I cannot trace the logical course of an argument whose premises I may have laid out. Whether I am a poet – for one can never become one – is something that posterity will have to decide. There is nothing else I can say about myself. One of the most difficult things to do is to paint a picture of oneself. 'Know Thyself' is a stern command.

Nor did he direct this perceptiveness only towards himself. From the earliest of the reflections and autobiographical jottings which he called 'Hottentottiana' he shows, as well as a penchant for aphorisms which stayed with him all his life, a remarkable maturity of public awareness for a schoolboy. Take, for example, the following:

The real mother of poetry may well be political freedom, the most vital condition for the poetic genius to flourish. True literature cannot prosper in a country where there is subjugation and bondage – by true literature I mean that which enters the life of the public, stimulating and inspiring as it goes.

Or this, from an address called 'Das Leben des Dichters' ('The Life of the Poet') delivered at the *Lyceum* in September 1826 – the sixteen-year-old schoolboy self-cast as poet, not yet as musician:

The poet stands above his surroundings, looking wistfully towards the radiance of the distant stars and making ready to open up his soul. When his three score years and ten have come – years that are in reality but minutes – he rises like a Phoenix, casting his plumage into the ashes, while his soul, freed of the dross of earth, rises in purity into the heavens.

Thus in the poet's life at its happiest is fused with life at its purest, which in turn is fused with life at its highest. The poet lives in the ideal world and works for the real world.

The poets of German romanticism would have welcomed him with joy as their disciple.

Schumann's final year at the Zwickau *Lyceum* was 1827–8, and in spring 1828 he took his public school-leaving examination, the *Abitur*. Standard qualification though it has since become, the *Abitur* in Schumann's day was still something of an innovation. Prussia, pace-setter in this as in so many things, introduced a uniform school examination in 1812; Zwickau had its own form of *Abitur* from 1821, but a law establishing a common *Abitur* for all the *Gymnasien* in Saxony did not come into force until 1830.

The examination posed no problems for Schumann, and he passed with the designation *'omnino dignus'*, roughly 'satisfactory in all subjects'. At the graduation ceremony each *Abiturient* had either to recite by heart a Latin or German poem he had composed for the occasion or deliver a formal address in Latin, German or French. Schumann's offering was a flowery Klopstockian ode in classical metre, seventy-six lines long, entitled 'Tasso'. His recitation was a disaster, as Flechsig related with relish:

One typical thing about him I must mention is that he had simply not learnt his poem for the graduation ceremony properly. He could not remember his lines and got completely stuck in the middle – but with an air of utter indifference. Passionate as he was when sitting at the piano, in other matters he could be casual and totally unconcerned.

Two days after leaving the *Lyceum* Schumann wrote to Flechsig in Leipzig:

School is now behind me and the world stretches out ahead. I could barely restrain my tears as I left the building for the last time. Yet my joy was greater than my grief. Now the real man within me must emerge and reveal his true nature . . . Pride of place in my mind belongs to Jean Paul. He is the one I set before all others, not excepting even Schiller (I cannot yet follow Goethe).

This mention of the name Jean Paul brings us for the first time into the presence of one of the seminal forces in Schumann's life and art, a writer whom he revered all his life, whom he set alongside Bach, proclaiming the two to be among the greatest geniuses in the history of German culture, and who in many ways embodies in literature the values that Schumann embodies in music.

Jean Paul Friedrich Richter was born in 1763 in a village in the Fichtelgebirge, hardly left the confines of his native Franconia during his whole life, and died in 1825 in Bayreuth, that town's only famous resident from the world of the arts until the arrival of Richard Wagner almost fifty years later. His roots are in eighteenth-century sentimentality, and his long, rambling novels belong to the context of the novel of sensibility, familiar to English readers above all through Sterne's *Tristram Shandy*. His high-flown, episodic manner, his rhapsodic syntax, his endless pattern-weaving and his highly-coloured, often exaggerated imagery make great demands on his readers' patience, while his whimsical humour, which has a certain heavy German charm, taxes one's tolerance.

Yet to many, especially in the age of nineteenth-century romanticism, he came as a liberating force, a writer who, through paradoxes, considered incongruities, the intermingling of the real and the imaginary and the juxtaposition of opposites, achieved a universality denied those unable to break out of the confines of the classicistic mould. His presentation of such dualisms found its most influential form in the device of the *Doppelgänger*, or double, which was later exploited with particular intensity by E.T.A. Hoffmann, Chamisso, Heine – and Schumann himself.

Jean Paul's name occurs frequently in Schumann's early diaries of 1827 and 1828, together with quotations from his novels. For the first book of 'Hottentottiana' (1828) he took the motto of Jean Paul's novel *Die unsichtbare Loge*, *'Der Mensch ist ein Gedankenstrich im Buche der Natur'* ('Man is an interpolation in the book of nature'), and modified it cleverly, if a little pretentiously, to read: *'Der Mensch sei kein Gedankenstrich im Buche der Natur, sondern ein Fragezeichen, das er sich beantworten muß'* ('Man should not be an interpolation in the book of nature but a question-mark for himself to answer'). In a characteristically extravagant comparison he described Jean Paul's unfinished novel *Flegeljahre* to Clara Wieck ten years later as 'a book which, in its own way, is like the Bible'. He would brook no criticism of his 'one and only Jean Paul', and not to respond to Jean Paul's message branded the offender as an irretrievable Philistine. This was what delivered the *coup de grâce* in his relationship with Liddy Hempel, as he said scornfully to Flechsig: 'When I thought of the things she used to say about Jean Paul, my vision of her as an ideal vanished. Let the dead rest in peace!'

So here he stood, not yet quite eighteen. Well read in the classics and in German literature; with an innate gift for music, yet more powerfully gripped at this moment by the claims of literature; sensitive, yet energetic in the pursuit of the aims to which he committed himself; outward-going and convivial, opening his heart to his mother and to his friends, yet also living in a world of his private fantasy, a world governed not so much by the values of life as by the values of art.

Yet already in his earliest diaries there speaks the voice of one avid for experience in every sphere, one who sought to absorb all these experiences into a pattern of understanding of the world at large, and, having interpreted this pattern, felt called upon to demonstrate how it should be refined, extended, even, if necessary, destroyed and re-cast. Self-confidence, a sense of vision and a claim to leadership communicate themselves through his youthful attitudes. As he said of himself two years later, adapting a line from the *Iliad*: 'It belongs to my nature to occupy first place.'

CHAPTER TWO

Reluctant Student

Although she had encouraged her youngest son to learn the piano, Christiane Schumann had no confidence in music as a career. 'An unprofitable pursuit', she called it. In her view Robert should attend the local University of Leipzig and study law – a *Brotstudium*, as the blunt German phrase has it – and her reluctance at the beginning to consider any other possibility has tended to be what posterity most readily remembers about her. His guardian, Gottlob Rudel, took the same line. So, it seems, did his elder brothers, who had inherited their father's practical business sense. Since it was clear that his next step would in any case take him to the university, and since, whatever his hesitations, he had at the moment no alternative subject to propose, he quietly allowed his family to assume that he shared their view. At the end of March 1828, two weeks after his *Abitur*, he took the coach to Leipzig to enrol in the faculty of law.

Second in size only to Dresden, the royal *Residenzstadt*, in the Saxon Kingdom, Leipzig had a population of some 45,000 at this time. A Slav settlement founded by the Sorbs in the seventh century, and a trading centre since the Middle Ages, it had gradually made itself into the commercial capital of Saxony, and from its markets at Easter and Michaelmas grew the tradition of trade fairs which survives to the present day. In the nineteenth century a number of industries developed – heavy engineering, especially the manufacture of railroad locomotives, scientific and musical instruments, and particularly publishing and bookselling, including music (Breitkopf and Härtel, Peters, Eulenberg).

The powerful rise in prosperity that took Leipzig to third place, behind Berlin and Hamburg, in the ranks of German industrial and commercial cities by the end of the century was a phenomenon of the 1860s and onwards, but the sense of a place on the verge of dramatic expansion already ran through the town in the earlier decades of the century. Where the elegant Dresden was dominated by the aristocracy, the industrious Leipzig drew its strength from the entrepreneurial bourgeoisie.

Among the rich moments of its historical past are Luther's disputation of 1519 with Johann Eck over the supremacy of the Pope, the association of Johann Sebastian Bach with the Thomaskirche, where he became cantor in 1723, and the immortalization in Goethe's *Faust* of the wine vault called Auberbach's Keller (now a restaurant). In the course of the eighteenth century, chiefly through the presence of a large number of influential thinkers and men of letters in Saxony, the prestige of the university grew rapidly, and in the middle of the century the city could lay fair claim to being the intellectual capital of Germany. When Goethe arrived there in 1765 from his native Frankfurt, at that time a larger and busier city than Leipzig, he found that his fine new clothes were out of date, that the dialect features in his speech made people look askance at him, and that the graces of polite society went far beyond what he had known at home. Not for nothing had Leipzig come to be known as 'Little Paris'. The dramatist Karl von Holtei summed up the situation thus:

There is only one city in Germany that can represent Germany; only a single city where one can forget that one comes from Hesse, or Bavaria, or Prussia, or Swabia, or Saxony; only one city where, amid the wonders of learning and the affluence of the business world, even a man who possesses nothing but his personality is honoured and esteemed. That city, in my judgement and in my experience, is Leipzig.

Unlike Dresden, where painting, sculpture and architecture held pride of place, Leipzig had its strength in music – performance, teaching, publishing. The centre of the city's musical life was the Gewandhaus, which housed, as well as the municipal library, the hall in which the orchestra that still bears its name gave its concerts from 1781 till 1884. This old Gewandhaus, together with a later building to which the concerts were transferred in 1884, was destroyed during air raids in 1943, but the orchestra remains famous to this day.

Since the summer semester at the university did not start until the beginning of May, Schumann stayed in Leipzig only long enough to enrol as a student, find himself lodgings, and make the acquaintance of a fellow-student called Gisbert Rosen, who was already settled in the city. Schumann and Rosen immediately felt attracted to each other, not least through their shared adoration of Jean Paul. Instead of going straight back to Zwickau, Schumann eagerly suggested that he should accompany his new friend part of the way to Heidelberg, where Rosen, disillusioned with his professors at Leipzig, now intended to study. They took the coach from Leipzig to Hof, from Hof to Bayreuth, where they stood in veneration before the grave of Jean Paul, then to Nürnberg, Augsburg, and eventually Munich.

Schumann kept a detailed account, in terms both of distance covered and money spent, of this and other journeys during his student days, and from his diaries it is clear that, although they had their earnest purposes, he and Rosen were not disposed to let the physical pleasures of life slip through their fingers. 'Pretty girls', he noted: 'Beautiful evening – effects of beer – Rosen and the girls of Bayreuth – huge quantities of beer'. And, darkly: 'Rosen's innocence in jeopardy'. He also recorded his verdict on various inns where they stopped for a meal. 'The "Goldene Sonne" at Bayreuth – mediocre', he notes. 'The "Blaue Glocke" at Nürnberg – bad; the "Weisses Lamm" at Augsburg – good and expensive; the "Kurprinz" at Landshut – good and cheap', and so on.

The most exciting moment of his visit to Munich was a meeting with Heinrich Heine, with whose poetry he was later to identify himself so closely. Heine, then thirty-one, had just become sensationally popular with his first two volumes of *Reisebilder*, including the *Harzreise*, and his *Buch der Lieder*. That two young students, totally unknown to him, could suddenly present themselves at his door and expect to be received had only been made possible by an introduction from an old friend of August

Schumann's, a businessman called Dr Heinrich von Kurrer, whom Robert and Rosen had visited on their way through Augsburg. 'Stimulating conversation – an ironic little man', wrote Schumann in his diary. Later in the day Heine even found time to escort his young visitors through the Leuchtenberg Gallery in the city.

Of this, his only meeting with Heine, Schumann later wrote more fully to Dr Kurrer:

I had expected a morose, anti-social individual who considered himself so superior to life and his fellow-men that he could not possibly adapt himself to their ways. But how different he turned out to be. Greeting me kindly, like a present-day Anacreon, he gripped my hand warmly, then showed me round Munich for a few hours. I would never have imagined this from the author of the *Reisebilder*. His lips, admittedly, were caught in a bitter, ironical smile – but a lofty smile at the trivialities of life, a mocking smile at small-minded men. It was this sense of satire, so evident in his *Reisebilder*, a feeling of deep resentment against life which penetrated to the core of his being, that made his conversation so fascinating.

From Munich Rosen went on to Heidelberg, while Schumann set out on his way back to Zwickau. Again his road led through Bayreuth. This time he called on Jean Paul's widow and received from her a portrait of the great man which he proudly sent home. 'If the whole world were to read Jean Paul', he wrote ecstatically to Rosen, 'it would become a better, but also an unhappier place. Often he has almost driven me to madness, but the rainbow of peace and his spirit of humanity keep loving watch over my tears, and my heart is wondrously exalted in a radiant transfiguration'. Lapses into purple prose like this reflect the dubious aspects of Jean Paul's influence, which sometimes provoked epigrams of an invincible tastelessness:

Nature is a handkerchief embroidered with the name 'GOD', on which man can dry his tears – tears of joy as well as tears of sadness.

At other times, still a teenager with the expansive idealism of youth, Schumann could turn an ingenious epigram:

Jean Paul often seems like the offspring of the wild, abandoned Dionysos and the Muses.

Or, in frivolous vein:

Girls are like new wine. When they are warm, they become lifeless and lose their glow. When they are cold . . .

Unfortunately the rest of the sentence in his diary is illegible, so the effects of frigidity are left to the imagination.

Schumann stayed in Zwickau only long enough – a matter of mere hours – to pack the things he needed. A letter to his mother on 21 May, a few days after his arrival in Leipzig, shows him homesick in the impersonal, aggressively intellectual metropolis yet determined to put a brave face on things.

I am well but not really happy, and I passionately long to return to the peace and quiet of the place where I was born and where I spent happy days in communion with nature. Where can I find nature here? Everything is overladen with art – there is not a hill, not a valley, not a wood where I can sit and give myself over to my thoughts. The only time I can be alone is when I lock myself in my room, and even then there is an endless racket going on down below.

Then comes the struggle to decide what to study. Law, a cold subject, depressing from the very beginning with its soulless definitions, does not appeal to me; I have no wish to study medicine, and no ability to study theology. Caught up in this endless conflict, I am vainly trying to find someone to lead me and tell me what to do. Yet I see I have no choice – it will have to be law. Dull and uninspiring though it be, I shall fight my way through. If a man has the will, he can do anything.

He and his old schoolfriend Emil Flechsig shared well-appointed rooms on the first floor of a house on the street Am Brühl – the street, incidentally, in which Wagner was born and which, then as now, was the centre of the Leipzig fur trade. Although both Schumann and Flechsig came from a comfortable family background, the accommodation they had chosen was beyond their means. Schumann proudly described to his mother their 'patriarchal style of living', and it soon became clear, for the first of many times, that his monthly allowance was not going to match his expensive tastes.

Above his desk hung portraits, in gold frames, of his father, of Jean Paul and of Napoleon. He had rented a piano for one ducat per month, but hinted to his mother, none too subtly, that he would appreciate the consent of his guardian to spending 400 thalers from his father's bequest on acquiring a new Stein grand. He read a good deal, went for a two- or three-hour walk every afternoon, played a regular game of chess with Flechsig in the evening, and also found time to take fencing lessons – not, he hastily assured his startled mother, because he anticipated having to fight a series of duels but because it was something of a social obligation in student circles. These were the days when the *Burschenschaften*, militant student corporations sustained by ideals of nationalism and political liberalism, claimed the allegiance of progressive young Germans, and displays of physical courage formed an inseparable part of their code of conduct. Schumann never concerned himself with the politics of the time in the direct way that, for example, Wagner did, but he saw the *Burschenschaften* in an interesting historical perspective, approving of the idea behind them while disliking the practical forms that their activity took.

To what extent the high moral tone in his letter of 21 May conveys his true intentions, and how far it is designed to allay her far from unfounded fears that he was not going to take his studies particularly seriously, may be debatable. According to Flechsig, Schumann's academic activities began and ended with his enrolment in the law lectures of Professor Wilhelm Krug and Professor Karl Otto: that was the only time, says Flechsig, that he went near a lecture hall. On the other hand, Krug later certified, when Schumann asked him to, that he had attended lectures 'with admirable diligence'. Given the formality and anonymity of the German university system and the various subterfuges to which this impersonality gave rise, attendance at classes was virtually impossible to check, and Krug, signing Schumann's student record at the end of the semester along with scores of others, would hardly have known whether he had attended regularly or not. Cynics might also point out that since a professor received a separate fee from each student who attended his lectures, he was only too eager to enrol as many students as possible. How often they actually attended in the course of the semester was a question delicately avoided, to the not infrequent benefit of professor and student alike.

Whatever he did not do, Schumann now began to devote a good deal of time to music, both composing and playing. Partly this was a way of helping to deaden the feeling of his homesickness. At the same time it introduced him, through a piano quartet that he formed with three fellow-students, to music in new media. Music can make bedfellows of the most unlike and unlikely spirits, and the trio of string players that he collected round him consisted of a student of literature called Friedrich Täglichsbeck, who played the violin, Christoph Sörgel, a twenty-five-year-old theologian from Bavaria who played viola, and, as cellist, the extraordinary Christian Gottlob Glock, described by Flechsig as 'an ancient character who had already been a student for seventeen years', initially as a theologian and later as a medic. Schumann's musical world was dominated at this time by Schubert, whose music he described as 'the tonal equivalent of a blend of Jean Paul, Novalis and E.T.A. Hoffmann'. When the news reached him of Schubert's death in Vienna in November 1828, he spent the whole night in tears.

The shadow of Schubert also hovers over his first surviving songs – six settings of poems by Justinus Kerner – written in the summer of 1828 and sent to Wilhelm Wiedebein in Brunswick for his opinion. Wiedebein, whose judgements carried considerable weight in the musical world, praised their 'truly poetic spirit' and concluded: 'You have received a great deal, a very great deal, from the hands of Nature. Make use of it – and the respect of the world will not be denied you'.

Flechsig, whose memories make highly entertaining reading, had a gently humorous view of Schumann the composer:

He used to adopt a most peculiar pose when composing. Since he perpetually puffed away at a cigar, the smoke always got in his eyes, so he sat at the piano with his mouth and the cigar butt pointing upwards, squinting downwards at his hands and making the most extraordinary grimaces. The cigar bothered him in other ways too. He liked to whistle or

murmur to himself the tune of the song he was composing, and to do this
with a cigar in one's mouth is well-nigh impossible.

Smoking and drinking – his diaries contain profuse
circumstantial evidence that women played a similar role – were,
as he saw them, indispensable stimulants. 'Heavy cigars induce
excitement and a poetic mood in me', he said. 'And if I have been
drunk and vomited, then the next day my imagination is livelier
and more vivid. While I am drunk, I cannot do a thing, but
afterwards I can'.

Though far from withdrawn or reserved in his social dealings,
Schumann had few regular, close friends apart from Flechsig and
the members of his piano quartet. A relative in Leipzig was his
brother-in-law Moritz Semmel, brother of Eduard Schumann's
wife Therese. Semmel was also a law student, and it was he who
had introduced Schumann to Rosen, but although his name
figures frequently in Schumann's diaries, it is never with any
special warmth. Semmel was of a rational cast of mind, and his
matter-of-factness often taxed Schumann's volatile imagination
and sense of fantasy.

Greater pleasure came from Dr Ernst August Carus and his
wife Agnes, the family he used to visit in Colditz during his
impressionable schooldays and who now lived in Leipzig, where
Dr Carus had become Professor of Medicine at the university. But
for all their undiminished kindness towards him, and in spite
of – perhaps because of – the idealized passion he had once felt
for Agnes, the Carus family was not really the company he now
needed. Even Flechsig was beginning to get on his nerves –
'ultimately just a pedant', he irritably called him, 'and on a big
scale. There is nothing I detest more, which is why I no longer
have any affection for him. He has no delicacy of feeling and no
character, just a rough, boisterous Bavarian temperament'.

But at the same time as he was complaining about poor
Flechsig, there appears for the first time in his diaries and in his
letters to his mother a name that was to become inseparable from
his own, the name linked to the moments of his greatest joy and
his deepest despair, the name that was to symbolize all the
rewards and all the antagonisms that life thrust in his path. The

name was Wieck. 'I am often at Wieck's, my piano teacher's', he wrote to his mother in August 1828, 'and every day I have the chance to meet the best musicians in the city'. In the detailed expenditure accounts that Gottlob Rudel required him to keep there appears an item for the same month: 'To Wieck – 20 thalers'.

Friedrich Wieck, then forty-three, was a remarkable character. Born in 1785 in a little place called Pretzsch, between Torgau, one-time residence of the electors of Saxony, and Wittenberg, the town from which Martin Luther launched the Reformation, he had been so poor and so sickly as a boy that only through the support of relatives and friends had he been able to attend the *Gymnasium* and, later, the University of Wittenberg, where he studied theology. Soon discovering that a career in the Protestant Church would benefit neither his parishioners nor himself, he took a job as private tutor to the family of an eccentric Saxon nobleman. Here he became interested in the piano through having as a fellow-tutor Adolf Bargiel, who later became a well-known piano teacher in Berlin and also, by a strange irony, the second husband of the woman Wieck was shortly to marry. This was Marianne Tromlitz, a nineteen-year-old pupil of his and a gifted pianist.

Wieck now resolved to make his career in the field of piano teaching. He was entirely self-taught, and by virtue solely of an unshakeable confidence in himself and an intolerant determination to bend the world to his will, he had made himself by the mid-1820s into the leading teacher of the pianoforte in Leipzig, able to pick and choose whom he would admit to his classes. At the same time he ran a music lending library and dealt in pianos and other musical instruments.

As his unsmiling resolution to claw his way to the top had earned him professional·success, so in his personal life it brought misery and disillusion. In 1824, after eight years of frustration, Marianne deserted him. Their first child had died in infancy and Marianne took the youngest, only a few months old, with her when she went, leaving him to bring up the remaining three of their five children, a girl and two boys, on his own. The eldest of these three was the one destined to make the name of Wieck famous in concert halls throughout Europe – Clara, child prodigy and virtuoso pianist, later, after years of devotion and almost unbearable mental suffering, to become the wife of Robert Schumann. The two must have met in Wieck's house at this time but Schumann makes no mention of her in his diaries or his letters. The nine-year-old Clara, for her part, was fully absorbed in preparing for the career that her father had mapped out for her. Wieck married again in 1828 and had three more children by his second wife, a woman almost twenty years younger. He died in Dresden, an honoured figure, in 1873, at the age of eighty-eight.

Both as a teacher and as a father Wieck was a hard taskmaster. Driven by the bitter memories of his deprived childhood and by the failure of his first marriage, he devoted his life, first to turning Clara into a virtuoso, then, as impresario, to organizing the brilliant concert tours that made her one of the most sought-after performers of the age. When asked why he did not make the same efforts for his other children, he replied that he only had one life to give away. His breathtaking self-confidence reached its height when, in a throw-away remark about the greatest virtuoso pianist of the day, he observed: 'I once told Liszt that if he had only had a proper teacher [Wieck himself, of course], he could have become the best player in the world'.

Yet, rigid and difficult though he could be as a person, Wieck the musician and teacher had a remarkable keenness of mind and held strikingly progressive views on the art of performance. In an age when virtuosity was equated with profundity and pyrotechnics were regarded as the touchstone of greatness, he insisted that musicality was what mattered, not muscle, and that the worship of technique for its own sake had perverted the musical values of performers and audiences alike. A four-line jingle expressed his guiding principle in a nutshell:

> *Des Kunstgesetzes erstes Kapitel*
> *Heisst: Technik als Mittel;*
> *Technik als Zweck,*
> *Fällt die ganze Kunst hinweg.*

(The first artistic precept to defend
Is 'Technique is but a means to an end'.
For when technique commands the day,
Art will simply fade away.)

Thus he taught his pupils to cultivate a sensitive, reflective style drawn out of an understanding of the music from within, not an obtrusive subjectivism forced upon it from without. This entailed studying not just how to acquire manual dexterity but also the foundations of harmony and other matters of basic theory. He held, for example, that in order to sustain a melodic line on the piano and achieve an even, delicate touch, one had to understand something about the art of singing, and he later elaborated on this principle in a little book called *Clavier und Gesang (Pianoforte and Song)*, published in 1853. His daughter Clara became, under his singleminded rule, the triumphant proof and justification of the rightness of his instincts and ideas, the living means by which he sought to reform the musical values of an ignorant and misled public.

As a new pupil of Wieck's, the eighteen-year-old Schumann was sent back to basics. 'He had to start doing five-finger exercises again, like a beginner', said the long-suffering Flechsig. 'The monotony of it almost drove me mad'. He was set on becoming a concert pianist, and showed an unwillingness to submit to the instruction in theory that Wieck also required – an unwillingness strengthened by the knowledge that, far from being a beginner in these matters, he had already composed a number of works himself and therefore deserved to be treated with special deference.

How long Schumann kept up his lessons with Wieck at this time we do not know, though when he came back to Leipzig in 1830 after eighteen months' absence, he appears to have picked up where he had left off. But very early in his first term at the university he had made a private resolve to stay in Leipzig as short a time as possible and then go to Heidelberg to join his friend Gisbert Rosen. The earliest practical moment to leave was the following Easter, but he broached the subject to his mother a long while earlier, half-seeking her consent, half-presenting her, as was his wont, with a *fait accompli*. 'I need to go to a different university', he told her: 'firstly for my own sake, because I do not feel at all well here and am simply vegetating; secondly, so as to make contact with different people; and thirdly, for the sake of my legal studies, because the most famous professors are in

Heidelberg'. In reality the famous professors in Heidelberg did not concern him in the slightest, nor did his physical or psychological state amount to one of vegetation. His real motives, often impulsive and fanciful, lay elsewhere. The façade of pseudo-reasons was erected for his mother's benefit.

Relieving his remaining months in Leipzig with vacation visits to his mother in Zwickau and his brother Karl's family in Schneeberg, and having with difficulty settled the debts that his immodest, un-student-like style of living had left unpaid, Schumann set out for Heidelberg in May 1829. He was in no hurry to arrive, and combined the journey with a leisurely tour of some beautiful parts of Germany he had not known before, among them the romantic, legend-laden stretch of the Rhine between Bingen and Koblenz.

In the coach from Leipzig to Frankfurt, the first stage of his journey, the motley collection of passengers included a secretary from the Prussian embassy returning to Berlin, a Jewish merchant from Frankfurt, 'who talked to me about leather and leathery things', a well-to-do old lady, an inveterate theatregoer, from Gotha, and a pair of inebriated French Jews, 'who managed to talk heatedly the whole night about nothing at all'. There was one travelling companion, however, to whom he took an immediate liking. This was the popular writer Wilhelm Häring, who published under the pseudonym Willibald Alexis.

Twelve years older than Schumann, Alexis was a much-travelled man who used the experiences of his journeys in journalistic pieces and in novels that derived from Sir Walter Scott; he had even passed off his early novels, published in the 1820s, a translation of Scott. He took pleasure in telling how he had met Goethe on three occasions, and how the great man had congratulated him on his essay 'Goethe as Critic'. Later, well after his encounter with Schumann, he wrote a series of historical novels, mostly set in Brandenburg, which have established his place in German literary history. He died in 1871, having spent the last twenty-five years of his life in a condition of mental instability.

With an infectious *joie de vivre* and a delight in his new-found friendship, Schumann told in excited detail the story of his journey with Alexis. 'The first thing I did', he wrote to his mother from Frankfurt, 'was to rise and shake off the dust of the coach like a Phoenix; the next was to consume a decent-sized steak'. Then they visited Goethe's birthplace, the Städel Art Institute, and some of the quaint, out-of-the-way corners of the city, still with an eye on lighter pleasures:

The girls in Frankfurt all have one feature in common – a kind of German melancholy, masculine in kind, which one often encounters in former imperial cities. Generally they have faces full of character; many are intelligent, few are beautiful – their noses are usually Greek, and often turned up. I do not like their dialect.

At the house of a writer and musician called Georg Döring the two friends met the beautiful English wife of Ferdinand Ries, Beethoven's favourite pupil. Madame Ries captivated Schumann, who likened her English to 'the lisping of an angel'. He seems, indeed, to have had a particular partiality for Englishwomen during his student days. A letter to Wieck later the same year mentions 'two eager, attractive English girls in the flower of youth' to whom he was giving piano lessons, and after a boat trip down the Rhine the following year, where there were fifty or so Englishmen and women on board, he told his mother: 'If I ever get married, it will be to an English girl'. Perhaps Jean Paul, whose eponymous hero Siebenkäs falls in love with an English-woman called Nathalie, is still lurking in the background.

The culmination of his lighthearted behaviour in Frankfurt came in an episode that he described to his mother:

The very first morning an irresistible desire came over me to play the piano. So I marched confidently into the premises of the nearest leading dealer and pretended to be the private tutor of a young English lord who wanted to buy a grand piano. I sat down and played the instrument for three hours to general amazement and applause, saying I would come back two days later with my master's decision on whether to buy it or not. By that time, however, I had long since arrived in Rüdesheim and was consuming the local wine.

From Rüdesheim he crossed the Rhine to Bingen, then travelled by boat past the romantic castles and the Lorelei rock down to

Koblenz. In Bingen, under the influence of the Rüdesheimer he had been drinking, he had a ghastly vision prophetic of a terrible moment still twenty years in the future: 'The moon was shining on the water. I fell asleep and dreamt that I had drowned in the Rhine'.

In Koblenz, after their high-spirited days together, he and Alexis had to go their separate ways – Alexis onwards to Paris, Schumann, turning back south, to Heidelberg. After his extravagant living of the last few weeks, he not surprisingly found himself almost penniless, and was forced to make the last fifteen miles of his journey, from Mannheim to Heidelberg, on foot.

By and large the year or so that he spent in this wonderful old town, from May 1829 till September 1830, was little more than a pleasant interlude in his life. He took the view that, on principle, a town with a university, like Berlin or Leipzig, was preferable to a university town, like Heidelberg. Students, he considered, needed to rub shoulders with the citizens of the workaday world beyond the lecture hall, and to experience a dialectical opposition to something outside themselves.

'On the other hand,' as he told his mother, 'Heidelberg has the advantage that the lyrical beauty of the countryside tends to divert students' minds from over-indulgence in sensual and intellectual pleasures. Hence the students here are ten times more virtuous than those in Leipzig'. His lodgings were somewhat cheaper than in Leipzig, so too was the cost of renting a grand piano, but meals became more expensive, because a gargantuan *table d'hôte* lunch of eight or nine courses, accompanied by wine, turned out to be *de rigueur*. Apart from the cost, Schumann complained about the time that it took to eat so much. 'Give me soup and a roast', he said, 'and I would be finished in six minutes. This way the meal takes an hour, and by the time one gets to the roast, one has almost killed oneself with eating'.

For a while his new professors at Heidelberg succeeded in demonstrating to him that law, for all its technicalities, should be seen as a humane discipline – an approach that seemed to have eluded the minds of the sages in Leipzig. The leading jurist in Heidelberg, a man for whom Schumann's enthusiasm knew no bounds, was Anton Friedrich Justus Thibaut, author of a famous book, *System des Pandektenrechts* (1803), on the subject of Roman law as administered in Germany at that time. It was less Thibaut's academic reputation, however, that captured Schumann's allegiance than his activities as an amateur musician, which included lavish musical *soirées* in his palatial home – Schumann talks of Handel oratorios sung by a choir of over seventy – and a book called *Über Reinheit der Tonkunst (On Purity in Music)*. In this quaint little treatise, published in 1825, Thibaut expressed reservations about the quality of 'modern' music – even Beethoven and Mozart – and pleaded for a canon of musical judgement that rested on Handel, Palestrina, Lassus and other old masters of Church music. Bach, strangely, left him less than enthusiastic. When the young Mendelssohn visited him a few years earlier and talked excitedly about Bach – 1829 was the year of Mendelssohn's famous revival of the St Matthew Passion in Berlin – Thibaut smiled and invoked in return the name of Vittoria.

Schumann had never succeeded in making ends meet in Leipzig, and nothing changed in Heidelberg. On 6 August 1829 he wrote an elaborate letter to Rudel, his guardian – one of many such missives – setting out in wearying detail the cost of his rent, meals, books, lecture fees, hire of a grand piano and so on, and demonstrating that his monthly allowance could not possibly cover these expenses. At the same time he asked for an additional sum so that he could go on vacation to Switzerland and Italy. He put the same request to his mother, enumerating twelve pressing reasons why such a journey was necessary: for example, that he would derive great practical value from it; that no student ever stayed in Heidelberg during the Michaelmas vacation; that in any case he had already made arrangements with two travelling companions – and a further handful of frivolous sophistries. If the money were not forthcoming, he added, he would just have to go out and borrow it, at 10% interest. The money duly arrived. It almost invariably did.

In spite of a good deal of bad weather he eagerly absorbed the beauties of Switzerland, especially the Bernese Oberland, and visited familiar tourist sights such as the places associated with the story of William Tell. For Italy, on the other hand, he could find hardly a good word. 'Swindling foreigners is the order of the day here', he wrote to his sister-in-law Therese. 'I find that the best thing is to pretend to be a Prussian, since the Prussians command the greatest respect'. He visited Milan, Verona, Padua and Venice, but the wonderful paintings, sculptures and architecture he must have seen left him almost completely cold. The sequences of jottings in his diary – 'miserable weather – paintings by Veronese, Tintoretto etc. – excellent meal – one palace after another – attractive, affectionate girl with a rose in her hair – rum – wine' and so on – show him as much concerned with personal trivialities as with works of art and moments of historical significance. His only memorable musical experience was a performance of an opera by Rossini in La Scala. 'For the rest', he wrote to Wieck, 'it is almost impossible to listen to music in Italy. You have no idea of the slipshod, yet full-blooded, passionate manner in which they rattle everything off'.

Back in Heidelberg in the autumn of 1829, Schumann became more and more aware that his commitment to jurisprudence was slipping away from him. He spent longer periods at the keyboard, sometimes practising as much as seven hours a day, and in order to find time for lectures and study, as well as for the country walks that were part of his daily routine, he had to get up every morning at four o'clock. After playing duets, particularly Schubert, with a friend called Theodor Töpken in the evening, he would extemporize. 'The thoughts simply flooded into his mind in a never-ending stream . . . These evenings, which often turned into nights, and which lifted us right out of the world around us, are something I shall never forget', wrote Töpken.

Schumann also unblushingly recorded in his diary the erotic success that his improvisation brought him. At a ball attended by a large company, a young Frenchwoman called Charlotte was so captivated by his playing that she burst out: *'O Monsieur Schumann, si vous jouez, vous pouvez me mener où vous voulez!'* Unfortunately for Charlotte, Schumann's thoughts wandered in the direction of a rival young lady called Lina, and he had no desire to lead Charlotte anywhere. More seriously, it was from situations like this, born of a spirit of fantasy and sheer exuberance, his musical imagination stimulated to a pitch of intense nervous creativity, that his first published piano pieces emerged – the 'Abegg' Variations and the *Papillons*.

All this industry at the keyboard received its triumphant recognition when Schumann played in public for the first time at a concert in Heidelberg in February 1830. The work he chose was the *Variations on the Alexander March* by Moscheles, a frighteningly difficult bravura piece which he threw off with great *panache*. 'The audience kept shouting "Bravo!" and "Encore!"', which put me into a state of nervous perspiration,' he wrote to his brother Julius. 'The Grand Duchess of Baden applauded especially loudly. You cannot imagine how popular I have become in Heidelberg, and how, without flattery, people respect and esteem me'.

The irresponsibilities and excesses that are staple ingredients of student life continued unabated.

Feb. 21: Fancy dress ball in the museum – Henriette in the black dress – foolhardy – stimulated by punch – home at 3 a.m. Feb. 22: Drinking session in my rooms – a dozen men from the Rhineland, Westphalia, Alamannia, Prussia – beer – slept till 11 – fancy dress ball that evening at the Sattlermüllerei – vulgar behaviour – Rosen – drunk – stayed till 5 a.m. – Anderson and Braun and the prostitute.

While it would be folly to regard such diary jottings – and there are pages and pages in a similar vein – as much more than circumstantial material, this last phrase cannot but call to mind the much-vented question of Schumann's later physical and mental disintegration, in particular the theory that his madness and his final general paresis were the products of syphilis. Given the time-span of the development of the symptoms in his later life, one would trace the source of the infection to his student days. But – and since the subject will re-emerge later, this needs to be stated here and now – nowhere in his letters or diaries, or among the reminiscences of fellow-students and others who knew him at the time, is there any awareness, suspicion or implication that he had contracted syphilis, or was receiving medical treatment – with mercury, for example – for a condition known, or thought, to be the result of syphilitic infection. His mode of life as a student, together with his own uninhibited diaries, hardly suggests that he practised the abstinence of a monk. But the documents yield no specific evidence for anything further.

In 1819, when he was nine, Schumann had experienced the wizardry of the virtuoso for the first time when his father took him to Carlsbad to hear the great Bohemian pianist-composer Ignaz Moscheles. Now, on Easter Sunday 1830, he made a journey to Frankfurt with Töpken for his second decisive confrontation with the unnerving power of musical genius – to hear the legendary Paganini. The inspired, almost demonic abandon of Paganini's violin playing worried him and seemed to deny the serenity that dwells in all great art, but the impact made by a performer so utterly possessed by his art, with the uncanny power to draw from his instrument sounds that others did not even know existed, was overwhelming.

It is a familiar story – the power of the dazzling pianist, the breathtaking violinist, the virtuoso singer, to sweep us off our feet through sheer exhibitionism, the shattering skill that can be lavished on a flimsy trifle. The performing musician, like the actor, is an intermediary. He can make a lot out of a little, can persuade us that there is more substance in what he is playing than there really is. If the truth be told, there is no great musical content in the concertos and other pieces of Paganini. But at this instant it was such music that drove the young and impressionable Schumann closer to the point of no return, the point of total commitment to art.

The pointlessness of his studying law any further received welcome confirmation from no less a person than the great Professor Thibaut himself, who told him that even if he did qualify to become a legal official of some kind, he would never reach a position of importance. Schumann delightedly passed this information on to his mother as support for the case that he was not meant for law, nor law for him. Christiane, who at the beginning had anxiously urged him to take up a *Brotstudium*, and not a subject which offered no economic security, had the wisdom to see that he had to follow the commands of his inner being. To be sure, she could not conceal a certain disapproval of what she saw as his self-centredness and his wilful disregard of what others, above all the older members of the family, might have to say to him. Sometimes she struck a moralizing, rather resentful tone. But her profoundest concern was to help him achieve what he felt he wished, and was able, to achieve. When he once read aloud to Rosen a letter he had received from her, Rosen remarked: 'You can be proud to have a mother like that'.

His final resolve reached her in a long letter of 30 July 1830. Making much of the unhappiness that befalls the man who commits himself to a career at odds with his true nature, and repeatedly invoking 'the power of creative imagination' that clamours for expression within him, he claims that in six years he can become the equal of any pianist in the world, given patience, perseverance and a good teacher. The 'good teacher', of course, is to be Wieck, into whose charge he wishes to give himself at the earliest possible moment:

Do please write to Wieck in Leipzig yourself and ask him outright for his opinion about me and my proposal . . . . Ask him to reply as quickly as possible.

You will realize that this is the most important letter I have ever written, or ever shall write. I beg you to grant my request and to send me a speedy answer. There is no time to be lost.

Goodbye, dear mother, and do not worry about me. God can only help us if we help ourselves.

Your most devoted son
Robert Schumann

Wieck's reply to Christiane's enquiry about her son's prospects said all that Schumann wanted. 'I undertake', asserted Wieck, 'that, given his talents and his imagination, I shall turn Robert into one of the greatest living pianists within three years. As proof of my powers I adduce the case of my own eleven-year-old daughter, whom I have just begun to bring to the attention of the world'.

When he left the university, having studied – 'been there', might be more accurate – for three semesters, he was given a certificate confirming his attendance and stating: 'As concerns his conduct, this was at all times proper and in keeping with the rules of the academic community. He was never charged with belonging to any proscribed student organization'. His fellow-student Eduard Röller recalled many years later in a letter to Flechsig that Schumann had expressed sympathy with the July Revolution of 1830, 'but without being a passionate democrat'. He did think it worth while to enter in his diary the song of the Strasbourg revolutionaries – *'Morts aux tyrans! Vengeance et liberté!'* – together with the satirical, anti-monarchist Lord's Prayer: 'Our ex-King, who art a rogue, cursed be thy name; thy Kingdom never come; thy will be done neither in France nor anywhere else etc.' But his political consciousness, compared, for example, with that of Wagner, who lived through the same events and passionately involved himself in the issues they raised, scarcely developed beyond the embryo.

Much of the short time left to him in Heidelberg seems to have been spent in efforts to put his financial affairs in order. Begging letters, unashamedly direct in tone, and often based on financial arguments of dubious credibility, went out to his mother, to his guardian and to his brothers, generally with the desired result so that he was able to pay back the various loans he had taken out. Whether this or other, undisclosed matters clouded his last weeks in Heidelberg we cannot know, but over his letters of this time, down to his first note to his mother when he finally reached Leipzig, there hangs a strange, introspective air of depression, of lassitude, as though something has happened to sour the joyful prospect of finally devoting his life to music. Whatever it was, he kept it to himself. 'He never had the openness and frankness', Röller remembered, 'to lay bare his thoughts and feelings, and thus reveal his true self'. It was a trait that people observed in him all his life.

He took two unhappy weeks to find permanent lodgings, and he had little money in his pocket. He even owed Wieck 20 thalers, and his mother, in response to his appeal, hurriedly sent him bed linen, household linen, coffee and sundry other necessities. The end of his letter of acknowledgment to her shows how close to despair he felt:

I am living like a dog . . . My hair is yards long and I want to get it cut, but I can't spare a penny. My piano is terribly out of tune but I can't afford to get a tuner. And so on and so on. I haven't even got the money for a pistol to shoot myself with . . .

Your miserable son
Robert Schumann

'Himmelhoch jauchzend, zu Tode betrübt', sings the lonely Klärchen in Goethe's *Egmont* – one moment in a transport of heavenly bliss, the next plunged into the depths of dejection. Such was Schumann's condition as his real existence, his real career opened up before him. And such it remained.

CHAPTER THREE

The World of Butterflies

I should like to paint a picture of his spiritual life, but I do not know him fully: he has hidden himself behind a heavy veil, whether consciously or unconsciously, which only men of mature mind can penetrate. I would not rank him among ordinary men: versatility and certain unusual characteristics single him out from the crowd. His temperament is the Melancholy, which is to say, he is given to emotion rather than to contemplation, tends to the subjective rather than to the objective. Strong powers of imagination but needs external stimulus. Not acute in perception or strong in reflective thought, leaning towards the artistic more than the speculative. Distinguished equally in literature and music, but no musical genius. Great perseverance; extremely well read in all branches of knowledge . . .

As a man, refined, free and natural in manner, kind. Does not rush into things but keeps apart and lives in his imagination. Broad in his sympathies and able to accommodate any situation. Harbours neither conceit nor distrust . . .

His love is pure and devout, and he has given honestly of this love: that he is pleasing to women, he knows. He is born to be a leader, though he assumes an air of diffidence. To him the earth is not so much a pleasure garden as a holy temple of Nature. He is religious without having a religion. He loves mankind and has no fear of fate . . .

Schumann's words. Part of a description of a friend, perhaps? Or of a figure in literature – a character from Jean Paul, or from E.T.A. Hoffmann? In fact, a self-portrait from his diary for 1830. Like all portraits it highlights certain features and underplays others, but the subject, an aspiring twenty-year-old musician as he arrived in Leipzig, on the threshold of a sometimes luckless, sometimes brilliant, yet short, ultimately tragic career, is clearly recognizable: a complex personality with whom, in common with many others, his new teacher Friedrich Wieck found it difficult to come to terms.

The Wieck family, consisting of the forty-five-year-old Friedrich and his second wife Clementine, aged twenty-six, with one child of their own and Wieck's two eldest surviving children by his first marriage, Clara (born 1819) and Alwin, lived in a big house in the centre of old Leipzig, Grimmaische Gasse No. 36. Here Wieck did his teaching. There happened to be at the time two vacant rooms in the house, which, after a few homeless weeks in the city, Schumann discovered and immediately took. In this way he found himself in almost daily contact not only with Wieck himself but also with his daughter, the girl who was to dominate his emotional life.

Clara Wieck, short, slight, almost fragile, was eleven, and about to be presented by her father to a musical world that was soon to lie at her feet. From the moment he discovered her precocious talent Wieck made her upbringing entirely his own responsibility, attaching scant importance to her general education or the development of her personality as a whole, and treating her almost as a trainer treats a performing animal. He allowed her only the most passing of contacts with her mother, who, finding his ways more and more intolerant and intolerable, left him in 1824 when Clara was five.

At seven Clara could read almost all the music that was put in front of her; at eight she played her first concerto – Hummel in G major – to a private audience, and made her first attempts at composing. In 1829 she played to Paganini, and two years later Wieck took her to perform before Goethe and other dignitaries in Weimar. Impressed by her confidence and by the power of her artistic personality, Goethe said admiringly: 'This girl has more strength than six boys put together'. Indeed, although Wieck laid the emphasis of his teaching method on the cultivation of inner-musical, as distinct from external, technical values, much of his time with Clara was devoted to strengthening her hand and arm muscles so that she could tackle the flamboyant bravura pieces essential to any performer's repertoire in this age. At the time Schumann came to Leipzig she was also taking lessons in theory and composition from Theodor Weinlig, cantor of the Thomaskirche, at whose hands Richard Wagner received his first and only formal lessons in musical theory the following year. A few weeks after Schumann's arrival she made her public debut at a Leipzig Gewandhaus concert, playing virtuoso pieces by Kalkbrenner and Herz (the *Variations brillantes* she played to Goethe), and a set of variations of her own on an original theme.

In the course of her eighth year Wieck started a chronicle of her activities under her own name, headed: 'My diary, begun by my father on May 7, 1827 and to be continued by Clara Josephine Wieck'. All the early volumes are in Wieck's handwriting and convey his views, not hers; only from 1838, and more particularly after her concert tour to Paris in 1839, does she express her own thoughts and allow her independent personality to emerge. When we add to these journals of Clara Wieck the joint diaries of Robert and Clara Schumann, with their account of her married life, of her concert tours and of her forty years of widowhood after her husband's death, we have an almost unbroken biographical-cum-autobiographical record of the seventy years of her careworn life.

Schumann first mentions Clara in his diary in December 1828, when she and her father played Czerny's *Rondeau mignon* for piano duet at a *soirée* in Wieck's house. But it is a purely matter-of-fact entry, on a par with 'Terrible weather – evening at the Carus's – wrote to Carl – shocking hangover' and similar lapidary observations. Not until the summer of 1831 do his references to her become more frequent and more intense, and even then it is with an air almost of reverence that he addresses her: 'I often think of you [he uses the form *Sie*, of course], but not as a brother thinks of his sister, or a young man of his beloved – rather, as a pilgrim thinks of a distant altar-piece' (from a letter of January 1832).

Fired, if somewhat intimidated, by Clara's brilliance,

Schumann applied himself to the routine of piano exercises that his teacher prescribed. But not, it seems, for long. After a few months he talked of going to Weimar and putting himself in the hands of the well-known composer and pianist Johann Nepomuk Hummel, a pupil of Mozart and Clementi. Wieck indignantly regarded this as an expression of no confidence, but since he was preoccupied with the, to him, far more important business of planning his daughter's concerts, the matter quickly passed from his mind.

Where he would have found the money to study with Hummel neither Schumann nor anyone else could know. He pawned the watch that his mother had given him, and tells her that he is having to sell the books from his library one by one in order to pay his bills. The same letter contains the information that he is contemplating an opera called *Hamlet*, on which he has set his hopes: 'The thought of fame and immortality gives me strength and stimulates my imagination'. Whether it was the thought of immortality or his imagination that lacked strength, *Hamlet* got no further. Nor did his career as a pianist. And the reasons why lead into an episode around which more conflicting evidence has collected and more conflicting theories generated than around any other issue in Schumann's life save that of his terminal disease and insanity.

Looking back on the years 1830–1 in the draft of a later autobiographical sketch, Schumann wrote: 'I played the piano six or seven hours a day. Then a weakness in my right hand, which became progressively worse, forced me to give up practising and abandon my plans to become a pianist'. In May 1831, however, reviewing in a letter to his mother the various forms that his career in music might take, he still gives it as his intention to become a pianist and a composer, so at the time the 'weakness' cannot yet have been decisive. In June 1832, again in a letter to his mother, he makes his first direct, if guarded reference to 'the strange misfortune which has befallen me', and which his brother Eduard, it appears, already knows about. Two months later he was deeply worried:

The whole house is like an apothecary's. I became anxious about my hand
but deliberately put off consulting an anatomist because I was afraid of
an operation – that is, because I thought he would say that the damage
could not be remedied . . .

The doctor told him to play the piano as little as possible and
recommended *Tierbäder*, 'animal dips', a treatment often
prescribed for paralysis of the extremities. It consisted of
immersing the affected part in the secretions of the thoracic or
abdominal cavity of a freshly-slaughtered animal and holding it
there as long as the natural warmth of the cavity lasted. 'It is not
the most attractive of treatments', Schumann admitted, 'and I am
afraid lest something of the animal's nature may get into my
own'. He could, indeed, make light of the whole procedure on
occasions: 'Afterwards my whole body feels wonderfully firm and
strong, and I have an urge to go and give someone a really good
hiding'. But by November he had resigned himself to the prospect
that his hand would never be cured. Electric treatment followed,
then sundry homoeopathic remedies, with a diet that totally
prohibited wine and coffee and permitted only a little beer.

But despite occasional flickers of hope it was all to little effect.
'Nine-fingered', he called himself, and gave the first closer
account of his ailment in a letter to his Heidelberg friend Theodor
Töpken in 1833:

I have a numb, broken finger on my right hand, and as a result of what
was in itself a trivial injury, coupled with my own negligence, the
impairment has become so serious that now I can scarcely use the hand at
all when I play.

In 1838 he told Clara that his 'injured hand' was getting slowly
worse, and that, to his horror, he could barely manage to stumble
through his own new compositions. The following year he
explained to Simonin de Sire, a rich Belgian who was among the
first of his foreign admirers, that the disability affected several
fingers, which had become so weak that he could scarcely use
them, but here he attributes the condition – evasively, one must
suspect – merely to having strained his hand by too much writing

and piano-playing in the past. To round off the historical record, there is a medical certificate in the military conscription records of Leipzig for the years 1841–2, which reports a total paralysis of the third finger of his right hand and a partial paralysis of the index finger. On the basis of this, combined with extreme shortsighted-ness and a tendency to attacks of vertigo, Schumann was declared unfit for military service, since he would have been unable to aim or fire a rifle. The document, signed by Dr Moritz Emil Reuter, who was one of the witnesses at Schumann's marriage to Clara Wieck in 1840, dates this condition from October 1831 and attributes it to the use of a 'mechanical device'.

But what actually caused the condition variously described as a misfortune, an injury and a state of paralysis? Over fifty years later the scholar Frederick Niecks, who sought out the personal evidence of surviving friends and colleagues for his biography of Schumann, asked the composer's widow about the matter. Clara, who was a mere twelve or so at the time, later talked only of the index finger and maintained that her husband had crippled it by practising on a very stiff dumb keyboard (Schumann's brother-in-law Moritz Semmel records that Schumann used to take on his travels a portable dumb keyboard, with springs fixed to the keys, in order to keep his fingers supple). But this explanation is unique to Clara, and although the army medical record does confirm that the index finger was involved, it does not confine the injury – nor did Schumann himself – to one finger.

The focus of attention then moves to the 'mechanical device' quoted in the military report. According to Schumann's first biographer, Josef von Wasielewski, who played under him in the Düsseldorf orchestra from 1850 to 1853 and had personal dealings with many of those close to him, Schumann hinted to a number of friends during his early months under Wieck that he had invented a mechanism which, attached to the hand, would make it possible to acquire a brilliant technique in a minimum of time. Indeed, already in Heidelberg he and Töpken had experimented with such devices. But in 1833, as Töpken later confirmed to Wasielewski, he confessed: 'We were at fault in trying to accomplish with these often reckless contraptions what a gentle, relaxed attitude would of itself have produced in the fullness of time'. The apparatus appears to have held the third finger back in a kind of sling, so that the other fingers could be exercised to achieve optimum dependence. As a result the tendons of his third finger, and also, it seems, of the index finger, became strained and permanently damaged. 'My third finger is completely stiff', he wrote in his diary in June 1832. Apart from its effect on his piano playing the disability must have made it difficult for him to grip a pen firmly, and would explain the painfully irregular and slovenly appearance of his handwriting, which, though somewhat firmer in his later years, never fails to test one's powers of decipherment.

In his book *Clavier und Gesang*, published over twenty years later, Wieck has a section in which he dissociates himself from a school of contemporary piano teachers that set store by mechanical aids such as the 'chiroplast', a device for making the hands flexible invented by Johann Bernhard Logier at the beginning of the century. In this section Wieck makes dark reference to a '"finger-tormenter" invented by a famous pupil of mine, which he employed behind my back, to the justifiable outrage of his third and fourth fingers'.* Although he mentions Schumann by name elsewhere in his book, he does not do so here, but it has always been assumed – perhaps too readily – that he had Schumann in mind. In any case, Schumann and Clara had by

---

*Quite apart from the question of the cause of the disability there is conflicting evidence on which actual fingers were affected. Part of the difficulty derives from differences of nomenclature – whether the hand is defined as having five fingers or a thumb and four fingers. Practice has varied in this between anatomists and musicians, between musicians in different countries, and from one age to another. The confusion has been compounded by English translators, who have sometimes taken over the German nomenclature without checking its precise meaning. One must know who is speaking, then when and where, in order to be able to interpret his utterance.

Over the term 'index finger' *(Zeigefinger)* – used by Clara and in the army medical report – there can be no misunderstanding. And since, whatever the nomenclature, the evidence always seems to refer to adjacent fingers, these would be the second (index) and third (cf. Schumann's diary reference above), the latter being the one treated – or maltreated – in the mechanical contraption. But Wieck's statement remains discrepant, whichever two fingers it refers to, and the discrepancies persist in biographies of Schumann, ancient and modern.

this time been married for thirteen years, and Wieck had long since made his peace with the son-in-law whose suit he had so tenaciously opposed, so he would have no cause to rehearse old arguments by exposing the culprit in public.

A totally different explanation of the injury to Schumann's hand was put forward as a rider to the diagnosis of his terminal disease – now generally accepted as accounting most completely for all the known symptoms – as syphilis. The standard treatment for syphilis in the nineteenth century consisted of administering doses of mercury, from which metal poisoning not infrequently developed. This showed itself *inter alia* in the form of headaches, nausea, depression, and numbness in the extremities; it was also one of the conditions for which *Tierbäder* were prescribed.

On this foundation the Schumann scholar Eric Sams built the theory that mercury treatment had affected Schumann's hand and fingers, and that he had thought up the 'finger-tormenter' as a means of overcoming the weakness. This contrivance would thus have been, not the cause of a condition but an attempted cure for it. And since Töpken was a party to the experiments, and must have known what lay behind them, the source of Schumann's primary infection must pre-date his stay in Heidelberg, which gives a *terminus a quo* of 1828–9 – his student days in Leipzig and his revelrous trip down the Rhine.

Attractive in its plausibility, such a chain of argument can only sustain a set of hypothetical circumstances – *if* Schumann had contracted syphilis, *if* he received mercury treatment for it, *if* poisoning then set in, and so on. And although he may have suffered from certain disorders that can be associated with mercury poisoning, there are other known symptoms which do not seem to have afflicted him. Then, did Wieck know or suspect that he might have syphilis? Could it have been the real reason why he would not tolerate the thought of Schumann marrying Clara? Indeed, did Clara herself know – assuming there was anything to know – and invent the story of the dumb keyboard years afterwards to protect his reputation, having borne him eight children in this knowledge? Has it something to do with her seeming reluctance to visit him in the mental asylum during his final years?

All we need say here – and we shall return to the subject when the symptoms of his deteriorating health overshadow all else – is that neither Schumann, nor Clara, nor any of the friends who observed him at the time, mention venereal disease, treatment for it, mercury poisoning or any other term in the equation. Clara never became infected, and all eight of their children were born without complications.

Although the occasional hope still flickered across his mind, Schumann knew by the end of 1831, or early in 1832 at the latest, that his vision of a career as a concert pianist could never become reality. The association of performance with composition had come to be taken almost for granted – Bach, Mozart, Beethoven, Paganini; in Schumann's own day Mendelssohn, Chopin, Liszt, later Brahms – and an inability adequately to interpret one's own works was a considerable handicap, both musical and social. But the matter lay beyond Schumann's influence. And in any case he was on the brink of other achievements.

Schumann was always quick to sense when he could profit from the expertise of others, even though he rapidly became sceptical of what they had to offer him, and in the summer of 1831 he embarked on a course of lessons in harmony and counterpoint with Heinrich Dorn, director of music at the Leipzig opera. Only six years Schumann's senior, Dorn was to become Wagner's successor as music director in Riga in 1839, and later in 1849 conductor of the Royal Opera House in Berlin. As Schumann never forgot his debt to his first musical teacher, Kuntzsch, so, despite the difference in their personalities, he acknowledged the value of the discipline to which Dorn had subjected him.

And discipline he needed. 'The first four-part chorale he had to do for me as a test of his knowledge of harmony,' said Dorn, 'was a perfect example of how to break all the rules of part-writing'. Connoisseurs of coincidences will enjoy the irony that thirteen years later, writing to Mendelssohn about *Tannhäuser*, Schumann said the same about Wagner, whom he accused of 'being unable to write four consecutive bars of music that are decently thought out'.

His studies in counterpoint took him as far as canon. 'For the rest', he wrote to his mother, 'Bach's *Well-tempered Clavier* is my grammar – the best there is. I have analysed the fugues one by one in the closest detail, which is of immense value and seems to strengthen one's whole moral fibre. Bach was a real man, a man through and through; there are no half-measures about him, nothing morbid – he composed everything as though for eternity'. His proud confession to Clara in 1838 is only one of many such later remarks: 'Bach is my daily bread. I refresh myself in his presence and perpetually draw new ideas from him'. And looking back in 1843: 'Bach and Jean Paul exercised the greatest influence on me in former times.'

Praising him for his diligence, Dorn later recalled his impressions of his young pupil:

He was a very handsome man, with blue eyes, which he tended to screw up a little. Roguish dimples appeared in his cheeks whenever he laughed . . . He gave the impression of being rather shy, and always kept very quiet.

The year 1831 marks Schumann's coming of age, and with it his accession to the substantial sum of money that his father had left him. He was now financially independent, and with this independence came a sense of responsibility. In his life as an artist too 1831 had a special meaning. It marked the publication of his Opus 1 and the launching of his career as a music critic.

Except for the very last period of his creative life, Schumann's compositions tend to come in clusters. From 1830 to 1839 he wrote only for the piano. In 1840 he devoted himself almost exclusively to song – the glorious year of *Dichterliebe, Frauenliebe und -leben* and other cycles. 1841 saw the composition of the First and Second (later revised to become the Fourth) Symphonies; then followed a period of chamber music – the three string quartets, the Piano Quintet and the Piano Quartet, all composed in 1842.

What underlies this phenomenon, and what motive forces guided his thoughts into the one or the other medium at a

particular moment, are matters that will take their place in the
biographical narrative. But we may already note, since it is a
broad observation about the course of Schumann's artistic and
psychological evolution as a whole, that the line of development
leads from the brief and fragmentary to the sustained and
rounded, from the fanciful and the evocatively novel to the
controlled and the traditionally self-justifying, from a music of
non-musical associations to a music of self-contained values, an
absolute music. In a word, it is a progress from romanticism to
classicism.

Schumann composed his Opus 1, the 'Abegg' Variations, in
Heidelberg in 1830, and they were published the following year by
Friedrich Kistner in Leipzig – 'a publisher whom I declare for the
benefit of posterity and all other composers to be a rogue', he
uncharitably recorded in his diary. 'Abegg' has two significances:
it is the name of a family in Mannheim, various members of
which Schumann had apparently come to know, and it spells a
sequence of notes, which, in waltz tempo, make up the theme on
which the variations are based:

A - B - E - G - G

[In German nomenclature B = English B flat, and H = English B.]

Apart from the occasional moment of chromaticism which
hints at the Schumann that was to come, and the technical
assuredness of the sometimes rather tinsel-like passage-work,
there is little of substantial interest in the music, which lives on
effective moments rather than on a sense of thoroughgoing
conviction, and is not free of the occasional gauche harmonic
progression. Basing pieces on the letters of a proper name was, of
course, not novel – BACH is the most familiar example, a motif
used already by Bach himself in *The Art of Fugue*: Schumann
later added his own studies on this theme in his *Six Fugues on the
Name of Bach* (Op. 60) for organ or pedal piano. His *Carnaval*

derives from the four letters ASCH, and there are instances in other works of private allusions smuggled into the music through combinations of notes which spell out groups of letters from individual names, including his own.

By the time the 'Abegg' Variations were published, *Papillons* (Op. 2) and other piano works, among them the *Toccata* (Op. 7), were already lying complete in his drawer. Compared with *Papillons* and everything that followed, the 'Abegg' Variations may seem conventional, even unpromising. Yet to Schumann they belonged, like the Intermezzi (Op. 4) and the Impromptus (Op. 5), with *Papillons* itself, to a single musico-poetic *genre* which he called just that – 'Papillon'.

What so persistent symbolic meaning did the image of the 'papillon' hold for Schumann? In a sense the question draws a predictable answer, for the ready associations that the butterfly evokes – delicacy, brilliance of colour, quick, darting movements in the warmth and freedom of sun-lit nature – can hardly be other than those in Schumann's own mind. And the most casual of glances at the twelve little numbers of the work shows the lightness, the playfulness, the fanciful changes of mood and direction as the music – or the butterfly – flits from one scene to the next.

But beyond this there runs through the work a programme, a sequence of events which the music mirrors – more accurately, of which Schumann's piece is the musical correspondent – and whose source he made clear in a letter to the poet and critic Ludwig Rellstab:

I feel I must add a few words about the origin of the *Papillons*, for the thread that is meant to bind them together is scarcely visible. You will remember the final scene of Jean Paul's *Flegeljahre*: fancy dress ball – Walt – Vult – masks – Vina –Vult's dancing – exchange of masks – confessions – rage – revelations – hurry away – concluding scene, then the departing brother. Again and again I turned over the last page, for the end seemed to me but a new beginning.

Almost without knowing, I found myself sitting at the piano, and one Papillon after another came into being.

The work is dedicated to his sisters-in-law, Therese, Rosalie and

Emilie. In a joint letter to them, to his three brothers and to his
mother he makes its origin and inspiration equally explicit:

Please read the closing scene of Jean Paul's *Flegeljahre* as soon as you
can. *Papillons* is actually a setting of this carnival to music. Does it not
faithfully reflect something of Vina's angelic love, of Walt's poetic
temperament and of Vult's sharp, brilliant nature?

In his own copy of *Flegeljahre* Schumann marked ten passages in
this final chapter with numbers that correspond to the first ten
items of the *Papillons*. The *'Grossvatertanz'* and the striking
clock in the Finale are his own invention.

Thus *Papillons* is a piece of undisguised programme music,
depicting the ball at which the twin brothers Walt and Vult, the
one an unworldly and over-sensitive poetic dreamer, the other a
forceful and independent realist, confront each other in their love
for Vina. At the end of Jean Paul's unfinished novel Vina gives
herself to Walt, and Vult, accepting his fate, leaves for ever. The
night of merry-making is over. In Schumann's magical Finale the
church clock strikes six, the last revellers make their way home
and all is quiet.

As Walt and Vult, the Faustian 'two souls' in Jean Paul's
breast, act out their roles according to their contrasting personalities, yet are in reality recto and verso of the same body
symbolizing the unity of the real and imaginary, of object and
subject, so Schumann was about to crystallize from his own
personality two fictitious characters to represent the different
sides of his nature. The divided personality, the *Doppelgänger*,
the *alter ego*, is a familiar symbol and technique in German
romantic writers from Jean Paul through Kleist and E.T.A.
Hoffmann to Grillparzer and Heine, both a demonstration of the
polymorphic nature of the individual human psyche and an
assertion of the transcendent principle of unitarianism.

A number of Schumann's earliest pieces, some since lost, some
unfinished, many of them in dance form (all but one of the
Papillons, like the 'Abegg' Variations, are in triple measure),
found their way into *Papillons*, as well as into the six *Intermezzi*

written the following year. These latter, which already show typical features of Schumann's piano style – the syncopated triplet patterns in No. 2; the double-octave call to attention, like a summoning trumpet (Nos 2 and 6); the sprightly Allegros with dry, dotted and double-dotted rhythms (Nos 1 and 4); the cross-hand intricacies in Nos 2 and 5 – incorporate material from earlier, unpublished vocal and chamber music. To this extent both *Papillons* and the *Intermezzi*, like the other early opus numbers, do not represent a sudden, successful departure from the adolescence of unpublishable juvenilia but a triumphant union of the romantic principles and impulses that made up the creative world in which he was living. At the same time, in the general context of the early nineteenth century they take their place alongside Beethoven's Bagatelles, Schubert's *Moments musicaux*, Mendelssohn's *Songs without Words* and similar collections of fanciful, mood-invoking miniatures in which one aspect of romantic pianoforte music finds such delicate expression.

Papillons received slightly patronizing but gratifyingly generous reviews from senior critics. The *Allgemeiner musikalischer Anzeiger* of Vienna praised the young composer for his originality: 'He belongs to no school but creates from within himself, shaping a new, ideal world through which he boldly, almost wantonly roams, at times with the most eccentric of gestures'. A letter from the venerable Hummel, to whom he had sent both the 'Abegg' Variations and *Papillons*, gave Schumann particular pleasure:

I am delighted at your lively talent. The only thing I might draw attention to is an occasional over-rapid change of harmony. Also you seem to surrender yourself perhaps a little too readily to the originality that you undoubtedly possess. I would not like this to become habitual with you, for it would detract from the beauty, the freedom and the clarity of a well-planned composition. But if you continue diligently and calmly, I have no doubt that you will attain your goal.

As the shadow of Jean Paul hangs over Schumann's earliest musical compositions, so Walt and Vult are godfathers to his first published piece of music criticism – a review of Chopin's Variations for Piano and Orchestra on the aria 'Là ci darem la mano' from *Don Giovanni*. It appeared in the *Allgemeine musikalische Zeitung*, the leading music journal of the day, in December 1831.

Much has been made of the remarkable vision that led Schumann in his very first public utterance to hail the genius of the as yet unknown and unplayed Chopin – who was a matter of four months older than the equally unknown Schumann. Indeed, when the question of Schumann the critic arises, most people can call to mind only this, his first article, with its famous challenge, 'Hats off, gentlemen, a genius!', and his last essay written in 1853 predicting the greatness awaiting the young Johannes Brahms. And to be sure, when one realizes the slightness of the evidence on which, in both cases, he staked his judgement – these Op. 2 Variations in the case of Chopin and Brahms' Opp. 1–5 (mainly piano works and still unpublished) – his instinct earns an almost uncanny justification. 'I do not think I err', he later wrote with pride, 'when I say that I was the first to draw attention to Chopin, this bold new spirit.'

Yet Schumann could wax equally lyrical over figures whose names barely survive today – Hermann Hirschbach, Norbert Burgmüller, Theodor Kirchner – and he failed ever to recognize two of the giants of his age: Wagner and Liszt. He had a keen sense of musical quality and craftsmanship *per se*: this underlies his unflagging enthusiasm for Mendelssohn and also for minor masters such as John Field and Sterndale Bennett. But his response to music, and his judgements on it, could as often be guided by what he felt to be a spiritual affinity to his own creative personality. He would turn aside almost involuntarily from what did not speak directly to his heart, for his concern was less to expose inadequacy and inferiority than to arouse enthusiasm for the virtues in which he so passionately believed and whose cause he so passionately advocated. In Chopin's *Don Giovanni* rhapsody he found an originality akin to his own – at times almost a reflection of his own world. And indeed, although their musical languages became more and more distinctive as their individual personalities developed, in harmonic idiom and in some aspects of the piano writing Chopin's Opus 2 has a good deal in common with the Schumann who was soon to emerge in the *Carnaval* (one of whose numbers is actually called 'Chopin') and the *Études symphoniques*.

Schumann's Chopin notice is headed simply 'Ein Werk II'. But subscribers to the conservative *Allgemeine musikalische Zeitung* found themselves reading something very different from that journal's usual reviews – so different, in fact, that Gottfried Wilhelm Fink, the editor, whose acceptance of the piece in the first place raised a number of uncomprehending eyebrows, felt constrained to follow it with a second notice of the same work. This, by an unnamed 'respected and honourable representative of the older school' – in fact Fink himself – followed conventional lines in its analysis, and concluded that Chopin's work was merely 'a piece of bravura and empty technical display'. Wieck called it 'clever and original' but added that 'almost all pianists and teachers consider it unintelligible and unplayable'.

Schumann thought otherwise. 'I consider Chopin's Variations to be not only one of the greatest piano works ever written but even, perhaps, one of the greatest of all musical works,' he wrote impetuously in his diary. But what was so different about the way he said the same thing in the august pages of the *Allgemeine musikalische Zeitung*? Let the opening of his 'review' speak for itself:

The other day Eusebius came quietly into the room. His pale features wore the enigmatic smile with which, as you know, he seeks to arouse curiosity. I was sitting with Florestan at the piano: Florestan is one of those rare musicians who seem to sense strange, new forces that lie in store. But this time even he was to be surprised.

With the words: 'Hats off, gentlemen, a genius!' Eusebius spread a piece of music out in front of us. We were not allowed to see the title. I turned the pages idly – there is something magical about the secret enjoyment of music unheard. Moreover, every composer seems to have his own musical handwriting – Beethoven looks different on paper from Mozart, just as Jean Paul's prose looks different from Goethe's. Here it was as though I were the object of strange stares coming from the eyes of flowers, of serpents, of peacocks, of maidens. Now and again it became clearer, and I thought I could detect Mozart's 'Là ci darem la mano' threading its way through a hundred chords. Leporello seemed to cast secret glances at me, and the Don hurried past in a white cloak . . .

Small wonder that the readers of the *Allgemeine musikalische Zeitung* were baffled. It sounded like the beginning of a short story, nothing like what they understood by a review. It offered no analysis, no musical examples – indeed, it seemed to say nothing at all about the work supposedly under discussion, except that the reviewer, a quite unknown young man, considered it a work of genius.

In literary context Schumann's little essay stands in direct line of descent from *Ritter Gluck, Don Juan,* the *Kreisleriana* and other works by E.T.A. Hoffmann, the writer second only to Jean Paul in Schumann's hierarchy. (He once toyed with the idea, according to his diary, of writing a 'poetic biography' of 'this confounded man Hoffmann'.) It is music 'criticism' of the romantic school, the philosophy of understanding not through analysis, the separation of subject from object, but through empathy, spiritual union, an invocation of the all-embracing oneness of the world, experienced through self-surrender to the values of art. 'Ein Werk II' tells us as much – perhaps more – about Schumann as about Chopin. But this is as it should be, for Schumann is as integral a part of the single, indivisible musical world about which he writes as is Chopin, and the whole cannot exclude any of its parts.

Here the figures of Eusebius and Florestan, scions of Jean Paul's Walt and Vult, having held animated conversations with each other in the pages of his diary for 1831, make their first public appearance in Schumann's writings. As pseudonyms for both sides of his personality, and as founder-members of the imaginary brotherhood of like-minded companions that he christened the 'Davidsbündler', they were to acquire in the coming years a special role as spokesmen for his own attitudes and views.

But already here Eusebius and Florestan present themselves as characters who reflect on music in the same spirit as Schumann composes it – a free, romantic spirit, rich in contrasts, that resists the dead weight of the conventional past and launches dazzling shafts of fantasy into new realms of the imagination. 'Kinder, schafft Neues!' cried Richard Wagner, despairing of contemporary composers who could only pour old wine into old bottles. It may be a far cry from the small-scale work of Schumann's piano pieces and songs to the immensity of Wagnerian music-drama, and alongside the giant figure of Wagner Schumann looks a minor figure. But his thought, both in music and in words, has its own originality: not the shattering originality of *Tristan und Isolde* or *Der Ring des Nibelungen*, yet an originality nonetheless – impulsive, personal, intimate.

Unhappily, this surge of creative vigour brought little assurance of stability, circumstantial or psychological, into his ways. A sense of restlessness and unease, compounded of various unrelated elements, was spreading over the surface of his life like a rash. The condition of his feeble right hand was a nagging source of depression, and he suffered a great deal from migraine. The energy and enterprise that his schoolfriends had so admired, like the abandoned frolics of his student days in Leipzig and Heidelberg, now gave way on occasion to a sombre introspection, sometimes accompanied by a withdrawal from the companionship of others. There was the occasional visit from members of the family, and he had a handful of friends he saw more or less regularly, like Moritz Semmel, Julius Knorr, with whom he played piano duets, the writer and later 'Davidsbündler' Willibald von der Lühe, and his long-standing drinking companion from Zwickau, Eduard Rascher, but these associations too tended to congeal, and the circle to become closed.

Wieck, with whom, in spite of the injury to his fingers, Schumann still had regular contact, was now devoting less and less time to his pupils and more and more to promoting Clara's concert tours. This took him away from Leipzig for considerable periods and deprived Schumann of the stimulus of his company. Then in the summer of 1832, after a profitable, if sometimes stormy nine months, Schumann finally gave up his composition lessons with Dorn, thus breaking another of the links that had given form and direction to his life.

Besides this there was the practical matter of his lodgings. From the time he arrived in Leipzig in the autumn of 1830 until 1836, when he found the rooms in the 'Rotes Kolleg' in the Ritterstrasse where he stayed till his marriage, he seems to have moved at least six times, the anticipated pleasures of each successive new apartment quickly wearing off. He does not appear to have stayed in the Wieck household much longer than six months, but exactly when and under what circumstances he left we do not know. Certainly he continued to be a regular visitor to the house even before he fell in love with Clara, for in a still fairly formal letter to her in February 1832 he describes with unfeigned joy how he used to tell fairy tales and adventure stories to her three younger brothers and play charades in their house.

Nowhere does the disharmony between the private and the public, between the growing self-consciousness of the young artist and the demands of society around him, become more apparent than in the changed style of his diaries. From his schooldays onwards Schumann had shown a penchant for epigrams – a partiality traceable in part to his conversance with Latin authors but more particularly to the influence of Jean Paul. Now, in place of the eager, breathless recital of journeys, faces, revelries and intellectual experiences that crowd his diaries of recent years, come solemn, studied utterances and extended fragments of autobiography, interspersed with the reflections of a man who seems to have lost much of his *joie de vivre*.

True, there was a period in 1832 when together with Rascher he developed an inordinate thirst for Bavarian beer, but this thirst, he solemnly assured his mother in May, was now permanently slaked, and his life set on a regular and sober course. His deeper worries about the future force themselves into his diary as terse, almost bitter reflections: 'The artist must always retain a balance with the outside world. Otherwise he will perish – like me'.

His self-centred despondency was deepened by a fear that gripped many parts of Germany at this time: the fear of cholera. The disease spread westwards from India through Russia and

Turkey in the early part of the century, and a wave reached northern and central Europe in 1829–30. Intensified by the Russo-Polish war of 1831, it claimed many hundreds of lives in Berlin and Vienna, and Schumann, who was haunted all his life by a morbid fear of falling victim to one epidemic or another, even had a dream in which he saw Wieck, Clara and himself meeting together for the last time before being struck down by the disease.

But sometimes a mood of optimism would suddenly radiate his world, as when he describes to his mother in a tone part playful, part genuinely happy the pattern of his daily round in the summer of 1932:

If I were to paint a picture of my domestic life, I might describe it as Italian in the morning and Dutch in the evening. My rooms are respectable, spacious and pleasant. At five in the morning I find myself able to leap out of bed like a deer. First I attend to my cash accounts, my diary and my correspondence. Then up to eleven o'clock I divide my time between studying, composing and reading: Lühe comes every day at eleven, a model of order and regularity. Lunch – then I read some French, or the newspapers. I take a regular walk between three and six, mostly by myself, in the direction of Connewitz [a village south of Leipzig]. Home by six, I improvise at the keyboard till eight, usually go to Kömpel's* and Wolff's for supper, then back home.

This snatch of autobiography, like most of his letters to his mother before he became twenty-one, still has something of the naïve, self-justifying, almost-too-good-to-be-true tone in which he habitually exaggerated his devotion to the study of law. But between the blithe, busy lines lurks a loneliness, a feeling of dissatisfaction, which only his creative urge could dissipate. 'I have always hated any form of inactivity', he wrote later in the same letter.

Not that the gay, self-indulgent Schumann of student days had vanished. A girl called Ottilie whom he had known in Leipzig

---

*Clara, in her edition of Schumann's *Jugendbriefe*, could not decipher this name with certainty. Neither of the two names appears in his Leipzig diary.

three years before now crossed his path again. At a Gewandhaus concert in aid of the Polish refugees who had been driven from their homes by the Russians, he caught sight of her across the hall: 'Ottilie gave me one long, hard look: I shall never be able to forget you. Her brother is in the Kaffeebaum restaurant every evening . . .' – characteristically abrupt, ejaculatory diary jottings that conceal a wealth of feeling and experience.

A pretty face never ceased to draw his glance. A number of years later he warned Clara: 'If we find ourselves strolling down a street in Vienna and an attractive figure comes towards me, so that I exclaim: "Look at those heavenly features, Clara!", or something similar – don't be shocked or get angry with me'.

His references to Clara at this time are full of respect and admiration, and he detects in 'Zilia', i.e. Cecilia, patron saint of music, as he now calls her, the same sudden swings from joy to melancholy, laughter to tears, that scarred his own spiritual life. Once he mentions that they stood arm-in-arm in Wieck's house. But there is no real inkling of what was to come. 'We are like brother and sister,' he described their relationship to his brother Julius in July 1832.

Among the plans for 1832 that he noted in his diary are a *Fantasie rhapsodique*, dedicated to Clara, of which no more is heard, a Fandango for piano, which found a place in his first Piano Sonata, and a set of studies on violin caprices by Paganini, which were completed and published later the same year. A piano concerto begun in Heidelberg and continued in Leipzig remained a torso. In addition he proposed to make a thorough analysis of the fugues in Bach's *Well-tempered Clavier* and to write a 'musical novel', with Cecilia (= Clara, a musical divinity), Florestan (= himself) and Meister Raro (= Wieck) as the principle characters, and 'the artist, the purity of art, supreme artistry and irony' as its generative principle. On this evidence the novel sounds as though it would have become a synthetic derivate of Jean Paul, E.T.A. Hoffmann and Goethe's *Wilhelm Meister* (which Schumann was reading at this time). But it was never written. Instead, the themes and the characters found their way into the company of Schumann's 'Davidsbündler' and came to life in the pages of his *Neue Zeitschrift für Musik*.

The *Six Studies after Caprices by Paganini* (Op. 3), like the second set of six written the following year (Op. 10), are instructional exercises 'arranged', as he put it, 'for pianists who wish to extend their technique in a variety of directions'. They were also instructional exercises for Schumann himself in that, on the one hand, they forced him to interpret the sometimes uncertain harmonic intentions of the original, and on the other, they extended his ingenuity in inventing pianistic equivalents of Paganini's string writing. A far cry from *Papillons*, they are the product of sheer hard work. For each study he provides detailed fingering, preparatory exercises and a commentary on specific technical problems. The result is a work that makes great demands on the performer, demands in many ways as formidable as those made by Liszt's more striking transcriptions of some of the same caprices.

How little Schumann's musical career had advanced by this time – or, more accurately, how narrow was its scope – is illustrated by a coincidence involving Richard Wagner. In December 1832 a Symphony in C by Wagner was played at a concert in the Gewandhaus. Clara afterwards wrote to Schumann: 'Herr Wagner has outstripped you, do you know? A symphony of his was played here, which is said to have been the very image of Beethoven's A major!' Schumann too, as it happened, was working on a symphony, in G minor, the first movement of which was given at a concert in Zwickau in November 1832. But it aroused little enthusiasm. Wieck found it 'well-constructed' but 'too thinly orchestrated', and although Schumann tried to remedy his inexperience in this latter department by taking lessons in instrumentation, the symphony was never finished. Almost nine years passed before he returned to the symphonic form.

Not only Wagner, who was three years younger than Schumann, but also Chopin, his precise contemporary, not to mention Mendelssohn, who was only one year older, had accomplished far more by this time than he. Although very little was yet published, Chopin had by 1832 composed waltzes, mazurkas, studies, the B minor Scherzo, the two piano concertos and a good deal else, while Mendelssohn, the prodigy, had behind him the incidental music to *A Midsummer Night's Dream, Fingal's Cave*, the String Octet, Book One of the *Songs without Words* and much else besides.

After spending some weeks of the winter of 1832–3 with his mother in Zwickau and his brother Karl in Schneeberg, Schumann went back to new rooms in Leipzig, this time in a large house given over in part to a popular restaurant called 'Rudolphs Garten'. He had frequented this restaurant for years, and the outlook from his rooms over the garden and the meadows beyond would, he hoped, help to bring him the peace of mind in which his art could be nurtured, a peace 'to which', in his words, he felt 'a kind of entitlement – a feeling I could share only with a serene and happy poet'. This peace of mind did not come. But Schumann could not know then that, like so many artists, he was able to create not only out of a condition of serenity and relaxation but also under stress, under the pressure of adversity, frustration and sometimes of despair.

Shortly after settling into 'Rudolphs Garten', where his student penchant for 'champagne nights', as he called them, continued undiminished, he had an experience which greatly intrigued him. A schoolteacher in Leipzig called Karl Julius Simon Portius had invented what he called a 'psychometer'. This, according to Schumann's description, was a machine which purported to reveal through magnetic forces the traits of an individual's character. The subject – 'victim' would be a better word – was first brought into 'magnetic association' with the machine, as Schumann put it. Then he was given an iron rod: if he possessed a particular characteristic 'fed into' the machine, the magnet in the machine would attract the rod; if he did not, it would repel it.

Since the middle of the eighteenth century and the time of the flamboyant alchemist and charlatan 'Count' Alessandro Cagliostro, cultured society in Europe had been fascinated by mechanical simulations of animal and human behaviour. In Paris Jacques de Vaucanson displayed a flute-player, a tambourine-player and – his masterpiece – a duck which ate, drank and quacked. Baron Wolfgang von Kempelen's mechanical chess-player was for years a much sought-after attraction in the courts of Europe. The most startling, however, and certainly most 'real' of these phenomena were the forces of hypnotism – 'animal magnetism', as he called them – released and exploited by Anton Mesmer. A belief in the magic powers of the lodestone goes back to antiquity but the 'enlightened' eighteenth century still applied it to the body as a cure both for external injuries and for internal disorders. Mesmer himself used it at first in his treatment of nervous diseases, abandoning it only when he realized that the healing power issued not from the magnet but from his own body.

Charlatans of all hues soon invaded the scene, and Portius seems to have been one of the more colourful. But Schumann took the psychometer utterly seriously, not least because it produced a character analysis which corresponded very much to his own assessment of himself. To his considerable satisfaction, the machine did not find him, as some people did, 'Secretive', 'Obsequious' or 'Determined', nor did the magnet react to 'Covetous', 'Crafty' or 'Dogmatic'. It did, however, respond strongly to 'Quiet', 'Shy', 'Sensitive', 'Original' and 'Predominantly Emotional'. It also diagnosed him as 'Hypochondriac', which he readily admitted.

In March he composed the piano *Impromptus* (Op. 5). Based on a theme by Clara and dedicated to her father, they are again cast in variation form. They reveal harmonic and rhythmic flashes of the Schumann that was to come, and some characteristically bravura piano writing, but Clara's rather insipid melody and Schumann's sometimes unconvincing bass line conspire to produce a work lacking fire and sustained conviction. We are still waiting for a true successor to *Papillons*.

The year 1833, already barren and unpromising, became darker as autumn approached. In July and August he suffered repeated fits of shivering, from which he took a long while to recover. Then in October his sister-in-law Rosalie, Karl's wife, died, and a month later his favourite brother Julius, who with Eduard had run the family business in Zwickau since their father's death.

Julius was twenty-eight, Rosalie a mere twenty-five. No family attachment of Schumann's approached in loyalty and intimacy that to his mother, and his relationship with Karl and Eduard, to whom he seems to have written only when he was short of money, rarely rose above the polite and the dutiful. But in his sisters-in-law he found sensitive companions with whom he could communicate without inhibition and without pretence. His dedication to them – Therese, Rosalie and Emilie – of a group of unpublished songs written during his student days, then of *Papillons*, was his way of showing his gratitude for their sympathy.

These two deaths plunged him into deep melancholy. The presence of sickness or death always released in him a morbid fear that fate had marked him down as the next victim, and the sudden loss of two relatives so close to him, both of them barely older than himself, paralysed his mind and his will. 'I will say nothing of these past weeks', he wrote to his mother:

I was little more than a statue, neither warm nor cold: by forcing myself to work, I gradually brought myself back to life. But I am still so fearful and timid that I cannot sleep alone, so I have taken in a good, honest fellow called Günther and am doing something for his education, which both attracts and cheers me. Can you believe me when I say I have not got the courage to travel to Zwickau alone, for fear lest something happen to me? Violent rushes of blood, indescribable fear, loss of breath, fainting fits – all come in quick succession, though less now than in the last few days. If you could imagine the apathy that this melancholy causes, you would, I know, forgive me for not having written sooner.

Months later, at the beginning of 1834, he still could not bear to be reminded of Rosalie or Julius. 'The mere thought of the sufferings of others', he wrote again to his mother, 'is so shattering as to drain me of all energy. Take care, therefore, not to tell me anything that might in any way upset me, *otherwise I must give up receiving your letters altogether*'. A chillingly brutal line in his diary expresses the desperation that gripped him in these dark days:

I was obsessed with the thought of going mad.

It is a frightening glimpse of the manic-depressive Schumann who twenty years later tried to drown himself. At this early moment the depressive state gave way mercifully quickly to the pleasure of new personal encounters, then to new creative plans. But as his life went on, these spells of depression became longer and deeper, making creative work almost impossible. This in turn intensified the feelings of hopelessness and failure in his personal life. Rarely, indeed, and increasingly so with the years, could Schumann be found in a mental condition that one would unemotionally characterize as 'normal'. Either God was in his Heaven and all was right with the world, so that he was carried along by a sense of elation, by a boundless confidence in his powers and in the success that they would bring; or everything was hostile, conspiring against him, forcing him deeper and deeper into the savage despondency which permitted no escape, and in which his mind became paralysed. And the leap from one extreme to the other, whether under a benevolent or a sinister star, could come with an abruptness as disconcerting to those around him as to those who followed at a distance the fitful progress of his creative life.

Rescue from the personal depression that hung over the turn of the years 1833–4 came in the form of two new friendships. One was with Johann Peter Lyser, a painter from Hamburg. Deaf since the age of sixteen yet devoted to music, Lyser wrote a number of attractive little stories, reminiscent of E.T.A. Hoffmann, about artists and musicians, collected in 1837 as *Neue Kunst-Novellen*. The other was with a pianist called Ludwig Schunke, who, for the tragically short time left to him – he died of consumption barely a year later – became one of Schumann's dearest friends. His father was a horn-player in the court orchestra at Stuttgart; he had studied in Paris with Kalkbrenner and Herz, came to Leipzig in 1833 and found himself lodging in the same house, Burgstrasse No. 21, as Schumann had moved into that September. 'A fine man and friend', Schumann described him, 'whose pleasure lay in seeking out the best and most beautiful things in life. I would willingly exchange all my other friends for him.' Schumann introduced Schunke to Wieck and his circle, where he met Carl and Henriette Voigt, rich patrons of the arts, who became closely involved in Schumann's life and art and also nursed Schunke through the last months of his suffering. Schunke played in several concerts at the Gewandhaus and lived just long enough to receive the dedication of Schumann's Toccata in C major, published in 1834.

Much as the friendships with Lyser and Schunke did, in personal ways, to lift him out of his despondency, their value was rapidly transmuted into artistic terms during the spring of the year that Schumann called in his diary 'the most important of my life'. The year was 1834. Its primary importance lies in a title – *Neue Zeitschrift für Musik*.

CHAPTER FOUR

Literature and Music

The groundswell of subjectivism on which the European romantic movement of the late eighteenth and early nineteenth centuries was borne carried with it a wave of speculative and critical thought on the principles that underlie the artist's creative activity. Wordsworth in the Preface to *Lyrical Ballads*, Coleridge in the *Biographia literaria*, Victor Hugo in the *Préface de Cromwell*, the articles by Novalis, Tieck, Friedrich and August Wilhelm Schlegel in the *Athenäum* – these are among the familiar utterances by men of letters on the values of the new, 'liberated' romantic art.

Composers too began to declare their intentions and attitudes, not content to leave their music to speak for itself. Weber, for example, was a regular contributor to cultural periodicals of the day; Berlioz and Liszt both wrote a great deal, and so, both expounding his own theories on art and society and publicizing his opinions on his fellow-composers, did Richard Wagner. It would not have occurred to Haydn or Mozart, let alone to Bach, to set about accompanying their music with explanations of aims and procedures, and even in the early nineteenth century it is tempting to say, with one's eye on Beethoven, Schubert, Chopin, that the greatest still did not do so. There is, after all, no reason why a painter or a sculptor or a composer should wish, or, indeed, be able, to express in words ideas and experiences that he has already been moved to express in colours, plastic forms or notes.

In the twentieth century, from Debussy, Stravinsky and

Schoenberg onwards, we have come to accept it as natural that a composer should, if he is so inclined, expound at length the purport of his own music, or interpret the musical scene around him, or both. He may, of course, have no desire to do so. Equally, whether acting on his own initiative or unwisely bowing to outside pressure, he may do it badly. Today we are richly endowed, under the rubric 'The composer has said . . .', with apologies, some harmless, some meaningless, some incoherent, some pompous, that make not the slightest difference to the meaning or the quality of the pieces to which they refer. But in the early nineteenth century it was not yet so, and the expository musician, or, like Tieck and E.T.A. Hoffmann, the musical *litterateur*, was a rarity.

In Schumann's day there were in Germany some half dozen influential music journals, carrying reviews of new music and concerts, general articles, short stories, poems and original musical compositions. The oldest and most prestigious was the *Allgemeine musikalische Zeitung*, founded in 1798 and published in Leipzig by Breitkopf and Härtel. This set the pattern for *Caecilia*, launched by the publishing house of Schott in 1824, the Berlin journal *Iris im Gebiete der Tonkunst*, edited by the poet Ludwig Rellstab (the man who gave Beethoven's Moonlight Sonata its name) from its inception in 1830, the *Allgemeiner musikalischer Anzeiger* of Vienna (1829) and others. As the urban middle classes grew, so activities like concert-going reached a broader public than that commanded by the eighteenth-century patrons, private or institutional, to whose commission Mozart, Haydn and their contemporaries worked. This in its turn created a market for the publicization and criticism of the activity of both composers and performers, on the one hand giving a kind of information service to growing audiences, on the other serving the commercial interests of the publishers.

In the days of its founder, Friedrich Rochlitz, a man whom Schumann much admired, the *Allgemeine musikalische Zeitung* had followed an open-minded and liberal course welcoming, for instance, the startlingly original manner of E.T.A. Hoffmann's essay on Beethoven's Fifth Symphony. But under the crabbed editorial policies of Gottfried Wilhelm Fink, things changed.

What appalled Schumann about most of the German journals of his time, in particular the *Allgemeine musikalische Zeitung*, was not so much their staid conservatism, or even their susceptibility to commercialism, as their utter lack of artistic standards, their inability to distinguish the good from the mediocre, and their ignorance of foreign music. As his friend Carl Banck put it:

It is clear that the criticism in this paper [the *Allegemeine musikalische Zeitung*] painstakingly avoids admitting the presence of skill or inspiration, and similarly turns away from any open opposition to mediocrity and incompetence. Its policy is one of the utmost tolerance, equally far removed from enthusiastic praise and critical censure. Its motto is 'Live and let live'.

This comfortable cult of the mediocre, as Schumann saw it, lay behind the critics' failure to recognize, for example, the genius of Chopin. And since, like Fink, they could not recognize genius when it stood before their eyes, they elevated for praise anything out of the ordinary they could find in run-of-the-mill works. 'Fink', said Mendelssohn, 'had the knack of finding shortcomings in what was excellent, and making out what was in fact feeble to be not entirely without merit'. On a personal level, Schumann suspected that Fink was deliberately ignoring his own music.

Against this background, part personal, part objectively critical, he gathered around himself a group of friends and planned a counter-attack. He describes his intentions for the first time in a letter to his mother as early as June 1833:

A number of cultured young people, mostly music students, have formed a circle round me, and I in turn have made the Wieck house its centre. Our main idea is to found a major new music journal, to be issued by Hofmeister [who published several of Schumann's early works]; the announcement and the prospectus will be issued next month.

The circle round Schumann consisted of Ernst Ortlepp, a music critic some ten years older than Schumann himself who had been living in Leipzig since 1831, J.P. Lyser, and Julius Knorr, a pianist whom he had known from his earliest student days. With his straight black hair, his pale, haggard features accentuated by the cigar dangling from his mouth, with his black pointed beard, his black clothes and his club foot, Knorr looked like Mephistopheles. In fact he was a lively and charming conversationalist, with the distinction of being the first to perform Chopin's 'Là ci darem' Variations in Germany. When Ludwig Schunke arrived in Leipzig shortly afterwards, he also joined the group.

The friends used to meet either, as Schumann says, in the house of Friedrich Wieck, which he still saw as a rallying-point for those with the true interests of music at heart, or in the famous old restaurant, the Kaffeebaum, now Kleine Fleischergasse No. 3.

The Kaffeebaum, with its baroque motif of the coffee tree above the entrance, had been a coffee-house since 1694 and became in the eighteenth and nineteenth centuries a popular haunt for Lessing, Goethe, Liszt and many other figures from the world of the arts. It was restored in 1967–8, and the little corner where Schumann and his friends sat over their drinks, arguing about the future of music and about the form that their new periodical should take, is still known as the 'Schumann-Ecke'.

From Schumann's own accounts one would picture an animated company grouped around him as their acknowledged leader, hanging on his every thought and pursuing the implications of his every utterance. In the field of the written word the initiative undoubtedly came from him. Working to his own pattern, setting his own pace and responsible only to himself and his ideals, he alone had the vision and the tenacity to formulate an artistic policy and carry it into effect.

But in social situations things were very different. Indeed, for all the enthusiasm of his schooldays and all the conviviality of his life-style as a student, he had even then never been extrovert, had seldom laid bare the deepest layers of his personality. It took a long while for others to come close to him, and the number of friends to whom he was prepared to grant a measure of intimacy was always small. From the early 1830s onwards his reserve became even more marked, leaving him with an existence almost hermetically sealed within an inward-looking world governed by three private, ego-centred principles – his love for Clara, his work on the *Neue Zeitschrift*, and his music. One person after another described this taciturn manner, amounting almost to a heedlessness, of the company around him, as one of his most noticeable characteristics, one which unsettled, even alienated, many who made his acquaintance. At times he seemed deliberately to cultivate this coolness in order to open up a distance, whether through a sense of insecurity or out of real lack of interest, between himself and others. Then he would suddenly cast off his fit of moodiness and rejoin the conversation as though he had never left it.

Whatever the psychological motivations, connected, as they may well be, with the manic-depressive syndrome that runs through his whole life, there does remain in his behaviour through the 1830s so marked an increase in his reticence and his unpredictable withdrawals from social gatherings that one feels tempted to seek some additional, clinical explanation. This returns us to the question of syphilis. For one of the recorded symptoms of mercury poisoning, along with physical manifestations like numbness and tremor in the extremities – which play their part in the discussion of Schumann's disabled right hand – is a personality change characterized by bouts of depression and an aversion to human contact. Later there were even moments, both before and after his marriage to her, when he rejected Clara.

A picturesque sketch of Schumann among his friends in the 'Davidsbündler' corner of the Kaffeebaum has been left by Franz Brendel, a music historian who succeeded Schumann as editor of the *Neue Zeitschrift* in 1845:

He used to sit sideways at the table, resting his head on his hand, his eyes half closed as though he were day-dreaming*, and frequently brushing back his long hair which fell over his forehead. Then, when an interesting exchange of ideas began, he would suddenly spring to life and become loquacious, so that we could watch him wake from his reverie and, as it were, rejoin the outside world.

Usually he drank beer, occasionally Rhine wine or champagne,

---

*This is the pose in which he is depicted in Johannes Hartmann's well-known bronze statue in Zwickau, erected in 1901.

and was rarely without a cigar in his mouth. After sitting through most of the evening in apparent detachment, he might rise abruptly to his feet and leave, without bidding his companions goodnight. Afterwards it often emerged that a musical idea had suddenly come to him, and that he had rushed home to write it down.

Powerfully built, with prominent features, Schumann had the slightly superior air of one absorbed in his own spiritual world. His characteristic pursing of the lips in a kind of inner smile, to be seen in various familiar portraits, was what gave his face its typical expression, while his blue eyes had a plain, almost impassive gaze. Conventionally dressed, he held himself very upright when he walked, but his gait was soft and loose-limbed 'as though his broad shoulders had no bones to carry', said Hieronymus Truhn, a correspondent of the *Neue Zeitschrift*. He was also extremely short-sighted and often used a lorgnette.

The composer Ferdinand Hiller, who came to know Schumann well, recorded his own memories:

Few of the artists I have known are more difficult to describe in their outer nature than Schumann. His manner in his dealings with people was the total opposite of that which characterizes his compositions. These are charged with all the emotions of his restless, agitated spirit, whereas in his social life his real ideal is silence.

One day in the summer of 1845 Hiller visited Schumann in Dresden with Franz Schubert, leader of the Dresden orchestra, and Félicien David, composer of the remarkable and once immensely popular symphonic work *Le Désert*. Schumann received them warmly. They sat down and waited in silence. Hiller and Schubert made a few remarks to each other to break the ice; Schumann and David listened but did not join in the conversation. 'After a while', Hiller recalled

I was beginning to feel hot and uncomfortable, when Schumann turned and murmured to me; 'David doesn't seem to talk much'. 'No, not much,' I replied. 'I like that,' said Schumann with a gentle smile.

He had a weak speaking voice, with no sonority, and when he did speak it was in plain, straightforward sentences. But what he held back in the social realm of the spoken word found eloquent expression in his hundreds of written articles and reviews, where, undistracted by others and meditating in his own terms, he could pursue the values which he sought to impress on the musical world.

Schumann's critique of Chopin's 'Là ci darem' Variations, published in December 1831, had introduced the figures of Florestan and Eusebius. Projections of different sides of Schumann's own personality, they enthused over the newly-discovered composer of genius and went in their excitement to a third character, Meister Raro, to seek his opinion of the new work. In the autumn of 1833 he presented these three as a group in an essay called 'Die Davidsbündler', originally meant for the as yet unborn *Neue Zeitschrift für Musik* but actually published, in three instalments, in the journal *Der Komet* between December 1833 and January 1834. The fiction of a group of characters discussing the values of true art merged with the real-life situation of the circle in the Kaffeebaum. As the thoughts of 'Florestan', 'Eusebius' and 'Meister Raro' were eagerly discussed by the friends at their table in the corner, so their own views and those of others who later joined them found their way into the pages of the new paper.

The relationship is akin to that between the fiction and the reality, some fifteen years earlier, of E.T.A. Hoffmann's 'Serapion Brotherhood', the gatherings of a *confrère* of literary and musical friends in Lutter and Wegner's wine-cellar in Berlin. From their impassioned conversations Hoffmann drew the format for the succession of stories and reflections that he put into the mouths of the members of his imaginary brotherhood. Seen as a literary technique by which a chain of stories is held together by a central character or a central circumstance – *Rahmenerzählungen*, 'stories within a story' – Hoffmann's *Serapionsbrüder* tales stand in the venerable tradition of the *Thousand and One Nights, The Canterbury Tales* and the *Decamerone*. But, more important in the context of nineteenth-century romanticism to which Schumann also belongs, the members of the Serapion Brotherhood came to speak for the constituent, sometimes conflicting elements of their creator's personality. In this way he could explore from different angles both his own subjective self and a selection of contrasting attitudes towards an objective situation or issue. Schumann, who had already absorbed the influence of Hoffmann's fantastic world in his schoolboy days, now discovered in the *Serapionsbrüder* a mode of lively self-expression and an attractive literary device.

In a letter to Heinrich Dorn he defined his ideal brotherhood thus:

The 'Davidsbund', as you have known for a long time, is only a romantic creation of the mind. Mozart was once as prominent a member as Berlioz is today, or as you yourself are, without there being an actual certificate of membership. Florestan and Eusebius represent my double nature, the two sides of which I seek to fuse together, like Raro. Behind *some* of the other masks there lie real people, and much in the life of the Bündler is drawn from reality.

As their leader conceived them and breathed life into them, the 'Davidsbündler' ('Men of David') formed a band of high-minded young men who, like the poet of the Psalms, took the field against the forces of entrenched barbarism and pledged themselves to break the paralysing grip of the cultural Philistines, especially those who took virtuosity for genius and technical skill for profundity. Looking back twenty years later, he described the inauguration of his idealistic 'Davidsbund' and the tasks that its romantic young reformers set themselves:

In Leipzig towards the end of the year 1833 a group of musicians, most of them young men, used to meet together every evening, almost as though by chance. Initially their motive was simply pleasure in each other's company. But soon they began to exchange ideas on the art-form that was meat and drink to them all, namely Music.

The state of music in Germany could hardly be said to be gratifying. Rossini still reigned in the opera house, and scarcely anything was heard on the pianoforte but Herz and Hünten. Yet only a few years had passed since Beethoven, Carl Maria von Weber and Franz Schubert were still living among us. True, Mendelssohn's star was in the ascendant, and wondrous tales were told of a Pole called Chopin, but not until later did either of them have a decisive effect on the course of events.

Then one day an idea flashed through the minds of these impetuous young men. Why, they thought, should we be mere idle spectators? Let us go to work to improve matters, and restore the true poetic quality of music. Thus the first pages of a new music journal came into being.

Schumann saw the activity of writing about music not as an exercise in detached observation or analysis but as a corollary, almost an organic extension, of the creative musical process itself. His grounding in literature, reaching back to his early knowledge of Latin and Greek, his readings in German literature and the entire ambience of the world of books in which his father lived, was firmer than that in music. Indeed, not until he had become a student at the University of Leipzig did the call to music finally prevail over the temperament that would have held him within the realm of literature. And even when this moment came he did not feel it as the rejection of one field of activity for another, the eclipse, in his own world, of one art by another, but as a natural intensification of a homogeneous artistic experience, the enrichment of a single, indivisible corpus of aesthetic impulses and insights.

His manner of writing about music thus amounts to a fusion of music and words in the spirit of Wackenroder, Novalis, Tieck and other German romantic writers whose thought was so influential during his formative years. Schumann himself made the point by once saying that he had learned more counterpoint from Jean Paul than from any of his music teachers. The indivisibility of the arts, destroyed by the classifying intelligence of the eighteenth-century rationalists, had to be restored, and the intrinsic oneness of art, philosophy and religion had to be demonstrated in an absolute context from which the relativities of time and space, of human mortality and imperfect understanding, had been banished. 'In the beginning', wrote Novalis in one of the *Blüten-staub* fragments, 'the poet and the priest were one. It is only later ages that have separated them. The true poet' – he might as well have said 'the true painter', or 'the true sculptor', or 'the true composer' – 'always remains a priest, as the true priest always

remains a poet.' Schumann stated the same principle in the first
number of his *Neue Zeitschrift für Musik*: 'We believe that the
painter can learn from a symphony by Beethoven, just as the
musician can learn from a work by Goethe'.

Here again Schumann reveals his affinity to E.T.A. Hoffmann.
On the one hand, as in his famous review of Beethoven's Fifth
Symphony in 1810, Hoffmann sought to lead his readers into the
romantic world of Beethoven's music by evocation and empathy,
appealing not to the faculty of cold, critical analysis but to the
power of emotion and imagination. In the same spirit, this time in
a framework of fiction, he wrote stories such as *Don Juan*, or
sketched half-real, half-imaginary situations like that in *Kreislers
musikalisch-poetischer Klub*, enshrining his aesthetic message in a
fantastic narrative or a scrap of fictional biography. He even
created, in the figure of the 'mad' Kapellmeister Johannes
Kreisler – inspiration   of   Schumann's   *Kreisleriana* – an
autobiographical *alter ego* through whom to live out the most
intense experiences of his own inner life as an artist. Schumann's
passionate Florestan and lyrical Eusebius, like the image of the
fraternal 'Davidsbund' as a whole, stand in the direct line of the
Hoffmannesque succession.

No less under the spell of Hoffmann, from his schoolboy days
onwards, was Richard Wagner, who in 1840, at the same age as
Schumann, turned his fascination to literary account in a trilogy
of short stories called *A Musician in Paris*. These attractive little
cameos convey their creator's philosophy of art through an *alter
ego* who suffers indignity and scorn at the hands of a philistine
public and dies with his personal creed on his lips: 'I believe in
God, Mozart and Beethoven, in the Holy Spirit and in the truth
of a single, indivisible Art'. One could imagine that Schumann,
who was certainly no less committed than Wagner to the values
and modes of expression of literature, might well have found in
literary miniatures of this kind a congenial medium for the affairs
of Eusebius and Florestan – indeed, of the whole circle of
'Davidsbündler'. But, strangely, he never took up the idea. Jean
Paul, Hoffmann and the other literary influences on his mind
found their way into his music, not into fiction.

In spite of what Schumann had told his mother in 1833,

Hofmeister showed no inclination to risk his capital by publishing the new journal that the group of enthusiastic young idealists offered him. When Schumann approached his brothers in the publishing business, Karl and Eduard, they also declined. Not until March 1834 did the Leipzig firm of Christian Heinrich Ferdinand Hartmann, former publishers of *Der Planet*, finally agree to take on the task. An editorial board was set up, consisting of Schumann, Wieck, Schunke and Knorr, and the first number, under the title *Neue Leipziger Zeitschrift für Musik, Published by a Society of Artists and Friends of Art*, appeared on 3 April 1834. Its motto, taken from the Prologue of Shakespeare's *Henry VIII*, makes it clear that this is to be no paper for those not prepared to think hard about the issues it raises:

> Only they
> That come to hear a merry bawdy play,
> A noise of targets, or to see a fellow
> In a long motley coat guarded with yellow
> Will be deceived.

A similar motto, taken from Goethe, Shakespeare, Jean Paul, Schiller or one of Schumann's other favourite authors, stood at the head of each issue of the journal. He collected quotations all his life, and at the very end, in the confinement of the mental asylum, he was still working on his *Dichtergarten,* an anthology of passages on music drawn from the great poets of all ages.

At the beginning Knorr was officially appointed editor-in-chief, but after only a few weeks sickness forced him to hand over to Schumann. By the end of the year Schunke was dead, Wieck withdrew his collaboration, finding the temper of the enterprise at odds with his conservative tastes – he in any case contributed a mere handful of brief reviews to the journal – and Knorr also resigned. This left Schumann in sole charge, and for a period of almost ten uninterrupted years from the beginning of 1835 he controlled its editorial policy virtually alone. The house of J.A. Barth took over publication from Hartmann in 1835 and ran the paper for two years; from 1837 until 1851, by which time Schumann had long given up his connection with it, it was published, still in

Leipzig, by the music firm of Robert Friese.

The *Neue Zeitschrift* appeared twice weekly as a folded sheet (four sides), 20 cm × 26 cm, each side generally printed in double columns. A quarterly subscription cost 16 groschen in Saxony, or 1 gulden, 12 kreutzer Rhenish.

The editorial introduction to the opening number tells readers what they can expect. There are to be historical and theoretical articles on all aspects of music, including teaching methods and new inventions; a review of other music journals; original literary pieces, such as short stories and poems on musicians and musical subjects; reviews of concerts and new published music; reports on musical events in Paris, London, Berlin, St Petersburg and other foreign cities; anecdotes and reflections on music taken from Goethe, Jean Paul, Novalis and other writers; and a comprehensive survey of contemporary musical life, including news of well-known musicians, announcements of concerts, and other items appropriate to a bulletin that might be called 'What's On In Leipzig'. Particularly interesting is the intention to give space to composers themselves to write about their work, about what has inspired, intrigued or incensed them, and to reply to their critics. 'If you want to penetrate the mind of an artist', says the editorial, 'you must visit him in his studio'.

Finally, in the spirit of the modern commercial 'Special Offer', an attraction designed to whet the appetites of hoped-for patrons, the editors announced that if things went well, a prize would be offered for the best pianoforte sonata sent to the paper. After Friese took over publication in 1837, music supplements became a regular feature, and a separate *Intelligenzblatt* carried advertisements.

So comprehensive does this survey of aims sound that it would seem to herald an encyclopedia rather than a periodical. Like all young idealists – the editors, apart from Wieck, were still in their twenties, and almost all their collaborators belonged to the same generation – Schumann and his friends tended to promise more than they could fulfil. In practice more columns of the *Neue Zeitschrift* came to be taken up with reviews of new music, books and musical events than with the more original material that the confident editorial had led readers to expect. To this extent the

Neue Zeitschrift differs little in outward form from the *Allgemeine musikalische Zeitung*, the *Revue et gazette musicale* and other contemporary journals. Indeed, given the musical life of the time and the public whose interest it sought to capture, one can hardly wonder that it was so.

But in manner, in its literary bent, above all in its commitment to a set of values and its rigorous pursuit of these values, the *Neue Zeitschrift* represented something radically new. As Schumann saw it, the music industry in Germany had over the past ten years become increasingly inbred, smug, even corrupt. Composers of originality were ignored, and the untutored public, misled by critics who were themselves miserably bereft of true artistic standards, worshipped at the shrine of showmanship and empty virtuosity. To Schumann this lamentable condition found its most pernicious form in the cult of the piano virtuoso which had spread over Europe in the 1820s and 1830s from Paris, musical capital of the world. For worse than the elevation of technical brilliance to an end in itself, which was already reprehensible enough, was that these keyboard gymnasts – Hünten, Henri Herz, Thalberg, Moscheles and the rest – also set themselves up as composers. And since what they wrote consisted of exercises designed to show off their own glittering technique, bedazzled audiences found themselves listening to music in which the presentation had become the substance.

True virtuosity, the marriage of consummate technical skill and profound spiritual understanding, was the ideal that Schumann kept before his eyes. Paganini, whom he had heard in Frankfurt in 1830, represented that ideal. So too, in their different ways, did Chopin and Liszt. In language reminiscent of Hoffmann, all three are linked together in the first number of the *Neue Zeitschrift* as artists

to whom music is the art-form which makes man feel the higher principle of his being and leads him from the common run of everyday life into the Temple of Isis, where Nature speaks to him in divine sounds which he has never before heard, yet which he at once comprehends.

As music periodicals were more often than not the house journals of music publishers, who stood to gain a great deal from the sale of the pieces written and played by these virtuosi, critics were under pressure not only to give such works as much publicity as possible but also to make their notices unexceptionably favourable. Their hands thus tied, they found it hard not to compromise their calling as independent arbiters of quality, and often failed in their duty towards the public. This was the situation that Schumann, through the proud independence, not to say outspokenness, of his *Neue Zeitschrift*, pledged himself to oppose. To this 'New Criticism' he then brought the novel stylistic qualities of his 'Davidsbündler' and the fanciful literary touch of 'Ein Werk II'.

His own words from the New Year editorial of 1835, just after he had taken the journal into his own hands, leave no doubt as to where he stood:

The age of mutual congratulations is slowly dying out, and we confess we have no interest in promoting its revival. A man who has not the courage to attack what is bad about a work can only half-defend what is good about it – you artists, especially you composers, cannot conceive what happiness it gives us to lavish upon you our unstinted praise . . .

But we do not see why we should behave differently from practitioners of the other arts, as of the sciences, where rival factions openly declare their positions and attack each other. Nor can we see how true criticism and the honour of music can be reconciled with an attitude of tolerance towards the enemies of music and the arts in general – that is, the talented who are merely facile note-spinners, the ten-a-penny talents (we can find no other word for them), and those with no talent at all.

Although, during the first years of his editorship, Schumann came to write more and more of the paper himself, he had a circle of *confrères* who made their own contributions – men like the deaf painter and short-story writer Johann Peter Lyser, Ferdinand Stegmayer, Kapellmeister at the Leipzig theatre, and the publisher Friedrich Hofmeister. The regular contributors usually signed their articles with pseudonyms or with ciphers – a common practice at this time. Some of these ciphers are immediately attributable – 'St' = Stegmayer, 'Hf' = Hofmeister, 'Knif' (*i.e.* Fink spelt backwards) = Knorr, who thereby conveyed that he saw himself as the opposite of the conventional editor of the *Allgemeine musikalische Zeitung*. Others cannot be ascribed with certainty. Schumann signed some of his own pieces simply with a number (2, 12, 13 and others). In addition he invents fanciful symbolical names in his descriptions of the meetings of the 'Davidsbund', which conceal known personalities: Eleonore, for instance, represents his Leipzig friend Henriette Voigt, while Felix Mendelssohn-Bartholdy appears as F. Meritis.

Of Schumann's own pseudonyms the most characteristic are the trio that had lived in his mind for several years – Florestan, Eusebius and Meister Raro. The name Florestan is taken from Beethoven's *Fidelio*: he represents Schumann the passionate idealist, impulsive, his mind overflowing with ideas, goading his fellow-'Davidsbündler' to 'slay all Philistines, musical or whatever'. 'My head is so full of ideas,' he bursts out, 'that I cannot actually form any of them'.

Eusebius, by contrast, the introspective, retiring soul who honours tradition and ponders the consequences of an action before he embarks on it, receives his name from the saint whose feast day falls on 14 February, two days after the feast of St Clara. Clara Wieck was now sixteen. At the time Florestan and Eusebius were born in Schumann's mind, she was twelve. Like all who knew her and heard her play, he marvelled. But neither then nor now, as he carried the spiritual lives of his two self-characterizations into the public world of his new journal, was there any hint of the future that they would share.

Schumann always delighted in obscuring the obvious, in inventing initials, anagrams, decorative pseudonyms like the 'Robert of the Mulde' and 'Robert Skuländer' of his schoolboy days, masks – the masquerade of *Papillons* and *Carnaval* – and other ways to conceal and mystify. Such mystifications are often spontaneous, even capricious in origin, and one must not expect a chain of associations with a consistent symbolic significance. None of the known saints that bear the name Eusebius gave Schumann a personal point of departure, none of their attributes has any referable relevance, still less is any of them known for an association with music. It would have sufficed for Schumann to have an innocent thought of Clara Wieck in his mind, then idly to notice the feast of Clara in the Church calendar, with the euphonius name of Eusebius close by, for him to make his

fanciful choice. The writer Wilhelm Häring, with whom
Schumann had once spent several happy days on a vacation trip
from Leipzig to the Rhineland, had chosen his pen-name
(Willibald Alexis) in this very way, taking the feast days of St
Willibald and St Alexis merely because they fell close together in
the month of July.

Nor did Florestan and Eusebius confine their existence to the
pages of the *Neue Zeitschrift*. Their names stood alongside those
of Chopin and Paganini as dedicatees of movements in *Carnaval*,
while Schumann's First Piano Sonata was originally published
under the mysterious rubric, comprehensible only to insiders,
'Dedicated to Clara by Florestan and Eusebius, Opus 11'. Only
five years later did Schumann issue this sonata in his own right
and under his own name. The individual numbers of the
Davidsbündlertänze are signed with the initials F. or E.,
sometimes with both: *Carnaval* was at first to be called *Fasching.
Schwänke auf vier Noten für Pianoforte von Florestan*, while
what came to be published as *XII Etudes symphoniques* had left
the composer's pen as *Etuden im OrchesterCharakter von
Florestan und Eusebius.*

Meister Raro, the third of the trio of Schumann's self-
projections as 'Davidsbündler', is charged with mediating
through his 'rare' wisdom between the extreme positions of his
two young friends. Initially, as Schumann had made clear in his
diary back in 1831, Raro embodied his Master, Friedrich Wieck,
but as Schumann's relationship to Wieck began to change, above
all under the tension caused by his deepening involvement with
Clara, so Raro acquired a broader, independent character and
came to utter many of the most deeply pondered conclusions of
his creator. After 1836, when Schumann and Clara openly
declared their love and the bitter four-year feud with Wieck
started, the name of Meister Raro disappeared for ever from the
company of the 'Davidsbündler' and from the pages of the *Neue
Zeitschrift für Musik*.

The volume and range of compositions reviewed in
Schumann's journal is immense. Many of these works have, in
the nature of things, been long forgotten. But since he had set
himself the task of raising the standards of taste of his

contemporaries, mediocrity had to be drawn attention to in order that excellence might be demonstrated. Similarly, since this task could only be carried out in terms of modern music, he spent comparatively little time on Mozart, Haydn and other eighteenth-century masters, seeing them as part of the assimilated tradition and not needing to be defended. He did, however, show his critical perception by pointing out in reviews of newly published scores of Mozart and Beethoven that not only were there many printing errors which could mislead the unwary but that groups of bars had here and there been omitted, destroying the whole form and meaning of the music.

Bach, on the other hand, for Schumann the greatest of the masters, source of never-ending wonder and practical inspiration, needed to be rediscovered and reinterpreted – one recalls Mendelssohn's famous performance of the St Matthew Passion in Berlin in 1829. Similarly, 'difficult' music, like middle-period and late Beethoven, demanded attention: there are articles on the E flat major Quartet and the C sharp minor Quartet and three separate contributions on the Ninth Symphony. Schumann's glowing review of Schubert's C major Symphony and its 'heavenly length' is well known, but he also returns time and again to Schubert's pianoforte music, little of which was known in the early 1830s. He wrote on Weber, Cherubini and Liszt, and gave a long account in 1835 of Berlioz' *Symphonie fantastique*, but said nothing about Wagner. Indeed, the *Neue Zeitschrift* as a whole has far less on opera – there is a rather disparaging account of Rossini's *Barber of Seville* and a merciless attack on Meyerbeer's *Les Huguenots* – than on pianoforte music, Lieder, or orchestral music.

The two composers to whom Schumann returns time and again, devoting more space to them than to any other, are Mendelssohn and Chopin. For the music of the former, from his *Songs without Words* to his orchestral music and his oratorios, as for the man himself, Schumann had an unwavering admiration, seeing in him a model of craftsmanship, discernment and taste. His attitude to Chopin, on the other hand, changed over the years. The ecstasy of 'Hats off, gentlemen, a genius!' gave way in the middle and late 1830s to a cooler tone, and beneath his notices of the countless waltzes, nocturnes, mazurkas and other piano works published between 1836 and 1842 there lurks a nagging disappointment that Chopin's art had not developed but retained a basic sameness of style. He even uses the word 'mannered'.

Through all Schumann's writings on music, whether in the *Neue Zeitschrift* or elsewhere, there runs a didactic purpose, the consciousness of a mission to raise the level of his readers' musical awareness by invoking above all the music of the glorious German tradition. It mattered less to him that the minutiae of his reviews of particular works should be appreciated than that new standards and values were transmitted, which would then find expression in the musical life of the community at large. His many aphorisms and maxims, such as those later collected as his *Advice to Young Musicians*, the theoretical companion to his *Album for the Young*, reflect the same concern. It was his way of resolving the disharmony that he had long felt between the artist and society, between the creative urges in him that clamoured for release and the outside world to which his activity was directed. For Schumann never saw the artist, however much he needed seclusion and composure, as the inhabitant of an ivory tower:

In the end an isolation from the world harms the artist. He accustoms himself to certain forms and mannerisms until he becomes an eccentric, a dreamer. For a while he may feel at his ease. But should a voice call out to him: 'Beware, my friend', he will begin to brood, to doubt himself, and pedantry is then followed by ill-humour, by hypochondria, that most deadly enemy of creativity.

In a moment of self-analysis he wrote to Clara in 1838:

Anything that happens in the world affects me – politics, literature, people. I reflect on these things in my own way, and these reflections seek an outlet in music. This is also the reason why so many of my compositions are hard to understand.

Schumann had no theory of composition, founded no 'school', perfected no image of 'the work of art of the future', Wagnerian or other. But neither was he content to enshrine his values in his music alone. And if it becomes increasingly characteristic, as the nineteenth century shows, for German artists to theorize about their art, to erect a superstructure of ideas on the practice of art, their own and that of their sympathizers, which embodies the values to which they aspire, then Schumann is very German. There is no clearer statement of the interplay in his life between composing music and writing about it than the plain biographical fact that the years of his tireless, often tiresome responsibility for the *Neue Zeitschrift für Musik*, 1834 to 1844, are also years of intense musical creativity. The literary and the musical, inseparable worlds to so many of the romantic persuasion, filled Schumann's thoughts and actions to the end.

CHAPTER FIVE

Masks and Realities

At the time the first number of the *Neue Zeitschrift für Musik* appeared on 3 April 1834, Schumann was sharing three rooms on the first floor of Burgstrasse No. 21 in Leipzig with his new friend Ludwig Schunke. They really needed only one room each but, as he wrote to his mother, since they would have disturbed each other when they played the piano, they had decided to rent a room in between for insulation. Schumann had grown philosophical about his crippled finger, and it disturbed neither his composing nor his improvising – an accomplishment which many had praised and to which he now returned from time to time. Work on the new journal demanded his entire energy, and for two months, normally the most dutiful of sons, he could not find time to write home. When he finally broke his silence, he began:

My dear, good Mother,
I have not died. If I had, you would certainly have read about it in our paper.

His last words to her in his previous letter had been: 'I'm growing a moustache. Don't be shocked!'

His health, physical and mental, seemed to be improving. Friends and collaborators surrounded him – he mentions the poet Karl Herlossohn, founder and editor of the journal *Komet*, the composer Ludwig Berger, an older man who had counted Mendelssohn and Heinrich Dorn among his pupils in Berlin, Christian August Pohlenz, cantor at the Thomaskirche in Leipzig, as well as Schunke, Lyser and the other faithfuls. The musical world was taking notice of the *Neue Zeitschrift*, and a certain confidence seemed justified. He claimed that he needed 600 thalers a month in order to live respectably but received in royalties, fees and interest on the money he had inherited from his father only 400 to 500 thalers. This he managed to supplement by writing articles for an encyclopedia, and with the reassurance of a substantial capital at his back he felt entitled to a feeling of quiet security.

A precious friendship, touching in its sincerity, sad in its brevity, enriched Schumann's life in the summer of 1834 – that with Henriette Voigt, the young wife of one of the wealthiest patrons of the arts in Leipzig. Carl Voigt, a successful business-man, kept open house for the musicians of the day, playing host to Mendelssohn, Chopin and many others. After each performance of Beethoven's Ninth Symphony in Leipzig he made an anonymous donation of 100 thalers to the orchestra, and on his death he left 6,000 marks to the Gewandhaus to ensure an annual, or at least biennial performance of the work. Henriette, one year older than Schumann, had studied the pianoforte with Ludwig Berger in Berlin, and lived for the arts. 'The artist needed to take only one step into her house,' read her obituary in the *Neue Zeitschrift*, 'to feel utterly at his ease. Portraits of the greatest composers hung on the wall behind the grand piano, and a fine music library was available to all. It felt as though musicians were the masters of the house, and music the goddess who ruled over it'. She was to die of consumption in 1838, at the age of twenty-nine.

Schunke, who had first met the Voigts at Wieck's house, introduced them to Schumann, who was captivated by the gentle Henriette in the extravagant, somewhat theatrical manner in which he responded to instant personal attractions. As a sixteen-year-old schoolboy he had conceived an idealistic passion for Agnes Carus, wife of a family friend in Colditz, revering her as an apotheosis of beauty and music. Henriette Voigt now aroused a similar romanticized emotion in him. As Beethoven's *Fidelio* had given him Florestan, so he called Henriette his 'Eleonore' and, intriguingly – perhaps with a glance at the slow movements of Beethoven's Fifth Symphony and 'Pathetique' Sonata, and Florestan's aria 'In des Lebens Frühlingstagen' in *Fidelio* – his 'A-flat spirit'.

The association of certain keys with certain moods, like that of sounds with colours, colours with scents, and other facets of synaesthesia, is a concept that Schumann probably received from E.T.A. Hoffmann. In the delirious keyboard improvisation with which Johannes Kreisler, Hoffmann's *alter ego*, stupefies his guests in *Johannes Kreislers, des Kapellmeisters musikalisch-poetischer Klub*, key follows upon key to the accompaniment of Kreisler's ecstatic commentary on the sequence of emotions and moods through which the music leads him, from the 'strange, rustling sounds' of A flat major pianissimo, through the 'agonized desire' of A flat minor to the frenzy of C major fortissimo.

Schumann felt the fascination of such mysterious 'correspondences', as Baudelaire called them in a famous poem, but he did not pursue the matter, and his interest remained whimsical, tangential. Although he had certain favourite keys, and key-relationships play an important structural role in his works, he made no systematic use of extra-musical associations in the manner of Hoffmann. There is a striking dominance of the key of D minor in the compositions of his final years – the Second Violin Sonata, the Introduction and Allegro for Piano and Orchestra, the Violin Concerto, the Overture to Goethe's *Faust* – but again one cannot read more than the most general of psychological meanings into this. His spirit, of the A-flat-major persuasion or any other, blew where it listed.

In the summer of 1834 an attractive eighteen-year-old girl called Ernestine von Fricken came to Leipzig to study the piano under Wieck. 'Her father,' Schumann told his mother,

is the rich Baron Ignaz Ferdinand von Fricken, from Bohemia, and her

mother is a Countess Zedtwitz. She is a childlike soul of wondrous purity,
tender and intelligent, devoted to the arts, extraordinarily musical and
passionately attached to me – in a word, the sort of woman I would
choose as my wife. But that is a long way off, and I have already given up
the thought of any closer relationship, easy though it might be for me to
achieve it.

Easy, and irresistible, it proved to be. They quickly fell in love,
and before the end of the year he had given her a ring and a
picture of himself to seal their secret engagement. To others who
knew her, Ernestine seemed far from remarkable. Long after
Schumann's death Frau Clementine Wieck, Wieck's second wife,
who saw her every day in the family house, recalled her as a fresh,
plump girl of little mental ability, while the music critic Carl
Banck, who became for a short while a rival of Schumann's for
the hand of Clara Wieck, described her as well-endowed
physically and highly responsive emotionally but with no
intellectual pretensions. In fact, she sounds not unlike Liddy
Hempel, the overwhelming but equally short-lived passion of his
student days. Perhaps this was Schumann's 'type'. Until, that
is – and it was about to happen – Clara took possession of his
heart and mind.

One may smile indulgently at the whole affair. But Ernestine
fulfilled at that moment an emotional need in Schumann for a
deep human relationship that would ensure his psychological
stability. A doctor he had visited the previous winter in the state
of grim melancholy that set in after Julius and Rosalie had died
told him: 'Medicines are no help in your case. Find yourself a
wife – she will cure you at once'. As he later admitted to Clara: 'I
desperately wanted a woman to cling to. So when Ernestine came
on the scene, I thought: She will be the one to save me'.

Wieck, who considered it his duty to act *in loco parentis* for
Ernestine, felt obliged to inform Baron von Fricken of what was
going on. First he assures the baron that the relationship, though
close, has so far been a thoroughly proper one – '. . . were I
able to speak to you personally, I could convince you that they
have never exchanged a kiss or even held hands'. Then he
proceeds in his letter to give an intriguing character study of the

young man who had once been his pupil, was soon forced to become his bitterest enemy and eventually became his son-in-law:

That the nature of their relationship should be so, reflects Schumann's character. It would take pages and pages for me to describe in detail this inspired and supremely intelligent composer and writer – his moodiness and obstinacy on the one hand, but on the other his nobility of mind, his enthusiasm, his splendid gifts.

The Baron immediately wrote to his daughter to warn her against any improper behaviour: 'By all means play pianoforte duets with Schumann, but no more'. It was too late. They had declared their love, letting only Henriette Voigt into their secret. When the news reached the Baron, he travelled to Leipzig and took Ernestine back with him to Asch, his estate near the Saxon-Bohemian border, but without reproach or recrimination – indeed, he seemed willing to accept their liaison.

Shortly afterwards, to the pining Schumann's joy, the Baron invited him to Asch. But suddenly everything began to crumble. While at Asch he discovered, presumably from the servants, that Ernestine, far from being the Baron's own daughter and the heir to his estate, was the illegitimate daughter of Countess Christiane von Zedtwitz, unmarried sister-in-law of the Baron, who, having no children of his own, had recently adopted her and given her his family name.

From this moment on Schumann's feelings for Ernestine changed, and by the summer of 1835 the chapter was closed. It is difficult to acquit him of at least a measure of dishonourable conduct in the affair. In 1853 he told Wasielewski that it was her illegitimacy which had led him to break off the engagement, a circumstance which, had he truly loved her, he would surely have thrust aside. In a later account of the episode to Clara he claimed that Ernestine betrayed his trust by concealing her illegitimacy from him. An even graver consideration, however, seems to have been his shock at discovering that Ernestine had no money of her own and no chance to earn any, which meant he would have to earn their daily bread 'like a workman'. Wasielewski suspected that his 'love' had been that of Schumann the 'Davidsbündler', in whom *Dichtung* and *Wahrheit*, imagination and reality, had no separate existence but fed one upon the other. To Henriette Voigt, however, his emotion had seemed utterly genuine.

Ernestine continued to love him and never understood why he left her: 'He wrote that I should save myself while I could, since he ruined everything he touched. That was all he said. I cannot think of any reason, and he gave me none'. In 1838 she married Count Wilhelm von Zedtwitz, an elderly relative of her mother's, who died only eight months later. Ernestine herself died of typhoid in 1844.

The whole affair came into the open again a few years later when Wieck used it to cast a slur on Schumann's character, and when Clara, for her part, anxiously wanted to know what had passed between the man she loved and the girl she had known and liked in her father's house. But by then the bond that held Schumann and Clara together had acquired a strength that could withstand such attacks and such knowledge.

The memory of Ernestine von Fricken is embedded in the work that sprang directly from the romantic relationship, a work among the most popular in the whole piano repertoire – the cycle *Carnaval* (Op. 9), composed 1834–5 and published in 1837.

The title speaks for itself. The twenty-two separate items that make up the work, some a mere page long or less, some more extended, each bear descriptive names related in some way to the imagined situation of a masked ball. To this extent *Carnaval* is a kind of richer, fuller, subtler *Papillons*. Sending a copy of the new work to the pianist Ignaz Moscheles in 1837, Schumann wrote:

It will be child's play for you to figure out the masked ball. And I need hardly assure you that the titles and the arrangement of the pieces arose *after* the pieces were already written.

The carnival associations of the cycle, and the side of his

personality with which Schumann wished to see it identified, were made even more explicit in the original German title: *Fasching, Schwänke auf vier Noten für Pianoforte von Florestan* (Schwank = jest, prank). In 1839, still attracted by the image they invoked, he brought the 'carnival' and the 'jest' together again in the designation of his Opus 26: *Faschingsschwank aus Wien*.

As published by Breitkopf and Härtel the work bore the title *Carnaval. Scènes mignonnes composées pour le pianoforte sur quatre notes*. Schumann explained the origin of these four notes in another letter to Moscheles:

Carnaval came into existence almost incidentally and is constructed for the most part on the notes A S [German *Es* = E flat] C H [= B natural], which make up the name of a little place in Bohemia where a musical friend of mine lived [i.e. Ernestine von Fricken]. Strangely enough, these are also the only musical letters in my own name. The titles I added later. Indeed, is not music sufficient unto itself, eloquent in itself? 'Estrella' [= Ernestine] is the kind of name one would put under a portrait so as to fix it more clearly in one's memory; 'Reconnaissance' is a scene of reunion, 'Aveu' a declaration of love, 'Promenade' a stroll such as one might take arm-in-arm with one's partner at a German ball. All this has no artistic significance. The only interest seems to me to lie in the various different spiritual states and moods.

Schumann set out in *Carnaval* itself the patterns that his four notes produced. Embedded in the work as No. 9 of the twenty-two items, under the name 'Sphinxes' – creatures assembled from parts of different animals, meaning different things to different people – are the three patterns, with German nomenclature:

No. 3 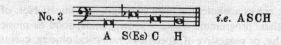 *i.e.* ASCH

These notes, unlike those of the 'Abegg' Variations, do not belong to any one diatonic scale, and the music ranges over seven keys in its exploration of the different sequences available. The result — and not only for this reason — is a kaleidoscope of moods and colours, imaginative little sketches that reflect the ever-changing configurations of the spiritual life of their creator. Certain pianistic mannerisms creep in, and the occasional structural idea, such as the extended sequential repetition of a rhythmic and harmonic pattern above a sustained pedal-point sometimes for twelve bars and more, may be taken to the point of diminishing returns, but one is left at the end with a rich experience of variety and swiftly changing impulses. Hence the problem, in the purely musical terms of both performer and listener, of not allowing the unity of the work to be splintered by the heterogeneity of its constituent parts. 'In *Carnaval* each new piece cancels out the last,' Schumann said to Clara, 'and not everyone can accommodate himself to that'.

At the same time, although the individual pieces are not musical representations of the titles they bear, and are thus not, in the narrow sense, programme music like *Papillons*, the names Schumann put to them could not but be those of persons and situations that had meant much to him in recent times. Chopin, Paganini, Florestan and Eusebius, Chiarina (= Clara), Estrella (= Ernestine), the 'Declaration of Love', the 'March of the "Davidsbündler" against the Philistines' — the associations need no labouring. But the experiences are in the music, not in the names. When Clara Wieck met Liszt in Vienna in April 1838 she played *Carnaval* to him. 'What a mind!' exclaimed Liszt. 'This is one of the greatest works I have heard.'

The primacy that Schumann claims for the music in his *Carnaval* — some of which, as often in his work, has its origin in earlier, unpublished dances and sets of variations preserved in his sketch-books — raises an issue central to the music of the romantic era as a whole: the issue of programme music. Not, of course, that 'programme music' – loosely understood as music inspired by, or suggestive of, specific extramusical objects, events or ideas – is an invention of the European nineteenth century. Moreover, in the deepest sense, almost all music exists in some way through its association with something outside itself, be that something descriptive, historical, psychological, religious or of any other origin. But only from the nineteenth century, and specifically the age of romanticism, does there arise a philosophy of composition that rests on the declared principle of grounding the piece of music on a phenomenon or an experience which has its own existence in another realm. Without this 'programme', in other words, the music would not have come into being, and thus cannot, to this extent, be separated from it. In so far as we are interested in the genesis of a particular work, our knowledge of the presence of such an external stimulus must needs form part of our assessment of that work.

Thus when Liszt writes an orchestral work called *Tasso* or *Hamlet*, and Richard Strauss a piece called *Don Juan* or *Macbeth*, the meaning of the work involves knowing at least something about the literary work, character or author who has inspired the composer to write music about him. The composer may or may not have worked to a detailed programme; his piece may be nothing more than a general evocation of what he sees as the essential meaning of his subject. But he starts from a declared point outside himself. And that this starting-point was typically to be found in literature is made explicit in the term 'symphonic poem' to describe the new genre of orchestral music. Schumann's *Papillons* belongs to the same spirit. So too, although the associations are not with the highways and byways of literature but with homely objects and settings – a hobbyhorse, a fireside, a child dropping off to sleep – do his *Scenes from Childhood*.

But whatever the objective interest of the programme, however great the historical figure, magnificent the literary work or famous the painted scene, the composer's work can ultimately only be heard and judged as music in its own right. In the last analysis there are only two kinds of programme music – that which is good, irrespective of its programme, and that which is poor, with even the noblest of programmes. The greatness of Beethoven's Pastoral Symphony is a greatness in music as 'absolute' as that of his Fifth or any other 'pure' Symphony. Which is not to say, however, that one's understanding of the Pastoral Symphony or any other great work of programme music is not the fuller and more satisfying for a knowledge of the extra-musical thoughts present in the composer's mind at the conception of his work and throughout its gestation.

The drawing of literary and pictorial associations into music reflects the romantic belief in the indivisibility of the world of the arts, the inspiration that can be drawn from one realm of artistic expression and transmuted into the values of another. Of even deeper significance in the context of the romantic nineteenth century as a whole is the contrary movement – that through which the values of music come to be seen as those which most perfectly express the aspirations of all artists in this age. 'Music is the most romantic of all the arts', wrote E.T.A. Hoffmann in his essay *Beethovens Instrumentalmusik*. 'One might even say, it is the only genuinely romantic art, for its subject is the Eternal'. In *Alte und neue Kirchenmusik* he takes this idea further:

No art is so complete an expression of the spiritualization of man as music – no other art speaks only and always the divine language of the spirit. Through the sounds of music we are brought into the presence of the highest and holiest things, of the spiritual power which kindles the spark of life in the whole of nature.

Jean Paul wrote in the same tone in the masked ball scene in his *Flegeljahre* from which Schumann had taken his *Papillons*:

A masquerade is perhaps the most perfect form in which life can enact the fancies of poetry . . . All things which are normally separate from each other, even the different seasons and religions, those who are friends and those who are enemies, are drawn into a single vibrant, happy circle. The circle revolves as though to the rhythm of poetry, moves in the sphere of music, which is the realm of the spiritual, as the mask is the realm of the physical.

Evocative language such as this kindled an immediate response in Schumann, a response that issued in his compositions as in his musical journalism. 'I detest anything that is not the product of a man's deepest impulses', he once said. That his own impulses were so strong and so varied, so unconditional in their demands, makes the romanticism of *Carnaval* and such works what it is.

Linked to *Carnaval* through the person of Baron von Fricken, Ernestine's adoptive father, and composed over the same period of months, are the *Etudes symphoniques* (Op. 13) – far grander and more difficult a work than *Carnaval*, and containing some of the most intricate piano music that Schumann wrote. At the same time as he was preparing the fair copy, according to his diary for the beginning of 1835, he also wrote out a set of variations – he called them studies – on the Allegretto of Beethoven's Seventh Symphony, which he had apparently composed a year or so before. This is listed in his own index of his works but has never been published, and we know it only from his sketch-books and from other fragments of manuscript.

The link between the *Etudes symphoniques* and Baron Ignaz von Fricken is the musical theme of Schumann's work itself. The Baron, an amateur flautist, had composed a Theme and Variations in C sharp minor for Solo Flute, of which he sent a pianoforte arrangement to Schumann asking him for his opinion. Schumann wrote a long reply, critical of a great deal of the music but polite and encouraging – he was, after all, addressing the man he saw at that time as his future father-in-law. The theme itself appealed to him as a basis for studies of his own, and having simplified it to a certain extent, he proceeded to compose a series of variations on it – some eighteen in all, it seems. Twelve of these he brought together, first as *12 Davidsbündler Studien*, then, more personally, as *Etuden im Orchester-Character, von Florestan und Eusebius*. The publisher Haslinger, in Vienna, insisted that they appear under a sober title and with the composer's real name, so they were finally issued in 1837 as simply *XII Etudes symphoniques*.

But they had still not reached their definitive form. In 1852, four years before he died, Schumann made a revised version, omitting Variations 2 and 9, re-writing the Finale and calling the work *Etudes en forme de Variations (XII Etudes symphoniques) pour le Pianoforte*. Six years after his death an edition by Wieck appeared with Nos 2 and 9 re-included. Then the 'Supplement' to the Complete Edition of Schumann's works, published in 1873, produced five more variations, which Schumann had not included in either of his own versions: modern editions usually incorporate these in the work. To round off the confusion, there also exists a manuscript sketch of the theme and eleven variations, some complete, some fragmentary, among them the five later published in the 'Supplement' from a different manuscript source.

In itself this chronicle of details might seem to interest only the student of source material or of the minutiae of Schumanniana. And to investigate, say, the relationship between successive drafts of a work assumes an involvement with detail that goes beyond what many might consider necessary for an appreciation of the finished work. But to survey, however summarily, the historical record of events behind the writing of the *Etudes symphoniques* cannot but intensify our understanding of Schumann's mind and of his mode of composition. The changing titles alone – the fanciful authorship of Florestan and Eusebius, the novel use of variation form for a set of studies, the choice, first of the descriptive term 'orchestral in character', then of the epithet 'symphonic', to connote the richly-coloured, expansive full-blooded pianistic style – show what was going through his mind. And the musical evidence shows him selecting from a body of material to arrive at the form that satisfied him, rejecting this, adding that, his conception of the expected 'final and definitive' statement changing with the supervention of new experiences, new associations, new dispositions of values. Schumann subjected his compositions to a great deal of revision. Even little moments of fantasy like the *Papillons*, seemingly so immediate, so spontaneous in their freshness, sometimes turn out to be reworkings of earlier songs or other discarded pieces, the results of concentrated refinement.

Schiller, in a famous essay, diagnosed a fundamental distinction in art between what he called the 'naïve' and the 'sentimental'. The former connotes pure, innocent, instinctive Nature, 'natural' nature, so to say, an ideal, moral state in which the moment unconsciously absorbs the accumulated meaning of history, and in which the artist of genius – Schiller's examples are the Greeks, Shakespeare and Goethe – is instinctively, effortlessly, 'naïvely' at one with the world. The latter lives by Mind rather than by Nature, with a morality drawn by the power of reason from a study of the processes of history, and with an urge to rediscover and re-create the unity which the 'naïve' artist has never lost. Schiller casts himself as this kind of 'sentimental' poet, who, he concludes, complements the 'naïve' artist: both are needed by mankind in order to achieve its goal, by the analogy that neither the realist nor the idealist can exist alone.

Seen in these terms the art of the nineteenth-century romantics, with their search for a lost unity and their self-conscious pursuit of subjective values, the appeal of composers to the conceptual inspiration of literature, and the invocation by poets of the abstract, supremely spiritual power of music, bears the unmistakably 'sentimental' marks of its age. Schumann the musician, steeped in romantic literature, the composer who claimed he had learned more about counterpoint from Jean Paul than from his music teacher, and who drew literary, pictorial and narrative associations into his compositions, lives in this same world. So does Schumann the writer, inheritor of the romantic philosophy of Art, of the urge to the aestheticization of reality, heir to the vision of a life transcended by the spirit and the values of music, seeking, as the 'sentimental' artist must, a higher, more real unity.

Behind its Florestan-Eusebius-symphonic exterior the music of the *Etudes symphoniques* enacts the search, upwards and outwards, to encompass this unity. As one variation-cum-study follows another in the grandest of grand manners, the music ranges over the whole gamut of moods, uninhibited in its inventiveness yet always in touch, through melodic or harmonic implications, with the theme, and always in quadruple rhythm. Canon and other contrapuntal devices (Nos 3, 4, 7, 8); the transference of the theme to the bass or an inner part (No. 2); the extended use of a single decorative metrical figure (No. 5): these are among the technical means by which Schumann varies his subject. And as agitation gives way to reflection, as serenity is shattered by passionate outburst, so the juxtaposition of violent, unprepared contrasts – how close we are again to the extremes of Schumann's own spiritual condition! – becomes a structural principle in itself. It is one of the most fiendishly difficult of Schumann's many difficult works to perform. Is it not appropriately so?

The *Etudes symphoniques* also posed difficulties for contemporary ears in its thought-content – as, for different reasons, had *Carnaval*. Schumann knew this, and replied approvingly to Clara when she wrote to him in 1838, rather apologetically, that she had decided not to play it at any of her recitals in Vienna:

You did right not to play my *Etudes*. They are not suitable for public audiences, and it would be pitiful if I complained afterwards that they had not understood something which was in fact not intended to be applauded in that way but only existed for its own sake.

We have come a long way since then. As Schumann extricated himself, successfully but none too honourably, from his commitment to Ernestine von Fricken, so Clara Wieck, consciously and irrevocably, moved closer and closer to the centre of his life. From the moment when he took up lodgings in the Wieck household he had marvelled at her piano playing, enjoyed her company almost as that of a younger sister, and come to take her presence as a matter of course. She, it soon became clear, felt a similar dependence on him, a feeling of which she abruptly became aware when faced with the fear that Ernestine was about to take him from her. She was confident and strong-willed, no weak, pallid creature, yet her father's incessant urgings and the unremitting pressure from which the virtuoso performer can never escape brought her at times close to collapse.

Above all there was the loneliness of such a life. She had never led the 'normal', open life of a young girl able to choose her friends and mix with others of her age, and the more famous she became, the more Wieck, half-father, half-manager, jealously guarded her like a performing animal whose only contact is with its trainer. Schumann represented to her the world outside, the world she knew so little about, either from experience or from education, and although she was still a child, he recognized in her a sympathetic intelligence with which he could communicate.

In the early months of 1835 Clara went on an extended concert tour of north German cities with her father. When she returned to Leipzig in April, Schumann saw her with different eyes: 'You seemed to me to have grown, to have become more unfamiliar. You were no longer the sort of child with whom I just wanted to laugh and play. You talked so intelligently, and I saw in your eyes a secret ray of love'. From this moment he knew that Ernestine could not survive the presence of Clara. Many years later he wrote to her: 'You are my oldest love. Ernestine had to come so that you and I could be united'.

They saw each other every day through the summer of that year. 'Clara's eyes and her love', he wrote. Then: 'In November our first kiss'.

Before the first of these two phrases in his diary stands one word: the name 'Chopin'. In September, on his way back to Paris from Carlsbad, where he had been visiting his parents, Chopin stopped over in Leipzig to visit, not Robert Schumann, the composer, but Clara Wieck, the young virtuoso about whom he had heard such remarkable things.

Chopin was at the height of his fame. He had left Poland for Paris in 1831, and in the space of a few years had turned himself into an immensely popular pianoforte teacher. Since his pupils were the children of the Parisian aristocracy, he quickly became, at twenty francs (£12) a lesson – more if he visited his pupils in their homes – and five lessons a day, extremely prosperous.

But his health was suspect. A delicate, sensitive nature, he found himself temperamentally at odds with the contemporary cult of the virtuoso, and had the previous year abandoned the hurly-burly of public performance for the quieter life of composing and teaching.

When Chopin arrived at the Wiecks' house in the old Grimmaische Gasse, Clara was not at home, and he waited a full hour until she returned. Since Clara spoke no Polish or French, and Chopin virtually no German, they will hardly have held an animated conversation, but she played him Schumann's recently completed Sonata in F sharp minor and two of his own Studies. He complimented her on her playing – for Schumann's music itself he had little sympathy – then played her one of his Nocturnes 'with the most delicate pianissimo', she recorded, 'but far too capriciously'. His poor state of health meant that he could only produce a forte with great effort, contorting his whole body in the process.

In October 1835 the *Neue Zeitschrift* carried a notice of his visit: 'Chopin was here, but only for a few hours, which he spent in private circles. He performs just as he composes – uniquely'. We have no record that he met Schumann at this moment. That he saw Mendelssohn we know from the latter's correspondence. A postscript to the notice in the *Neue Zeitschrift*, signed Eusebius, reads: 'Florestan rushed towards him. I saw them arm-in-arm together, floating through the air rather than walking'. But it sounds rather like an extravagant vision than a statement of a real meeting.

The following summer, however, Chopin passed through Leipzig again, and this time the two men spent a day in each other's company, to Schumann's great joy. Chopin played some of his Studies and Mazurkas – 'incomparable pieces', wrote Schumann to Heinrich Dorn – and parts of a new Ballade in G minor, which he dedicated to Schumann. But it was a fleeting, one-sided encounter. To Schumann it meant a lot, to Chopin very little.

Of far more significance was Schumann's relationship to Mendelssohn, who arrived in Leipzig from Düsseldorf at the end of August to take up his appointment as director of the

Gewandhaus concerts. Among major – or minor – composers Felix Mendelssohn-Bartholdy is one of the few about whose personality and public life scarcely any of his contemporaries had a bad word to say. He had to counter the hostility of the anti-Semites and the surliness of those who envied him his wealthy background – the two groups are not unnatural allies, as Wagner made painfully clear – but he did so without sacrificing the generosity, the sincerity and the enlightened sense of duty that gained him the loyalty and respect of a very wide circle of friends and acquaintances. He wore his Judaism lightly and effortlessly shrugged off most of the gratuitous personal sneers levelled at him.

His friend Eduard Devrient, the famous actor, who helped persuade the formidable Zelter to allow young Mendelssohn to conduct the historic revival of Bach's St Matthew Passion in Berlin in 1829, tells a charming anecdote. Walking back with Devrient after the successful interview with Zelter, Mendelssohn turned excitedly to his friend and cried: 'To think that it has been left to you, an actor, and me, a Jewish boy, to revive this greatest of all Christian music!'

True, he may have lacked, except in rare flashes, the will, or the power, to surrender unconditionally to the power of fantasy that inspired him at such moments as the Overture to *A Midsummer Night's Dream* and some of the earlier *Songs without Words* – moments which remind one that in his youth he had been as enthusiastic about Jean Paul as Schumann. He also showed little inclination to concern himself with the theory of music or with academic matters of aesthetics. But as a practical musician, as choir trainer, orchestral conductor and teacher, he had a devoted following. He was only twenty-six when he came to Leipzig and he died at the age of thirty-eight, but during these twelve years of association with the Gewandhaus orchestra he made their concerts into events of paramount importance in the musical life of Germany. Restrained and unostentatious in his manner as a conductor, nudging and persuading his fifty players towards the interpretation he sought rather than driving them before him in relentless pursuit of his aims, he achieved performances of a new clarity and subtlety over a far broader repertoire than his predecessors had countenanced. 'His movements were short and precise, and often barely visible,' said Ferdinand Hiller, who conducted himself at the Gewandhaus in 1841-2, 'for he stood with his right side towards the orchestra. A glance at the leader, a quick look in this direction or that, was all he needed'. Cultured and refined, he was a professional to his finger-tips. Nor could he bear idleness. If the conversation was proving unprofitable, he could be caught looking repeatedly at his watch, thinking what better use he could be making of his time.

Typical of Mendelssohn's integrity and sense of propriety was his reaction on receiving the invitation to Leipzig. Such a position would, he knew, give him the freedom to do all those things of which a true conductor dreamed, and most men would have seized the offer without a second thought. Mendelssohn, however, first replied that on no account would he accept the post if it involved dismissing a present incumbent. Learning that this would not in fact be the case, he then asked that Christian Pohlenz, who was employed as an occasional conductor, should receive a generous sum in compensation for being asked to retire. Only when this too was settled did he agree to come.

Before he arrived in Leipzig, Mendelssohn would have known of Eusebius' aphorism on the Overture to *A Midsummer Night's Dream* in Schumann's first 'Davidsbündler' essay of 1833, as well as of the review in the *Neue Zeitschrift für Musik* of his six *Songs without Words* (Op. 30). So he could have hardly looked forward to meeting Schumann with other than appreciative thoughts in his mind.

Henriette Voigt introduced the two men to each other in the Gewandhaus itself, and Schumann recorded the occasion in the rapid, breathless style in which he often wrote his diary – the style of *Papillons,* one might call it:

I told Mendelssohn I knew all his compositions well; he made a modest reply. Deep understanding in all he did and said, from the smallest things to the biggest. His judgement on musical matters, particularly on compositions, the most profound and cogent that one can imagine. His was for me the highest praise – he was the supreme arbiter. His life a work of art – perfect. His handwriting, too, the image of his spiritual harmony. Honest in all things; not influenced by flattery, nor capable of any.

In the spiritual fraternity of the 'Davidsbündler' Mendelssohn received the transparent code-name F. Meritis, and his activities, from his performances with the Gewandhaus orchestra to his foundation of the Leipzig Conservatoire in 1843, were closely and admiringly followed in the pages of the *Neue Zeitschrift*. Of his debut before the Gewandhaus audience in October 1835 Eusebius-Schumann wrote to Chiara-Clara: 'A sudden hush came over the audience. F. Meritis appeared. A hundred hearts leapt up to greet him at this very first moment.' The concert that followed consisted of Mendelssohn's own Overture *Calm Sea and Prosperous Voyage*, a Scene and Aria for Soprano from Weber's *Der Freischütz*, Spohr's Violin Concerto No. 8, the Overture and Introduction to Cherubini's opera *Ali Baba* (with choir), then, after the intermission, Beethoven's Fourth Symphony. It was a remarkably modern programme: the pieces by Mendelssohn and Cherubini had been written in the last few years, and even the Beethoven was only a little over thirty years old. Mendelssohn, like Berlioz, Liszt and Wagner but unlike Schumann, conducted with a baton – a recent innovation in the concert world which symbolized the emergence of the interpretative conductor from the mere time-beating, corrective role he had played hitherto, initially from the harpsichord, later from the front violin desk.

When, a few years later, he came to learn of Schumann's liaison with Clara, Mendelssohn showed great sympathy for the lovers – as did Liszt, incidentally, but few others. 'He is so understanding and good', Schumann wrote to Clara. Indeed, the initiative for contact between them came more frequently from the senior and more famous man, who, despite his reservations, more than once showed himself ready to put his influence behind a wider acceptance of Schumann's music.

Musically these two great figures in nineteenth-century German music were poles apart, and knew it. In Mendelssohn the composer Schumann admired quality of imagination and craftsmanship, and, as a practical musician, commitment to great music and to high artistic standards. Mendelssohn, on his side, had an affection for Schumann the man but both a general suspicion of writers on music – even if they praised his own – and a less than complete enthusiasm for Schumann's compositions. He once remarked to the violinist Joachim: 'It is remarkable that a man who has created such beautiful things can also be so awkward' – an awkwardness above all, Mendelssohn made clear, of instrumentation. He did not even like her husband's Piano Concerto, Clara Schumann confessed much later. But beyond dispute is the profound sense of loss that Schumann felt when he heard of Mendelssohn's death in November 1847. 'As one always feels when in the presence of a prodigy', he wrote, 'he seemed to be those three inches taller than everyone else. Yet he remained so good, so modest.'

Mendelssohn has been called the Romantic Classicist – though Classical Romanticist might be more accurate. Either way the focus rests on his *oeuvre* as a whole – which is to say that his symphonies, his *Songs without Words*, his oratorios, his chamber music and the rest form parts of a consistent, unified corpus. The classical urge, if one may so denote the desire to express oneself in classical forms and cultivate the patterns of thought that these forms demand, had from the beginning made itself felt in Schumann also. But there is a vital difference. For against Mendelssohn's homogeneity stands, in Schumann, a dichotomy, a cleavage in his creative imagination between the part fantastic, part lyrical romantic world of *Papillons, Carnaval, Kreisleriana* and the songs, and the formal classical idiom of his symphonies, his operatic and dramatic works, his chamber music and his contrapuntal exercises in fugal and other forms. A few works – the *Etudes symphoniques*, perhaps – may span the divide. In essence, however, the direction of thought, and the forms in which the thought finds expression, are different in either camp, and the rationale of either side requires its own description and evaluation.

Thus in the same months of 1835 as he was working on *Carnaval* and the *Etudes symphoniques,* Schumann completed two piano sonatas, both begun two years earlier. The Sonata No. 1 in F sharp minor Op. II was first published in 1836 as *Pianoforte Sonata. Dedicated to Clara by Florestan and Eusebius* and reappeared four years later under Schumann's own name. He drew some of his themes from earlier, unpublished pieces, using a 'Fandango' of 1832 as the basis of the first Allegro, and for the slow movement the melody of an even earlier song, 'An Anna', written in 1828, the year he left school. This was material already in stock, so to speak, and he completed these first two movements in 1833. But he took a long while to come to terms with the remaining two movements, and the work as a whole suffers both from an unevenness rooted in the spasmodic manner of its composition, and from the pervasive impression of a composer labouring to perform a task unsuited to his powers, a task he should not have set himself. There are attractive moments – Liszt found the slow movement very appealing – but it lacks the overall formal grasp, the broad, single-minded vision of the total work that the genre requires. Which is to say, it is a sonata in name only. This is virtually what Ignaz Moscheles, one of the leading pianist-composers of the day, is saying in his sharp-sighted review, written at Schumann's request, for the *Neue Zeitschrift für Musik* in 1836:

This work is the true symbol of a force that has sprung up in our day and is spreading everywhere – the force of Romanticism. It is, I am sure, the product of a single mind, although the title-page bears two names. In their writings Florestan and Eusebius often put forward contrary views so as to widen the area of their discussions and allow themselves scope for humour. The composer of this sonata seems to have chosen these twin brothers to motivate the contrasting elements in his work. But the difficult task he has set himself can be resolved only through a sustained and determined effort, and he must direct his considerable creative powers towards the achievement of a greater clarity.

This was only a diplomatic way of repeating his blunt description of the work in a letter to his wife as 'interesting but difficult, very laboured and somewhat confused.'

The composition of the Sonata No. 2 in G minor (Op. 22) spans an even longer period than that of its predecessor and bears palpable resemblances to it. The oldest material comes in the Andantino, which also goes back to a song written in 1828, called 'Im Herbste' (the poem, like that of 'An Anna', is by Justinus Kerner, of whom he made a number of settings during his schooldays at the *Lyceum* in Zwickau). Two years later he adapted the melody as a piano piece called 'Papillote' (he probably came across the word, meaning 'curl-paper', in the masquerade from Jean Paul's *Flegeljahre*), then reworked this, in its turn, into the second movement of his Sonata. The first and third movements date in their essence from the summer of 1833; the whole work was completed, as Schumann recorded in the only reference to it in his diary, in October 1835.

But this was still not the end of the matter. Four years later, at Clara's bidding, he returned to the Finale, a brilliant Presto in 6/16 marked 'Passionato'. 'It is too difficult', she complained, 'and the public, even the connoisseurs for whom you write, will not understand it'. So he replaced it by a new Rondo, and the Sonata, dedicated to Henriette Voigt, finally appeared under the imprint of Breitkopf and Härtel in 1839.

Among the rest of the detritus left from earlier attempts at piano sonatas are a work in A flat (1830), of which two movements are preserved in manuscript, and another in B minor (1831), the sole surviving movement of which became the Allegro, Op. 8. A further isolated sonata movement in B flat dates from 1836. This catalogue of fits and starts, of first, second and third thoughts, tells its own tale. 'Schumann's career as a composer of sonatas evidently began as uneasily as it continued,' as one critic put it.

If Eusebius has breathed his reflective, lyrical nature into the slow movements of the F sharp and G minor Sonatas, then the Allegros and the Finales belong to the headstrong Florestan. The opening of the first movement of the G minor Sonata is marked

So rasch wie möglich, 'As fast as possible'; shortly before the end comes the superhuman injunction *Schneller*, 'Faster', and sixteen bars later, *Noch schneller*, 'Faster still'. This is not Schumann instructing the performer but Florestan wildly responding to the music. Time and again Schumann has recourse to the urgent phrase 'faster and faster', building up his climaxes by almost frenzied accelerandi and fortissimi which cause all but the most intrepid – or most blasé – of performers to turn pale with fright.

After a performance of the F sharp minor Sonata by Anton Rubinstein in Vienna in 1884, the sharp-tongued Hanslick wrote:

The slow movement had an ideal beauty – an unforgettable moment of perfect ecstasy. The Finale, on the other hand, hit us like a hurricane, so that not even listeners who knew the work thoroughly could always keep pace with it, and were in places left to guess what he actually played.

The amateur who has grappled with this movement – let alone with the original Presto Finale of the Second Sonata – will know, like Hanslick, how much is usually surrendered to the imagination.

Such passages of sustained and mounting intensity, often built on the extended, even mechanistic repetition of rhythmic patterns and harmonic sequences, are in Schumann a compensation. They do duty for the lack of a broad sense of structure which would motivate from its own inner principles the climaxes and the whole formal meaning both of the individual movement and, in sonatas, symphonies and other essays in multipartite classical forms, of the relationships between the movements. The sudden arrest of the forward sweep of a movement by the interpolation of a sequence of adagio bars – as though Eusebius were to interject a few quiet remarks after the tempestuous Florestan had talked himself into an excited state of temporary exhaustion; the use of a pedal point or an extended plagal cadence at the end of a movement – as in the discarded Presto of the G minor Sonata – to prevent the music from hurtling onwards into formless infinity and to bring it to a considered close: these are other surrogate devices to remedy the absence of a commanding and comprehensive formal intelligence. They are characteristics that reveal the heart of Schumann's music.

CHAPTER SIX

Clara

In 1835 Schumann was beginning to compose more purposefully and powerfully. The *Neue Zeitschrift für Musik*, which claimed the greatest share of his energy, was gaining a name for itself both within Germany and abroad, and the loss of early collaborators like Lyser and Knorr had been quickly made good. True, the break with Ernestine von Fricken had left him with a certain uneasiness, but the arrival of Mendelssohn in Leipzig quickly raised his spirits again as he envisioned an exciting partnership in pursuit of a common artistic goal. All this optimism, however, was paled by the radiance that suddenly flooded his world from the most glorious, most irresistible, yet most harrowing, even destructive emotional experience of his whole life – his love for Clara Wieck.

Time has tended to lay on the story of Robert and Clara Schumann a soft veneer of romantic idealism. Clara, the musical prodigy, little more than a child when she entered Schumann's life and still in her teens when her love for him was publicly revealed, is portrayed as the adoring young maid who meekly surrendered to the difficult, often morose and depressed composer, with whom, after years of frustration and opposition, she finally came together in perfect harmony.

The reality is less romantic. But it is no poorer in psychological interest for that. Indeed, precisely because it is impossible almost from the beginning to imagine any other outcome in their relationship than that they must eventually become man and wife – their appeals to destiny seem more than just despairing hopes – the history of their life together, and the struggles that preceded it, take their meaning from a framework of inevitability.

Whatever unexpressed and uncomprehended feelings may have touched them before, the catalyst in their first confession of love for each other was the episode between Schumann and Ernestine von Fricken. Confronted with the black reality that she was on the point of losing him, Clara came close to despair. At that moment she was no match for the older girl. Later, however, Schumann revealed that Ernestine had written to him: 'I always thought that you could love only Clara, and I still think so'. 'She saw things more clearly than I did,' he added.

In 1838, long after the chapter was closed, and obsessed by his pitiless struggle to prevent Schumann from marrying Clara, Wieck dragged up the affair with Ernestine in order to cast a slur on Schumann's character. Far from showing resentment, Ernestine spiked Wieck's guns by assuring him that they had been nothing but friends who were brought together by a common love of music. It was a magnanimous lie that says much for Ernestine's character.

Soon after their first kiss, proudly noted by Schumann in his diary, Clara went with her father on a recital tour of a number of towns in Saxony, among them Zwickau. Schumann travelled there to hear her and later wrote to her of his happy memory: 'It will be three years ago tomorrow that I kissed you that evening in Zwickau. I shall never forget that kiss. You were so sweet. And at the concert, Clara, sitting there in your blue dress, you could not even look at me. I can see it as though it had happened today'. In this state of blissful blindness he could not conceive that anything could impede their happiness. That Clara was only sixteen and could not marry without her father's consent seemed the merest technicality, for, so he thought, he had no reason to doubt that his old teacher, the wise Meister Raro of the 'Davidsbündler' and co-editor of the *Neue Zeitschrift* at its inception, would do other than give them his blessing.

Wieck had no intention of doing anything of the kind. Aware

of what was going on, with Schumann constantly seeking an opportunity to be alone with Clara in the house, he sent her away to Dresden in January 1836, so that, as he claimed, she could impress the Saxon aristocracy with her genius. This, of course, achieved nothing. In February Wieck, who as well as organizing Clara's recitals and giving pianoforte lessons still carried on his trade in musical instruments, happened to be called away from Leipzig on business for a few days. Seeing his opportunity, Schumann at once took the coach to Dresden. Friends found a way to circumvent the precautions that Wieck had taken, and the two spent a few precious hours together.

When news of this secret tryst reached Wieck on his return to Leipzig, he flew into a rage, told Clara that he would shoot Schumann if he came near her again, and wrote to Schumann in a tone that made it impossible for the poor suitor to think of ever setting foot in the house in the Grimmaische Gasse again. 'If your father had known me better', he later wrote to Clara, 'he would have saved me a great deal of suffering, and never written me that letter. It made me two years older'.

This letter marked the declaration of a war that was to last over four years. From February 1836 until September 1840, when Robert Schumann and Clara Wieck were finally married, the proud, intolerant, unyielding father pitted his strength against his teenage daughter and his one-time pupil, stopping at nothing to keep them apart and finally being compelled, not by conversion or by circumstance but by legal injunction, to accept his defeat.

That the hard-bitten Wieck survived the battle with few scars, setting himself up in Dresden soon after as a teacher of renown and living on unperturbed to the age of eighty-eight, need cause no surprise. In her resolution and resilience, Clara, sometimes presented to the popular imagination as a delicate, helpless creature at the mercy of events and the will of others, came of the same stock as her father. And although her incessant travels left her tired and lonely, she had her career to hold on to, the awareness of exceptional gifts that could not be left to wither.

The most vulnerable, because physically and psychologically the least stable, circumstantially and professionally the least secure, was Schumann himself. No longer the convivial, outward-going character that the diaries of his student days reveal, yet the very opposite of assured and self-sufficient in his withdrawal into himself, he needed something, somebody, to support him in his weakness. People may have been starting to take note of his journalism, while *Papillons, Carnaval* and the *Etudes symphoniques* betokened the stirrings of a musical imagination which forced on him, though as yet on few others, the realization of a creative power soon to fill his whole existence and set him among the great composers of his age. But at this moment he counted for little. He had no career as a performer by which to court publicity, like Paganini, or Liszt, or Chopin, nor had he the gifts of a conductor or an organizer, like Mendelssohn and Wagner, or of a teacher, like Wieck. Above all, he could not escape the nagging awareness of appearing to the world at large as inferior to the brilliant young girl, nine years younger, in whose company alone he could contemplate his survival. All Germany knew Clara Wieck; all Germany certainly did not know Robert Schumann. When Chopin had stopped over in Leipzig the previous year, it was to see and hear her, not him.

It was in this depressing mood of personal and artistic inadequacy that he received the news of his mother's death on 4 February 1836. The sense of loneliness settled even more oppressively over him when Clara left Dresden with her father for Breslau a few weeks later and did not return until April. One sad, bitter phrase in his diary says it all. *'Trübes Jahr 1836,'* he wrote: 'cheerless year'.

Schumann had last seen his mother in December, when he went to hear Clara play in Zwickau. For some time she had been ailing; her letters to him had become more and more infrequent, their content stranger, a mixture of pious sermonizing and elaborate self-pity, leaving a disturbing impression that virtually nothing had been said. We do not know exactly how old she was but it must have been close to seventy. Since her husband's death ten years earlier she had continued to live in the family house in Zwickau, where her son Eduard still carried on the publishing and bookselling business of Gebrüder Schumann. The distant,

melancholy mood of her final years permeates her very last letter
to Robert, written shortly before Christmas 1835, which ends:

My memories are my treasure, and if young people of your age are rich in
what you hope for, then those of my generation are rich in what they have
lost. Spend your holiday in joy and happiness, and pass thus into the New
Year also. I shall pray for you, for my two sons and for all who love me.
And I beseech God to forgive all those who misjudge and offend me.
Remember me to Clara, and especially to dear, good Reuter [a doctor and
friend of Schumann's]. Think of me on New Year's Eve. I shall be
thinking of you all with affection.

Usually she signed herself 'Your loving mother C.S.' Here, as
though concluding a formal business letter, she took her strange
leave of him as 'C. Schumann, *née* Schnabel'.

Schumann did not go to her funeral. He had an intense fear of
death, and when someone close to him died, he became numb,
helpless, almost suicidal. So it had been at the time of his sister
Emilie's tragic death in 1825 and when his father died a few
months afterwards; so it had been again when he lost his favourite
brother Julius in 1833. That he had always had a frank, sincere
relationship to his mother, sending her excited reports of his
vacation trips, confiding to her his anxieties about the future,
about Ernestine, about Clara, seeking her opinion on his work –
all this made a public display of grief unbearable.

Only the thought of Clara gave him hope. He paid a short visit to
Zwickau a few days after his mother's death. Waiting in the coach
station late at night for the post-chaise to take him back to
Leipzig, he wrote to her:

I can scarcely keep my eyes open. For two hours I have been waiting for
the coach. The roads are in such a bad condition that I may not be able to
leave until two o'clock . . .

   It has been a hectic day – my mother's open will, accounts of how she
died and so on. But beyond the darkness I always see your radiant
countenance, and then I can bear things more easily . . .

   My first task in Leipzig will be to put my external affairs in order. My
internal affairs are settled: perhaps your father will not turn his back on

me when I ask for his blessing – though there is a great deal to be thought out and settled. Meanwhile I shall put my trust in the benevolent spirit that watches over us. Fate has intended us for each other. I have known it a long time, but I did not have the courage to tell you earlier, or to hope that you would understand . . .

It is dark in the waiting-room here; the passengers next to me have fallen asleep. There is a blizzard raging outside. I am just going to nestle in the corner, put my head on the cushion and think only one thought – you.

Lebe wohl, meine Clara.

Dein Robert

The self-deceiving hope that her father might in the end 'not turn his back' on him only shows how much he underestimated their adversary. Having brought Clara back to Leipzig from Dresden, Wieck virtually put her under house arrest. He forced her to hand over all Schumann's letters and promise to break off all contact with him. An entry in his diary for June 1836 reads laconically 'Exchange of letters'. Until September the following year not a word, spoken or written, passed between them.

Wieck's implacable and increasingly malicious opposition to the relationship between his daughter and Schumann is usually put down to the basest and most selfish of motives. The jealous father, so the argument runs, with the encouragement of his second wife who now had three young children of her own and had pushed her stepdaughter into the background, could not bear the thought of losing control over Clara. He had devoted his life to turning her into the *Wunderkind* she had become: the thought that the fruits of all this invested effort would now no longer be his to enjoy made him fortify his defences with all the weapons he could lay his hands on.

Wieck was an established musician and now, in his fifties, had no need to worry about the future. The fears he had about Clara's future derived rather from a sense of injured pride, of being denied the continued praise of the world for having nurtured her gifts to their glorious florescence, than from any financial considerations. At the same time he was concerned that the considerable fees Clara now received should not be squandered by an adventurer with an eye on her money. As long as she was under twenty-one she could not marry without his consent, and he held in trust all the money she earned. So on all counts, and not least in the future interests of Clara herself, he found it the most convenient and most correct policy to exercise his proprietary rights over her for as long as he could.

These were matters of principle. Wieck did not produce them as a response to Schumann's encroachment on his preserve, and that Schumann was the unhappy man to come into collision with them was, in a sense, an accident. Any but the richest and most celebrated suitor would have been treated in the same way. Indeed, a young musician and friend of the Wieck family, Carl Banck, who tried to take advantage of Schumann's banishment and edge his way into Clara's favour, met with the same iron-fisted rejection and left Leipzig soon after.

But there may also have been other thoughts about Schumann in Wieck's mind. One conviction was that Schumann, who, though comfortably settled with his income from the *Neue Zeitschrift* and with the legacies he had received from his parents, was notoriously fickle in financial matters, wanted Clara chiefly for her money. His affair with Ernestine von Fricken had a mercenary streak in it which made Wieck's mistrust, exaggerated though it may have been, far from unjustified. Reminiscing to Clara in a letter of February 1838 on the circumstances of his break with Ernestine, Schumann did not conceal the dismay he had felt on learning that she was not the heir to the Baron's fortune. What, he asked, would become of his artistic career in a situation like that? And what, Wieck could have been forgiven for thinking, would become of his daughter's money in the hands of a man like this?

Suspicions of this kind received unfortunate support from Schumann's known indulgence, not always moderate, in beer and wine, which could readily be accommodated in an image of undisciplined pleasure-seeking. Nor was his mental instability a secret. Clementine, Wieck's second wife, told Frederick Niecks in her old age that the effect of drink on Schumann's known tendency to states of depression made his friends afraid that he might one day throw himself out of a window, and they watched him anxiously.

There also remains the unmentionable but often mentioned question of syphilis. Wieck had observed almost daily the course of the injury to Schumann's right hand. He was horrified by the mechanical contraption that Schumann and his friend Töpken had devised and he must have known things about the whole affair that we no longer know – things best kept secret. If the paralysis in Schumann's fingers was due to mercury poisoning, Wieck would not have needed to be told the likely reason for the treatment, and a father who suspected such a disease would hardly blind himself to the consequences for his teenage daughter. We shall never know for certain. But Wieck's extreme behaviour over the four years of his opposition to the marriage can attract only explanations of an extreme nature.

Schumann's only completed work in 1836 was the last of his three pianoforte sonatas, that in F minor Op. 14, dedicated to Moscheles. It appeared in print the same year, which is why it bears an earlier opus number than its predecessor, No. 2 in G minor, not published until 1839. Schumann designed it as a five-movement work with two Scherzi and with a slow movement consisting of variations on an Andantino by Clara. The original publisher, Haslinger of Vienna, found this too unconventional and persuaded Schumann to omit both Scherzi and allow the work to appear in three movements, not as a sonata but under the title *Concert sans orchestre*. Both Liszt and the dedicatee considered this a misnomer, and said so. Schumann showed no inclination to concern himself with the piece again until three years before his death, when he published it as a four-movement *Troisième grande Sonate*, leaving out Scherzo I (which was published posthumously in 1866), making Scherzo II the second movement and the Andantino variations the third. The furious Finale, with its characteristically headstrong injunction 'Prestissimo possible', was originally notated in a breathless 6/16

measure, like the superseded Presto of the G minor Sonata, but
for his 1853 edition Schumann changed this to 2/4. He also
reduced from six to four the number of variations in the third
movement.

All three of Schumann's pianoforte sonatas belong to the same
musical world, reflect the same sequence of first, second and
sometimes third thoughts, spring from the same wells of
unbridled impetuosity and delicate lyricism, use a common
musical vocabulary and draw on a common pool of harmonic and
rhythmic techniques. They have the same power to dazzle by their
virtuosity and the same tendency to drag, and all have their
moments of undisguised indebtedness to the pianoforte sonatas
of Schubert.

Maybe the relative oblivion into which the F minor Sonata has
fallen has something to do with its greater unevenness and its
more obtrusive repetitiousness – though homogeneity and
conciseness are hardly the hallmarks of its fellows either. That the
G minor is both the most popular of the three and the shortest
may carry a moral.

In the autumn of 1836 Schumann chanced to make the
acquaintanceship of an English musician who for a short time
became very attached to him. This was William Sterndale Bennett,
something of a prodigy as composer and pianist at one time styled
the English Mendelssohn.

Bennett had greatly impressed Mendelssohn in London in 1833
when, at the age of seventeen, he played a pianoforte concerto of
his own in D minor. In 1836, at Mendelssohn's invitation, he
came to Leipzig with a number of his scores, played his C minor
Concerto at a Gewandhaus concert with great success, and in the
end stayed in the city no less than eight months. During his stay he
had an unusual opportunity to savour a sense of patriotic pride,
when he was among the crowds who thronged to admire the
'steam-carriage' that had just arrived from England for the new
railway line from Leipzig to Dresden.

Shortly after Bennett's arrival Mendelssohn introduced him to
a circle of musicians that used to dine at the fashionable Hôtel de
Bavière, among them Ferdinand David, leader of the
Gewandhaus orchestra, the young French pianist Stamaty and

Robert Schumann. Schumann introduced him in turn to Carl and
Henriette Voigt, to the barons of the publishing houses of
Brockhaus and Breitkopf and Härtel, and to Walther von
Goethe, the great poet's grandson, of whom Bennett wrote: 'He
speaks English *a little better* than I do German – which I don't
speak at all'.

Schumann was greatly taken with the lively young Bennett. He
visited him frequently in his lodgings, invited him to share his
daily constitutional and glowingly described him as 'an out-and-
out Englishman, a splendid artist and a beautiful poetic soul'. In
January 1837 he devoted his editorial in the *Neue Zeitschrift* to
Bennett's works and dedicated the *Etudes symphoniques* to him
the following year.

Of Schumann the composer Bennett has less to say in his letters
and diaries than of Schumann the man, but for the latter he
clearly had a considerable affection, appreciating above all
Schumann's love of good living. A few days before returning to
England he achieved the unlikely feat of mentioning Schumann
and cricket in almost the same breath. 'Well, I'm off on
Monday,' he wrote in his diary:

Called yesterday on Madame von Goethe, dined with Benecke, and
played at Cricket with some Englishmen, which made the Germans stare
very much, as they never saw the game before – we had English bats and
balls. *8 o'clock evening.* Schumann has been to spend an hour with me
and drink a bottle of Porter. I am sorry to part from him, for I think he is
one of the finest-hearted fellows I ever knew.

And it is Schumann with the ever-present cigar in his mouth that
he commemorates in a jolly little canon – in far from impeccable
German – that he presented to him:

(*Herr Schumann is a merry cove,*
He smokes cigars where'er he rove.
Three decades old, I would suppose,
With short-clipped hair and stubby nose.)

Schumann and Bennett corresponded for a number of years afterwards, and Bennett, who wrote a comically ungrammatical German, paid two more visits to Leipzig, but he never met Schumann again.

A work with its roots in the same year of 1836, virtually a sonata in all but name, is that which now bears the title *Fantasie*

(Op. 17). 'Fantasie' was a favourite appellation of Schumann's. The diary for 1832 contains references to a *Fantasie rhapsodique* and a *Fantaisie satyrique*, both unexecuted; in 1837 came the well-known *Fantasiestücke* (Op. 12), the *Kreisleriana* (Op. 16), with the subtitle 'Fantasien für das Pianoforte', and in 1853 a *Fantasie* for Violin and Orchestra, Op. 131, while the first movement of the Pianoforte Concerto was written in 1841 as a self-contained piece also with the simple title *Fantasie*. The word evokes associations of a freely roaming imagination, which in the piano *Fantasie* (Op. 17) takes the form of a semi-programmatic work in three movements. There are also unmistakable terminological and musical echoes of Schubert's 'Wanderer Fantasie', echoes still heard in Schumann's *Arabeske, Blumenstück* and *Humoreske*.

The *Fantasie* was originally to be called *Obolen auf Beethovens Monument (Mites towards Beethoven's Monument)*: 1. 'Ruinen' ('Ruins'); 2. 'Trophäen' ('Trophies'); 3. 'Palmen' ('Palms'). Earlier he had thought of calling the three movements 'Ruine' ('Ruin'), 'Siegesbogen' ('Triumphal Arch') and 'Sternbild' ('Constellation'). Such changes of mind – he often changed the dedication of his pieces also – are characteristic of the volatile Schumann. The music may evoke now one image or set of associations, now another. Of the first movement of the *Fantasie*, marked 'To be performed with passion and a sense of imagination throughout', he said in 1838: 'I consider it the most intense thing I have written'. A year later he wrote to the composer Hermann Hirschbach: 'Have a look at the first movement of my *Fantasie*. Three years ago I considered it the summit of my achievement. Now I think otherwise'.

After this movement, with its romantically styled middle section 'In the manner of a Legend', comes the great March in E flat, while the Finale, the shortest of the three movements, is, unusually, the slow movement, reminiscent in its conclusion of the serenity of Beethoven's Sonatas Op. 109 and Op. 111. Liszt, indeed, regarded the whole *Fantasie* as 'worthy of Beethoven'. In Schumann's world the 'Fantasie', the free imagination, darts to and fro at will and makes its own rules. Its form is its content, and it does not submit willingly to pre-formed expectations or external formal constraints.

The immediate impulse for the composition of the *Fantasie* was the action launched in 1835 to raise funds for a memorial to Beethoven in Bonn – hence the original title. Schumann proposed to write a sonata – more precisely, he wanted Florestan and Eusebius to do so – and donate the proceeds of its sale to the fund. He had precise ideas on how the work should look. It was to have a black binding, he instructed the publisher, with gold lettering and a motif of palm leaves embroidered round the title; the dedication on the title page was to read 'For the Beethoven Memorial, from the Composer and the Publisher'. He also intended to quote in 'Palmen' the Adagio of Beethoven's Seventh Symphony, but no trace of this remains in the printed score. He soon abandoned the whole romantic project, however, and when the work was finally published in 1838, as *Fantasie*, with a dedication to Liszt, it had lost the invocative titles to the individual movements and all reference to Beethoven. Instead it carried as a motto a quatrain by the romantic poet and philosopher Friedrich Schlegel:

> *Durch alle Töne tönet*
> *Im bunten Erdentraum*
> *Ein leiser Ton gezogen*
> *Für den, der heimlich lauschet.*

(Through all the sounds that make up the patchwork of the earthly dream there runs a soft, persistent note that he who listens secretly can hear.)

'The "note" in this motto', Schumann wrote to Clara in 1839, 'must be you'. And the *Fantasie* is, indeed, intimately bound up with their relationship. 'You can only understand the piece', he said to her, 'if you transport yourself back to that unhappy summer of 1836 when I renounced you'.

At this moment, living in the same town as Clara yet forbidden to have any dealings with her, depressed and frustrated, he saw no hope for the fulfilment of their love. 'Clara loves me as sincerely as ever,' he wrote to his sister-in-law Therese in Zwickau, 'but I have completely given up'. And Clara, unable to know or influence the desperate thoughts in his mind, still uneasy over the episode with Ernestine and unsettled by the advances of Carl Banck, was beginning to fear in his silence a withdrawal, a resignation under the burden of unbearable strains.

But their love was too strong to break. Neither of them, even in their blackest, most tormented moments, found the despairing strength to part, and Wieck too was to discover his powerlessness. The first movement of the *Fantasie* Schumann described to Clara in 1838 as 'a deep-felt lament for you'. But a year later he could happily assure her: 'Now I have no reason to compose such unhappy and melancholy music any more'. The *Fantasie* had now become Clara's in a positive, profoundly optimistic sense, the mystic sense of the motto from Friedrich Schlegel.

In the Adagio at the end of the first movement there is a quotation from Beethoven's song-cycle *An die ferne Geliebte*:

Beethoven:

Nimm sie hin denn, die-se Lie-der

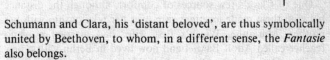

Schumann:

Schumann and Clara, his 'distant beloved', are thus symbolically united by Beethoven, to whom, in a different sense, the *Fantasie* also belongs.

Liszt first played the work to Schumann in March 1840. At the end of the first movement, Liszt said,

Schumann remained perfectly silent in his chair . . . which rather disappointed me. So I asked him what impression my rendering of this movement had made on him, and what improvements he could suggest, since I was naturally anxious to hear the composer's ideas on the reading of so noble a composition. He asked me to proceed with the March, after which he would give me his criticism. Such an effect did my playing of this movement have that he jumped up from his chair and, with tears in his eyes, cried. 'Wonderful! Our ideas on how these movements should be played are absolutely identical, but you, with your magic fingers, have brought these ideas to fulfilment!'

By the time the *Fantasie* was published, the crisis days of 1836 were past and Schumann could give it its optimistic *envoi*, but it was conceived in the despair and disillusion that pursued him through much of that year. Even in 1837 they were still capable, under the stress of their separation, of hurting each other. In the summer of that year Schumann had fits of suspecting that Clara's will was weakening under her father's iron determination. His rival Carl Banck had reappeared – 'I thought that one day I would read of your engagement in the newspaper', he told her. This made him contemplate taking revenge on her by throwing himself into the arms of another woman, as he literally put it. Earlier, to Clara's indignation, he had declined to review her recently published Piano Concerto in the *Neue Zeitschrift*, passing the task to a friend from Schneeberg called Ernst Becker. Becker's perfunctory notice of her work offended Clara. Even more hurtful was that Schumann followed Becker's curt review with lengthy notices of his own on other recent piano concertos, including ones by Henri Herz and Sterndale Bennett. 'That he should forget himself in this way deeply offends me,' she wrote to Banck. 'How could he write so much about Bennett's concerto yet not find a single word to say about mine?'

One of Clara's few sources of comfort, although the distance between them made meetings rare, was her relationship with her mother. Marianne, Wieck's first wife, had married a piano teacher called Adolf Bargiel and now lived in Berlin with a new family of her own, but Clara always found in her a sympathetic listener to her troubles.

On one visit to her in Berlin in February 1837 Clara met, as well as Spontini and a number of leading musicians, the romantic author Bettina von Arnim, one-time friend of Goethe, Beethoven and Madame de Staël, and one of the most vivacious literary personalities of the mid-nineteenth century. Bettina's husband, the aristocratic writer Achim von Arnim, had died in 1831, and the gregarious Bettina, now fifty-two, left the Arnim country estate of Wiepersdorf, outside Berlin, for the company and the stimulating intellectual life of the Prussian capital. She made her entry into literature in 1835 with what is still her best-known and best-loved book, *Goethes Briefwechsel mit einem Kinde (Goethe's Correspondence with a Child)*, a charming series of fanciful letters, fashioned out of a few pieces of genuine correspondence that had passed between them. Bettina had been warmly received by Goethe in Weimar in 1807, when she was twenty-two, but her behaviour towards Goethe's wife Christiane was not a model of tact, and in 1811, after an unpleasant, albeit stupid incident between the two women, Goethe broke off all contact with her. Some years later, however, when the memory of this fracas had faded, Goethe allowed her to write to him again, even accepting from her in 1824 a design she had made for a memorial to him. She formed her own clay model, and the marble figure, made at the expense of the grand duke of Weimar, stands in the Städel Institute in Frankfurt. A woman of remarkable versatility, she also set a number of Goethe's poems to music. In her diary of the Berlin visit Clara called Bettina 'a highly intelligent, passionate woman, but as regards music full of false judgements. She brims over with humour'. Of Clara Bettina said: 'It is a scandal that a girl of seventeen should be so accomplished'.

But Clara was mature beyond her seventeen years, and strengthened by the sympathy of her mother and the practical willingness of friends to help her cause behind Wieck's back, it was she who made the first bold move to cut the knot of suspicions and frustrations that threatened to squeeze the life out of the love that she and Schumann had created.

In August 1837 she gave a recital in Leipzig, playing, among others things, three of the *Etudes symphoniques*. Schumann was in the audience. 'I had eyes only for you', she told him. 'Yet I did not have eyes for you, because I was not allowed to'. After the recital she approached Ernst Becker, whom she had also caught sight of in the hall, and begged him to ask Schumann to return to her the letters that her father had forced her to send back to him over a year ago. A few days later Becker came secretly to the house with a message from Schumann that he would not let her have his old letters back but that she could have new ones instead. Becker had brought the first of these with him, and handed it to her. The letter itself filled one side of the sheet, which was folded inwards and sealed. On the back, the first words that Clara read, was a message that conveyed not only Schumann's sufferings of the past months but also an anxious hesitancy, an apprehension lest that which he so desperately wanted might have gone for ever: 'After endless days of silence, days of pain, of hope, of despair, may these words be received with love. If this last is no more, I beg that this letter be returned to me unopened'.

The text of the letter addresses her with the formal 'Sie', which alone symbolizes the gulf that has opened up between them:

13 August 1837

Are you still loyal and resolute? Unshakeable as is my faith in you, even the most steadfast of men begins to waver if he hears not a word of that which is the most precious thing to him in all the world. For that is what you are to me. I have thought it all through a thousand times, and everything tells me that, if we want it so and if we act, it must truly come to pass. Just write 'Yes!' and tell me if you are willing to give your father a letter from me on your birthday. He is now favourably disposed towards me and will not turn me away if you plead on my behalf.

I am writing this as the sun rises. Would that but one more dawn separated us. Above all things hold fast to this: *It must truly come to pass, if we want it so and if we act.*

Tell not a soul of this letter, otherwise all could be lost. Do not forget your 'Yes!' I must have this assurance before I can consider the next step.

All this, as it lies before you, comes from the depths of my heart, and I append to it my name

Robert Schumann

These were the first words he had addressed to her for a year and a half.

The following day Becker brought back Clara's 'joyful 'Yes!' She added: 'I, too, have felt for a long while that *it must be so*. Nothing in the world shall distract me, and I will show my father that a young heart can be resolute too'.

In future years Schumann and Clara regarded this day, 14 August 1837, as their secret engagement day. It was also the day of St Eusebius.

With the collusion of Nanny, an old servant in the Wieck household, secret messages passed between them, and three weeks after their 'engagement', as Nanny was accompanying Clara home from a visit to friends late in the evening, Schumann waited in the shadows. 'The first time we saw each other again', she wrote to him later,

you were so formal, so cold. I wanted to be more affectionate but I was too agitated and could barely control myself. The moon lit up your face when you took off your hat and drew your hand across your forehead. It was the most wonderful feeling I had ever had – the feeling that I had found what was dearest to me again.

All doubts now banished, filled with a new happiness and optimism, Schumann prepared his letter to Wieck and gave it to Becker to deliver. It is an intense, moving document, in part a tortured account of his own sufferings, in part an affirmation of the matchless beauty of the love that binds him and Clara, and in part an appeal to Wieck, as a devoted father, to allow their relationship to continue. 'With all the profound emotion which an anxious, loving heart can command,' he ends, 'I beseech you to grant us your blessing, to be a friend again to one of your oldest friends, and the best of fathers to the best of daughters'.

The following day Wieck summoned him to his house. 'Wieck's reply was so confused', wrote Schumann to Becker later the same day, 'such an ambiguous mixture of concession and rejection, that I now have no idea what to do – *no idea at all*'. Wieck's only written reaction to Schumann's approach – he apparently sent no answer – was a laconic note in the diary he had long kept in Clara's name, which said: 'On my birthday there arrived among other things a letter from Schumann. To write about it would take pages'.

After the interview Schumann wrote to Clara in a state of desperation:

My meeting with your father was terrible – His frigidity, this maliciousnes., this farrago of contradictions. He has found a new way of destroying me – by plunging the whole dagger into my heart, hilt as well as blade: I don't know which way to turn. You must fear the worst from him . . . I am utterly lifeless, so embittered, my noblest feelings so humiliated . . . In vain do I seek some excuse for your father, whom I always held to be an honourable and humane person . . . He will give you away to the first man with money and a title who comes along, believe me . . . I cannot remain long in this state – my constitution will not stand it.

And, already foreseeing that they might have to seek their happiness without Wieck's consent, he added:

If he drives us to the limit and refuses to permit us to marry after a year and a half or two years, then the authorities will unite us. God forbid that it will come to that.

But it did.

In the years that followed Schumann stumbled from one psychological crisis to another, at one moment recovering the strength to hope, at the next slipping back into despair. Yet Clara suffered even more. Denied the presence of the man she loved, she could not renounce her affection and respect for her father, who had jealously devoted his life to her career and the cultivation of her gifts but had now convinced himself that another man, an outsider of no great stability of character or security of position, was about to snatch his life's work from him. He knew that if he carried his opposition to Schumann too far, he ran the risk of undermining Clara's health and peace of mind, and thus the concentration on which her success as an artist depended. She knew that he desired her happiness. He knew that his behaviour was achieving the very opposite. Small wonder that Schumann found his utterances 'a farrago of contradictions'.

Soon after the final break with Schumann Wieck took Clara on an extended recital tour to Vienna, where she had enormous success, financial as well as musical. Her third recital, Wieck recorded in the diary, was attended by 800 people and brought in 1035 gulden. Among the audience was the famous poet and dramatist Franz Grillparzer, who afterwards wrote a poem in her praise. She also met Liszt and played him Schumann's *Carnaval*, to his great admiration. Of the impression made by Liszt himself at the keyboard Wieck wrote: 'He cannot be compared with anybody – he is unique. His appearance at the piano beggars description. His passion knows no bounds, but frequently he offends one's sense of beauty by distorting the melody and pedalling too heavily'.

A special honour bestowed on Clara during this stay in Vienna was her appointment by the Austrian emperor to the rank of Kaiserlich-Königliche Kammervirtuosin – a rare distinction in conservative, Catholic Vienna for a woman who was both a foreigner and a Protestant. As a result she found herself more and more in demand. But it was a lonely life. 'I go nowhere', she wrote: ' – never to dances and only rarely to the theatre. Yet I never have a moment to myself. Father is at home almost the entire evening, and when he isn't, the Prince comes (my former neighbour), with a cursed servant who sits all day by the window and keeps watch on the house when I am on my own . . . The only balls I have attended have been three private occasions. Strange – I have no liking for young men. They are all so insipid, so unintelligent: in a word, there is only one Robert'.

Wieck's role on Clara's tours was partly that of chaperon, partly that of manager. Managers and agents, indeed, were beginning to emerge as a separate race at this time, and although we hear little criticism of Wieck himself, musicians often resented the way these administrators thrust themselves between the artist and his public. And, inevitably, the greater the artist, the more obtrusive his advisers. It worried Mendelssohn, for example, to see Liszt caught up in the manoeuvrings of these parasites when he played in Leipzig in 1840. 'Unfortunately', wrote Mendelssohn to Moscheles,

even Liszt is now set round by a manager and a secretary who administer his affairs so abominably that the whole audience was incensed. It cost us all a great amount of trouble to smooth things out before his second recital. The publicity, the alterations, the prices, the programme, in fact, everything that Liszt had not attended to personally, was wrong, and the normally placid Leipzigers were furious. In the meantime, I think, they have calmed down, and Hiller, Härtel, Schumann and I have done our best to counteract the effect these administrators created.

With the covert help of old Nanny, who had accompanied Clara and her father on the tour, letters found their clandestine way from Vienna to Leipzig and from Leipzig to Vienna every few days, sometimes every day. But seven long months went by before Schumann and Clara saw each other again.

During this time he completed some of his best-known cycles of pianoforte pieces – the *Davidsbündlertänze* (Op. 6), the *Fantasiestücke* (Op. 12), the *Kinderszenen* (Op. 15), the *Novelettes* (Op. 21) and the *Kreisleriana* (Op. 16).

The *Davidsbündlertänze* sprang from the happiness that attended his reunion with Clara in August 1837. They are of a piece, unrevised products of a single, unerring impulse. 'If ever I was happy at the piano', he wrote to Clara, on one of whose *Soirées*, Op. 6 he based the opening of the first number, 'it was when I was composing these'. The spiritual condition of their birth – they are all mood pieces of one kind or another – is captured in a motto that stood beneath the title in the original edition.

> *In all und jeder Zeit*
> *Verknüpft sich Lust und Leid:*
> *Bleibt fromm in Lust und seid*
> *Dem Leid mit Mut bereit.*

(Joy and suffering go hand in hand at every moment. Be upright in joy, and steadfast in the face of suffering.)

Indeed, the *Davidsbündlertänze* are as immediate a piece of spiritual autobiography as any of Schumann's compositions. 'They abound with wedding thoughts', he told Clara later. The first edition, brought out in 1838 by Friese, publisher of the *Neue Zeitschrift,* was entitled: *Davidsbündlertänze für das Pianoforte, Walther von Goethe zugeeignet von Florestan und Eusebius.* Each of the eighteen dances, alternately lively and reflective, is signed either 'F' or 'E', sometimes both. In 1850–1 Schumann reissued the work as *Die Davidsbündler, 18 Charakterstücke,* without the verse motto and the individual ascriptions to Florestan and Eusebius, and with a few modifications of musical detail. A third edition made in 1862, after Schumann's death, claimed to incorporate the variants of the first two versions into a final definitive reading.

Thematic reminiscences of *Carnaval* peep through the *Davidsbündlertänze,* as flashes from *Papillons* light up *Carnaval,* and all three share a penchant of Schumann's for inconclusive endings in his whimsical miniatures. Such endings may even lie in a different key from the opening, as in the *Davidsbündler* Nos 10 and 16. Probing, ambiguous openings also have their place:

(No. 9)

The *Davidsbündlertänze* is the last work in which Schumann made Florestan and Eusebius take public credit for a musical composition. They belonged to a period which had now virtually come to an end, a period in which Schumann made ostentatious display of the conflicting extravagancies within his enthusiastic imagination. Eusebius made sporadic appearances in the *Neue Zeitschrift* until 1839; Florestan appeared for the last time in

1842. Meister Raro, with his original associations of Friedrich Wieck, had abruptly disappeared in 1836, the time Wieck first intervened to take Clara out of Schumann's grasp. The characters remain, the creative conflicts persist. But the exteriorization of their individuality in the Jean-Paulesque world of openly flaunted masks is fading.

Born of the same elation as the *Davidsbündlertänze*, the same sudden confidence of a creative vision that needs neither preparation nor qualification, are the eight *Fantasiestücke* (Op. 12), published in March 1838 by Breitkopf and Härtel. With a range that embraces the fleeting mystery of 'Traumes Wirren' and the hesitant charm of 'Warum?', the whirling, chromatic breathlessness of 'In der Nach' and the extrovert happiness of 'Ende vom Lied', these are among Schumann's most popular pieces. He took his title from E.T.A. Hoffmann, whose *Fantasiestücke in Callots Manier* brought together a number of stories and sketches on music and musicians, written in a fanciful but penetrating, sometimes psychologically disturbing manner. Hoffmann's invocation in his title of the seventeenth-century French engraver Jacques Callot takes the associations of Schumann's pieces back still further, inviting us to hold side by side in our minds a vision of Callot's prints, with their freedom, their variety and their extraordinary concentration of figurative detail in a minute space, and the sounds of Schumann's highly original musical sketches, equally free-ranging and equally intense in the expressiveness of their individual moments. Schumann's *Fantasiestücke* do not enact a plan, like *Papillons* or *Carnaval*, nor do they have recourse to the variation-form so typical of his pianoforte music. Their unity, like that of Callot's engravings and Hoffmann's stories, is a unity not of substance but of imagination, the same unity that holds together Schumann's wonderful song-cycles – works that were only a few years away, and towards which his musical development was leading.

As in *Carnaval*, the titles of the individual *Fantasiestücke* were not starting-points for a music yet to be written but fanciful designations of pieces already composed. Sitting at the keyboard in front of his finished manuscript, Schumann would let his restless imagination wander over the field of pictorial or narrative associations that the sounds brought to his mind, anxiously reading into the notes a meaning that would relate to his own condition. Even the observation that all the movements but one are in flat keys could be made to bear a significance. His poetic commentary on 'In der Nacht', for instance, centred on the story of Hero and Leander. 'You know how it goes', he wrote to Clara:

every night Leander swims across the water to his beloved, who waits in the lighthouse and lights the way for him with a torch. It is a wonderful, romantic old legend. When I play 'In der Nacht', I cannot get the picture out of my mind – first, how he dives into the sea. She calls, he answers. He swims through the waves and arrives safely at the other side. Then comes the cantilena, when they embrace; then he has to return but cannot bear to part – until night again shrouds the whole scene in darkness.

'It is astonishing how it all fits', he wrote to his pianist friend Carl Krägen. It is not, of course. There is no limit to the fictional descriptive patterns that can be draped over a given musical composition. But they are also all private, arbitrary, self-oriented. No one could see in 'In der Nacht' a portrayal of the story of Hero and Leander – no one but Schumann, that is.

He poignantly described the autobiographical meaning of the *Fantasiestücke* to Clara in terms of 'Ende vom Lied', the last piece: 'I thought that, now I had reached the end, everything would revolve itself in a merry wedding. But as I thought of you, sorrow came over me, and the result was a chime of wedding bells mingled with a death knell'. Like the joyous march of 'Ende vom Lied' that suddenly melts into a pianissimo coda, it could be an image of Schumann's whole life.

During the early months of 1838, when Clara and her father were still in Vienna, Schumann felt an optimism about the future which, though to be cruelly frustrated in his and Clara's personal life, sustained the happy creativity of late 1837. That Clara could write to him and receive letters from him was the only concession Wieck had made to them, but it was enough for them to give each other the support they desperately needed. Clara even suggested that they might establish themselves in Vienna; here, she told him, the financial prospects, public appreciation and the social scene in general were a lot more attractive than in Leipzig, where Wieck would in any case forbid them to stay together.

In March 1838 Schumann wrote to Clara that, 'as though he had suddenly grown wings', he had just composed

some thirty droll little things, from which I have selected a dozen or so and called *Kinderszenen*. You will enjoy them – though you will have to forget that you are a virtuoso. They have titles like 'The Bogeyman's coming', 'By the Fireside', 'Catch-as-catch-can', 'Pleading Child', 'Ride a Cock-horse', 'From far-off Lands' and so on. You can see what they're like – and they're all easy to carry off.

He was brimming over with music at this time. To his friend Becker he wrote: 'I feel I could almost burst with music – I simply have to compose. So strong is my urge that even if I were cast on to a desert island in the middle of the ocean, I could not stop'.

As published in September 1839 the *Scenes from Childhood* (Op. 15) consist of thirteen little pieces, all in simple episodic form, all with allusive titles like those he quotes in his letter to Clara, and all with the naïve charm that has given them a special place in the affection of musical households. Unlike the later *Album für die Jugend*, which really are written for children, the *Kinderszenen* are addressed to adults – 'reminiscences of a grown-up for grown-ups', Schumann put it. But he also wanted their appearance to match their content, and he put to Wilhelm Härtel, the manager of Breitkopf and Härtel, a detailed list of requests concerning format, size of type, ornamentation and so on. As for the other three works of his that Härtel published in 1839, he received for the *Kinderszenen* a fee of three Louis d'or.

Schumann first saw the *Kinderszenen* and the *Novelletten* (Op. 21) as a single collection of pieces, a direct expression, like this whole group of works from the *Davidsbündlertänze* to the *Kreisleriana*, of the inspiring and all-consuming presence of Clara. In style and form, as in their range of moods and emotions, they can be set alongside the *Fantasiestücke*, though they are perhaps less spontaneous, less fresh than the earlier collection. 'I have composed a frightful amount for you in the past three weeks', he wrote to Clara: 'jests, Egmont stories, family scenes with fathers, a wedding – in short, most endearing subjects. The whole thing I have called "Novellettes", because your name is Clara, and "Wieckettes" does not sound attractive enough'. This last allusion is a typical piece of Schumannian whimsy. The English soprano Clara Novello had recently had a tumultuous reception at two of Mendelssohn's Gewandhaus concerts, above all for her singing of Handel. With the love of one Clara in his heart, and the voice of another Clara ringing in his ears, he took the latter's surname and playfully added a diminutive ending to it, producing a 'little novelty'.

The collection consists of eight such 'little novelties', without titles, originally published in four pairs in July 1839 (four of the *Albumblätter*, Op. 124, were composed at the same time: Schumann would often write piece after piece, in a sudden burst of energy, until the vein of inspiration was exhausted, then assemble from them his collection of the moment, leaving the rest for inclusion in later works or simply as unused fragments). They are much more substantial than the *Fantasiestücke*, the *Kinderszenen* or any of the other collections in this group – more elaborately sectionalized, perhaps more deliberately cogitated in consequence, as unmistakably Schumann in rhythmic and harmonic vocabulary as his more pointed, maybe more immediately captivating imagistic sketches, but somewhat more serious in tone. Schumann described them to the composer Hermann Hirschbach as 'closely linked, written in joy, for the most part cheerful and on the surface, with just a few moments in which I plumb the depths'. And to Clara, earlier: 'You appear in the *Novelletten* in every possible circumstance, in every irresistible form . . . They could only be written by one who knows such eyes as yours and has touched such lips as yours'.

Finally in this burst of creativity that sublimated Schumann's energy in the first half of the year 1838 came the *Kreisleriana*, Op. 16. So impatient was he to see the work published that, instead of giving it to Breitkopf and Härtel, who still had others of his works in production and could not promise to have it ready before the following year, he gave it to Haslinger in Vienna, who brought it out a few months after receiving the manuscript.

The eight movements took him only a matter of days to write. 'You and the thought of you play the dominant role', he told Clara just after he had finished, 'and I intend to dedicate them to you – to you as to no one else. You will smile when you recognize yourself in them'. And in another letter: 'Play my *Kreisleriana* sometimes. You will find a wild, unbridled love there in places, together with your life and mine, and many of your glances. The *Kinderszenen* are the opposite – peaceful, tender and happy, like our future . . .' In their published form the *Kreisleriana* were dedicated not to Clara but to Chopin. The *Kinderszenen*, unusually, have no dedication.

Lurking behind the title of Schumann's Op. 16 is the bizarre, schizophrenic character Kapellmeister Johannes Kreisler, the figure invented by E.T.A. Hoffmann to embody his vision of the musician in the clutches of society, the struggle between the divine values of art and the Philistinism of a smug, uncultured public. Hoffmann, who changed his third name from Wilhelm to Amadeus in reverence for Mozart, and who composed operas, symphonies, chamber music and a good deal else, led a Jekyll-and-Hyde existence as a judge in the Prussian civil service by day and a carouser and storyteller by night. Likewise Kapellmeister Kreisler, Hoffmann's *alter ego*, hovered between the scornful despair of serving a society he despised and the emotional turbulence of his inner life, the frustrations of a doomed love and his devotion to the true spirit of art. One moment he is lost in dreams, in a soft, unreal world of yearning; the next he raves against the forces that drag him back into a hated 'reality', and indulges himself in wild, grotesque behaviour that seems to prove, to all but the few who understand him, that he is mad.

From Schumann's schooldays the figure of Kreisler, like the eerie, sinister stories with which Hoffmann's name is most immediately associated, had gripped his mind like no other literary creations save those of Jean Paul. Now, twenty years later, he could read the joys and sufferings of the tormented Kreisler into the music he had written, matching the love and the misery of the unhappy Kapellmeister with his own longing for fulfilment and his illusions of happiness, making a mirror of his own spiritual condition.

Like the eight *Novelletten*, the eight items of *Kreisleriana* bear no titles. Half of them – Nos 2, 6, 7 and 8 – are in the rondo form for which Schumann had a particular penchant. This form, in essence an expression of the episodic principle on which almost all Schumann's pianoforte music rests – with the self-explanatory exceptions of variation, sonata, fugue and other classical exercises – also predominates in the *Novelletten*, underlies all four *Nachtstücke*, Op. 23, and on a more extended scale, the *Arabeske*, Op. 18, the *Blumenstück*, Op. 19, and the *Humoreske*, Op. 20.

'Of all these things I like the *Kreisleriana* best,' wrote Schumann to his Belgian friend Simonin de Sire. And they are, indeed, Schumann at his best. The mood passes from the headlong agitation of the first movement to the alternating serenity and passion of the second, from the gently rocking 6/8-rhythm of the sixth to the furious 2/4 of the seventh and the scampering 6/8 scherzo of the last (the G minor theme that he later re-used in the Finale of his First Symphony). Yet from this diversity emerges a remarkable unity. To turn the page from one movement to the next is not, as in the *Davidsbündlertänze* or the *Kinderszenen*, to make a new beginning but to move from one stage in the exposition of a story to the next, to absorb a pattern of ever-changing emotions held within the subjective, yet somehow also objective unity of an artist's personal experience – the experience of Schumann, of Hoffmann, of Johannes Kreisler. For at this moment they are all one in an ambiguous blend of calm and unease, of assurance and mystery expressed in the chromaticism of the beautiful opening of the last section of the longest and most intense movement in the work (No. 2):

*   *   *

Sehr innig und nicht zu rasch

Hoffmann could not have composed such music. But he would have recognized why his name was associated with it.

CHAPTER SEVEN

'Hail wedded love, mysterious law...'

In May 1838, shortly after Schumann finished the *Kreisleriana*, Clara returned to Leipzig from Vienna. She had been away for seven months. Yet ironically this long absence had coincided with a sudden burst of musical activity on Schumann's part, alongside his continued devotion to the organization of the *Neue Zeitschrift*. True, he was now contributing fewer articles of his own to the journal than at the beginning, and he wrote still fewer in the remaining years before he finally gave up the editorship in 1844. But April 1838 still found him giving his usual extended survey of musical life in Leipzig during the previous winter season, and in June came his review of the last works of Schubert, which had just been published – the 'Grand Duo' for piano duet and the last three pianoforte sonatas.

Already the previous year friends had urged him to leave the *Neue Zeitschrift* to others and devote his time to composing. But apart from the financial aspect – the publisher, Friese, paid him about 600 thalers a year, which was a good half of his annual income – he still needed the stimulus of writing words as well as notes. Literary associations, whether of Jean Paul and E.T.A. Hoffmann in his pianoforte music, or of Goethe, Heine, Eichendorff and the other poets from whose verse he was soon to fashion some of the finest of the world's Lieder, never left his mind.

Although Clara stayed in Leipzig some six weeks before leaving again, this time for concerts in Dresden, she and Schumann were apparently not allowed to see each other. After she had left, the same irony repeated itself. 'How strange it is,' he wrote to her a few days later. 'Since you have been away, I can compose again. Yet all the time you were here, I could not'. At such moments he was sustained by a false optimism that Wieck could not hinder their happiness much longer. The graph of his emotional condition, and with it his mental health, plunged and soared many times before, on 12 September 1840, their goal was finally reached. In July 1838 he wrote to himself in his diary: 'Never forget what Clara has borne for your sake'. She could have written the same.

Vienna had brought Clara fresh successes, and when Wieck, as a crafty delaying tactic, hinted that he might permit her to marry Schumann provided they did not live in Leipzig, Schumann convinced himself, characteristically but illusorily, that the Austrian capital could do the same for him. Although he was a Saxon, and felt that he belonged to Saxony as to nowhere else, Leipzig was beginning to feel provincial, in spite of Mendelssohn and the Gewandhaus. Vienna, with a population of well over a quarter of a million – almost twice as big as Berlin, and over seven times the size of Leipzig – had a music-loving public far superior in knowledge and discrimination to any other in the German-speaking world, and must surely, he thought, welcome the prospect of adding him and his *Neue Zeitschrift* to its musical life. And when Clara finally joined him there, so his thoughts ran, his personal happiness and professional fulfilment would be complete.

So at the beginning of October he set out along the same route – Dresden, Prague, Vienna – as Clara had taken almost exactly a year before. It was a journey not without incident, as he wrote to her a few days after his arrival:

Shortly after leaving Prague I had a whole series of misadventures and felt like a proper schoolboy. In the first place I arrived in Vienna without my hat, which blew off in the night twelve miles this side of Vienna. But I could easily have lost my head too. For at one of the stops two coaches drove off without me. I chased after them as hard as I could. No one heard my shouts, and my strength was just on the point of giving out when I finally caught up with the second chaise, jumped on to the step and clung to the door as the horses galloped along. After I had crouched there in this terrible position for a few moments, the door I was holding on to suddenly flew open. Heaven knows how I managed to hang on. If I had fallen off, it would have been all up with me.

He could have taken it as an omen of what was to come. The fine buildings, above all St Stephen's Cathedral, impressed him, as did the many beautiful women, and he walked reverentially through the streets, breathing the spirit of Haydn and Mozart, of Beethoven and Schubert. He found life more expensive than in Leipzig, though he was able to find a room on the first floor of a house in the Schön Laternengasse, which cost only 22 gulden a month.

But as he had overestimated the welcome that would await him in Viennese musical circles, so also he had naïvely failed to envisage the obstacles that would be put in his way. Vienna already had an *Allgemeiner musikalischer Anzeiger* of its own. The publishers did not relish the thought of a competitor, nor had they forgotten that the *Neue Zeitschrift für Musik* – Schumann himself, not to disguise the fact – had said some caustically uncomplimentary things about their *Anzeiger* back in 1834. The city was in any case riddled with cliques and coteries, bristling with self-defensive instincts released by the attempted intrusions of their rivals, and even more strongly aroused by the invasion of a brash, foreign intruder. 'I must refrain from expressing my real opinion about musical conditions here,' he wrote to Oswald Lorenz, his deputy editor in Leipzig. 'If I did, I would be offending against the rules of hospitality'.

Nor had he given thought to the political climate in Austria. This was the era of Metternich, to some an oracle of diplomatic inspiration, to others the incarnation of reaction and oppression, but at all events responsible for a rigid censorship of the written word and consequently for the restriction of freedom of thought. Already seeing what this would mean if his journal were really to be published in Vienna, Schumann warned Lorenz not to accept any contributions that might offend the authorities: 'You have no idea what power the censor wields here. It reminds one of those secret courts of the Middle Ages'.

Moreover, the inward-looking political conservatism of Metternich's Austria bred a suspicion of outsiders, and

Schumann, as a foreigner, had no certainty that he would be granted permission to take up permanent residence in Vienna. Reserved and unsure of himself, he made no close friends who could have helped him over these hurdles, and as his spirits flagged, so unhappiness and disillusion began to edge out the optimism that had sustained his letters to Clara in recent months. As time went on, he realized that Wieck would implacably oppose their marriage for as long as the law allowed, that is, until Clara became of age, and his inner discord began to show itself in suspicions that Clara was holding back in her total commitment to him out of a lingering sense of loyalty to her father. When she pointed out in her letters, with good justification, the difficulties that would face him in Vienna, he virtually accused her of wavering in her affection and thus created a climate of misunderstanding which fed still further the pessimism that always threatened to stifle him.

As 1839 arrived, Schumann grew more and more aware that his thoughts of a future in Vienna were an illusion, and that he could do nothing but return, defeated, to Leipzig. Clara's enviable yet dispiriting independence was brought home to him again when she set out in January with her old companion Nanny, though for the first time without her father, for a six-month stay in Paris. Here she lodged at first in a hotel in the rue Michadière where Pauline Viardot-Garcia, the famous operatic soprano who later championed the cause of Wagner's music in Paris, was also living. The two leading French piano manufacturers, Erard and Pleyel, anxious that Clara should use their instrument at her concerts, each presented her with a grand piano on which to practise: the Erard, she found, had an uncomfortably hard touch; the Pleyel was easier, but both were very different from the German and Austrian instruments she was accustomed to. Later she moved to the apartment of her Leipzig friend Emilie List and her family in the rue Navarin.

Wieck had planned this conquest of the musical capital of Europe as the climax of Clara's career – more exactly, of his and Clara's career. She played to great applause in the Salle Erard and met all the best people, including Meyerbeer, the king of Parisian music, who was very well-disposed towards her. At a dinner in

Meyerbeer's house she met the remarkable novelist and critic Jules Janin, and also the great Heinrich Heine, who had been living in political exile in Paris since 1831. Whether Heine remembered being visited in Munich by the excited, eighteen-year-old Robert Schumann and his friend Gisbert Rosen back in 1828, we cannot know; he makes only perfunctory reference in his diary to meeting 'the pianist Clara Wieck'. She found him 'a melancholy and unhappy man, who faced the terrible prospect of going blind. He spoke with great bitterness about Germany'.

For the rest she met many of the leading composers and performers in the French capital – Paer, Stephen Heller, the thirteen-year-old prodigy Georges Mathias – and played to private gatherings at the homes of ambassadors and similar *haute volée*. She also made the acquaintance of the young Charles Hallé – founder of the famous Manchester orchestra that bears his name – and it was Hallé's company that, to their shared delight, she first played through the *Kinderszenen*, which Schumann had just sent her.

But she did not like the Parisians, whom she found affected, colourless and trivial. They, for their part, while marvelling at her skill, considered it strange and improper that a girl of nineteen should be allowed to travel abroad in this way without her father, or at least a proper chaperon. In fact, one reason for the visit had been an ignoble ruse on Wieck's part to force Clara to recognize, under the pressure of her loneliness in a strange city, how much she depended on him and how little Schumann could offer her.

The ruse failed. Not for the first time Wieck miscalculated, unable to see how unshakeable was Clara's love, and how strong this love made her. In May she wrote a long letter to her father from Paris. In its poignancy, its affectionate honesty and its depth of sympathy, moving in a young girl who had been reared in such confined, hothouse conditions yet who had seen far more of the world than the lover nine years her senior, this letter says all there is to be said:

It is a passionate love I have for Schumann, yet I love him not simply out of a feeling of rapture or passion but because I find him a fine man, and because I believe that no other would love me so purely or understand me so completely as he. On my side I believe I could offer him perfect happiness, for no woman could understand him as I do. Everyone has his peculiarities, but must one not just accept these? I know what Schumann lacks, and that is a friend, a man of experience to help and support him. Remember that Schumann has never gone out into the world, so how can you suddenly expect him to be successful? O father, I wish you could be his friend – you would not find him ungrateful, and would certainly respect him. Do you think I could love him as I do if I did not respect him? Do you think that I do not recognize his faults? But I recognize his virtues too . . .

All we need for our happiness is a secure income, however small, and your consent. Without this latter I would be deeply uneasy and unhappy, as would Schumann also, who is so sensitive a person. I could not bear this. Dear father, will you promise me your consent if Schumann can prove that he has an income of 1000 thalers? If you will but give us hope, we shall be happy, and Schumann will woo me in a new spirit . . .

I can never leave him, nor will he ever leave me. I could never love another man. Give me your word, I beg you, and tell me openly what you require of us . . .

At the time Clara wrote this, Schumann, dejected and disillusioned, was back in Leipzig. But there had been one glorious moment during his unprofitable and ever lonelier months in Vienna.

Not long after his arrival he had walked out to the Währinger cemetery to lay a flower on the graves of Beethoven and Schubert, which are almost side by side. 'Although it had not been vouchsafed to me', he wrote in the *Neue Zeitschrift* in 1840, 'to know in life these two masters, whom I revere the most among modern musicians, I would have dearly loved to have beside me, as I stood there, somebody who had been close to one of them – in particular, I thought, a brother. On my way home it suddenly occurred to me that Schubert's brother Ferdinand, whom he had highly esteemed, was still alive'.

So shortly afterwards, already aware that Ferdinand Schubert was in possession of a large number of his late brother's unpublished manuscripts, Schumann called on Ferdinand and was shown, to his joy and astonishment, an immense amount of musical material, including dramatic works, masses and several symphonies. Among these latter was the manuscript score of the

'Great' C major. Schumann persuaded Ferdinand to send it to Mendelssohn in Leipzig, and Mendelssohn conducted the first performance at the Gewandhaus the same year. In 1840 Schumann wrote a pioneering account of the work in the *Neue Zeitschrift*, comparing it to a four-volume novel by Jean Paul and praising its 'divine expansiveness', its power not only to envelop the listener in its magnificence but also 'to make him continue, as it were, the creative process in his own mind'.

Schumann's piano music owes much to Schubert, in vocabulary and musical form as well as in the attachment of *Papillons, Carnaval* and so on to the lineage of the *Moments musicaux*. Moreover, his discovery of Schubert's C major Symphony played its part in the genesis of his own Symphony No. 1 in B flat, a work conceived among optimistic thoughts of spring and fulfilment that made him write excitedly to Clara: 'You have inspired a symphony in me!' It was three years before this inspiration bore fruit, but his months in Vienna did produce more pianoforte music. There was the new Finale for the G minor Sonata, to replace the original Presto that Clara had considered too difficult, and the four not particularly memorable or well-matched *Klavierstücke* – Scherzo, Gigue, Romanze and Fughette – published in 1841 as Op. 32. The four *Nachtstücke* (Op. 23) owe their name, like the *Kreisleriana*, to E.T.A. Hoffmann, who published two sets of mysterious tales under this title in 1816-17. 'While I was writing these pieces,' Schumann wrote to Clara, 'I kept seeing funeral processions, coffins and unhappy, distraught figures. When I had finished and was pondering over a title, I always came back to *Funeral Fantasia* – is that not strange?' At one time he thought of calling the four movements 1. 'Funeral Procession'; 2. 'Weird Company'; 3. 'Night Revels'; 4. 'Round with Solo Voices'. Musically they are little more than a pallid reflection of the *Kreisleriana*, less intense in their lyrical moments, more perfunctory in their energetic sections, for which a somewhat palling reliance on diminished sevenths bears much of the blame.

With the *Faschingsschwank aus Wien*, Op. 26, on the other hand, we return to the uninhibited, extrovert world of the masked ball and *Carnaval*. Four of its five movements were written in

Vienna around carnival time, i.e. Shrove Tuesday, the fifth after Schumann's return to Leipzig. All are in flat keys, like so much of Schumann's most characteristic music. The complete work, variously styled by him as 'a grand romantic sonata' and 'a romantic showpiece', was published in 1841.

The latter designation speaks for itself. The full range of Schumann's piano skills – vigorous rhythms, extended syncopations, full chordal writing to simulate orchestral effects, moments of subtle counterpoint, brilliant passage-work – is on exuberant display, while the explicit romanticism lies in his return yet again to the world of E.T.A. Hoffmann by giving the *Faschingsschwank* the subtitle *Fantasiestücke für das Pianoforte*.

As for the 'grand romantic sonata', it is less helpful as a definition than revealing of how Schumann viewed the classical term and wished to invoke it for a collection of such 'fantasy pieces.' Thus the opening Allegro is a long-drawn-out movement in rondo form; then follow a slow Romanze, only 25 bars long, and a two-page Scherzino in 2/4 time, which moves in an almost unbroken dotted rhythm from start to finish; the fourth movement, Intermezzo, is a typical whirling episode marked 'Mit grösster Energie', while the Finale, in many ways the strongest and most satisfying of the five, is cast in sonata form, with a lyrical second subject among the most beautiful of all Schumann's melodies:

Of the pianoforte works Schumann wrote in Vienna there remain three substantial single pieces, all extended examples of the rondo principle: the *Arabeske* (Op. 18), the *Blumenstück* (Op. 19) and the *Humoreske* (Op. 20). The one appears to have followed on the heels of the other in a spurt of activity which had an ulterior motive: 'I am composing very intensely at the moment,' he wrote at the end of the year to the publisher Joseph Fischhof, 'and hoping to elevate myself to the rank of favourite composer of all the women in Vienna'.

The popular *Arabeske* is a light, conventional rondo, the three appearances of its principal theme separated by two episodes in minor keys. The *Blumenstück*, by contrast, consists of nine sections, some repeated, others not, arranged – like the blossoms of the title, perhaps – in seemingly haphazard order, and sustained from beginning to end by an almost uninterrupted flow of semiquavers. There are occasional slight variations of tempo, and two of the sections are in the relative minor of the main key of D flat major, but an air of sameness hangs over the whole piece.

Schumann drew a charmingly delineated distinction between these two works and the 'Grand Humoreske', as he called it: 'Op. 18 and 19 are fragile – they are for women. Op. 20 strikes me as more substantial'.

'More substantial' the *Humoreske* undoubtedly is, if by 'substantial' we mean – dispassionately – large-scale. It is comparable in length to the piano sonatas and to the *Fantasie* (Op. 17) – itself virtually a programmatic sonata in three movements – and almost as long as all eight *Fantasiestücke* or all eight *Kreisleriana* put together. The key signature of two flats stands throughout almost the whole work, but formally it defies description, let alone analysis, so splintered is it into a myriad fragments of different size and character. In so far as one or two of these fragments reappear in the course of the work, though quite irregularly, it is possible to invoke the rondo principle, but beyond this one can only call on the term episodic – in these circumstances a supreme understatement. Schumann's idiosyncratic use of the double-bar makes a definite section-alization problematical, since while it invariably accompanies an incisive change of mood and tempo often made precise by a metronome marking, it also punctuates, for example, modulations within a single section. Where the former, so to speak, might be compared to a full stop, the latter would correspond to a comma. But by any reckoning there are over twenty sections of contrasting character, some extended, others of merely a few bars, deploying virtually all the formal and pianistic techniques known from his other works down to this point, and with numerous reminiscences of them. Indeed, it has a special interest as a kind of repository of Schumann's thoughts, moods, quirks and other factors of his creative personality, thrown together almost spontaneously, with little regard to extended principles of construction. Whatever unity there is, is emotional, not formal. It is like the musical counterpart of a novel by Jean Paul.

These productive moments could not, however, disguise the pointlessness of staying in Vienna. In March he wrote to his former landlady, Frau Johanne Devrient, to ask for his old rooms back:

Vienna, 10 March 1839
Monday

My dear Madame Devrient,
If you hear someone ringing the bell and asking you to take him back into the house where he used to feel so at home, it will be me.

At the end of the month, just as he was about to leave, he received news from Therese, his sister-in-law, that his brother Eduard had fallen seriously ill in Zwickau and would not live long. He hurriedly set out on the journey back, but by the time he reached Zwickau, Eduard had died. He was only forty-two. Schumann wrote to Clara:

Last Saturday, at half-past two in the morning, I clearly heard an ensemble of trombones play a chorale as I was in the coach – that was the moment he died. All these strains have left me quite numb, and I cannot find anything to say . . . Eduard was the only one left on whom I could rely as a kind of protector. He always kept his word, and we never exchanged a word in anger.

Eduard had held part of his younger brother's capital in trust, and Robert, constantly aware that he needed a secure financial foundation before he could marry Clara, feared for a while that Eduard's death might have unpleasant consequences. In the event his fears proved groundless, and he inherited some 1,500 thalers from Eduard's estate to add to the 3,500 thalers that Eduard had been holding in his name.

Of the five children born to August and Christiane Schumann only two were still living – Robert, now approaching twenty-nine, and his second eldest brother Karl, in Schneeberg, who had remarried after the death of his first wife Rosalie. Robert's relationship to both Karl and Eduard was correct rather than affectionate. But death always comes at the wrong moment. And with his vision of a future in Vienna dashed, the separation from Clara growing daily more oppressive, and Wieck's hostility to their longed-for happiness becoming more and more stubborn, Eduard's loss struck harder than that of Karl ten years later, when his life had become more stable.

Back in his old rooms in the seclusion of the 'Rotes Kolleg', their restful outlook on the grass and trees belying their situation in the centre of a bustling city, Schumann busied himself with the day-to-day affairs of the *Neue Zeitschrift*. But his earlier *élan* had slackened. In part, no doubt, this stemmed from his preoccupation with personal problems and the strategy for solving them. Beyond this, however, the *Neue Zeitschrift* now found, like all crusading journals, that after a while the point of its originality, its 'New Criticism', was becoming blunt. One cannot live in a state of continuous novelty, any more than one can live in a state of permanent revolution. As Florestan and Eusebius had made their contribution to Schumann's development as an artist and been granted honourable retirement, so his journal, among whose contributors he had always been the dominant personality, already had its most influential years behind it. But he did not formally give up the editorship until 1844. The paper itself, surviving a number of mergers and changes of title, continued to appear till 1943; it was then reconstituted under its original name in 1949 as a state music journal of the German Democratic Republic. A rival *Neue Zeitschrift für Musik* is published as the organ of the Robert-Schumann-Gesellschaft in Düsseldorf.

Schumann's return to familiar surroundings also stimulated him to take up improvisation again, an activity in which he could conceal to a large extent the ineffectuality of his paralysed fingers. Sitting at his piano by the large window overlooking the Hof, with a copy of a Raphael Madonna on the wall, together with portraits of Bach, Beethoven, Clara Wieck and his friend the late Ludwig Schunke, he would play on into the middle of the night, often to the not unqualified approval of Frau Devrient. Oswald Lorenz, deputy editor of the *Neue Zeitschrift*, recalled listening to him:

He had a strange style of playing, the very opposite of a virtuoso manner, with its grand display of passionate intensity and abrupt contrast. In fact, such a manner would have been quite unsuited to what he played, which rarely seemed to be independent, self-contained pieces but rather the random products of free fantasy, compositions still waiting to be written down.

He tended to play everything with the sustaining pedal slightly depressed, so that the inner parts in particular became blurred. He composed at the piano, and cigar butts were strewn along the music rest, but he did not smoke while playing. Most of those who have left accounts of hearing him say that he played almost exclusively his own compositions or, as Lorenz described, what seemed to be improvisations. He also arranged 'quartet mornings' and 'quartet evenings' in his room as a means of extending his and his friends' experience of chamber music.

In the world of orchestral and instrumental music the Gewandhaus concerts under Mendelssohn were still the backbone of musical life in the city. Earnest occasions though they were, they also had their unexpected moments. Once, to general bewilderment, the second half of a concert suddenly turned out to consist, contrary to what the published programme promised, of all four overtures to Beethoven's *Fidelio*, played one after the other. In the first half a visiting young violinist had been so scornfully received that he shrank from facing the audience for his solos in the second half and crept away in shame. When he could not be found after the interval, Mendelssohn decided to fill the gap by repeating the two *Leonore* Overtures he had conducted in the first half and adding the other two, which he had not rehearsed.

Although he mentions starting work on two quartets, the only pieces Schumann completed during the remainder of 1839 were the *Three Romances*, Op. 28, for piano, for which both he and Clara had a special affection.

In April 1839, at the time Schumann returned to Leipzig, Clara was still in Paris, outwardly successful but inwardly lonely and unhappy. Wieck played with calculated craftiness on the poor girl's distraction, in one letter threatening to disown and disinherit her, in the next making an emotional appeal to her sense of obligation to him. Clara could not conceal her distraught confusion in her letters to Schumann, and since their letters frequently crossed, he would unwittingly find himself responding to questions and anxieties that had already been superseded by the time he was confronted with them. His desolate reactions, in turn, only confused her further.

The ebb and flow of his emotions, the surges of hope followed by bouts of depression, even by doubts of Clara's commitment to her love, eroded both his strength and his will. On his birthday he wrote to her in Paris: 'Today I have entered my twenty-ninth year, and the greater part of my life may well lie behind me . . . at all events I shall not live to a great age – that I know for certain'.

Clara's point of no return was reached in June. Wieck sent her a list of impossible conditions under which, he said, he would consent to her marrying Schumann. They included withholding all the money she had so far earned – a total of 7,000 thalers – and paying it to her only after five years, together with 4% interest (Wieck was nothing if not correct in his financial dealings); a renunciation by Clara of any rights to her father's inheritance; and – a gratuitous insult – a legal certification of Schumann's income. Indignantly Clara replied that she would have nothing to do with such a dishonourable and offensive business. Schumann had in the meantime found the strength to draw up a petition to the courts that he and Clara be allowed to marry. To his signature on this petition, in full knowledge of what she was doing, Clara now added her own.

Armed with this document, Schumann made one last, hopeless attempt to conciliate Wieck, who did not condescend to reply in person. Instead a letter came in Frau Wieck's hand saying that her husband wished to have nothing more to do with him. With the help of a lawyer, Wilhelm Einert, a petition was made ready for the Appellationsgericht and submitted in July, accompanied by statements of Schumann's financial position and other evidence that he was a fit person to look after his bride. Einert assured him that the case was bound to succeed but that because the court also needed to hear Wieck's side, the process might take longer than they would like. It was over a year before the promised judgement was delivered.

Not that they were without friends and supporters throughout this time. Some had belonged to Schumann's world for many years, like Julius Knorr, with whom he used to play piano duets in his earliest days in Leipzig, and the faithful Carl Becker, in whom he and Clara had confided from the beginning. Then there was Dr Moritz Emil Reuter, a physician who acted as a kind of factotum, always ready to help in bringing the lovers together. Reuter was the doctor who signed the medical certificate concerning Schumann's injured right hand, on the basis of which he was exempted from military service. Others came from the ranks of the *Neue Zeitschrift* – the brotherhood of former 'Davidsbündler', one might call them – like the poet of many pseudonyms Anton Wilhelm Florentin von Zuccalmaglio (known to readers of the *Neue Zeitschrift* as 'Saint Diamond' and 'Gottschalk von Wedel, the Village Sexton'), the composer and pianist Alfred Julius Becker, who had found his way into Schumann's company by way of Mendelssohn and Henriette Voigt, and the critic Ernst Ortlepp. Mendelssohn himself, like the Voigts, was also confident of a happy outcome and gave the lovers his encouragement.

A touching gesture came from Clara's mother, who lived with her second husband in Berlin. In a generous letter to Schumann she looked forward to meeting the man 'who has completely captured the heart of my beloved daughter'. In July he travelled to Berlin to meet her, carrying with him portraits of Clara and himself, the complete *Neue Zeitschrift* to date and some of his recent compositions – 'so that she can really get to know me'. She was greatly taken with him and wrote to tell Clara so; she had also written to Wieck, she said, appealing to him not to stand in the way of his daughter's happiness but, hardly surprisingly, had had no reply. 'How happy I shall feel,' she ended, 'when the two of you are united!'

In August Schumann and Clara saw each other for the first time in almost a year. Each new day in Paris added to her burden, and when she finally decided to leave, the industrious Dr Reuter arranged a secret rendezvous for them in Altenburg, a town between Leipzig and Zwickau. Starting out on her long journey on the 14th, she arrived in Altenburg on the 18th. From here they travelled together the twenty-five miles or so to Schumann's brother Karl and his family in Schneeberg, where they spent three happy days.

Clara recorded in her diary her resolve to make a domestic success of her future life with Schumann. But at the same time she added firmly: 'I shall not give up my playing. If I did, I would never forgive myself'. She meant it at the time. Gradually, however, as their family grew larger and as Schumann's fight against his deteriorating health imposed greater and greater strains on all around him, her career slowed down and finally came to a complete stop. But as long as her husband lived, she put his well-being and his interests before all else, and in this she saw the great difference between herself and her father. Of him she wrote, seeing through to the heart of his inflexible and difficult character: 'He is a very good man, and he has done for me what not many fathers would readily do. But he has never known a noble and beautiful love, and cannot understand what it is like'. Clara's mother agreed to come to Leipzig and look after her until the legal arguments had been settled, so as to forestall any danger that the moment she set foot in the city again, her father might order her to return to his own custody.

Wieck now began to behave like a man who had taken leave of his senses. When, as the first step in its procedures, the Appellationsgericht called a meeting of the three parties in order to convince itself that there was no chance of a mutually agreed solution, Wieck did not turn up. The court then fixed a date in October, a month hence, for the official hearing. Clara's mother, whose husband was in poor health, decided to return to Berlin and took Clara with her.

Learning that Clara was to give a recital there shortly afterwards, Wieck tried everything to spoil her chances of success. He wrote to Stadtrat Behrens, who had given her permission to use his grand piano for the occasion, warning him that 'since my daughter has accustomed herself to the hard touch of English pianos, she will ruin any other instrument'. He even wanted the King of Prussia to intervene in the name of paternal authority to prevent her playing at all. Instead His Majesty personally attended her recital in the famous Schauspielhaus on the Gendarmenmarkt, 'and applauded her virtuoso performance loud and long', wrote the critic of the *Neue Zeitschrift*. So energetically did she play that in her final piece, Thalberg's bravura 'Moses' Fantasia, a bass string snapped. 'But I could not help laughing,' she wrote to Schumann, 'and in the end I was even quite pleased, because it added to the overall effect!'

In a further letter to Behrens Wieck went so far as to describe his daughter as 'an immoral girl who has been seduced by a miserable wretch', while his public behaviour in Leipzig, Dr Emil Reuter wrote to Clara, 'has become as ludicrous as it is offensive to those forced to witness it'. He sent poison-pen letters to acquaintances in towns where Clara had been invited to play – Hamburg, Bremen, Lübeck – to undermine her reception in advance. But to no avail. Her recital programmes now usually included items by Schumann – the *Kinderszenen,* the *Novellettes* or one of the Sonatas – which she would slip in between pieces by Beethoven, Scarlatti, Mendelssohn and popular minor composers such as Moscheles and Thalberg. Also in her repertoire were works by Chopin, including the two concertos, and some of Liszt's transcriptions of Schubert songs.

When the day of the October hearing arrived, Wieck again did not appear. As his reason he gave the fact that, since he had not attended the meeting of the conciliation tribunal in September, that particular stage in the proceedings had never properly taken place. Einert, presenting the case on Schumann's and Clara's behalf, pointed out how ridiculous and dishonest this claim was, but the court, reluctant to move too hurriedly where the legal dependence of a daughter on her father was involved, agreed to defer the matter again, this time until December. Clara went back to Berlin with her mother; Schumann, tense, worried, apathetic, his musical life dried up, dragged out his days in Leipzig.

Wieck, by contrast, returned to his home in Dresden and embarked on a hate campaign against the couple who dared to oppose his will. Sensing that he could not win, he composed a libellous 'Declaration', accusing Schumann of moral depravity, of being a drunkard, of pursuing Clara for her money and so on. To Clara herself he sent a letter, bearing the false signature of one Lehmann, with further insults against Schumann and threats of the dire consequences of associating with him.

On 18 December the Appellationsgericht finally met to consider the substantive case. All three parties were present. Clara described the scene in her diary the same evening:

I could not look at my father in court without feeling a deep sense of compassion. All his efforts, his many sleepless nights, the 'Declaration' on which he had spent months of work – it was all to no avail. He burst into violent fits of rage, and several times the judge had to order him to be silent. I shuddered each time this happened, and could scarcely bear to see him subjected to such humiliation. He glowered at me in fury, but only once did he say anything against me . . . This day has divided us for ever, or at the very least destroyed the tender bond between father and daughter. My heart too feels as though it has been torn apart.

Robert conducted himself very well, with all his natural calmness, which was the best way of countering my father's rage. I love him now more than ever, for he has suffered himself to be insulted in public for my sake.

Wieck's cardinal objections to the marriage, as he stated them to the court, were that Schumann could not afford to support Clara in a proper manner; that neither as composer nor as music critic had he achieved, or was he likely to achieve, a position of any significance that would guarantee his financial future; that he was a drunkard; and that both he and Clara had previously had romantic attachments, which demonstrated at least their inconstancy, if not also their immorality. (This last slur on their characters can only refer to Schumann's affair with Ernestine von Fricken and Clara's friendship – fostered, be it remembered, by Wieck himself – with Carl Banck.)

On 4 January 1840 the Appellationsgericht finally handed down its verdict. It dismissed all Wieck's objections out of hand, save one – that relating to Schumann's alleged drunkenness. This, the court decided, was a serious matter that had been neither proven nor disproven, and Wieck was given time to produce more evidence to support his allegation. There were many, from his fellow-students at Leipzig and Heidelberg to the brotherhood that gathered in the Kaffeebaum, who knew that he was a heavy drinker, and his diaries make no secret of the fact. More than once during his early days in the 'Rotes Kolleg' he had disgraced himself by trying to drink his way out of his melancholy. But in spite of Wieck's efforts to persuade her, the good Frau Devrient refused to incriminate him.

Although Wieck's charges against him were basically mere insults, and his financial situation, though not opulent, was secure enough, Schumann could not repress his sense of inferiority to Clara in outward qualification and public esteem. He was known merely as the composer of a number of interesting but not widely acclaimed pianoforte pieces and as the editor of a music journal. Back in 1838, when Clara received the honorary title of 'Kaiserlich-Königliche Kammervirtuosin' from the Emperor of Austria, he had written to his sister-in-law Therese of his desire to achieve something comparable. Now, when his personal honour

1 Zwickau, Schumann's birthplace: a mid-19th-century engraving.

2 Dresden: a contemporary print of the Saxon capital, where Robert and Clara Schumann lived from 1844 to 1850.

Zwickau d: 1 Januar 1828.

Meine gute Mutter!

[handwritten letter in German cursive]

Ich bleibe

Ihr
gehorsamer und dankbarer Sohn
Robert Schumann

4 Clara Wieck, aged fifteen: an engraving made in 1835.

5 Portrait of Schumann by Kriehuber, Vienna 1839.

3 *Left:* Schumann's earliest extant letter, written on 1 January 1818 to his mother. The text reads: 'My dear Mother, Now we are starting a new year. I shall always try to study very hard in this new year and work hard in school, so that you will always be pleased with me, like my teacher. Do not feel offended if I have sometimes caused you grief, but I shall make an effort day by day to cure my faults. Thank you for the nice presents you gave me for Christmas. What I wish most is for God to keep you and the children. I remain your obedient and grateful son, Robert Schumann.'

Robert and Clara Schumann, 1850.

7 Schumann's original musical score for 'The Merry Peasant' from his 'Scenes from Childhood', op.68.

8 The Leipzig Gewandhaus. Many of Schumann's works were first performed here; Mendelssohn was chief conductor of the Gewandhaus orchestra from 1835 until his death in 1847.

9   Photogravure of Schumann in 1850.

10   Carl Jäger's portrait of Schumann, based on a photograph.

11   Schumann's children. At the back Marie (seated) and Elise; in the front, from left to right, Ludwig, Felix, Ferdinand and Eugenie. Julie is not in the photograph. Emil died in 1847 when he was eighteen months old.

12 Inselstrasse No. 15, Leipzig. Robert and Clara had rooms on the first floor of the house after their marriage in 1840.

13 The house in Bilker Strasse, Düsseldorf (now No. 15), where the Schumanns lived from 1852 until Robert's suicide attempt and removal to the asylum at Endenich.

4 Drawing of Schumann by Jean-Joseph-Bonaventure Laurens,
853. Above Schumann's dedication to Laurens is the violin melody of
ιe third movement of his D minor Trio.

15 The chorale to the words 'Wenn mein Stündlein vorhanden ist' ('When my hour of parting comes'), written by Schumann in the asylum at Endenich.

16 The asylum in Endenich, outside Bonn, where Schumann died. Engraving, c.1850.

and status were under public scrutiny, and thinking it would also give satisfaction to Clara – who was certainly not without ambition on his behalf – he approached a friend in Jena, a writer on music called Gustav Adolph Keferstein, with the tentative idea that the university there might consider awarding him an honorary doctorate for his services to music. Keferstein found that the university would look favourably on such a proposal, and on 17 February Schumann submitted his *curriculum vitae* to the dean of the Faculty of Arts. One interesting plan he mentions in this is a study of Shakespeare's relationship to music – a project he referred to more than once in the course of his life, though nothing ever came of it. A week later – a breathtaking expeditiousness by modern standards – he was awarded the degree of *Doctor philosophiae honoris causa*.

None of this, of course, impressed Wieck. Unable to prove his accusations, he appealed against the court's judgement *in toto*. In March, however, the court confirmed its rejection of his arguments, leaving him only the forlorn possibility of substantiating his charge of drunkenness. Gradually he realized the hopelessness of his position. In default of any further protests and appeals on his part the court deemed him to have withdrawn his objections to the marriage, and on 11 August 1840 Robert Alexander Schumann, aged thirty, and Clara Josephine Wieck, aged twenty, were given legal permission to marry. The battle had lasted over four years.

Ever prone to mystical, symbolical interpretation, Schumann conferred a special significance on the date of this victory. The following day, 12 August, was the feast of St Clara, the 13th that of St Aurora (i.e. the new dawn), and the 14th that of St Eusebius – a holy trinity.

Some of these long, last weeks of waiting they had spent with Clara's mother in Berlin, where they were often to be seen together at the theatre and at musical gatherings in the Mendelssohn family villa in the Leipziger Strasse. For the rest the gloom in Leipzig had been relieved not only by Mendelssohn's Gewandhaus concerts and such events as Wilhelmine Schröder-Devrient's performance in *Fidelio* in April, but also by the sensational appearance on the scene of Franz Liszt.

Liszt was on his way back to Paris from Vienna, following the same route, via Prague and Dresden to Leipzig, as Clara had taken three years earlier. He gave two recitals in the Gewandhaus, and in the intervening seven days spent a great deal of time in Schumann's company. He had a high opinion of Schumann's music – unlike Chopin – but found that whatever he included in his programmes did not arouse the sort of enthusiasm to which he was accustomed. It was too advanced, he thought, too far beyond the taste of conventional audiences. As a result, he later confessed to his shame, he only rarely included an item by Schumann in his concerts. The same difficulty had troubled the composer Louis Spohr, who wrote to Schumann that his wife, a professional pianist, found the *Etudes symphoniques* hard to play and could not understand them properly. Of Schumann's works Liszt ranked *Carnaval* particularly high, considering that it would eventually take its place as the equal of Beethoven's 'Diabelli' Variations.

It was a long time since Schumann had felt so elated. 'Liszt becomes more and more of a giant every day', he wrote to Clara.

This morning he played at Härtel's again and made us all tremble, then jump for joy . . . It is an incredible life here at the moment – nothing but dinners and suppers, music and champagne, Counts and beautiful women. In short, he has turned our lives upside down.

Contrary to the impression that the overworked epithet 'brilliant' may give, Liszt's power as a pianist lay not only in the muscular but also in the delicate and subtle. 'As a proof of this', wrote the pianist Anton Strelezki, who came to know Liszt a number of years later,

I can assure my readers that, having once heard him play his own arrangement of the 'Erl-King', I was surprised to notice that, as he left the piano, not a trace of perspiration or fatigue was noticeable on his face or hands. Only a few weeks after this I heard the same piece played by Anton Rubinstein, and from his appearance at the end you would think he had just come out of a shower that he had taken with his clothes on. And yet Liszt's rendering was just as vivid as Rubinstein's, and his fortissimo had the same tremendous power.

The concert programmes of nineteenth-century virtuosi raise many a disbelieving eyebrow today. Liszt, for instance, opened his first Gewandhaus recital with his arrangement of the Scherzo and Finale from Beethoven's 'Pastoral' Symphony. Even Schumann had his reservations about the wisdom of this choice. 'Nevertheless', he conceded, 'the audience did have the opportunity to feel the presence of the maestro at the keyboard, and were satisfied to have seen the lion shake his mane'. Liszt followed this with his Fantasia on Themes by Pacini and some pieces by Chopin.

At his second recital Liszt began with Weber's *Konzertstück* for piano and orchestra (playing both the solo part and the orchestral accompaniment of a concerto at the same time was a normal practice):

Pianist and audience seemed to be in a particularly lively mood, and the enthusiasm both during his playing and at the end surpassed almost everything that this city has seen. Starting with majestic power and grandeur, like a column advancing on to the battlefield, he pressed on and on until he reached the point where he stood triumphant at the head of the orchestra and led it boldly into the fray. It was as though he were that very general himself to whom we compared him in outward appearance, and as though the applause at the end were a tumultuous shout of 'Long live the Emperor!'

The rest of the recital consisted of Liszt's own compositions – his Fantasia on Themes from *Les Huguenots* and some of his transcriptions of Schubert songs. At a third recital, which he gave without fee for the musicians' benevolent fund, he honoured the three leading Leipzig composers of the day with a programme devoted to their works: Mendelssohn's D minor Concerto, some studies by Ferdinand Hiller and ten items from Schumann's *Carnaval*. In his review of the occasion Schumann noted, with some surprise, that Liszt played almost all these pieces from the music.

Leipzig was too provincial to detain Liszt for long. Schumann proudly made him aware of the cultural and artistic eminence of the city, with its university, its 150 bookshops and its thirty cultural journals, but Liszt found it all too bourgeois. 'There are no princesses or duchesses', he complained.

But whatever pleasure and encouragement such moments as

Liszt's visit brought Schumann, they were only incidental to his joyful awareness that, even under the strain of the protracted law suit, his musical powers were returning. Once again, unpredictably yet characteristically, he was lifted from a state of torpid pessimism, his personal and creative life blocked in stagnant hopelessness, to a condition of unaccountable but irrepressible elation. The first word that something new and wonderful was dawning comes in a letter to Clara: 'I am ecstatic, brimming over with music, as always in February [Schumann had a selective memory]. You will be amazed what I have done in this time – *not* things for piano, but I'm not going to tell you yet!' A few weeks later he gave away the secret to his friend Töpken: 'In the last few weeks I have been writing only for the voice. So utterly at the mercy of the ebb and flow of melody am I that I feel almost swamped, oblivious to all the disgraceful things going on around me. I fear I shall not be able to bear this exhilaration for long'. He bore it long enough to compose, in a space of mere months, over 120 songs, among them some of the most glorious in the whole repertoire of Lieder.

The 'disgraceful things', of course, referred to the machinations of Friedrich Wieck. But having tried all possible and impossible ruses to undermine the love that bound his daughter to Schumann, Wieck could now only creep away in defeat.

Schumann received the court's decision in Leipzig. Clara was on a concert tour in Erfurt and Weimar – her last appearances as Clara Wieck – and knew nothing at that moment. The next day he travelled to Weimar and suddenly presented himself in the drawing room of the house where she was staying. Keferstein, who had arranged Clara's tour, described the scene: 'It was a touching moment, moving for all those present. The jubilation went on and on, a scene of sheer bliss and rapture. His eyes shining through his tears, Schumann embraced first his fiancée, then the whole company, one after the other, becoming merrier and more talkative than I had ever seen him'.

One of the last people to visit him at his old rooms in the 'Rotes Kolleg' was the pianist Amalie Rieffel, a friend of Clara's, who described the impression he made on her:

His appearance has nothing in particular to commend it. He looks like a good, honest citizen. Just now and again his mouth takes on a sardonic twist, his brow darkens, and he suddenly becomes interesting! His nature is the same – quiet, unassuming and so simple that one would not dream of suspecting he possessed any particular ability or intellectual talent. He speaks quietly, in short, unfinished sentences; he also has a friendly, attractive smile and frequently nods his head slightly as he talks.

The wedding – 'with organ, without hymns', the register states – took place at 10 o'clock on Saturday, 12 September 1840 in the Protestant village church of Schönefeld, outside Leipzig, where a schoolfriend of Schumann's Zwickau days, August Wildenhahn, was pastor. Wieck, needless to say, did not attend, but Clara's mother came from Berlin. Ernst Becker and Dr Moritz Reuter were the witnesses. Also present at the simple service were Clara's friends Emilie and Elise List, Ferdinand Wenzel, a 'Davidsbündler' from Kaffeebaum days, Assessor Herrmann, who had helped with the legal presentation of the case, and Frau Carl, *née* Tromlitz, sister of Clara's mother, in whose house Clara found sanctuary during her stays in Leipzig.

After the wedding Schumann and his bride, together with their guests, went back to the Carls' house in Leipzig. Clara wrote in her diary:

People danced a little. There were no revels, but every face radiated a deep sense of inner contentment. Nothing occurred to spoil the day, which shall be recorded in this diary as the most wonderful and most important day of my life . . . A new life is opening up, a wonderful life . . . I have always had a firm faith in God, and I shall keep this faith for ever.

The following day, 13 September, was Clara's twenty-first birthday, the moment when she would in any case have become free to manage her own fortune and marry whomsoever she chose. With the time needed for the banns to be read, 12 September became the earliest possible Saturday for the wedding to be held. But Schumann would hardly have failed to savour the irony, the supremely satisfying poetic justice, that united him and Clara on the very last day left to them to assert their love in defiance of the insanely jealous father who had done all in his power to destroy it.

CHAPTER EIGHT

'Liederjahr'

In the popular imagination the names Robert and Clara Schumann invoke the image of perfect partnership, a marriage of ideally blended souls, complementary, serene. The reality is less perfect, less smooth. Paradoxes cleft their relationship from the beginning. He was thirty, she twenty-one, yet while hers was a household name in the whole of musical Europe, his was little known even in his own country. He had led a free, hedonistic life, dependent on no one, at liberty to define his own goals; she had been protected from the world, held in jealous confinement, reared for a single purpose. He was widely read and sought intellectual influence; she had had a restricted education and lingered far behind him in knowledge. Above all, conscious of her powers and of her responsibility to her art, she was at the summit of her public career, while he, till now a composer only of pianoforte music, most of it small-scale if highly original, stood at the threshold of a glorious summer of musical creation. The points of stress, of divided interest, were many, and they did not lie concealed for long.

Shortly before their wedding Schumann had found an apartment for them in Leipzig on the first floor of Inselstrasse No. 5, not far from his old rooms in the 'Rotes Kolleg'. One of his first acts was to open a 'Marriage Book', a diary which, he wrote on the first page,

shall record everything that concerns the two of us in our life together –

our hopes and desires, the things we want to ask each other but cannot put into words, and our ways of restoring harmony between us in case we should misunderstand each other. In short, this little book is to be our true and faithful friend, to whom we confide everything and from whom we have no secrets.

With a formality that may make us smile today he concluded: 'If you concur with these sentiments, my dearest wife, then write your name beneath mine and let us say together, as a talisman, the three words on which all earthly happiness rests: Diligence, Thrift, Loyalty'. Under this, in Clara's handwriting, stands the simple phrase: *'Dein Dir von ganzer Seele ergebenes Weib Clara'* ('Your utterly devoted wife Clara').

There is something very characteristic about Schumann in this. He was always a meticulous keeper of records. As a student he made detailed accounts of all his expenses and kept special travel-diaries in addition to his regular domestic chronicle; he had a project-book full of names, dates and notes on literary works, a notebook with plans for future compositions, a huge collection of literary quotations ('Mottosammlung') for use in the *Neue Zeitschrift*, an index of no fewer than 4,700 letters that he had received between 1833 and 1854 (the letters themselves, carefully numbered and collected into twenty-eight volumes by Schumann himself, have been lost since the end of World War II), and other similar compilations and catalogues. Most of this material lies in the archives of the Robert-Schumann-Haus in Zwickau and has never been published in full.

In the second week of their marriage Schumann and Clara began to study Bach's *Well-tempered Clavier* together. For him this was a chance to share and renew his devotion to the composer he revered above all others; for her it was a moment of revelation, a profound enrichment of her musical education. From Bach they turned to Beethoven's symphonies and Mozart and Beethoven overtures, then to the Haydn and Mozart quartets, which they played together at the keyboard. Equally concerned to broaden Clara's general education, he introduced her to Goethe, Jean Paul, Shakespeare and other classics of world literature. She would also discuss with him her own compositions, chiefly piano music and songs, which had their own modest charm. Like

Mendelssohn with his sister Fanny, they even shared in the composition of a work – the song-cycle to poems by Rückert, published in 1841 as Schumann's Op. 37. Schumann wrote nine of the songs, Clara the other three, though in these too one suspects that Schumann's refining hand may have been at work.

The practical problems involved in reconciling their different musical needs soon became apparent. They both had grand pianos in their rooms, which meant that when Clara needed to practise, Schumann could not concentrate on composing. 'These thin walls are a real irritation', runs a curt remark in the family diary. Clara gave way, but not without a feeling of dissatisfaction. 'I am getting behind with my playing, which always happens when Robert composes'. To which he could only reply: 'It is my fault, but I cannot alter it. Clara realizes that I must cultivate my gifts and am now at the height of my powers, and that I must use my youth while it lasts. Such is the situation when two artists marry – one cannot have everything'. But he knew the price he was asking her to pay: 'Too often my songs have been bought at the cost of forcing her to keep silent, or of pretending she was not there'.

'My songs'. In these two words lies the essence of the year 1840 for Schumann the composer. Back in February he had hinted in letters to Clara and others, in phrases of barely concealed ecstasy, that he was composing for the voice. Not only that, but a torrent of lyrical melody was surging through his mind: 'Since yesterday morning I have written almost twenty-seven pages of music – something new [the song-cycle *Myrthen*, Op. 25] – about which I can say no more than that I was laughing and weeping for joy the whole time'. In March he sent Clara two of the songs which he had published earlier that month in the music supplement to the *Neue Zeitschrift* – his first songs to appear in print.

The flood of inspiration knew no end. As well as the twenty-six songs of *Myrthen* (eight of the poems are translations of Burns, five are by Rückert, three each by Goethe and Heine) the month of February alone also produced the nine Heine settings of the *Liederkreis*, Op. 24 – in sum over a song a day. After Liszt's visit to Leipzig in March he resumed with the Heine songs of Op. 49, then completed the twelve Eichendorff settings of the *Liederkreis* Op. 39 by the middle of May. He wrote at that moment to Clara:

'I have again composed so much that it seems almost uncanny. But I cannot help myself – I feel like singing myself to death, like the nightingale. There are twelve Eichendorff songs. But I have already forgotten them and started something new'. The 'something new' was the cycle *Dichterliebe*, sixteen settings of Heine, finished, together with three other Heine songs, by the end of the same month.

June, by which time it had become clear that Wieck could no longer sustain his fabricated objections to his daughter's marriage, found Schumann mentally exhausted again, but in July he found new strength, repeating what he had earlier said to himself in moments of lethargy: 'Take hold of yourself and set about your task with all the strength you can muster!' In four weeks he composed the *Frauenliebe und -leben* cycle, the three separate Chamisso settings of Op. 31, the five songs, Op. 40 (settings of Hans Andersen in Chamisso's translation) and four of the six songs to poems by Robert Reinick, Op. 36. By the time the year was out, he had produced no fewer than 138 vocal items, mostly for solo voice but also for two and three parts, such as the four duets for soprano and tenor, Op. 34, and the three two-part songs, Op. 43. He also thought of writing an opera on E.T.A. Hoffmann's story *Doge und Dogaressa*, but the idea came to nothing.

This obsession with a single form has its origin, not in an area of technique or in a conjunction of external circumstances but in the psychology of Schumann the man and Schumann the musician. In 1838, in a letter to Clara that goes to the heart of his spiritual life, he wrote: 'Everything that goes on in the world concerns me – politics, literature, people. I ponder it all in my own way, then it has to find a release, a path of expression, in music'. Politics, public activity in general, indeed, played an insignificant part in his life. He committed himself to no political cause – there were many to choose from – aligned himself with no philosophy, struck no public stance on social and moral issues, as Wagner inveterately did. Nor had he any taste for the work of the practical administrator, like Mendelssohn. In the few public positions to which he was appointed – as teacher of composition at the new Leipzig Conservatoire in 1843, for instance, or as director of music in Düsseldorf in 1850 – he showed no inclination to conceptualize the nature of his task and scant ability to communicate with, let alone to inspire, the musicians entrusted to his care.

The 'literature' and 'people' in his letter, on the other hand, that sought their 'path of expression' in his music, lie at the centre of the creative consciousness that led him from the world of piano music to the world of song. Over almost all Schumann's music from *Papillons* to *Kreisleriana* and the *Faschingsschwank aus Wien* there hovers a literary presence, discernible not necessarily in the simple, direct guise of descriptive programme music – though this is part of it – but through the persistent awareness of literary analogues and literary values in the composer's mind. To be sure, each finished work is to be assessed by criteria proper to music. At the same time we know that dominating his imagination were visions of Walt and Vult from Jean Paul's *Flegeljahre*, or of E.T.A. Hoffmann's unhappy, love-sick Kapellmeister Johannes Kreisler. The events related by Jean Paul and Hoffmann were as heightened events from life: life and art are indivisible. This is what Schumann 'ponders in his own way' and allows, in one set of pianoforte pieces after another, to 'find its release' in music.

But the experience of life through art, of reality through fantasy, now gave way before the pressure of the profoundest emotional encounter of his life. Allusions and hidden meanings no longer sufficed: the masks of the dancers at the masquerade had to fall, emotions were openly declared, realities proudly acknowledged. The songs of 1840, the year of his marriage, are Schumann's love-songs to Clara. The words of the poems expose the fluctuating moods of the sophisticated lover – his excited anticipation of seeing his beloved, his suffering under the misery of separation, his frightened vision of being deprived of the consummation of his passion, perhaps even by death. Yet everything springs from, is contained by, and moves inexorably towards, this love. Such is the world of the poems by Heine in the *Liederkreis*, Op. 24, and such is the world, experienced in personal reality, for which Schumann finds 'a path of expression' in his music.

The *Dichterliebe* cycle is an even more intense autobiographical statement – more sincerely and intensely autobiographical in Schumann's music, indeed, than in Heine's poems, with their self-pitying, semi-ironical flavour. In the title alone – which is Schumann's, not Heine's – lies his equation of poet and musician, both in himself and as a symbol of the unity of all art, and also his identification with the joys and sufferings that sustain the poems he has selected. For unlike the nine poems of the *Liederkreis*, which form a self-contained group within the section 'Junge Leiden' in Heine's *Buch der Lieder*, the sixteen songs of *Dichterliebe* have been freely chosen from the sixty-six poems of the section called 'Lyrisches Intermezzo'. Their unity is not narrative, like Schubert's *Die Winterreise*, nor musically cyclical, like Beethoven's *An die ferne Geliebte*, but purely and simply emotional – the ebb and flow of love, its power, its moods, its situations. Love in action, as it were.

Schumann's self-exploration through these or any other poems, and his overt self-expression in his music to them, lead as naturally to the composition of groups of songs, rather than individual settings, as the inspiration of his piano music had issued in collections of variations, of carnival scenes, of *Fantasiestücke* and *Nachtstücke*. The focal point, be it a situation, an emotion, an idea, or perhaps his experience of the world of a particular poet, is irradiated from different angles, sometimes fixed with a dazzling light, sometimes with a subdued glow. Hence also the episodic manner of the individual pieces themselves, as the composer roams over his chosen area, his imagination lighting now on this view, now on that.

So it is also with the *Frauenliebe und -leben* cycle, to texts by the romantic poet Adalbert von Chamisso – a self-contained group of nine poems given this title by the poet himself, of which Schumann, with his customary licence, set only eight. Here it is the woman's happiness and yearning that rule, not the man's, and as the piano postlude at the end of the last song returns to the music of the first, so the circle of love closes round her and her beloved. The emotions, as she revels in the wonder of her love, are Clara's:

(*Frauenliebe und -leben*, Op.42, No.2)

Although the deepest roots of Schumann's preoccupation throughout 1840 with the art of song lie in his spiritual biography, it also reflects a constant feature in his mode of working, viz. the urge to explore to their limits the parameters of his chosen form of the moment. For almost ten years he had devoted himself to nothing but piano music; now he had nothing in mind but songs. In the coming few years it was to be the same story with orchestral symphonies and chamber music. It is as though he wanted to feel a complete mastery of one genre before moving to another – a feeling both that what he wanted to express could be fully conveyed in the form of the moment, and that this form, once conceived and created, encompassed everything that at that moment he wanted to say.

Maybe this is a statement of his limitations. Maybe it even implies that he was aware of these limitations. He came only slowly to the larger forms – almost reluctantly, one might feel, and under pressure, both from within and without. Certainly Clara is soon heard urging him to write a symphony, and he eventually completed four symphonies, seven concertos or similar extended works for soloist and orchestra, an opera and many substantial choral compositions. But, fine music as they contain, few, if forced to choose, would wish to retain them at the expense of his piano music and his songs. In originality, in beauty – in everything, indeed, that makes for his greatness as a composer – Schumann had reached his peak by the 'Liederjahr' of 1840. What followed, *pace* the occasional return to the heights in moments such as the Piano Concerto, was a slow decline, the companion of the irreversible deterioration of his physical and psychological condition.

This watershed in Schumann's creative life becomes the more prominent with the realization that what at first appears as a substantial change of interest from piano music to song represents in fact, as Schumann conceived the two genres, merely an organic extension of a single lyrical continuum. The lyricism of his piano pieces is the lyricism of the Lied. 'Träumerei' or 'Warum?' are as much 'Songs without Words' as any of Mendelssohn's. And as poetry and music are but two designations of a single creative activity, allowing Schumann to call the last of his *Kinderszenen* 'The Poet Speaks', so the sphere of instrumental music merges into the sphere of vocal music, leaving the last of the *Fantasiestücke* with the title 'The End of the Song'.

In practical terms this means that the pianoforte part in these songs is not an 'accompaniment' but, in a very real sense, the song itself, with the vocal line pointing, underlining and above all, through the presence of the words, intensifying and conceptualizing. 'I have no faith in a singer of Schumann's songs', said Grieg, 'who does not appreciate the fact that the piano has quite as great a claim to attention as the singer himself'. This lies at the root of the often-observed feature that the vocal line and the piano part so often share the melody. It is not that the piano doubles the melody given to the voice but rather that the voice underscores the melody that already crowned the piano part. Likewise the postludes that follow the singer's final words – that at the end of *Dichterliebe*, say, or *Frauenliebe und -leben* – are not merely perfunctory closing bars but miniature piano solos, codas with their own self-generated musical significance, like those with which he so frequently brings his piano pieces to a close.

This doubling of the melody in the piano part is still a characteristic of Schumann's style many years later. The charming if at times rather flat *Fantasiestücke* (Op. 73) for clarinet and piano, for example, written in 1849, contains extended passages in which the piano duplicates the clarinet part, following it high and low through chromatic melodic movement and dotted rhythmic patterns; likewise the three *Romanzen* (Op. 94) for oboe and piano, and the *Märchenbilder* (Op. 113) for viola and piano.

Three years after the 'Liederjahr', in a review of a collection of Lieder by Theodor Kirchner, Schumann himself stressed the complementary nature of the vocal and piano parts:

Related to the development of literature, there has arrived also in the realm of song-writing a new epoch to succeed that of Schubert, one which has put to its particular profit recent advances in the sphere of the accompanying instrument, the piano. Kirchner himself calls his pieces 'Songs with Pianoforte', and we must not overlook this. The voice cannot achieve everything by itself, or convey everything by itself. Alongside the impression made by the song as a whole one must permit the specific subtleties of the poem to emerge, whereby at the same time the vocal line must not be allowed to suffer.

With a passage like this in one's hands, and with the sound of the superb songs of 1840 in one's ears, it is hard to believe that Schumann had in fact long held a low opinion of song as an art-form. Throughout the 1830s he had clung to the belief that it was in instrumental music that the real prospects of progress lay – absolute music, as it were, not a form, like song, that had its genesis in something outside music. His own piano music was part of this progress. But perhaps he sensed by 1839 that he had said in this genre all that he had to say. An originality that feeds on itself will soon die. It was this lack of development, this persistent preoccupation with the unchanging, unmistakable techniques of the miniaturist, that disappointed him in Chopin, of whom he concluded in 1841: 'Novel and inventive though he is in externals, in the form of his pieces, in his special effects, he remains in essence the same, so that we fear he will never achieve higher things than he has already achieved.'

As late as June 1839 we still find him confiding to the composer Hermann Hirschbach: 'All my life I have regarded vocal music as inferior to instrumental music, and never considered it great art'. But vocal music quickly became for him a linear extension of instrumental music, of his own piano music, and as the formal frontiers between them crumbled, so the stigma of inferiority vanished. Words and music became one, fused by the power of the love that made Robert and Clara Schumann one.

What, then, did Schumann, a man well versed in literature, ask of the poetry he chose to set? How did he approach it? And what is the relationship in his songs between poetry and music? *Pace* the limitations inherent in any such generalization, one may distinguish two approaches to the art of song-writing. One was defined by Karl Friedrich Zelter, Mendelssohn's teacher, close friend of Goethe and one of the most influential figures in German musical life at the turn of the eighteenth century. 'When I want to set a poem to music', said Zelter, 'I seek in the first place to penetrate the meaning of the words and form a living picture of the scene. Then I read the poem aloud until I know it by heart, and in thus reciting it over and over again, I find that the melody comes of its own accord'. In other words, the music is an illustration or interpretation of the text, an extension of its meaning into a new medium. The meaning of the music is by definition bounded by the meaning of the text, and the composer sees himself as a kind of servant of the poetry, putting his music at the service of the pre-existing, pre-eminent verse.

This was the conception that Goethe expected in those who set his poems to music, an approach that led him to see in composers like Zelter and Reichardt his ideal song-writers. It expresses the principles in the mind of Gluck when he stated that, as he worked on his operas, he tried to forget that he was a musician. And it is the basic philosophy that underlies the songs of Hugo Wolf. As Gerald Moore once put it: 'We believe that Goethe, if he could, would have sung "Anakreons Grab" as Wolf sang it'.

The other approach proceeds from a belief in the autonomy, and ultimately the supremacy, of the music, in the inevitability that the composer, if he is true to his art, must follow wherever his music takes him, whatever the minutiae of the text that is his starting-point. In Mozart's phrase, referring to the libretti of his operas: 'Poetry must be the obedient daughter of music'. Or as Schumann put it: 'The poem must wear the music like a garland, or yield to it like a bride'. In such a song the music grows upwards and outwards from the text and acquires a life of its own, making the poem, however great, seem like an excuse for writing music, a verbal means to a musical end.

Moreover, as the great age of European song dawned at the beginning of the nineteenth century, the form began to evolve from that of a predominating melody supported by a formal harmonic accompaniment, as a sculptured head rests on a plinth, into a totality of voice and instrument, poetry and music, in which the piano part receives its integral, autonomous, inalienable role in the communicated 'meaning' of the song. What we are defining, or circumscribing, of course, are the Lieder of Franz Schubert, most precious of all the jewels of romantic song-writing.

The world of Schubert's Lieder was Schumann's inheritance. No doubt Beethoven's *An die ferne Geliebte*, in its poetic theme as in its musical expression, also had its place in his mind (the return in the piano postlude to the melody of the opening song is a specific detail), while the lyricism of Mendelssohn's *Songs without Words* brought their own delight and their own influence. But it is in the direct line of descent from Schubert, to whom his piano music already owed its own debt, that Schumann's songs have their true place, like those of Brahms and Richard Strauss after him.

If, therefore, in this philosophy of song-writing, the music 'takes off' and leaves the text behind, the question of the choice of poem becomes secondary. The composer uses the poem as a means of stimulating his musical imagination, and his responses to poetry, as to any external stimuli, will vary with the movement of his susceptibilities and his psychological needs. At one moment a certain poet may seem to speak for his spiritual condition, at another he may find his emotions mirrored in a different source. The question of literary quality does not yet enter the argument. Schumann could very rarely set texts by nondescript poets. Schubert could, and did, turning from Goethe to Wilhelm Müller, or from Heine to Rellstab, in almost spontaneous response to what caught his fancy. And it is a commonplace of musical knowledge that the greatest poetry does not necessarily evoke the greatest music – indeed, it may evoke none at all.

Schumann's deep-rooted literary experience set its own standards in his choice of poets. Forty-two of his songs, by far the largest contingent, are settings of Heine, the memory of whom had retained its vividness from the one occasion, in 1828, when they had met. He coined the term 'Heinismus' to denote a quality of proud irony that he found in the poet, and used strophes from his poems as mottos for a number of issues of the *Neue Zeitschrift*. A diary entry in March 1833 records setting some Heine poems to music. The settings have not survived, but the entry itself is a fascinating confusion of literary and musical terminology: 'Wrote music poems to songs by H. Heine and dedicated them to him' *(Musikalische Gedichte, mit untergelegten Liedern von H. Heine, verfasst und Heine zugeeignet).* Already at this time the text had been swallowed up into the music, and the language of music had become the language of literature. Heine, incidentally, who had been living in exile in Paris since 1831, can hardly have known of this dedication. He never wrote to Schumann, whom he could have known of only as an editor and critic, and he had no opportunity of hearing his songs.

Heine's *Buch der Lieder* is a stylized, fictionalized, sentimentalized exercise in emotional autobiography, rich in lament and suffering but also in bitterness and a self-indulgent irony. This sophisticated mixture had in it much that spoke directly to the anxious, lonely, often distraught Schumann of early 1840. Above all, however, it was the delicate yet firm structure of the little poems, their drooping elegance and appealing naïveté, to which his creative powers responded. The form of the poetry was so simple, so direct, that it lent itself to whatever music-oriented purpose the mood of the moment induced. Having touched his emotions, the poems surrendered to him to treat as he wished, without direction, without constraint. Sometimes music and poem move together, the one supporting the other; sometimes – more often, and more characteristically – they are in deliberate tension, dissimilar patterns superimposed the one on the other. But everywhere the music leads, rules, dominates, and the poem can only submit.

Thus the first song of *Dichterliebe*, the beautiful, fragile 'Im wunderschönen Monat Mai', sets the two identical strophes of Heine's poem to two identical melodic patterns: the four lines of verse in each strophe yield eight bars of music, two bars to each line. The 'yearning and desire' of which the last line of the poem speaks find their musical expression in the languishing dominant seventh on which the song ends, a poignant musical question to which there is no resolution, any more than there is an answer to the question in the last line of the poem – 'Will my love find fulfilment and rest?'

At the other extreme stands 'Ich grolle nicht', the seventh song in the cycle. Here Schumann's musical emotion takes savage hold of him, and he wrenches the poem apart as his declamatory passion forces itself out. A juxtaposition of the words Heine wrote and the words Schumann set tells its own story:

Heine: *Ich grolle nicht, und wenn das Herz auch bricht,*
Ewig verlornes Lieb, ich grolle nicht.
Wie du auch strahlst in Diamantenpracht,
Es fällt kein Strahl in deines Herzens Nacht.

Das weiss ich längst. Ich sah dich ja im Traum
Und sah die Nacht in deines Herzens Raum,
Und sah die Schlang', die dir am Herzen frisst,
Ich sah, mein Lieb, wie sehr du elend bist.

– again two formally identical strophes.
   The text of Schumann's song becomes very different:

Schumann: *Ich grolle nicht, und wenn das Herz auch bricht,*
Ewig verlor'nes Lieb,
Ewig verlor'nes Lieb, ich grolle nicht,
Ich grolle nicht.
Wie du auch strahlst in Diamantenpracht,
Es fällt kein Strahl in deines Herzens Nacht,
Das weiss ich längst.

Ich grolle nicht, und wenn das Herz auch bricht,
Ich sah dich ja im Traume,
Und sah die Nacht in deines Herzens Raume,
Und sah die Schlang', die dir am Herzen frisst,
Ich sah, mein Lieb, wie sehr du elend bist.
Ich grolle nicht,
Ich grolle nicht.

One cannot ask what 'right' Schumann has to make free with Heine's poem in this way. In one sense he has none. He laid hands on it uninvited; it does not 'need' Schumann's music for its existence, and it becomes neither a better nor a worse poem through the superimposition of music – Schumann's or any other – upon it. *Mutatis mutandis* the poem can do nothing for the quality of the music; having inspired the composer's imagination, it has fulfilled its role and must leave the stage to whatever that imagination creates, be it superb or mediocre. Song, by this philosophy, is simply music, no more, no less, and must be judged as such. Faithfulness to poetic form, as in 'Im wunderschönen Monat Mai', makes for a very different kind of song from 'Ich grolle nicht', but it is not a criterion of quality, merely a statement of a formal relationship.

Also a formal relationship, here internal to the music itself, is that between the keys of the various songs. Keys and key-relationships have psychological significance for Schumann. He also worked private meanings and allusions into them, as he did into note-patterns, which lays upon the singer who transposes the songs the obligation to retain the internal key-relationships. As it stands, *Dichterliebe* is written for tenor voice. The nature of the poems hardly makes them a woman's songs, though Schumann actually dedicated the cycle to the great prima donna Wilhelmine Schröder-Devrient.

Heine is customarily thought of as Schumann's poet, as Mörike was Hugo Wolf's. But although he did set more poems by Heine than by anyone else, they all come in the 'Liederjahr' of 1840 with the exception of 'Tragödie', written in 1841. After that, strangely, he never returned to him. Likewise his settings of Chamisso, Geibel and Justinus Kerner all belong to 1840, together with the *Liederkreis* Op. 39 to poems by Eichendorff.

This latter, which has in it some of the best known of all German Lieder, is perhaps the most beautiful of Schumann's song-cycles – richer, fuller, more intense than its companions. 'The Eichendorff cycle is my most romantic music ever, and embraces much of you, dear Clara, within it', he wrote to her. The piano part is of an unmatched subtlety, and the vocal line is more independent and more dramatic. Schumann's freedom of attitude towards the poems, on the other hand, remains unchanged. In certain songs – 'Auf einer Burg', 'Wehmut' – he sets Eichendorff's text as it stands, repeating nothing and changing nothing. In others he alters the words, changes the syntax, repeats word-groups at will – all in response to the dictates of his musical imagination.

Take the very first song, 'In der Fremde'. The first four lines of Eichendorff's poem Schumann sets 'straight', as two evenly balanced couplets. The second half of the poem runs thus:

> *Wie bald, wie bald kommt die stille Zeit,*
> *Da ruhe ich auch, und über mir*
> *Rauschet die schöne Waldeinsamkeit.*
> *Und keiner mehr kennt mich auch hier.*

In the song this becomes, with Schumann's additions in roman type:

> *Wie bald,* ach *wie bald kommt die stille zeit,*
> *Da ruhe ich auch,*
> Da ruhe ich auch,
> *Und über mir rauscht die schöne Waldeinsamkeit,*
> Die schöne Waldeinsamkeit,
> *Und keiner kennt mich mehr hier,*
> Und keiner kennt mich mehr hier.

Apart from the effect of the insertions, Schumann dislocates Eichendorff's second and third lines, changes *'rauschet'* to *'rauscht'* and rewrites the last line. In 'Süsser Freund, du blickest', from *Frauenliebe und -leben*, he completely omits one of Chamisso's strophes, then repeats just two words from the penultimate line of the final strophe to round off the song. In 'Du Ring an meinem Finger', from the same cycle, he not only repeats word-phrases but invents additional words to fill out the melody in his mind. Can one any longer describe such songs as 'poems set to music'?

Schumann's eighteen songs to texts by Goethe cover the years between the early 'Der Fischer' (1829) and 'Nachtlied' (i.e. 'Wandrers Nachtlied') of 1850, but the poet to whom he most frequently returned in the course of his life was Friedrich Rückert. Starting with five settings in the collection *Myrthen*

(1840) and ending with 'Die Blume der Ergebung' (1850), he composed twenty-seven solo songs to Rückert texts, a corpus second in size only to that of his Heine settings. Beyond this he set Rückert a number of times between 1846 and 1849 for various vocal combinations, including the *Adventlied* (Op. 71) for soprano, chorus and orchestra, and returned to him in 1853, the last year of his superfluous creative life, in the three trios for female voices, Op. 114.

Rückert's poetry owes a great deal to folk-song, and its openness and simple directness, both in subject-matter and form, was of a kind to stimulate Schumann's lyrical inventiveness without restricting the freedom of treatment that he claimed. Where Heine's verse, for all its superficial naïveté and cultivated sentimentality, is sharp, pointed, with the metallic edge of a penetrating individual intelligence, Rückert's is soft, blurred at the edges, less distinctively personal. The bitter-sweet tone of Heine's *Dichterliebe* poems struck a special chord in Schumann's mind as he swayed between hope and despair in his fight for Clara, while Rückert's gentler, blander verse relaxed rather than provoked him. At the same time the many poems in which Rückert speaks with the voice of a woman or a young girl obsessed with thoughts of her lover helped to broaden the emotional range. To Schumann he was a true 'poet for all seasons'.

'I have written enough songs – over a hundred', he wrote in the family diary in November 1840, 'but I find it hard to stop'. As he had earlier explored the field of pianoforte music to its limits, so now, at the end of the glorious year of song, the year of Clara – for the lyricism and the love are one – the music still pulsing through him was about to flow into fresh moulds.

CHAPTER NINE

The Classic and the Romantic

In both personal and musical fulfilment, the years 1840–1, embracing the months before Schumann's marriage and his first year together with Clara in Leipzig, were the happiest in a life not rich in happiness. He was as sensitive as ever to contrarieties, as aware as ever that, in spite of now being Dr Schumann, of enjoying the personal approval of men like Liszt and Mendelssohn, and of having made the *Neue Zeitschrift für Musik* a force to be reckoned with, his role to the public at large was that of the man who had married the famous Clara Wieck. But as Clara's presence brought him strength to face his day-to-day reality, circumstantial and psychological, so the sheer urge within him to compose, the discovery of a new fluency, fed his steadily rising confidence.

Life in their apartment in the Inselstrasse ran a course that Robert and Clara faithfully recorded in their joint diary. Things were quiet, comparatively uneventful. Old acquaintances called – Emilie and Elise List, Frau Devrient, Dr Reuter, Mendelssohn – and there were evenings of music-making, sometimes at the Inselstrasse, sometimes at the house of friends. 'Every day I give thanks to God for the happiness of being able to call such a wonderful man my own,' wrote Clara. And Robert: 'My wife is the very incarnation of modesty, generosity and love. Everyone can see it'.

'Everyone' now included Friedrich Wieck, who could not blind himself to the couple's happiness. That he could not, or would not, share it was Clara's one cause for sadness. He ignored the letter of congratulation she sent him on his fifty-sixth birthday in August 1841 and Schumann's news shortly afterwards of the birth of their first child. It was a joyful occasion for her when three years later, with his second granddaughter already born and his son-in-law's fame growing, he threw off his resentment and offered an eagerly accepted peace.

Schumann's preoccupation with composition through the winter of 1840–1 demanded a sacrifice from Clara which she could understand but which left her sorrowful. For the moment she had exchanged the hectic round of the virtuoso, with its nervous strains but stimulating rewards, for the unaccustomed quietness of domestic responsibility, and her husband's absorption in his work felt to her like neglect, even indifference. 'For the last few days', she wrote in the diary in February 1841, 'Robert has been very cool towards me. True, the reason is a gratifying one, and no one can be more deeply concerned with all he does than I am, but at times this coldness hurts me, for I am the last to deserve it. Forgive this note of complaint, my dear Robert, but emotions sometimes have to take precedence over reason'.

Gradually, however, through this outwardly calm, ordered period in their lives, Clara resumed her regular piano practice. Her years of training had left too deep a mark, her sense of professional commitment had made her will too firm for her ever to doubt that she would eventually return to the concert platform. She was deeply devoted to her husband, but her artistic fulfilment had a life of its own. Nor could financial considerations be ignored. Her recital fees were now her own, and although Wieck's allegations that Schumann wanted to marry Clara for her money was grotesquely unjust, she could still earn far more than he did.

Plans for a visit to Russia were put off for the present. Practical arrangements for such tours had formerly been attended to by Wieck, who had the businessman's financial sense and tenacity. Clara did not, and Schumann still less so. But in March 1841, to the enthusiastic welcome of a faithful public, she returned to the Gewandhaus to give her first public performance since her marriage – a Piano Duo by Mendelssohn (Op. 92), which she and the composer played together, the Adagio and Rondo from Chopin's Second Piano Concerto, one of Mendelssohn's *Lieder ohn Worte*, Schumann's Allegro, Op. 8, a sonata by Scarlatti and, as the obligatory bravura finale, Thalberg's 'Moses' Fantasia. The most important item in the concert, however, had no piano part. It was the music that had so dominated its composer's mind in recent months as to make him, so she thought, indifferent and 'cold' towards her – the music of Schumann's Symphony No. 1 in B flat major, now receiving its first performance, with Mendelssohn conducting.

Since the unfinished G minor Symphony of 1832, the first movement of which had been played in Zwickau at the time, Schumann had made no foray into the field of orchestral music. Unsure of himself in the presence of the larger forms, and lacking the enviable fluency of a Mendelssohn, he had approached Christian Gottlieb Müller, a violinist in the Gewandhaus orchestra – the same man, incidentally, who had given the seventeen-year-old Richard Wagner lessons in harmony a few years earlier – for help in orchestration. But this had not advanced his development. He had sufficient self-knowledge at that time to realize that his true musical nature found its expression in small forms, and these, moreover, in the realm of a single instrument. In essence the 'Liederjahr' of 1840 is an extension of the same philosophy.

But partly because the alternative to self-repetition would have been silence, partly out of ambition to explore new and larger fields, and also, it would seem, because Clara led his thoughts in that direction, Schumann now began his advance into the realm of extended classical forms – symphony, oratorio, concerto, chamber music, opera. True to his manner of concentrating on one set of problems at a time, he moved from one area to the next only after having said all he had found to say. As 1841 became his 'year of the symphony', so 1842 was dominated by the string quartets, the Piano Quartet and the Piano Quintet; various pieces involving woodwind instruments came in 1849, the two violin sonatas followed each other in 1851, and so on.

Clara's share in launching Schumann's symphonic career can

be surmised from an entry in her personal diary a year before their marriage:

I am sure it would be best if he composed for orchestra; his imagination cannot expand sufficiently on the keyboard . . . All his compositions are conceived orchestrally, which is why, I think, the public does not comprehend them, for the melodies and figuration are so intertwined that it is difficult to hear the beauties of the work. My greatest desire is that he should compose for orchestra – that is his true field. Would that I could succeed in persuading him to do so.

The notion that his concentration on piano music had cramped his imagination may have reflected Clara's own thinking, but Schumann himself said just that in a letter to Dorn about the same time: 'I often feel like crushing the piano to the floor – it restricts my thoughts too much'.

It was a classic misconception. For as the demands of the grand classical manner had already exposed in his piano sonatas the incompatibility of his darting, impulsive imagination with the sustained grasp of a single, extended formal principle, so the claims of symphonic form presented themselves as a challenge to which it was not in his nature to rise. That he should long to find a place in the symphonic pantheon alongside Mozart and Beethoven, Schubert and Mendelssohn, expresses an ambition of which there was no need to feel ashamed. The wonder is that he should have so mistaken the nature of his gifts as to believe it possible.

To try to give a fool-proof definition of 'symphonic', in other than an obvious formal sense, is otiose. But any music lover can 'feel' the drama, the conflict, the spiritual universality embraced by the symphonies of Mozart and Beethoven, and can 'feel' that, except perhaps in a few privileged moments from his 'Great' C major, Schubert's lyrical symphonies do not share this universality – still less do the charming and elegant symphonies of Mendelssohn. The beauty of this music is not in dispute – how can one be deaf to the beauties of Schubert's 'Unfinished' symphony or Mendelssohn's 'Scottish' and 'Italian' Symphonies? The principle at stake, measured by the highest criteria – the only ones by which one can measure – is that of the truly 'symphonic', as real and apprehensible a criterion as the 'epic' or the 'dramatic'.

There is little for surprise in this. What confronts us is in essence the antithesis of classic and romantic. In the particular context of German music in the early mid nineteenth century it involves a movement away from the abstract formal symmetry that had sustained the symphony of the eighteenth century towards a conception of form governed by the imaginative impulse of the moment, the spiritual unity of the experience that had inspired the act of artistic creation. Formal unity thus becomes a product of subjective vision, and whatever the source of the vision, the form and nature of the work of art is the expression of the relationship between the artist and his chosen subject. The uniqueness of the relationship then forms the final link in the chain of the romantic argument.

It is against this background that the programme symphony and the symphonic poem emerge – Berlioz' *Symphonie fantastique*, Liszt's *Tasso, Les Préludes* and so on. It is also the invocation of such literary, narrative or pictorial associations that releases orchestral sketches like Mendelssohn's *Hebrides* Overture, much of Schumann's most characteristic piano music – and, above all, the Lied. For as a symphonic poem or illustrative 'Concert overture' starts from a point outside music, so also a song owes its genesis and the direction of its movement to the poetic text. This is the sense of Liszt's description of Schubert as *'le musicien le plus poète que jamais'*. Far from simply 'setting to music' a series of poetic strophes, Schubert created their musical equivalent – one might even say their musical substitute. Not by accident does the great age of German Lieder, from Schubert through Schumann to Brahms and Hugo Wolf – the same is true of opera, from Weber to Richard Wagner – coincide with the age of German romanticism.

One would not need to digress in this way just in order to affirm what one knows already: that Schumann is a romantic composer. But the excursion helps to provide a context within which to relate his symphonic aspirations to the non-symphonic nature of his musical personality, illustrating the implications of these gifts in particular and the ethos of romanticism in general. And it is both sad and revealing that Schumann should have thought that, his romantic *Flegeljahre* behind him, he was standing at the threshold of 'classical' status, with his greatest achievements yet to come. 'One of the things that make me happy', he said at the end of 1841, after completing his D minor Symphony, 'is the awareness that I am still a long way from my goal but feel the power to achieve higher things'.

Liszt, writing in the year before Schumann's death, already perceived the dichotomy between his nature and his aspirations:

No one can fail to recognize that instead of venturing, conquering, discovering, Schumann strove to reconcile his romantic personality, torn between joy and pain, and often driven by a dark urge towards the fantastic and the bizarre, with the modalities of classical form, whereas the clarity and symmetry of such forms lay beyond his characteristic spirit . . . This struggle against his true nature must have caused him great suffering, and it has stained even his most beautiful pages with the blood that has flowed from the open wound.

That Schumann considered the piano 'restricted his thoughts too much' is a thought that leads even more deeply into the nature of his music. Down to 1845 he composed entirely at the piano. But his piano music is not as often unmistakably and inimitably pianistic as is that of the two great original composers of piano music in the nineteenth century – Chopin and Liszt. Even Mendelssohn's, in both its lyrical and bravura moments, is more pianistic. The persistent thickness of texture of Schumann's piano music, like the technical demands it makes in its successions of massive chords, its full-blooded leaps from one register to another, in short, the sense that it is pressing towards the limits of what two hands can encompass – this tempts one to think that Schumann hears such music in terms of full orchestral sound.

At the same time his orchestral timbre is for the most part an undifferentiated mass, like the aggregate tonal product of his piano music – indeed, often sounding like perfunctorily orchestrated piano music.

That he composed at the piano hardly touches the issue. So did Mussorgsky and Ravel – but one would not think of the former primarily in terms of piano music, whereas the latter, one of the finest of composers for the keyboard, is at the same time one of the great masters of the orchestra.

And as Schumann's piano music is so often not characteristically pianistic, so his orchestral music is so often not characteristically and individualistically orchestral. It is music virtually dissociated from the medium for which it is written, evolved at the keyboard as a matter of convenience and preference. His quartets are music for string quartet but not string quartet music; the *Fantasiestücke* Op. 88 are pieces for clarinet but not clarinet pieces; while Op. 70, for instance, is inscribed by the composer as being for horn and piano, cello and piano or violin and piano.

To be sure, much of Bach's music is 'absolute' in this sense, and Bach scored and rescored many of his works for different combinations of instruments. But Schumann is not Bach, nor did he make transcriptions of his pieces in the way Bach did. The literary and other non-musical associations of his music also create a totally different set of initial circumstances. He moved from one musical genre to another as he sought to extend his experience, but the burden of his message remained the same, a message expressed more fully, more naturally, more beautifully in some genres than in others.

Interesting and significant in this connection is that, unlike Liszt, and in spite of the perfect opportunities it offered to a composer steeped in poetic experience and imagistic fantasy, Schumann wrote no tone poem or other piece of orchestral programme music. The nearest he came to it was in the late concert overtures like *Die Braut von Messina*, but these have the quality rather of incidental music, like Mendelssohn's *Midsummer Night's Dream* Overture, than of programme music as usually understood. The programmatic impulse found expression in his piano music; corollarily his orchestral music confined its existence to abstract, classical forms.

At the time he wrote his First Symphony, brimming over with music, Schumann saw before him the challenge of symphonic form and would stop at nothing less. The flourish of the opening bars, peremptorily summoning the attention of the audience, like the fortissimo chords at the beginning of the G minor Sonata, the second Intermezzo and other piano pieces, conveys his undisguised confidence:

'I composed this symphony', he later wrote to Spohr, 'at the end of the winter, with that springtime *élan* that returns every year, right into old age. I did not attempt to depict or describe anything, but the season in which it was born did, I am sure, affect the form it took and help to make it what it is'. So also, specifically, did a poem by a minor writer, one Adolph Böttger, which describes how the mist and gloom of winter give way before the blossoming of spring – a scene in which Schumann could instinctively detect a personal symbolic meaning. Both the sketch, which took only four days, and the manuscript score are headed 'Frühlings-Symphonie', and, as though Florestan and Eusebius were still looking over his shoulder, he originally thought to call the four movements 'Frühlingsbeginn' ('Coming of Spring'), 'Abend' ('Evening'), 'Frohe Gespielen' ('Merry Playmates') and 'Voller Frühling' ('Fullness of Spring'). In its published form the symphony bore none of these fanciful tags.

An irrepressible *joie de vivre* throbs through the whole work, right down to the characteristic 'poco a poco accelerando' with which the Finale gallops to its close. His orchestra – two flutes, two oboes, two clarinets, two bassoons, four horns, two trumpets, three trombones, timpani and strings – is that of Beethoven's Ninth Symphony and Schubert's C major. Mendelssohn uses smaller forces – two horns instead of four, and trombones only in the last of his five symphonies (the 'Reformation') – yet his scoring has a brilliance and a variety that Schumann rarely achieved.

That he had had only sketchy instruction in the craft of orchestration is of little relevance. So had Wagner. The real issue lies in the nature and quality of the musical ideas themselves. Where Tchaikovsky had a mastery of the orchestra that modifies the conceptual shortcomings of his symphonies, Schumann had not. On the contrary, his limited range of orchestral colour and the frequently unrelieved, almost claustrophobic sameness of the sound-texture over page after page, only intensify one's uneasiness. Excessive doubling – of woodwind by strings, oboes by clarinets, etc., – an over-heavy bass, product of the obtrusive persistence of the double-basses *arco*, the frequent recourse to string tremolo: these contribute much to a textural monotony. Taking the shadow for the substance, Weingartner and Mahler both rescored Schumann's symphonies, thinking to make the texture less opaque and the basic substance clearer, rather as a restorer removes overpainting and varnishing that obscure the surface of an old picture. They may have found it an instructive exercise, but it made no difference to the nature of the originals.

It was something of a disappointment to Schumann, elated in the pride of his immense creativity, that his First Symphony should meet with a mixed response. Clara, who, together with Mendelssohn, took part in the concert, wrote as enthusiastically as ever to her friend Emilie List: 'I have never heard a symphony received with such applause'. Alfred Dörffel, historian of the Gewandhaus concerts, on the other hand, recorded that, though struck by its originality, the audience, like the orchestra, found much of the work strange and not immediately accessible:

Almost every instrument had awkward passages that were difficult to perform and therefore spoiled the players' enjoyment of the work as a whole. In particular the second violins in the Finale were required to execute figurations proper to the pianoforte rather than the violin. The flautists too had cause for complaint. The only completely satisfied performer was Pfundt, the percussionist, who found to his delight that the score demanded three tympani instead of the usual two.

Hardly was the scoring of the First Symphony finished than Schumann, still in his jubilant 'spring' mood, plunged into the symphonic Overture, Scherzo and Finale (Op. 52), virtually a symphony minus a slow movement. At one stage he designated it as such. Originally he had called it a suite, and when he offered it to the Leipzig publisher Hofmeister (who rejected it), he explained that 'what distinguishes it from a symphony is that the individual movements can be played separately'. 'We do not know what to call it', wrote Clara in the family diary at the beginning of May. A few days later Schumann noted: 'The orchestration of the Sinfonietta is finished'. The entire work had taken a mere three weeks to write.

The constant changes of title – it had already happened with some of his piano pieces – are revealing. For if the individual movements can be performed separately, what remains of the concept of symphonic unity? To be sure, it was common concert practice at the time to play individual movements from symphonies and concertos. But this was to extract elements from works that had been conceived as integrated wholes – like an altar triptych, each panel of which has its own inner logic but where the full, planned meaning of the work derives from its totality. Schumann, by contrast embodies the episodic principle, agglomeration rather than unitarianism. The whole is less than the sum of its parts.

Within a matter of days he had also finished a piece for piano and orchestra that he called *Phantasie in A minor* – later the first movement of the Piano Concerto, whose second and third movements were not written for another four years. Then, still before the month of May was out, he started at a furious pace on the sketch of yet another work. 'Robert's mind is caught up in a whirl of activity', noted Clara on Whit Sunday.

Yesterday he began another symphony. I have not heard anything of it so far but at times I catch the sound of a fiery D minor in the distance, and I can see from the way he acts that it will be another work drawn from the very depths of his soul. Heaven is favourably inclined towards us, and even Robert cannot be more blissfully happy at his work than I am when he finally shows me what he has composed.

He showed it to her on her birthday, 13 September. It was the Symphony in D minor (Op. 120).

The extraordinary energy of 1841 had still not quite exhausted itself. In October a 'little symphony in C minor' was running through his head, and although he never scored it, he did complete the sketch the following month. Then there was his first foray into the realm of choral music, a setting for chorus and orchestra of Heine's triptych of poems, 'Tragödie', which he all but completed, then laid aside; later he used it in song form in volume four of his *Romanzen und Balladen* (Op. 64). Finally, on Christmas Eve, he wrote a lullaby which subsequently found its way as 'Schlummerlied' into the *Albumblätter* (Op. 124), published in 1854. Ideas for an opera also came into his mind, and from this time dates his acquaintance with Thomas Moore's romance *Lalla Rookh*, in which he found the captivating story of Paradise and the Peri. 'Perhaps it can be turned into something attractive in music', he reflected. Two years later he finished an oratorio on the subject. And throughout this time he continued to edit the *Neue Zeitschrift* singlehanded, putting together for each week's two issues the various news items and reviews from his contributors, and occasionally, though now less often than in the past, adding articles of his own.

Though chronologically the second of Schumann's four symphonies and originally announced as such, the D minor was revised ten years later and only published in 1853. By that time two other symphonies had already appeared, numbered 2 (in C), and 3 (in E flat), so that the D minor became No. 4.

It was largely the indifferent reception of its first performance in the packed Gewandhaus hall in December, at which the Overture, Scherzo and Finale were also heard for the first time, that led Schumann to withdraw it. And this reception, in turn, owed much to the circumstances of that concert. For besides Schumann's two orchestral works the programme included two pianoforte works by Liszt, played by the wizard himself – the *Fantasy on Themes from Lucia di Lammermoor* and the *Hexameron* for two pianos, with Clara as his partner. Liszt inevitably commanded the lion's share of attention. 'The duet', wrote Zuccalmaglio in the *Neue Zeitschrift für Musik*, 'aroused excitement of unparalleled proportions. All the normal conventions of applause were broken, giving way to a frenzy of enthusiasm'.

It was a situation - sad, slightly bitter - that epitomized so much in Schumann's life and work. For almost two years he had enjoyed a condition of relative psychological equilibrium and released an unbroken stream of musical compositions - over 130 songs in the 'Liederjahr' of 1840 and now, in the following year, three symphonic works, with thoughts of more large-scale pieces to come. Suddenly, when the moment for public recognition arrived, an ironical conspiracy of circumstances cheated him of his reward - ironical above all because his own Clara had played a part in frustrating his success. And as for the role of Liszt, it was virtually impossible for anyone to survive on the same concert platform, or for any music other than his own to be left ringing in the audience's ears at the end of an evening. To include Schumann's two earnest, rather dully-scored orchestral pieces in the same programme as two examples of Liszt's dazzling piano writing was almost an act of masochism.

For Liszt the virtuoso and Liszt the private citizen both Robert and Clara had the same admiration and affection as before. But they disliked his retinue of camp-followers and disapproved of the flamboyant egocentricity that he cultivated in his social life. His music, furthermore, they found intolerable. 'I can only call his compositions terrible,' said Clara: 'a chaos of excruciating dissonances, with a perpetual rumbling in the deep bass and tinkling in the high treble, with boring introductions and so on. I could almost detest him as a composer'.

A particular originality of Schumann's D minor Symphony lies in the derivation of much of its musical substance from a few seminal ideas used rather like motto themes. This became a favoured technique of his. The themes are often first stated in the slow Introduction - three of his four symphonies open this way - and the result, as in Beethoven's Fifth Symphony and, later, in Tchaikovsky, is a kind of consolidated monothematic unity. The so-called *idée fixe* in Berlioz' *Symphonie fantastique*, of which Schumann wrote a long, glowing review in the *Neue Zeitschrift*, may also have influenced the course of his thoughts.

In its original form the Scherzo ran into the Finale without a break; otherwise the movements were separate. In the version of 1851, however (that almost always used in present-day performance), Schumann's urge towards a unitarian conception has produced a continuous work in six sections – the four movements proper, with introductions to the first and fourth. The thematic links between the first and last movements are also drawn more tightly together.

But the most striking later revision of the work involves the orchestration. Schumann had behind him by 1851 a year's experience of conducting a variety of music with the orchestra in Düsseldorf, which might have been expected to help refine his own none too subtle orchestral technique. Instead he set about rescoring the first and last movements even more thickly, doubling parts and giving more prominence to woodwind and brass. Wasielewski, who was the leader of the Düsseldorf orchestra at the time, tells that Schumann came to him one day with the original score of the symphony and asked him to copy the string parts on to fresh pages of manuscript paper; he then added the new woodwind and brass parts. One would scarcely recommend it as a mode of scoring. He commended the symphony to his Dutch 'Davidsbündler' friend Johannes Verhulst as 'better and more effective than before', but we may be forgiven for raising a hesitant eyebrow.

On 1 September 1841, as Schumann was coming to the end of his work on the D minor Symphony, Clara gave birth to their first child, a girl called Marie. 'We were beside ourselves with happiness', wrote the proud father in the family diary. 'How proud I feel to have a wife who has not only given me her love and her art but now also a gift like this!' Marie's godparents at her baptism twelve days later – Clara's birthday – were Schumann's one surviving brother Karl, Clara's mother, Mendelssohn and Frau Devrient, Schumann's former landlady. Marie never married. She continued to live at home after her father's death and became a piano teacher; she stayed with her mother until Clara died in 1896, and later moved to Interlaken, in Switzerland – like her youngest sister Eugenie, also unmarried and also a piano teacher – where she died in 1929.

Schumann was a devoted, almost doting father. On Marie's first birthday the following year he opened a diary in her name, dwelling lovingly on little sentimentalities:

You were happy and lively almost the whole time, with your pretty blue eyes and dark lashes. You have learnt to crawl around the room very quickly and are very agile. You can even stand up by yourself, though of course you cannot yet walk properly or talk. But your singing is farther advanced, with definite intervals and phrases. At the back of this diary, where the staves have been ruled, you will find some of the little tunes that I used to sing to you at the piano. We shall make up a lot more together : . . .

The happiness of the young family grew when, early in 1842, they received a joint invitation to go to Bremen and Hamburg – Schumann to supervise a performance of his First Symphony, Clara to play again in cities where she had had such success two years before.

For Clara, wife and now mother, this meant the chance to return to the career which she had put into the background but had never dreamt of renouncing. If she were to withdraw for too long, people would forget her in favour of some new prodigy like the twelve-year-old Anton Rubinstein, who was dazzling European audiences at that moment, and the bloom would vanish from her own playing. *'Rast ich, so rost ich'*, she recalled: 'If I rest, I rust'. For Schumann the invitation brought particular satisfaction in that it was addressed jointly to him and Clara. So often he had been made to feel that the outside world saw him merely as the consort of his more famous wife.

But the occasion turned sour. The concerts were a moderate success, no more. Clara played Bach, Mendelssohn and Liszt, with little pleasure, on a mediocre instrument. Then came an invitation to the court at Oldenburg – an invitation to Clara alone. Finally, reviving an intention she had had two years earlier, Clara decided to travel on from Hamburg to Copenhagen, leaving her husband to return home to Leipzig and to their six-month-old daughter – also alone.

It was the first separation of their marriage, and it brought bitter unhappiness to them both. At Kiel, where she was due to play on the first evening of her journey to Denmark, Clara felt so miserable that at the very last minute, with the audience already in their seats, she feigned sickness, and the house manager had to send the disgruntled patrons home, leaving her to pay for the ticket refunds out of her own pocket. In Copenhagen, fortunately, she recovered her composure and gave a series of recitals, successful both financially and artistically. Among the more entertaining characters she met in the Danish capital was the fairy-tale writer Hans Christian Andersen, 'a man of poetic, childlike nature, still fairly young, very ugly – in fact, the ugliest man you can imagine, yet of very interesting appearance. It takes some time to get used to his personality'.

Schumann meanwhile, during the four weeks of his loneliness, reflected disconsolately on the fate of a man forced again to play second fiddle and be deprived of the security and peace of mind that he needed for his work. 'The separation has once more brought home to me my strange and difficult position', he wrote to Clara. 'Must I neglect my talents in order to act as a companion to you on your tours? Should you leave your gifts to stagnate, while you are still young and strong, because I am tied to my journal and my piano? We must at all costs find ways of cultivating our talents side by side'. In his diary he noted: 'Pitiful life . . . Dreary time . . . Composition out of the question . . . I don't know what's the matter with me'. He even seriously considered going with her to America for a few years.

During Clara's absence in Denmark Schumann had a visit from another ambitious, frustrated young Saxon composer who had come to Leipzig to see his family – Richard Wagner. Wagner, whose thoughts were occupied with the subject of Tannhäuser, had just left Paris after the first of his failures to take the musical capital of Europe by storm. The following year he was to become Kapellmeister at the Royal Court Theatre in Dresden, and when the Schumanns moved to that city in 1844, he saw a good deal of them.

But the two men were radically different, both as personalities and as musicians, and although each sensed a certain quality in the other, they had difficulty in understanding each other – Wagner the voluble, egocentric, outgoing enthusiast, Schumann the hesitant, withdrawn, introspective brooder. Of this meeting in April 1842 Wagner wrote:

Schumann is a highly gifted composer but an impossible person. I visited him on my return from Paris, told him about my experiences there, talked about the state of musical life in France, then about that in Germany, talked about literature and politics, but for almost a whole hour he hardly uttered a word. One cannot always do all the talking oneself. An impossible person.

Schumann reciprocated a few years later in his diary: 'Wagner has a great flow of words and his head is chock full of ideas, but no one can listen to him for long'.

With Clara's return in April he regained his peace of mind and the zest for composing that had filled him the previous year. As 1841 had been his 'Year of the Symphony', so 1842 became the 'Year of Chamber Music'.

The immediate stimulus for this change of direction came from the quartets, first of Haydn and Mozart, then of Beethoven, which he and Clara studied closely, one by one, at the keyboard. 'June, apart from a few oppressive days and nights, was a delightful month', he wrote in their diary, 'and I have been busy in a new field, completing and copying out two string quartets'. These were No. 1 in A minor and No. 2 in F major. A third, in A major, followed shortly afterwards, and the three works, dedicated to Mendelssohn, were published the following year by Breitkopf and Härtel as Op. 41. This was not his first excursion into the realm of the quartet, but his plans of early 1838 and 1839 – 'I have begun two quartets – they are as good as Haydn's, I can assure you' he wrote at that time to Clara – had come to nothing.

Whether Schumann's string quartets are in fact 'as good as Haydn's' is an idle question. But one thing is apparent. Whereas Haydn's are genuinely music for stringed instruments, Schumann's are like piano music transferred to strings. Much of the passage-work is of keyboard rather than string character, long stretches of the music have a monophonic nature that recalls a pianistic technique, and the imitations, sequences and other contrapuntal devices have a similar familiarity derived from his piano music. He never returned to the string quartet, and wrote no other chamber music that did not involve – indeed, did not rest on the supremacy of – the piano.

An ironical postscript to this was added by Schumann himself through his attitude to the composer whom he had originally regarded as the great genius of the age – Chopin. Secure as Chopin's place in musical history was, in Schumann's eyes he had failed to develop, confining himself to piano music. 'Unfortunately', wrote Schumann in the *Neue Zeitschrift* in 1837, 'he totally neglects any compositions of larger proportions'. (Strangely, although he must have known them, he says nothing about Chopin's two concertos.) When, however, Chopin obliged in 1841 with a composition 'of larger proportions', namely the Sonata in B flat minor, Schumann waxed caustic: 'To call it a sonata, as Chopin has done, is sheer caprice, almost downright arrogance, for he has simply yoked together four of his wildest offspring, trying to smuggle them under this name into a setting to which they would otherwise have never found their way'. One master of the piano miniature reproaches a fellow-master of the same genre for being just that! Schumann's piano sonatas may look formally more like classical sonatas than Chopin's (the Funeral March Schumann found 'by and large repellent'). Whether many, for this or any other reason, would wish to claim that they are musically superior . . .

Shortly after finishing the last of the three quartets, Schumann sketched and completed the Piano Quintet Op. 44 – a mere five days for the sketch and two weeks for the finished score. Almost exactly a month later, also after taking five days over the sketch, he completed the Piano Quartet Op. 47, and before the end of the year a Piano Trio, published as Op. 88 under his favourite title *Phantasiestücke für Pianoforte, Violine und Violoncello*.

The Quintet is the most satisfying and most popular of Schumann's chamber music works. The reasons lie on the surface. Here is verve, enthusiasm, serenity, charm, and above all a sense of utter conviction, the feeling that the whole work is 'of a piece', that Schumann saw its entire course from the very moment of its joyful opening bars. Unlike, say, the piano sonatas and the string quartets, or even the symphonies, all of which contain attractive music in microcosm, the Piano Quintet offers an experience of beauty not only in the parts but also in the whole.

In essence this is an achievement felt in the spirit rather than demonstrated in the letter. But the last section of the Finale, heralded by a sustained chord, fortissimo, of the dominant seventh, unifies the work in a strikingly original way by setting against each other in counterpoint the opening themes of the first movement and the final movement, like the statement of the subjects of a double fugue (see opposite, page 219).

One can hardly resist the conclusion that both the success and the pervasive happiness of Schumann's Piano Quintet have their source in his relieved return to a world in which the piano is king. There are barely half-a-dozen bars in the whole work in which the piano is silent, and the work could as well be defined as a domestic concertino with string accompaniment.

Scarcely had Schumann finished the Piano Quintet than he started work on the Piano Quartet, sketched at the end of October 1842 and written out over the following weeks. As completely dominated by the piano as the Quintet, but less heroic, less enthusiastically singleminded, it suffers from the comparison with its grander fellow through the very reduction of the string parts from four to three. The relationship between piano and strings becomes even more unequal, that is to say, the opportunities for violin, viola and cello to display an independent personality against the strength of the piano, or even to underscore particular motifs which contribute to that strength, become less productive. The doubling of parts, from which, given Schumann's approach to the medium, there is no escape, falls more heavily on three instruments than on four, while the musical texture, as thickly woven as ever, becomes as an ensemble less expansive and less rich. Comparison with the piano quartets of Mozart, Beethoven or Mendelssohn, with their lighter and less dominating piano parts, will show that Schumann's is not the only philosophy of the exercise. Brahms' three works in the genre use the piano in a greater variety of ways – to accompany a lyrical melody, for example, to produce an antiphonal effect in

interplay with the strings in concert, sometimes only to provide a sustained bass above which the strings can embroider their own melodies.

The predominance of phrases of four bars and multiples of four works towards the same centripetal concentration of vision and effort, whereas much of his piano music shows a greater independence of phrase-length, often based on syncopated rhythms, themselves expressive of his impulsive, quixotic fantasy. In the confines of an abstract, traditional genre, it seems, the pressures of order and symmetry bore the decisive influence on the form of his musical argument.

By the end of 1842 Schumann had worked himself into a state of nervous exhaustion. The psychological effect was predictable. More familiar though his name had become to the musical public in recent years, his standing was still far from that of a Mendelssohn, or even of a Spohr. Much remained to be done. 'In a community where I cannot be first', he had said, ten years earlier, 'I would rather be nothing at all than second or third'. His ambitions had not waned.

But his enforced idleness also had economic consequences. Clara was expecting another child and could not take on any concert engagements. Apart from the interest on the capital Schumann had inherited from his father, and also, presumably, on that which Wieck had accumulated in Clara's name from her recitals as his dependent daughter, their only regular income came from Schumann's editorship of the *Neue Zeitschrift für Musik*. The sale of compositions, like Clara's concerts, had supplemented the family budget, and the thought that this source might dry up made him even more tetchy and morose. His resentment of the inferiority of his public status *vis-à-vis* Clara returned, a resentment exacerbated by a nagging self-reproachful suspicion that she was sacrificing her artistic future on the minor altar of domestic dependence and maternal responsibility. At the same time he knew that only this sacrifice could preserve his own creative personality and mediate in the conflict between himself and the world in his struggle to find, as a man and as a musician, a *modus vivendi* with the personal and professional realities around him.

His unease and his bouts of brooding silence left their mark on Clara also. In November she wrote in the diary:

> For some days I have been in a state of depression – I do not think you love me as you used to, and I often have the feeling that I do not satisfy you . . .
>
> The thought that you would have to work in order to earn money I find terrible, for you could never be happy that way. Yet I can see no alternative as long as you prevent me from pursuing any possibility I might have to earn some money.
>
> Forgive these impulsive words, dear Robert, but my feelings for you go even deeper than this. Kiss me – do not be angry. And if you can, go on loving me, at least a little. For your love is my life.

It therefore seemed something of a mixed blessing when at the beginning of 1843 Mendelssohn invited him to join the staff of a new Royal Music Conservatoire in Leipzig, which was to admit its first students in a few months' time.

Mendelssohn's appointment to the Gewandhaus in 1835 at the age of twenty-six – it is hard to realize that he was only twenty at the time of his performance of the St Matthew Passion – had put the musical life of the city on a new level. But this new standard depended on his personal presence. If he were to leave or die, Leipzig music could slump back into its former mediocrity. So in order to secure the continuity of the new-won excellence, the enlightened King Friedrich Augustus II appointed him Royal Saxon Kapellmeister and charged him with the establishment of a music school, donating 20,000 thalers for the purpose. The plan finally came to fruition in April 1843, when the school was formally opened by the King's minister Paul von Falkenstein, and the first twenty-two students took up their studies. Among them was a young violinist called Joseph Joachim.

Under Mendelssohn as director, who himself taught solo singing and composition, the Conservatoire started with a basic staff of five: Moritz Hauptmann for harmony and counterpoint; Carl Ferdinand Becker, a co-founder of the *Neue Zeitschrift für*

Musik, for general music lectures; Ferdinand David, leader of the Gewandhaus orchestra, for violin; Christian August Pohlenz, cantor of the Thomaskirche, for organ and choral singing; and Schumann for composition, score-reading and pianoforte. Further teachers were appointed as the school grew.

The philosophy of the Conservatoire was to provide not a specialized instrumental training but an all-round education in both the theory and the practice of music. No students, whether from Germany or abroad, were accepted without an entrance examination or for less than one whole year; the complete course lasted three years, and discipline was strict. Of the 63 students who joined in the course of the first year, 47 were men and 16 women, but there was no thought of coeducation, and separate classes were held for the young men and the young ladies. The building itself, a modest two-storey house erected in the courtyard of the Gewandhaus, stood until 1887, when bigger premises were built elsewhere in the city.

Yet attractive though the prospect may at first have seemed, and although for the first few months he devoted himself whole-heartedly to his new and unfamiliar duties, Schumann could never have been a successful teacher. Although, in theory, he had a view of music that assumed the involvement of art in the life of the community – the philosophy behind the *Neue Zeitschrift*, indeed, rested on the principle of raising the standard of public knowledge and appreciation – this view did not imply to him any obligation to take part in the practical promotion of his opinions. He stated what he believed, and left it at that. To persuade, to explain, to see the matter from the standpoint of the humbler mortal, of the pupil anxious to learn – the prerequisites of any teacher – was not his way.

His uncommunicativeness alone posed difficulties. Freely as he could express himself in writing, when he could set his own pace and soliloquize without interruption, the pressures of a conversational situation made him insecure, inhibited, finally reducing him to almost complete silence. Wasielewski remembered what he could be like:

As a student at the Conservatoire at the time I had the opportunity to witness his behaviour for myself. On one occasion I was told to go to one of his pianoforte classes and take the violin part of Schubert's B flat major Trio, with one of the students playing the piano part. The whole lesson passed off with Schumann saying hardly a word, though I remember very clearly that there would have been reason enough for him to do so.

Again, one must not equate diffidence with lack of interest, or silence with disapproval. He had a genuine interest in seeing the new Conservatoire succeed, and his so-called 'Project Book' contains notes for future activities that he considered the institution might usefully undertake, among them an edition of the works of Bach and the establishment of a music library. He also envisaged the foundation of a kind of national 'Society of Musicians', which should make itself responsible for producing authentic editions of the classics, forbidding the 'modernization' of old music, doing away with unnecessary foreign titles and musical terms, and similar reforms. But he could only commit such thoughts to paper. Never could he have argued them in person before the body to whom in his imagination they were addressed.

Schumann's activity at the Leipzig Conservatoire lasted only a short while. In January 1844 it was interrupted by a four-month tour of Russia with Clara, then finally brought to an end in the autumn of that year by his breakdown and his move to Dresden. By and large it was not a particularly happy or profitable episode. And as a venture into the field of practical music-making, it set a sad precedent for his disastrous years as conductor of the Düsseldorf orchestra in the last stage of his active life.

For reports make it uncomfortably clear that he was a bad teacher, incapable of giving advice on specific matters such as phrasing, fingering and dynamics, and restricting himself to general, unhelpful remarks. Sometimes he gave the impression of barely paying attention to what was going on. Louis Ehlert, one of his pupils, related that after he had played him a piece, all that occurred to Schumann to say, absentmindedly, was 'It's very odd. Whenever you strike a high E flat, the window pane rattles'.

A few weeks after Schumann joined the Conservatoire, Clara gave birth to a second child, also a girl, christened Elise. Her mother had somehow found the time in recent weeks to compose a number of small piano pieces, but, wrote the proud father, 'Clara herself sees her principal occupation as that of mother, and I believe she is happy in this role'. Family friends like Mendelssohn, Emilie List, the Voigts and old Frau Johanna Devrient visited them in the Inselstrasse, and the rich musical life of the city ensured that they were regularly seen in cultural circles.

The spring of 1843 also brought Schumann a personal encounter with Berlioz. Berlioz was on a concert tour of Germany, conducting performances of his own works before audiences often at a loss to know what to make of them. He had already given two concerts in Dresden and had met Wagner there, but the two were very different in character and had little predisposition to understand each other's music. Wagner even suspected, like many men of ambition who cherish grand designs, that Berlioz was jealous of the success of *Rienzi* and *Der fliegende Holländer*.

Schumann had no such ambivalent feelings towards Berlioz, whose music he had known since 1835. 'It was a pleasant meeting,' he wrote in his diary:-

Berlioz conducted excellently. There is a good deal in his music that is insufferable, but also much that is extraordinarily ingenious, even inspired. He often seems to me like the powerless King Lear – in fact, his features, otherwise very fine, also bear a trace of weakness around his mouth and chin. Paris must have corrupted him. Unfortunately he knows no German, so we do not talk very much. I had imagined him to be more vivacious, more fiery, but he has an attractive smile. For the rest he is a true Frenchman – always drinks water with his wine and eats stewed fruit.

As a kind of postscript to the 'Chamber Music Year' Schumann wrote a set of variations for the unusual combination of two pianos, two violoncellos and horn. Shortly afterwards, for no stated reason, he revised it as a piece for two pianos alone and published it as such (Op. 46) the following year.

But his one substantial work of 1843 was in a form totally new to him, a form which, like its predecessors symphony, string quartet and piano quintet, he now grasped as a fresh challenge. This was the secular oratorio *Das Paradies und die Peri* (Op. 50), for solo voices, chorus and orchestra.

'I must tell you', he wrote on 3 June to Eduard Krüger, a writer on aesthetics who contributed regularly to the *Neue Zeitschrift*, 'that I have recently written hundreds of thousands of notes, completing on Ascension Day the largest composition I have yet undertaken. The subject is "Paradise and the Peri" by Thomas Moore – an oratorio, but for cheerful people, not for a place of prayer.' Writing to his Dutch friend Verhulst a few days later, he called it not only his biggest work so far, 'but also, I hope, my best . . . The whole idea is so poetic, so pure that it filled me with inspiration'.

The Irish romantic poet Thomas Moore established his reputation with a graceful, if lightweight collection of lyrics called *Irish Melodies* in 1807. In 1817 he published *Lalla Rookh: An Oriental Romance*, which brought him a popularity second only to that of Byron in an age captivated by tales of the East and by orientalia of all kinds. This was the age of Coleridge's *Kubla Khan* and of John Nash's Brighton Royal Pavilion, in Germany of Friedrich Schlegel's *Über die Sprache und Weisheit der Indier*, Goethe's *West-Östlicher Divan* and Rückert's *Die Weisheit der Brahmanen*. In music there had also been works with Eastern settings, such as Félicien David's once overwhelmingly popular 'Ode-symphonie' *Le Désert* and Niels Gade's cantata *Comala* – not to speak of Mozart's *Seraglio* and *Magic Flute* at the end of the preceding century.

Moore's *Lalla Rookh* consists of four narrative poems in rhymed couplets, linked by prose interpolations telling of the journey of the Indian princess Lalla Rookh from Delhi to meet her betrothed, the King of Bucharia. The king turns out to be one and the same as a young poet called Feramorz, who accompanies her on the journey, and with whom she falls in love. The second of Feramorz' poems is 'Paradise and the Peri', a symbolic tale of salvation through ceaseless striving, in which the Peri, a spirit cast out from heaven, can only be forgiven and re-enter Paradise if, as the poem puts it, she

> *brings to this eternal gate*
> *The gift that is more dear to Heaven.*

After offering two gifts that are rejected, the Peri finally brings the tear of a repentant sinner. This proves to be the gift that Heaven seeks, and she is received back into Paradise. It recalls the chant at the end of Goethe's *Faust*:

> *Wer immer strebend sich bemüht,*
> *Den können wir erlösen*
>
> (He who ever strives and toils,
> Him we can redeem.)

Sensing that this story, with its sentimental mixture of symbolic motifs, oriental colours and lavish imagery, might stimulate Schumann's musical imagination, his old friend Emil Flechsig made a translation of Moore's text and gave it to him. This, with modifications and the addition of original material of his own, then became the starting-point of Schumann's composition.

Each of the three parts of the work – the first and third have nine numbers, the second has eight – is a seamless web, aria running into quartet, accompanied recitative giving way to chorus, in an unbroken lyrical flow. Its immediate formal antecedents are, on the one hand, Mendelssohn's *Erste Walpurgisnacht* (1830), and on the other recent 'through-composed' romantic operas such as Marschner's *Der Vampyr* (1828) and Wagner's *Fliegender Holländer* (1841). The vocal line of some of the solo parts has a grace and beauty that recall Schumann's great songs of 1840, but the orchestral writing is rarely more than conventionally supportive, an undistinguished base on which the vocal parts rest, or, at moments of climax, a consolidation and reiteration of the argument sustained by the chorus.

It is in the choral writing itself, however, that the conflict between the needs of the medium and the nature of Schumann's creative gifts shows itself most patently. Flechsig's German translation of Moore's poem has scant dramatic quality – indeed, scant quality of any kind – but this cannot excuse the almost total lack of dramatic sense in Schumann's music. A single phrase of a few words is repeated over and over, tossed to and fro from one voice to another, split up into individual words which are themselves then repeated and exchanged between the parts. All the stuff of oratorio texts, the cynic may observe – but it provides no alibi for musical shortcomings.

Mendelssohn shows in *Elijah* and *St Paul*, as Handel had shown in *Israel in Egypt, Judas Maccabeus, Messiah* and many other works, that dramatic effectiveness in oratorio is not precluded by the repetitive, non-dramatic conventions inherent in the manner in which they set texts to music. The drama – the same is true of opera – lies in the music. No one could dream, from the libretti of *The Magic Flute* or *Parsifal* – that of *Das Paradies und die Peri* has a vocabulary and a spiritual ambience uncannily similar to the latter – what drama-laden music they were to bear. Schumann's oratorio, the work he sadly considered his best at that moment falls, as a whole, by the same token. The obverse of the originality of the continuous musical texture in each section of the work is the sameness, an undifferentiated musical mass dominated by its least satisfactory constituent – the chorus.

The first performance of the work at the beginning of December 1843, in aid of the new Conservatoire, also marked Schumann's debut as a conductor. The rehearsals had been less than totally satisfactory, largely, it seems, because Schumann lacked the necessary experience and authority. The soprano Livia Frege, who sang the part of the Peri, wrote to Clara: 'If your good husband could only make up his mind to argue a little and insist that people pay better attention, things could be put right at once'. But the première itself and a second performance a week later were received with great applause, and the congratulations of David, Niels Gade and other musicians of judgement strengthened his sense of achievement.

Perhaps the happiest result of this success, however, came in the form of a letter, totally unexpected, from his father-in-law in Dresden:

Dear Schumann: 15 December, 1843

Tempora mutantur et nos mutamur in eis.
We can no longer continue to be remote from each other in the face of Clara and the world. You too are now a father – what need is there for

long explanations? In matters of music we were always of one mind – I was even your teacher, and it was my statement that set you on your present career. I do not need to assure you of my respect for your talent and for your fine achievements.

I await with joy your arrival in Dresden.

> Your father,
> Fr. Wieck

Slowly but surely Wieck had come to realize, not only that the love between his daughter and Schumann had an inner resilience on which he could not lay hands, but also that the man whose integrity and ability he had so bitterly impugned was gradually becoming a force to be reckoned with. Wieck's world rested on the pillars of ambition and achievement. Whatever private emotions may have moved him, such as the thought of the grandchildren from whom he had cut himself off, his change of heart expressed in essence a grudging admission of his son-in-law's public achievements: editor of an established music journal, composer with a growing reputation, and newly-appointed teacher at the Conservatoire. Earlier this same year he had already asked Clara to tell him of any new works of Schumann's that were to be performed in Leipzig, and he came across from Dresden to hear *Das Paradies und die Peri*. 'Your husband and I are determined people', he wrote to her; 'we must be allowed to go our own ways, but we are both men of principle. Consequently it cannot surprise him if I seek to do justice to his creative power and his industry. Come to Dresden soon and perform your husband's Quintet'.

Three days after Wieck's letter arrived, Schumann and Clara did go to Dresden, and the formal reconciliation – the moment for which Clara had so desperately longed – was sealed. Never had she resigned herself to having to pay for her devotion to her husband with the prospect of a life-long alienation from her father. But the savageness of his opposition to her marriage, together with the personal abuse which he had showered on Schumann, left scars that would never heal, and destroyed the prospect of anything beyond a dutiful relationship of interest and respect.

A growing reputation may be very gratifying, but as Schumann was made to realize, it does not always find expression in economic terms. He and Clara led a full social life and already had two children to care for. 'We spend more than we earn', he noted frankly in the family diary, and although plagued by the anxieties and complexes that always accompanied such moments, he found himself facing once more the unwelcome but hitherto unfailing answer to the situation – a concert tour by Clara.

Even before their marriage there had been talk of an extended visit by Clara to Russia. Plans for her to go at the beginning of 1841 had been put off because of the uncertainties of the political situation, while the thought of going the following year was thwarted by the knowledge that Liszt also proposed to be there at that time. To give the impression of competing with Liszt would invite disaster. The winter of 1843–4, when Clara was pregnant with Elise, also had to be allowed to pass – these successive hindrances, one suspects, being secretly welcomed by Schumann as manifestations of a *force majeure* that was frustrating what he was pleased to see frustrated.

But now, finally, with Mendelssohn having helped to persuade Schumann of the benefits that a Russian tour would bring, they left their children in the care of Schumann's brother Karl in Schneeberg and set out in January 1844. Clara gave recitals in various ports of call along the route – Berlin, Königsberg (now Kalliningrad), Riga, Dorpat (now Tartu) – but the rigours of the journey, with primitive hotels and temperatures well below zero, made Schumann unwell. Still resentful of the interruption to his composing – 'My next plan is for an opera, on which I am passionately anxious to start' – he caught a chill in Dorpat because of the thin bedclothes. 'The hotels here are very bad,' wrote Clara to her father:

one can hardly eat the food, and many things are simply not available, except for tea and coffee, which are both good. The worst thing is the terrible beds. Eiderdowns are unknown, and all we have are thin coverlets, though the rooms are heated. My husband caught a chill in the night: we are not used to such scanty bed-coverings, except at the height of summer – and here the temperature stays twenty degrees below zero, day in, day out.

It took a week before he felt well enough to continue the journey, and they finally reached the ice-bound Russian capital on 4 March. Compared with Mendelssohn, or Chopin, or Wagner, Schumann was not a much-travelled man. But on all his journeys, from the high-spirited jaunts of his student days onwards, he kept a detailed and keenly observed record of what he saw and heard, and his 'Reisetagebuch' of the journey to Russia shows how responsive he was to the scenes, and above all to the people, around him.

The tour turned into an almost unqualified success. On Liszt's visit the previous year the audiences had packed the hall for his first recitals but became smaller and smaller as time went on. With Clara it was the reverse, so that, as every performer would wish, she left the city at the height of her popularity with an eager public clamouring for her return. She was received by Tsar Nicholas I in his winter palace one morning and played to him and his family for two whole hours. Other members of the aristocracy also paid their respects. A special pleasure came with the appearance of Adolph Henselt, a young German composer whose work Schumann had praised some years earlier in the *Neue Zeitschrift* and who was now court pianist to the Tsar. And to his utter surprise and delight he found still living in the city a seventy-year-old uncle, Karl Gottlob Schnabel, his mother's eldest brother, who had emigrated from Germany as a young man to serve as a medical officer in the Russian army. He also made the acquaintance of Glinka.

A rather tart impression of Schumann and Clara in Petersburg society was recorded by one J.K. Arnold, who remembered them from an evening in the home of Alexis Lvov, composer of the Russian national anthem:

Clara Schumann displayed masculine strength and feminine instinct in both her conception and her execution of the music, although she is only twenty-five years of age. However, one could hardly describe her as a charming or particularly likeable woman. Both she and her husband spoke French with a Saxon accent, and German like worthy Leipzigers. As to Schumann, he was silent and withdrawn the whole evening, as usual. When the two Counts Vielhorsky or his host Lvov asked him a question, he just muttered something unintelligible. Clara was a little more communicative and answered everything for him. Most of the time he sat in a corner close to the piano, his head bowed. His hair hung down over his eyes, and he wore a severe expression; he looked as though he were whistling softly to himself.

Schumann's sense of satisfaction with his Russian experience emerges with undisguised directness from the letters that he sent to Wieck back in Dresden. 'We have now been in St Petersburg four weeks,' he wrote at the beginning of April:

Clara has given four recitals and has played before the Tsaritsa; we have met many distinguished people and seen a great number of interesting things. Each day brings something new, and when we look back, we can be content with what we have achieved.

That he included himself in this achievement was due in part to the financial success of Clara's recitals, in part also, however, to her successful performance of his Piano Quintet, the *Kreisleriana* and a number of other pieces. But during the four-week stay in Moscow that followed, spells of his old melancholy returned, and even of the morose suspiciousness of Clara that had clouded the tense years of their battle against Wieck – irrational moments when, saying nothing but acting as though offended, he made her feel she had done something wrong, had neglected or somehow been unkind to him. He also suffered fits of dizziness, which long, lonely walks did little to alleviate.

Significantly and sadly expressive of these moods of depression, and alarmingly prophetic of the permanent darkness that was to settle over his mind a mere ten years later, is a set of five poems on historical associations invoked by the Kremlin, a complex of buildings which held a strange, almost sinister grip on his imagination. Deprived of the peace and solitude he needed for composing, yet seeking an outlet for the confusion of emotions that pressed upon him, he returned to the world of poetry in which he had lived as a schoolboy, before music became the dominant force in his life.

Yet now, as then, the literary and the musical were only two sides of a single creative urge. In a revealing phrase he described these poems to his father-in-law as 'concealed music, since I had neither the time nor the tranquillity necessary for composing'. They have a disturbing flaccidity and tiredness about them, as though his concentration, the power to shape convincing poetic symbols and artistic forms, had eluded him, leaving a loose assemblage of lines and images unguided by a central intelligence. Had the 'concealed music' issued in notes rather than words, the result, one fears, would have borne an uncomfortable resemblance to the often curiously uncoordinated compositions of his final years.

From Moscow the couple returned briefly to St Petersburg, then set out on the long journey home. After an absence of four months they saw their children again at the end of May. 'For a long while we could not get used to being back in Leipzig again,' wrote Clara in the diary: 'everything seemed so empty, so desolate, in spite of being back in our old home with our children. Robert, moreover, continued to feel unwell, as he had in fact throughout the tour, although it had been kept in the background.'

But in August, shortly after a not very rewarding visit from Hans Andersen, who showed little interest in a group of Schumann's songs that Livia Frege sang for him, he became seriously ill. He had taken up his teaching again at the Conservatoire and still had nominal responsibility for the *Neue Zeitschrift*. Also, after years of doubt and indecision, he had finally begun to compose the music of what eventually emerged almost ten years later as *Szenen aus Goethes Faust*. All this work now proved too much for him. On top of these physical demands came an incident that showed again how pathologically predisposed he was to take offence where none was intended.

In November 1843 Mendelssohn had temporarily given up the direction of the Gewandhaus concerts and gone to Berlin; Ferdinand Hiller was appointed in his place but left after the 1843–4 winter season. For 1844–5 the committee then called on the composer Niels Gade, a Danish musician seven years Schumann's junior, who had settled in Leipzig some years earlier and made himself universally popular. Schumann knew and liked Gade and had reviewed some of his compositions in the *Neue Zeitschrift*, but he felt that he should have been offered the post first. Not that he would, or could, have accepted it. And everybody knew, as he did, that he would have been totally unsuited for the job. But he chose to feel offended and allow the imaginary insult to prey on his mind, which made his physical and psychological state still worse. Purgatives and sundry homoeopathic remedies achieved nothing. 'A terrible week has just passed,' wrote Clara in October. 'Robert got no sleep; his imagination conjured up all manner of horrible scenes, and in the morning I would find him bathed in tears. Only with great effort could he drag himself across his room. He had utterly given up hope'. It was a nervous breakdown that brought him to a state of almost total collapse.

Unable to work, professionally slighted, deprived of the personal comfort and musical encouragement of Mendelssohn, now in Berlin, the friend whose career radiated the success and the harmony that his own life had never known, he found nothing to keep him in Leipzig any longer. He resigned from the Conservatoire – which in any case had seen little of him throughout the year – gave up the editorship of the *Neue Zeitschrift* and, following the advice of his doctor and the promptings of Wieck, decided to move with Clara to Dresden.

The move marks a deep incision in the ineluctable deterioration of his creative powers and the disintegration of his mental stability. It was in Leipzig that he had studied, that he had composed all his greatest piano music and songs, that he had founded and edited the *Neue Zeitschrift für Musik*, that he had met his wife, that he had acquired whatever reputation he had. And although it now had nothing more to offer him, and he, at this moment, had nothing more to offer it, Leipzig still remained, he wrote, 'a very important city for music, and I would advise any young man of talent to go there, for it offers so much music – so much good music, moreover'.

On 13 December 1844, with their two young children – Clara was expecting a third – they left Leipzig and moved to Dresden.

CHAPTER TEN

Uncertain Intermezzo

Like Leipzig, Chemnitz (today Karl-Marx-Stadt), Zwickau and many other places in this area, Dresden was a Slav settlement. It became capital of the duchy of Saxony in 1485, and from then onwards its importance steadily grew, notwithstanding the vacillating policies and mixed political fortunes of the dukes themselves. In 1806 the Elector Friedrich August III threw in his lot with France against Prussia and the allies and was rewarded by Napoleon with the title of King, an honour that cost him half his territory after Napoleon's defeat. But the cultural life of the capital went on without any noticeable disruption. In his *Encyclopedia of Saxony* Schumann's father characterized the city of 1814 thus:

In size and population Dresden belongs to the third rank of European cities. It has no great trade fairs like Leipzig or Naumburg, no extensive industries like Chemnitz, Zittau, Plauen and other towns, and no mining like Freiberg. But as the capital of a beautiful and populous state, it is a place much frequented by visitors, a centre of luxurious living, of good taste, of art and scholarship, and of pleasure.

Though only 70 miles from Leipzig, Dresden breathed a totally different atmosphere. Leipzig was a city of middle-class values, a focus of industry and commerce, the seat of one of the leading universities of the time and, partly through this, partly through the related prosperity of publishing and the book trade, a self-conscious intellectual centre with a civic pride in promoting the arts, especially music. Dresden, by contrast, home of the Saxon court and redolent of aristocratic tradition, took its status for granted and enjoyed its privileges *ex officio*, setting at the heart of its artistic life not music but the visual arts, and furthering the activities of painters rather than musicians. With this air of somewhat smug relaxation in the ambience of beautiful buildings and superb paintings went a softer, milder climate – the area between Dresden and Meissen produces wines of no mean quality – which offered its own contrast to the harsh and often unfriendly weather of Leipzig.

The prospect of a gentler climate was in itself an inducement, psychological as well as medical, for Schumann and Clara to leave Leipzig. He was sick, nervous, depressed, full of doubts, the epitome of everything negative, and although his departure, as he wrote in his diary, 'had not been without tears, there was actually little left to keep me there beyond the consideration that it was my birthplace'. (It was not, of course, but it must have felt as though it were.) They found themselves an attractive ground-floor apartment at Waisenhausstrasse 35, in the Altstadt – the whole street was destroyed in 1945, along with the rest of the centre of Dresden – but his first months in the city did nothing to lift the darkness of his depression.

Dr Helbig, a homoeopathic physician whose advice he sought soon after his arrival, wrote a long note which not only diagnoses his condition at that moment but also reveals frightening symptoms of a progressive physical and psychological disintegration. 'As soon as he embarked on any mental activity', wrote Helbig,

he began to tremble and feel weak, and his feet became cold. A sense of apprehension would come over him, combined with a strange anxiety about dying, which took the form of a fear of high mountains and tall buildings, of metal implements, even keys, of medicines, and of being poisoned. He suffered a great deal from insomnia and felt at his worst in the mornings. Since he used to pore over any medical prescription until he found some pretext for not taking the medicines in question, I prescribed cold douches, which improved his condition to the extent that he became able to resume the only work he knew, viz. composing music. Since I had on several occasions encountered a similar set of symptoms in men who concentrated to excess on one particular activity – businessmen, for instance, who spent all their time adding and subtracting figures – I advised Schumann to turn his mind now and again to subjects other than music. He took up things like natural history and physics but after a few days pushed them aside, retreated into his shell and devoted himself to his musical thoughts again.

Particularly instructive for the observer were, on the one hand, the auricular delusions with which Schumann, a man with a highly-developed aural sense, was afflicted, and, related to this, the peculiar nature of his psychological life. The ear is the sense most active during periods of darkness, the last to cease functioning and the first to awake, capable of reacting to whispers even while a man is still asleep, the sense most closely linked with the emotional faculties and with the forces controlling prudence, revenge, aggression, and also the appreciation of music. Anyone who reflects on the characteristics of night and darkness and compares them with Schumann's psychological life, will at once find certain things understandable. When we consider that the eye could not perceive light, nor the brain understand ideas, if the former could not create light in itself, or the latter evolve ideas in itself, then we shall begin to grasp the nature of Schumann's auditory delusions.

Apart from the interest that attaches to the explicitly clinical aspects of this depressing account, and to the recognition of the pathological symptoms that beset Schumann with pitiless persistence until his death, Dr Helbig's report reveals *en passant* how different a person Schumann had become over the last few years. Gone were the *joie de vivre* and the sense of confidence which, despite fits of depression and self-doubt, had shone through his personal and creative life in the years surrounding 1840, the year of his marriage. Gone were also the versatility and intellectual drive, the literary insights and energies that had made up so much of his artistic personality and significance. Composition, says Helbig, was now 'the only work he knew'. The desire to concern himself with theoretical or historical issues in music, and thus with the music of others, had left him. Still less was he disposed to meditate on wider questions of philosophical or social relevance, indeed, to occupy his mind with anything that would shake his introverted fixation on the struggle to compose. He even seemed to recognize the danger himself, commenting on his nervous exhaustion in a letter to the teacher and critic Eduard

Krüger: 'I think I must have been too preoccupied with my music'. And whatever one's view of the quality of the music he wrote during this time in Dresden and later, it rarely breathes the spontaneity and freshness, the air of an art open to, and in a sense dependent on, a world outside itself, that fill the piano pieces and songs of earlier years.

The music that preoccupied Schumann at the time he moved from Leipzig to Dresden was a setting of the final scene of Goethe's *Faust*, the first part to be written of what he completed in 1853 as *Szenen aus Goethes Faust*.

Goethe is a name that recurs again and again in Schumann's diaries from the earliest times onwards. In 1831, after a convivial evening stimulated by Chambertin and champagne at his favourite haunt of Rudolphs Garten in Leipzig, he produced the fanciful equations Epicurus = Don Juan: Plato = Faust to represent the relationship between practice and theory. Later the same year he expressed Goethe's eminence more soberly: 'Just ask yourself – what is the most beautiful thought there is? It is life, pure life – like Shakespeare, like Goethe, like Mozart'. Strangely enough he did not set many of Goethe's poems – far fewer than of Heine, Rückert, Eichendorff or Chamisso, for example, and even of minor poets like Geibel and Kerner.

During his tour to Russia with Clara in the opening of 1844 he read *Faust* closely – not that there is any other way in which one can read this greatest of all works in German literature – and first thought, as he had with *Das Paradies und die Peri*, in terms of an opera. But to encompass the meaning of so huge a work in operatic form – indeed, to convey even a fraction of its poetic, dramatic and philosophical significance – was an insuperable task, and to use Goethe's text in any other spirit would have seemed to him an act of betrayal. The only possibility lay in intensifying through music the meaning of chosen moments in the work, moments of intense symbolic power. The greatest of these is the 'Apotheosis of Faust' that brings the drama to a close. Schumann started work on his music after returning from Russia, was forced by his desperate state of health to abandon it for months – 'I was in the grip of sinister demons', he wrote to Verhulst – until finally, in the course of the summer, he found the strength to complete what he had started.

But as though uncertain of his own powers, and in awe of the masterpiece he had laid hands on, he then put the music away. 'The scene from *Faust* lies in my drawer', he wrote to Mendelssohn in September. 'I am too afraid to look at it again. It was the sublime poetry of this concluding scene that moved me to undertake the task, and I do not know whether I shall ever publish it'.

It remained in his drawer for another three years, when he took it out and added three more sections to it. Shortly afterwards, in June 1848, the complete scene was given a private performance in Dresden. After this occasion he sent the editor and publisher Alfred Brendel an interesting comment on the philosophy of his undertaking:

What gave me the greatest pleasure was to hear from many people that the music had made the meaning of Goethe's text clear to them for the first time. For I was often afraid I would hear the rebuke: 'What is the point of writing music to poetry that is so perfect?' On the other hand, for as long as I have known this scene I have felt that its effectiveness could be enhanced precisely through the medium of music.

Its first public performance, appropriately, was at a concert in August 1849, given as part of the centennial celebrations of Goethe's birth.

Between 1849 and 1850 Schumann added to this final scene a Part I in three sections 'Szene im Garten ['Scene in the Garden']; Gretchen vor dem Bild der Mater dolorosa ['Gretchen before the Image of the Virgin Mary']; Szene im Dom ['Scene in the Cathedral']) and a Part II, also in three sections ('Sonnenaufgang' ['Sunrise']; 'Mitternacht' ['Midnight'] and 'Fausts Tod' ['Faust's Death']), and in 1853, as a not very convincing afterthought, an Overture. The complete work was neither published nor performed during his lifetime.

In his approach to Goethe's text Schumann assumes the same freedom as in his song settings, selecting, omitting and repeating lines at the prompting of his musical whim. The garden scene between Faust and Gretchen, for instance, takes the 'He loves me – He loves me not' episode from Goethe's 'Garten', omits the last two dramatic lines of Faust's final speech, then rounds off the movement with phrases from Mephistopheles and Marthe taken from Goethe's next scene, 'Ein Gartenhäuschen.' The famous closing 'Chorus mysticus', on the other hand, with its eight short rhyming lines, is made by repetition of lines, word-groups and single words to extend to a choral and orchestral movement of over 250 bars.

Like almost all Schumann's large-scale works, and like his later music in toto, the *Szenen aus Goethes Faust* have moments of attractive detail, flashes of the lyrical beauty in which he had earlier revelled, but lack the sense of central control, of total vision, that commands attention from beginning to end. It is not a matter of the frequent rhythmic monotony, or the undistinguished instrumentation, or the stolid choral writing, but of the lack of a sense of compulsive inner unity. Brahms meant just this when, after playing the accompaniment for a performance of the work in 1859, he wrote to Clara:

The *Faust* went quite well, but it was tiring to sit for three hours at the piano, playing the accompaniment, without being able to move or say anything. To perform the whole work on a single evening, even with orchestra, does not seem a good idea to me, and you should try to prevent it rather than encourage it. The third part makes a greater impression by itself than when it follows the other two parts. Besides, the various numbers rarely have much connection with each other.

Harsh words – and Clara tried to convince herself that they were unjust. Schumann himself set his *Faust* above *Das Paradies und die Peri* on the grounds of its superior poem, 'which forced me to exert myself more'. But it is not within the power of Goethe's genius to guarantee that his poetic masterpieces will unfailingly inspire musical masterpieces.

A measure of the shortcomings of Schumann's *Faust*, particularly in the achievement of the dramatic fervour by which he set so much store, emerges from a comparison of his 'Chorus mysticus' in the final scene with that of Liszt in his *Faust Symphony*. There is hardly an area – harmony, orchestration, above all the creation of emotional intensity and a sense of inescapable drama – in which Liszt does not prove himself, at

Schumann's expense, to be the profounder interpreter of Goethe's poem, the truer messenger of its spiritual meaning and beauty. The supervention of Mahler's Eighth Symphony has revealed even more mercilessly the struggle of Schumann's *Faust* for survival.

Schumann's diaries for 1845 now show him absorbed in fugue, canon and the other devices of counterpoint. 'February 2 – continually engrossed in the study of fugue with Clara'; 'February 18 – busy with fugal studies the last three weeks'; 'February 21 – passion for fugue' – there are a host of such entries. 'I find it strange and quite remarkable,' he wrote, 'that almost every motif that forms in my mind has the characteristic of lending itself to various kinds of contrapuntal treatment. It is not that I start with the slightest intention to compose such themes – it just happens that way. There seems something basic and natural about it'. He arranged for a pedal keyboard to be attached to his piano, and composed two sets of Studies and Sketches for Pedal Piano (Ops 56 and 58) and the Six Fugues on BACH for Organ or Pedal Piano (Op. 60) – his only pieces for organ.

Social life in the new surroundings that Schumann and Clara had chosen brought many difficulties. Indeed, drifting further and further away from a world in which he could find no proper place, Schumann often gave the impression of wanting to avoid his fellow-men. He came to know some of the painters, sculptors and architects in the Saxon capital, but his interest in their company soon waned. The birth of a third daughter, Julie, in March 1845 also made him look inwards rather than outwards. He went on long country walks with Clara alone, and friends who had not seen him for some time were alarmed by his deterioration, both physical and psychological. 'When I visited him in Dresden', said the music critic Gustav Keferstein, 'he looked very poorly. He was in such a state of nervous exhaustion that already at that time I was deeply worried whether he could live much longer'.

That his mental faculties were beginning to degenerate was also the impression he made on Max von Weber, Carl Maria von Weber's son, who lived in Dresden with his widowed mother. He had fits of bad manners, forgot the conventions of polite society and talked about musicians and general questions of art in a

rough, intolerant tone. Max von Weber belonged to a circle of
artists and musicians that used to meet in the Engel tavern in
Dresden, in much the same spirit as the 'Davidsbündler' had
congregated in the Kaffeebaum in Leipzig. Schumann joined the
group for a while but soon lost interest, and his behaviour, as
Weber describes it, certainly taxed the goodwill of his
companions:

Generally he sat at a little table facing the wall, with his back turned to
everything going on in the place, holding the handle of his beer mug in his
hand and totally absorbed in his own thoughts. His lips were pursed, and
it looked as though he were whistling quietly to himself, although there
was no sound to be heard. The others respected his qualities, and most of
them were prepared to accept the way he deliberately cut himself off, but
some were apprehensive of him because their attempts to draw him into
the conversation had been so brusquely and rudely rejected.

On another occasion that Weber recalled, Schumann waxed
scornful at the expense of Cimarosa, calling his *Matrimonio
segreto* 'canary music' full of *Haarbeutelmelodien* ('periwigged
tunes'). At this Carl Lipinski, leader of the Dresden court
orchestra, protested in his broken German: *'Alle Ehr', Doktor,
Sie seien sehr respectabeler Componist, wollte aber, wüssten
einen zu recommandiren uns, der schriebe Haarbeutelmusik von
der* Matrimonio segreto' ('Much respect, Doctor, you be very
honourable composer, but wish you recommend us one who write
periwig music like *Matrimonio segreto.'*) 'Whereupon,' Weber
continued, 'Schumann got to his feet without replying, picked up
his hat, put it on and hurried out of the room without a word to
anyone, while Lilpinski muttered: "Remarkable composer but
coarse man, not nice companion".'

A particular embarrassment in Dresden, which might have been
expected to be the opposite, was the presence of Friedrich Wieck,
who had been living in the city since 1840 with his second wife.
Wieck's earlier animosity towards Schumann had passed, but it
had not given way to cordiality, while Clara was disturbed by the
sight of her father desperately trying to turn his new daughter
Marie into the prodigy that Clara herself had been. 'She plays
well', Clara admitted, 'but she lacks the spark of inspiration, and
her playing always strikes me as mechanical and listless'. So

immovable was Wieck's suspicion of Schumann's personal and musical influence that when Schumann founded a choral society in Dresden a few years later, he forbade Marie and his other pupils to attend its meetings.

The source of musical influence in Dresden at this time, however, lay not with Robert Schumann, still less with Friedrich Wieck, but with a man whose real career had only just begun, a man destined to transform the face of European music and become not only one of the greatest composers the world has known but also one of the most demanding and most controversial – Richard Wagner.

Wagner was three years younger than Schumann. The two first met, it seems, in the summer of 1831, when Schumann wrote the single word 'Wagner' in his Leipzig diary, and Wagner contributed a number of articles to the *Neue Zeitschrift für Musik* in the course of the 1830s. Shortly after Wagner returned from Paris in 1842, they met again in Leipzig. Wagner, not surprisingly, did all the talking, while Schumann, he recalled, 'sat there for almost an hour and barely spoke a word.' 'A highly gifted musician', was his verdict, 'but quite impossible as a person'. Schumann's opinion of Wagner the man was a mirror image of the same scene: 'He possesses an immense gift of the gab and ideas simply pour out of him, but it is impossible to listen to him for long.' Obviously Schumann stopped listening long before Wagner stopped talking.

Wagner and his wife Minna had been in Dresden since his appointment as Kapellmeister to the royal court orchestra in February 1843. They were far more lavishly accommodated than the Schumanns, occupying a large villa in the broad Ostra-Allee (now Julian-Grimau-Allee), overlooking the Zwinger. The previous year both *Rienzi* and *Der fliegende Holländer* had had their premières there, so the basis of his reputation had already been laid. At the time Schumann arrived, he was working on *Tannhäuser* with a speed and a sureness of purpose that Schumann could never match in his extended works.

In his autobiography *Mein Leben* Wagner describes his relationship to Schumann during their shared years in Dresden as 'very friendly and with a sense of mutual sympathy and trust'. They saw each other from time to time in a circle of artists and musicians – among them Eduard Bendemann, Schnorr von Carolsfeld, Julius Hübner, the architect Gottfried Semper, the sculptor Ernst Rietschel and the composer and conductor Ferdinand Hiller – that met to discuss the latest developments in the arts. Schumann was also present when Wagner read his newly completed libretto of *Lohengrin* to this company in November 1845. But their meetings were sporadic and unplanned – amicable but not cordial. And although Schumann came to admire *Tannhäuser*, he remained critical of Wagner's style and method both now and after they had left Dresden. Wagner, for his part, who commented on Schumann's 'quite remarkable awkwardness' when he conducted, was somewhat more generous, finding Schumann's music both thoughtful and attractive. At the same time his tone has something patronizing about it, the tone of a man who feels he can afford to look down on the efforts of lesser mortals around him.

One thing the two men did have in common, however, was a dissatisfaction with the state of musical life in the Saxon capital. For both of them the standard was set by Leipzig, and for all the progressive brilliance of Dresden in the visual arts, as a musical centre it was a sluggish backwater. Weber, who had been Kapellmeister there some fifteen years earlier, had had so little confidence in the musical forces at his disposal that he arranged for the premières of his three great operas to be given elsewhere – *Der Freischütz* in Berlin, *Euryanthe* in Vienna and *Oberon* in London.

The energetic Wagner set about overcoming this mediocrity by introducing into the operatic repertoire and concert programmes works that would raise the standard of public taste – a didactic intent similar to that which underlay the editorial policy of the *Neue Zeitschrift für Musik*. Schumann, less forceful by nature, and with no official position to use as a springboard, tried with Ferdinand Hiller to set up a scheme of orchestral subscription concerts on the lines of those at the Gewandhaus. The first concert, at which the fourteen-year-old Joachim played Mendelssohn's Violin Concerto, took place in November 1845, but the scheme as a whole aroused little enthusiasm. Schumann had hoped to attract Leipzig concertgoers to these occasions as well, but musical interests were well catered for in Leipzig, and if the Leipzigers did go to Dresden – which happened rarely enough – it was not for music. 'Things are unbelievably hidebound here', he wrote to Mendelssohn. Even the orchestra made difficulties: 'They refuse to play any Beethoven symphonies at such special concerts because they are afraid it would prejudice their Palm Sunday concert and thus their pension fund, which receives the proceeds'. In any case the subscription concerts depended for their existence less on Schumann than on Hiller, who conducted them, and when Hiller left Dresden in 1847 they came to a predictable end.

The contrapuntal studies with which Schumann occupied himself during the early months of 1845 doubtless had their pedagogical value as a technical discipline but they issued in no great original creative work. Towards the summer, however, his mind cleared and his strength returned, and in the course of the rest of the year he not only finished the Piano Concerto but also, just before the onset of a year's creative barrenness and desolation, laid the foundations of his Second Symphony.

Schumann's inscription on the manuscript of the Piano Concerto reads: 'First movement, a self-contained movement, written in Leipzig in 1841 and called "Fantasie"; the other movements written in Dresden in May and July 1845.' At the time he was working on the 'Phantasie', he described it as 'something between a symphony, a concerto and a large sonata', adding, with an eye on the flamboyant works that excited the contemporary public: 'I realize I cannot write a concerto for a virtuoso, so I must think up something else'. Its first performance was in Dresden in December under Hiller, the second in the Gewandhaus on 1 January 1846, under Mendelssohn. On both occasions Clara played the solo part.

Formally and conceptually, the 'something else' amounts to an equivalence in terms of soloist and orchestra to the multi-sectioned pianoforte works like the *Fantasie*, the *Humoreske* and other pieces of that period. As the unity of these pieces, with their romantic, evocative titles, rests not on a calculated formal balance between constituent parts, as in the classical sonata, but on the often mysterious centripetal power of their creator's imagination – in other words, a unity not structural but spiritual, almost biographical – so the Piano Concerto also is held together by a pervasive joyous emotion that surges through the work from beginning to end.

The original 'Fantasie' had a life of its own and would have survived, one imagines, as a single-movement work alongside the later *Introduction and Allegro appassionato* (Op. 92) and the *Concert Allegro with Introduction* (Op. 134). But in order to rank as a concerto, it needed to be bigger, as Clara charmingly reveals: 'Robert has added a fine last movement to his *Phantasie for Piano and Orchestra in A minor*, so that it has now become a concerto'. Schumann would often change the title of a work in the course of its composition, or from one published edition to the next, and use conventional terms in an idiosyncratic way, like calling his F minor Sonata a 'concerto without orchestra'. At the same time these were days when new forms were demanding new appellations – like tone-poem – and established terms being made to accommodate works very different from those hitherto associated with, and expected from, such terms – Liszt's B minor Piano Sonata, for instance.

That the first movement of Schumann's concerto dispenses, for example, with the opening orchestral tutti may be an immediately arresting characteristic but it is neither an innovation nor an experiment on Schumann's part. In Beethoven's G major Piano Concerto the solo instrument makes the first statement, while the 'Emperor' Concerto opens exactly like Schumann's, with a fortissimo chord tutti followed by a flourish for the solo instrument. In his two piano concertos and his violin concerto Mendelssohn likewise launches the soloist into the principal theme at the very beginning of the work. No, the originality of Schumann's concerto lies, as with all his music, in the originality of his lyrical romantic imagination, not in individual features of structure or formal conception. And his Piano Concerto, perhaps uniquely among all his extended works, sustains this originality throughout its three movements with a sureness of touch made the more miraculous by the length of time over which it was composed and the alarming deterioration of his physical and mental condition.

A mere two months after finishing the Piano Concerto, Schumann wrote excitedly to Mendelssohn: 'For a few days now my mind has been throbbing to the sound of trumpets and drums.

I wonder what it will lead to'. What it led to is revealed by Clara in her own letter to Mendelssohn; 'My husband has recently been very busy, and at Christmas he surprised and delighted me with the sketches of a new symphony. He is utterly possessed by music, and as a result it is impossible to do anything with him – I like him that way'. Later Schumann confessed his own sombre memories of this time:

I wrote the symphony in December 1845, when I was far from well, and I have the impression that one cannot but hear this in the music. Only in the last movement did I begin to regain my strength, and when the work was finished, I actually did feel better. But otherwise, as I said, it reminds me of a dark period . . .

It was the Symphony No. 2 in C major, Op. 61.

Of all Schumann's symphonic works this is the most purely classical, the most 'absolute', in both approach and manner. It is, of course, as subject to the ebb and flow of his subjective confidence and his psychological fortunes as all the rest of his music, but it has not the dependence on external, non-musical stimuli, or the episodic, associative, sometimes programmatic manner that accompanies this dependence. Put another way, and *pace* its musical virtues, it aims at an objectification of experience and a sustained classical ethos which contradicts the vivid, impulsive romantic emotionality that lies at the heart of Schumann's genius. He has conquered, for a moment, his true nature. In so doing, he has stifled his spirit and become less like himself.

The same may be, and has been, said about the other two great German lyricists of the romantic nineteenth century, Schubert and Brahms, who also often seem in their symphonies and other works in classical forms to be doing violence to the real essence of their creative personalities. But whereas Schubert and Brahms, not without cost, both succeeded in assuming the grand manner and in striking at times a tone of heroism and drama, Schumann not only hardly ever did so, but sacrificed almost his entire spontaneity and originality in the attempt.

Generalization quickly becomes overstatement, but if one

invokes the four symphonies, the violin and violoncello concertos, the string quartets, the piano sonatas and most of the other chamber music, one can hardly avoid asking whether it is in these ideal, abstract forms that the real Schumann resides, or whether it is in the intimate lyrical world of his romantic piano music and his songs.

Moreover size had a fatal appeal to many musicians – and not only musicians – in the nineteenth century, and many were seduced to the belief that big was not only beautiful but also *per definitionem* great. Schumann had in his mind at this time a number of plans for operas. A few years earlier *Faust* in this form had been abandoned. In 1844 he had commissioned a libretto from Oswald Marbach based on Byron's poetic 'Tale' *The Corsair* but composed only the opening chorus. Now he thought of a *Singspiel* on Goethe's epic poem *Hermann und Dorothea*, and also wrote to the poetess Annette von Droste-Hülshoff asking for a libretto to set. A year later he started work on *Genoveva*, the one opera he actually completed.

Whether the example of Wagner had an influence on this preoccupation with large-scale stage works we cannot tell. Certainly nowhere in nineteenth-century music is the cult of size and grandeur more defiantly celebrated than in Wagner's music dramas. But Schumann's preoccupation with large forms had its own roots in his personal and artistic biography, and followed its own sad path of development.

The classically formal character of the C major Symphony may reflect the frame of mind in which he had immersed himself in the study of counterpoint during the early part of 1845. There is also an historical interest, here as in the D minor Symphony – Liszt, Wagner and Tchaikovsky are among his companions – in his use of a motto theme which recurs as a unifying principle throughout the work. But the music does not rise to the originality, let alone the potentiality, of the thought, and the symphony as a whole, for all its attractive moments, leaves an impression of strain, the work of a man carrying out an obligation with no great conviction.

Although the symphony already existed in essence by Christmas 1845, it was October of the following year before Schumann found the strength finally to complete the score.

Mendelssohn conducted the first performance at a Gewandhaus concert in November. It was tolerably well received but as the last item in a long programme that included two performances of the overture to Rossini's *Wilhelm Tell* it found the audience less fresh and alert than they might have been. It was, after all, modern and therefore demanding music, which, like any contemporary art, required the concentrated attention that must always accompany unfamiliarity. Played earlier in the programme, Schumann thought – and seeming to imply that Mendelssohn was at fault in this – it might have made a greater impression. When asked for his own assessment of it, he replied: 'It's a real Jupiter'. How many would think of setting it alongside Mozart is perhaps a question better not asked.

Apart from finishing the C major Symphony, the only music that Schumann found the strength to compose during 1846 was two groups of part-songs (Ops 55 and 59). As well as the condition that Clara described as his 'nervous ailment', he was suffering from auditory hallucinations – a continuous droning and roaring in his ears, coupled with the conversion of every noise he heard into a musical sound. Composition in such a state was unthinkable. In May he went to stay with his old Leipzig friends, Major Serre and his wife, on their estate at Maxen, outside Dresden, in the hope that a change of surroundings might alleviate his distress. But he now became prone to fits of vertigo, and his hypochondria grew worse. 'He is unable to put the thought out of his mind that whenever he looks out of the window he cannot help seeing the mental asylum of Sonnenstein'. Clara had little idea, when she wrote these words in her diary, how tragically close was the moment when her husband's world was itself to be bounded by the walls of a mental asylum.

Clara herself was finding the strains of such a life harder and harder to bear. In February 1846, in the middle of one of Schumann's worst periods, she gave birth to Emil, her fourth child, who died little over a year later from glandular atrophy. In September they moved to a larger apartment round the corner on the first floor of the Reitbahnstrasse No. 20, where two more children were born during the four years they lived in Dresden. Both Clara and Robert were devoted to their young family but

Clara sometimes wondered where, even whether, she would find the strength to look after both them and her chronically sick, deeply depressed husband. 'And what will become of my own work?' she wrote plaintively. 'I do not know whether things can always go on like this'.

In the summer Schumann began to suffer from sudden rushes of blood to the head. Thinking that the sea air might be beneficial, he spent July and August on the North Sea island of Norderney, meeting on his journey there the famous Swedish soprano Jenny Lind, who was in Hamburg to sing Donna Anna in Mozart's *Don Giovanni*. The physician who tended him on Norderney noted that among the manifestations of his depressed state were a persistent 'preoccupation with the abdominal region'. Given the nature of the disease whose grip might appear to relax for a moment but could never be broken, one could readily speculate on what form this affliction might have taken – but it can only remain speculation. 'Schumann's terminal disease', wrote Dr Richarz, director of the psychiatric clinic where Schumann spent the last two years of his life, 'was not primarily a specifically mental sickness but a gradual, inexorable deterioration of the structure and functions of the entire nervous system. His physical degeneration was only one manifestation of this'.

Little by little, however, his condition on Norderney improved, and in the autumn he returned to Dresden in a relatively stable frame of mind which, with only a few relapses and attacks of vertigo, lasted miraculously through most of the following year. With this improvement Clara's hopes rose for a resumption of her own career, the main question being to decide where, apart from the ever-faithful Leipzig under Mendelssohn's regime, she would be most warmly received. What more ready answer than Vienna – scene of her triumph nine years ago as the eighteen-year-old Clara Wieck, darling of the imperial court and toast of the musical *cognoscenti*? She would also, she reflected, be able to act as ambassador for her husband's music, playing his piano and chamber works herself and arranging for his symphonies to be included in concert programmes. So in November 1846, filled with an optimism that it seemed at times would never return, they set out together, with their two eldest children, for a three-month stay in the Austrian capital.

It proved one of the greatest disappointments of their lives. Vienna, which enjoyed – or suffered from – an *embarras de richesses* in things cultural and artistic, had a short memory. The city's homage to Clara in 1837 had been sincere enough, but many musical events had come to the city since then and been carried away, like the memory of her playing, on the waters of the Danube.

She gave four concerts in the Gesellschaft der Musikfreunde. The first two – which included Beethoven's C major Concerto, Chopin's Barcarolle and A flat major Polonaise, and, of Schumann, the Piano Quintet and the Andante and Variations for Two Pianos Op. 46, with Anton Rubinstein taking the second part – barely covered expenses. Before the third Clara suffered the indignity of being asked for a subsidy of 100 guilders out of her own pocket in order to guarantee the solvency of the enterprise. She played Schumann's Piano Concerto, and Schumann conducted his First Symphony. The hall was far from full, the reception of the works cool and perfunctory, and such applause as there was seemed meant for the performers rather than the composer. The famous critic Eduard Hanslick, a man well-disposed to Schumann's music, recalled the melancholy occasion in his memoirs:

I went to see the Schumanns yesterday, together with two other faithful and sympathetic admirers of Schumann's music. We sat there uncomfortably for a while without saying anything, each of us depressed at how cool the response to the wonderful concert had been. Then Clara finally broke the silence, bitterly complaining about the audience's indifference and lack of appreciation. Whatever the rest of us tried to say in order to pacify her only succeeded in making her even more bad-tempered. Then Schumann made the unforgettable remark: 'Don't worry, Clara dear. In ten years everything will be different'.

It was an optimistic guess. And ten years proved to be more than Schumann had.

Among the audience at this unhappy concert was Jenny Lind, who had arrived in Vienna the day before. Earlier that year Clara, as a favour that Mendelssohn asked of her, had taken part in a concert in Leipzig at which Jenny Lind had sung. Dismayed by the failure of Clara's first three Vienna concerts, Jenny impulsively offered to return Clara's favour and sing at the last one, due to be held in a few days time. Clara gladly accepted. When the evening came, the memory of earlier disappointments weighing on her mind and her spirits no higher than her expectations, she found to her astonishment that the hall was packed. The reason was a cruel one. It was not Clara that the masses had come to hear but the 'Swedish nightingale'.

In the social sphere too Vienna now offered more disappointments than pleasures. To meet Grillparzer again, whose admiration for Clara's playing had not waned, proved a happy occasion, but Adalbert Stifter, then on the threshold of his career as one of the great Austrian novelists and short-story writers, made a pallid impression on them. Of Schumann's views on Meyerbeer, who also happened to be in the city at this time, and whom he was not always successful in avoiding, the less said the better. Flotow, composer of the opera *Martha*, had equally little to offer him. The poet Eichendorff he unfortunately met only at the very end of his stay, so that what seems to have started on a level of cordiality and even enthusiasm – 'Your husband's songs have breathed life into my poems', he said to Clara – was not given a chance to unfold.

Once before, at the time of Clara's earlier success there, Schumann had thought of making Vienna his new home. But Vienna gave him no encouragement. Now Clara too was made to share the feeling of not being wanted. 'How differently we felt when we left from when we arrived', runs the last entry in her diary. 'At that time we thought we would find a refuge there but now any desire to do so has completely gone'. It was at least some consolation to them that two concerts she gave in Prague on the way back to Dresden were received with enthusiastic applause not only for her playing but also for the works of Schumann that were included – the Piano Quintet, the Piano Concerto and some of his Eichendorff songs.

There were indeed signs here and there that people were beginning to sense the presence of an important composer. After only a few days back in Dresden with their two smallest children – the two-year-old Julie and the tragic little Emil, whose glandular condition was already alarming – they set out for Berlin. Here Schumann was to supervise preparations for a performance of *Das Paradies und die Peri*, while Clara was to give two recitals. At one she played Schumann's Piano Quintet, and to a private gathering his Piano Quartet, among the guests being the singer Henriette Sontag, Fanny Hensel, Mendelssohn's elder sister, Clara's long-standing friend and patron Count Redern, and the poet Emanuel Geibel.

After the unhappy experience of Vienna Berlin seemed a haven of friendliness and appreciation, especially for Clara. The reunion with her mother, who never lost her affection for Schumann and faithfully offered the young couple whatever support she could, brought a moment of great joy, while on a different plane she revelled in the company of the King and Queen of Prussia, the Duke of Mecklenburg and others of the nobility, Bettina von Arnim, the sculptor Schadow, the singer Pauline Viardot and other luminaries of the cultural establishment. Happy though they were to go back to their children, Dresden could not but seem staid and provincial in comparison.

In June 1847, for the first time in three years, Schumann's physical and mental condition permitted him to celebrate his birthday in something like traditional style, and the following month Zwickau honoured him with a special charity concert, at which he was invited to conduct his C major Symphony, the Piano Concerto – with Clara as soloist – and the recently completed *Beim Abschied zu singen* (Op. 84) for chorus and wind instruments. The Sunday after the concert, as they were walking through the town, a group of townsfolk suddenly appeared, blew a triple fanfare on their instruments and cheered them to the echo, while hundreds of others flocked to the scene and joined in the celebrations. 'It was like a carnival', wrote Schumann to the publisher Friedrich Whistling, 'and we were fêted as never before, which, coming from my own town, filled me with delight'.

A picture of Schumann's daily round at this time was given by the housekeeper Fräulein Emilie Steffen to Frederick Niecks, when he was collecting material for his biography of Schumann in the late 1880s. He led an ordered life with regular habits, said Fräulein Steffen. He would work through the morning, then often take a walk with Clara; after lunch he returned to his work until six in the evening, when he repaired to Dauch's tavern nearby for a glass of beer and a perusal of the day's newspapers. By eight he was back home for supper. Clara usually spent these two hours practising. Old Fräulein Steffen remembered him as withdrawn and usually absorbed in thought but also as a devoted paterfamilias who found time to show little gestures of affection and appreciation to the members of his household, including Fräulein Steffen herself.

Yet relatively stable and relaxed though Schumann's health and state of mind had for the moment become, he managed to produce very little music in the course of the year – a revision of the final scene from Goethe's *Faust* originally written three years earlier, the short choral piece *Beim Abschied zu singen*, a piano trio (No. 1 in D minor, Op. 63) and a handful of songs. In a sudden moment of inspiration in April he sketched the overture to his opera *Genoveva*, but it was eight months before he wrote another note of the work.

The end of 1847 also brought two moments of special sadness. One was the departure of Ferdinand Hiller for Düsseldorf, where he had been appointed director of music. Hiller, just one year younger than Schumann, enjoyed an effortless popularity wherever he lived and worked. Born into well-to-do circumstances, he had been a friend of Berlioz, Chopin and Liszt in Paris in the 1830s, and was regularly in the company of Schumann and Mendelssohn in Leipzig, where he conducted the Gewandhaus concerts in the 1843–4 season. In Dresden he made his comfortable home a centre of musical activity where Wagner, for one, felt very much at ease. Among his composition pupils at the Conservatoire in Cologne, which he founded in 1850 and where he died, were Engelbert Humperdinck and Max Bruch.

But a greater shock, which coincided almost to the day with Hiller's departure, was the death of Mendelssohn. On 1 November Niels Gade, the current conductor of the Gewandhaus orchestra, arrived from Leipzig with the news that Mendelssohn, who was a mere thirty-eight, had had a stroke – the third in two weeks. 'He has no fever, Gade says', noted Schumann in his diary, 'but his speech is incoherent, and the doctors are at a loss what to do. People in Leipzig are very worried about him but we all hope it will pass over'. Three days later he was dead. Only a few months earlier his sister Fanny, to whom Clara in particular had become attached in Berlin, had also died of a stroke. 'Our grief is intense', wrote Schumann –

for we valued him not only as an artist but also as a man and a friend. His death is an incalculable loss to all who knew and loved him. A thousand fond memories spring to mind, making one want to exclaim 'Why has Heaven done such a thing?' Yet to be snatched away in one's prime and at the peak of one's power – should one not be happy to die thus? – But if I were to review all the qualities that endeared him to us, I should never finish. I feel as though our grief over his death will last as long as we live.

Two days later, in the curt, mnemonic style that he used in his diary, he recorded his visit to Leipzig to pay his last respects:

In M's house – his children playing with their dolls downstairs – the dead man, noble soul – his brow – his lips – the smile on them – he looked like a glorious warrior, like a conqueror, as though some 20 years older than those still alive – two veins standing out prominently on his head – laurel wreaths and palms.

The following afternoon, 7 November, 'a mild, spring-like day', Schumann joined the five other pallbearers to carry Mendelssohn's body from his home in the Königstrasse to the Pauliner Kirche – on the right Schumann, Moscheles and Gade, on the left Moritz Hauptmann, cantor of the Thomasschule in Leipzig and teacher at the Conservatoire, Ferdinand David, leader of the Gewandhaus orchestra, and Julius Rietz, also a teacher at the Conservatoire. As the cortege moved slowly through the crowd-lined streets on its hour-long journey, two instrumental ensembles each played in turn the March in E minor from Book V of the *Songs without Words*. At the service in the church the choir sang two choruses from *Saul* and, as a last farewell, the final chorale from Bach's St Matthew Passion. After the funeral the body, watched over by David, was taken in a special train to Berlin and buried in the family vault in the Alter Dreifaltigkeitsfriedhof, near the Hallesches Tor.

With his prosperous background, his prodigious gifts and the ease with which he moved in the ranks of German and foreign nobility, Mendelssohn had been the idol of many and the envy of most. For Schumann, who so often started from a consciousness of his own inferiority in the public mind, it had sometimes been difficult to keep his admiration free from thoughts of his own under-privileged status. Mendelssohn, he knew, was so much more versatile, so much more effective. Nor could he help knowing that Mendelssohn did not greatly care for some of the larger works by which he set great store, such as the Piano Concerto and the C major Symphony. But the sense of impoverishment to his own life and to the musical scene in general went deep.

The presence of death around him always affected Schumann's ability to work, and for the rest of November he had little to show. Shortly before Christmas, however, he regained a serenity of mind in which to take up again the large-scale project that had lain fallow since the summer, a project with which he struggled, with furious energy but also with persistent anxiety, to complete over the coming months – his opera *Genoveva*.

From the period when his mind had been utterly absorbed in the task of setting words to music, the wonderful 'Liederjahr' of 1840, Schumann constantly returned to the prospect of writing an opera. At that time he was turning with bewildering rapidity from one poem to the next, from one poet to another. 'I have again written so much', he once told Clara, 'that it sometimes seems quite uncanny'. In this mood of enthusiasm he contemplated again an opera based on the story *Doge and Dogaresse* by his beloved E.T.A. Hoffmann, and spent many hours trying to put together a scenario and a satisfactory libretto, but failed and never returned to the idea.

In the course of the next few years he approached a number of writers with requests for texts, and in 1844 actually began work on Oswald Marbach's libretto from Byron's *The Corsair*, but hardly got beyond the opening chorus. His Project Book lists a host of subjects that he considered suitable for operatic treatment –

Faust, Till Eulenspiegel, the Nibelungenlied, the singers' contest on the Wartburg, Abelard and Heloise, Maria Stuart, Kalidasa's Hindu drama Sakontala, the Peasants' Revolt of 1525, the Blacksmith of Gretna Green and many more. His thoughts even strayed towards Arthurian legend, and he was somewhat put out when Wagner suddenly produced his text of *Lohengrin* in 1845: 'For a year or so I had been contemplating a work on this very subject, or at least a similar one from the age of the Round Table – but now I can throw it in the fire'.

In the spring of 1847 he came across the five-act tragedy *Genoveva*, written four years earlier by Friedrich Hebbel, a dramatist who invested his characters with a powerful psychological realism. He also found an earlier, very different drama on the same subject by the romantic poet Ludwig Tieck, on which he now also drew, asking the poet and painter Robert Reinick, whom he had come to know in Dresden, to assemble a libretto from the two works. Reinick made two drafts but Schumann rejected them both as creating too sentimental a story, and ventured to approach Hebbel himself for advice. Hebbel, as it happened, was planning a visit to Dresden that summer, and Schumann eagerly sought a meeting with 'the greatest genius of our day', as he called him.

In effect it was a non-meeting. Hebbel wrote that Schumann suddenly turned up, said he was delighted to make his acquaintance and asked whether he could be of any assistance. 'Yes, you can,' replied Hebbel. 'Can you tell me where I can find the nearest cab? I'm in a hurry'. If he had had the time, he later wrote to Princess Marie Wittgenstein, he would have advised Schumann to follow the original legend for his *Genoveva*, rather than adapt Tieck's drama or his own. Even the brevity of their encounter had shown Hebbel that he would scarcely have found Schumann a congenial companion. 'I could not have behaved otherwise towards him,' he confessed in the same letter, 'because he was not only determined in the way he kept silent but was unpleasant about it as well, seeming not to listen either'.

So, not surprisingly, Hebbel showed little interest in associating himself with any opera based on his play, and in the end Schumann made his own arbitrary use of Reinick's drafts to produce a work described simply as 'Opera in 4 Acts after L. Tieck and F. Hebbel'. Wagner, to whom he proudly showed his libretto, did not think much of it, but the suspicious and hypersensitive Schumann resented Wagner's criticism, thinking, said Wagner later, 'that I was trying to ruin his most effective moments'. So he persisted, for better or for worse, with his own version. Act One he completed in a flush of enthusiasm in a mere ten days over Christmas 1847 and New Year 1848, Act Two between January 21 and February 4. Two and a half months later he went back to the work, writing Act Three between April 24 and May 3, and Act Four between June 15 and 27. After the final double bar stands the inscription *'Vollendet den 4ten August 1848'*.

The whole opera, therefore, text and music, was written in a series of sudden bursts in little more than a year from the moment he first encountered Hebbel's play. And the very same day that he orchestrated the final chorus, he started work on a new dramatic project, the melodrama *Manfred*. Small wonder that, looking back on these periods of intense creativity and on the moments of triumphant exhaustion that followed them, Schumann called 1848 his 'most fruitful year'. Small wonder too that he counted it something of a miracle to have found the strength and the concentration to finish *Genoveva* without collapsing under the strain. 'I lost every melody as soon as I had thought of it', he later wrote, 'and what I heard inside my head took too much out of me'.

The legend of Geneviève of Brabant is a typical example of the widespread story – versions are found in French, Scottish and Scandinavian ballads, as well as in English and German sources – of the chaste wife falsely accused of infidelity, repudiated and condemned to death by her husband, then finally reconciled with him when her innocence is proven and the villain who has slandered her is killed. In Hebbel's drama it is the psychology of this villain, Golo, servant of Genoveva's husband, the Pfalzgraf Siegfried, that holds the centre of attention, whereas Tieck concentrates on the scenes of the narrative legend itself, above all those in which mysterious and supernatural elements dominate.

In trying to put together his libretto, Schumann found himself caught between these two totally different interpretations of the subject matter. In intellectual terms, the terms of psychological motivation, Hebbel's intense, almost grim drama gave him a satisfaction that he would have dearly sought to convey, even to intensify, through his music. On the other hand the episodic panorama of scenes assembled by Tieck, allusive and associative in style rather than soberly consequential, had an atmospheric quality that appealed to his sense of the impulsively imaginative and colourful.

The result is an unnatural compromise. The stuff of drama was not in Schumann's blood, either as a writer or as a composer, and while the flights of fancy stimulated by the romantic motifs in the story allowed his imagination to roam freely, the achievement of a firm delineation of character in the principal roles lay beyond him. In consequence the conflict of principles and personalities on which drama depends, be it spoken drama or music drama, is not there, and the work's power of survival is undermined from the outset.

Hanslick, who broke more than one lance for Schumann's music and praised where praise was due, summarized the matter with characteristic bluntness, revealing not only the problem about *Genoveva* but also how it reflects the personality of its creator:

It all corresponds to the romantic in Schumann – the medieval atmosphere, miracles and mysticism, Christian piety, even reminiscences of folksong ... Schumann's libretto is weak and uninteresting, particularly in its characterization of the main figures. Without Hebbel's keen psychological motivation Golo has turned into a conventional theatrical villain, Genoveva into a long-suffering bore, and Graf Siegried into a simpleton. As for the music, it suffers from the central, incurable condition of being undramatic. Whole passages from Golo's or Siegried's part could be transferred to Genoveva, or vice versa, without making the slightest difference, so similar is everything.

The melodic line is almost entirely lacking in plasticity, while the poverty of the rhythm is even more striking – wherever one opens the score one sees in the vocal parts row upon row of notes of equal value, or arranged in regular patterns, generally crotchets. The very sight of the page puts one off with its lack of varied note-values and rhythmic contrasts. The best part of the opera is that which has nothing to do with the stage at all, namely the Overture.

Hanslick concludes, remorselessly yet sadly:

Genoveva bears the unmistakable marks of the brooding manner and the agonizing lack of concentration that characterize Schumann's third period, features that can be proven by reference to the excessive appoggiaturas, syncopations, pedal points, the weakness of the rhythm and the melodic line, and other points of detail.

The undramatic nature of *Genoveva*, the sameness of its music over a span of action that calls for psychological and emotional differentiation, underlies what contemporary writers said about the first performance. Franz Brendel, for instance, writing in the *Neue Zeitschrift für Musik*, complained of the 'absence of light and shade', as a result of which 'our sensitivity becomes dulled'. Johann Christian Lobe, editor of the *Allgemeine musikalische Zeitung*, still the most prestigious musical journal of the day, described each act, despite its division into numbers, as 'a single through-composed song', and drew the same conclusion as Brendel:

To treat every aspect of a through-composed opera as of equal importance is bound to lead to monotony, and weary both the ear and the mind. This neglect of dramatic considerations must strike the neutral observer as a lack of experience in such matters rather than as an inspired innovation.

But so preoccupied was Schumann with thoughts of drama that he turned with barely a pause from *Genoveva* to a subject that had lain in his mind since his student days – Byron's *Manfred*.

It is not difficult to see what attracted him to Byron's 'Dramatic Poem in 3 Acts', with its overtones of the Faust story, its Shakespearean mixture of blank verse and rhyme, its interplay of earthly characters and supernatural spirits, and the atmosphere of romantic extravagance and legend that envelops the medieval hero, illegitimate son of the great Holy Roman Emperor

Frederick II. As a literary work, it is just what Byron called it – a poem, to be read, not a drama to be performed. It has no plot, no consequential action, but consists of a web of psychological musings and quasi-philosophical reveries spun round the gloomy hero who is caught in an ineluctable but only partly revealed syndrome of sin and guilt. In the end death has mercy on him, and as he lies in the monastery, he murmurs to the Abbot: 'Old man – 'tis not so difficult to die'.

Radically abridging and adapting Byron's text in the German translation by a Silesian pastor called Karl von Suckow, Schumann composed music to fifteen separate, mainly short numbers, preceded by an Overture. His treatment is not operatic, however, but rather in the nature of incidental music, and the result is a kind of melodrama. There are musical choruses for various groups of spirits but Manfred himself does not sing – he declaims his words against the orchestral and choral accompaniment. The Overture and the first section of four numbers were finished in November 1848, the remaining numbers, in two further sections, the following spring.

One cannot but understand Schumann's choice of Byron's poem as a form of self-identification with its confused and tormented hero, driven to distraction by the spirits whose presence he has commanded. 'On no other work did I lavish so much love and devote so much strength as Manfred', he said later. Wasielewski recalls how, as Schumann was reading Byron's poem aloud a few years after, his voice suddenly faltered, his eyes filled with tears, and he was so overcome with emotion that he could not continue. Richard Pohl, a young man who helped Schumann with some of the poetic texts he later set, remembered him conducting the Overture at a Gewandhaus concert in 1852:

He was deeply serious; utterly absorbed in the score, quite forgetting the audience and paying little heed even to the players of the orchestra, he lived in his music, identified himself with his task, became himself Manfred, so to speak. I felt that this, more perhaps than any other work, had been written with his heart's blood, that here he had spoken to us from his innermost soul.

Putting such reminiscences together, and reflecting on what we now know of his physical and psychological condition, we can feel the sinister significance he found in the words of Hamlet that Byron set at the head of his poem:

> There are more things in heaven and earth, Horatio,
> Than are dreamt of in your philosophy.

It was Schumann's declared intention to have the work performed on the stage. Since Byron had had no such thoughts, and since Schumann's inability to present theatrically dramatic characters was manifest, the idea becomes doubly incongruous. Yet in 1852 no less a person than Liszt took it upon himself to present it in the Weimar Court Theatre as a drama-with-music, and a few other towns later followed his example. But there was little chance that it could establish itself in this form. The essence of the work – which in any case barely extended to forty pages of short score – is contained in the Overture, itself the only extensively developed piece of music among the sixteen separate choral and orchestral numbers.

Curiously enough, six years earlier, after finishing *Der fliegende Holländer*, Wagner had written the prose draft of a five-act opera on the same subject. He called it *Die Sarazenin (The Saracen Woman)*, developing an episode in Manfred's life that he had come across in an historical work. It is hard to believe that Wagner did not know Byron's poem, but he makes no mention of Byron at this point in his autobiography, and his draft is for an expansive dramatic work far removed from the brooding, inward-looking world of Byron and Schumann.

Less than a day separated Schumann's completion of *Genoveva* and his absorption in the poem of *Manfred*. But between preparing his text and starting on the music, he composed, in a mere fourteen days, the forty or so little piano pieces that comprise the *Album für die Jugend* (Op. 68) – music as far from the world of romantic drama as one can imagine, and both the first and best-known of a number of his works designed for educational use.

A didactic strain formed part of Schumann's personality. It was less overtly and consistently in evidence than, say, in Wagner or Berlioz, perhaps also than in Mendelssohn, but it could take very precise and concrete forms. The whole enterprise of the *Neue Zeitschrift für Musik*, devoted to the education of public taste and the elevation of musical standards, had rested on a didactic premiss. Now, at the other end of the educational spectrum, so to speak, and through the immediate stimulus of the needs of his own children, he turned his mind for the first of a number of moments – though they were only moments – to the theoretical and practical instruction of the proverbial 'young musician'. 'The pieces that children usually learn in their piano lessons', wrote Clara in the family diary, 'are so bad that it occurred to Robert to publish an album of such little pieces of his own'.

There were now four children in the Schumann household, of whom the two eldest, Marie and Lischen (Elise), aged seven and five, were already of an age to need such pieces. Julie was three, while little Ludwig, who had been born at the beginning of that year, was not yet one. The following year, 1849, he put together twenty-eight songs in a *Liederalbum für die Jugend* (Op. 79), while among his last works is a set of three piano sonatas 'für die Jugend' (Op. 118), each dedicated to one of his three daughters.

The forty-three little pieces of the *Jugendalbum*, divided into a group for beginners and a group for more advanced players, have found their way into instructional collections the world over. In Schumann's original plan, however, they were to be supplemented by extracts from works of other composers, from Bach to Spohr. Moreover in the sketch-book that contains the majority of the published pieces Schumann also jotted down a number of the *Musikalische Haus- und Lebensregeln* – 'Instructions to Young Musicians', as they are usually known in English – which he published on their own in the *Neue Zeitschrift* in 1850 and added to the second edition of his *Jugendalbum* the year after. His conception was thus of a composite educational exercise involving both precept and example, the training both of the intellectual and the physical faculties.

While the charm of these pieces is evident, and while they must be judged by the canon proper to the purpose for which they were written, the sense of a certain sameness soon creeps over one. This has its origin in features such as an excessive amount of repetition of phrases and motifs in the individual pieces, a degree of rhythmic monotony – not a single item is in triple measure – and a concentration on the near keys. Towards the end, at least, his notional 'more advanced' pupil might have profited from an introduction to a realm beyond that bounded by four sharps and three flats.

The *Jugendalbum*'s adhortatory companion, the *Musikalische Haus- und Lebensregeln*, offers a quaint pot-pourri of the entertaining, the obvious and the sage. 'See to it that your instrument is always in perfect tune' and 'Should anyone place a new composition in front of you and ask you to play it, first read it over' is advice close to the superfluous – though, by stating what should always be the case, it unwittingly reveals for the historical record what often was not the case. Other recommendations have a relevance as keen for the student of today as for the pupil in Schumann's mind. 'Practise thoroughly the fugues of the great masters, above all those of J.S. Bach; let the *Well-tempered Clavier* be your daily bread' – who would not say 'Amen' to this? Or: 'Never play bad compositions – and never listen to them unless absolutely obliged to do so'. And: 'Sing regularly in choirs, especially the middle parts. This will make you musical'.

Occasionally we confront a warning that all musicians might take to heart – especially critics: 'Do not judge a composition on a first hearing. That which pleases most at first is not always the best. Masters call for study'. And there are thoughts remarkably progressive for their time: 'Listen attentively to all folksongs. They are mines of beautiful melody and will give you an insight into the characteristics of the different nations'.

Schumann's practical energies also found an outlet at this time in the Dresden Choral Society, the 'Verein für Chorgesang', which he had a hand in founding at the beginning of 1848. This was a mixed choir of between sixty and seventy singers that grew out of the male-voice choir, the 'Liedertafel', which Hiller used to conduct. It met every Wednesday evening, and Clara accompanied at the piano.

Like the 'quartet mornings' he used to hold in his bachelor days in the 'Rotes Kolleg' in Leipzig, Schumann viewed the choir's meetings chiefly as occasions for the detailed study of classical and modern works, not as rehearsals for public concerts. He was in any case a diffident chorus-master and conductor, and his concern lay with the educative value, both for his choristers and for himself, of the works by Palestrina, Bach and Handel, as well as modern cantatas by Mendelssohn, Hiller and Gade, that he studied with them. The availability of a captive choir also led him to compose in the course of this and the following year a considerable number of part-songs for various combinations of voices, and three extended works for chorus and orchestra, including a setting of Rückert's *Adventlied* (Op. 71). Clara, meanwhile, though at the beck and call of her four young children, and anxious to create an atmosphere in the apartment that her husband would find conducive to his work, still had a handful of pupils and managed to give an occasional recital in the course of the year.

In March 1848, with Schumann in a state of exhaustion after composing Act Two of *Genoveva* in a mere fourteen days, an incident occurred – erupted, one might rather say – in the family circle which, far from bringing the pleasure it was expected to, caused general embarrassment and started the disintegration of what had been a warm, almost ardent relationship. This was the unexpected arrival in Dresden of Liszt.

Liszt was on his way from Vienna to Weimar to take up his first post as Kapellmeister to the Grand Duke Karl Alexander. First he presented himself to the surprised but gratified Wagner in the spacious official apartment in the elegant Ostra-Allee, where he lived with his wife Minna. Then, similarly unannounced, he appeared before the startled Schumanns in their far more modest rooms in the Waisenhausstrasse, some half a mile away. Schumann's admiration for the great virtuoso might have waned a little since their first meeting in 1840 but he felt both the pleasure and the compliment of the visit, and Clara hurriedly arranged a party for that same evening in his honour. At Liszt's request, Schumann's D minor Piano Trio was to be played at the party by Clara, Ferdinand David and Johann Grabau, principal cellist of the Gewandhaus orchestra. The painters Eduard Bendemann and Julius Hübner were among the hastily invited guests. So too was Wagner, who left his own account of the occasion.

When the appointed time arrived, all the guests were present except the Prince of Denmark. They waited almost two hours, then, in irritation, the performers started on the first item of their programme, Beethoven's Trio in D major. 'As we reached the last page', wrote Clara in her diary, 'the door suddenly flew open and Liszt rushed in'. Having finished the Beethoven, the players turned to Schumann's trio, which Liszt much enjoyed. They then played his Piano Quintet, but over the meal that followed, Liszt rather disparagingly described the work as 'a bit Leipzig-like', which strained the already tense atmosphere still further. He then sat down at the piano himself 'and proceeded to play so abominably', said Clara, 'that I felt utterly ashamed at having to stay and listen, instead of leaving the room at once, as Bendemann did'.

In the wild and unpredictable manner characteristic of him, Liszt then launched into a disquisition on the relative merits of Meyerbeer and Mendelssohn, to the latter's disadvantage, although he was well aware of the affection and admiration that Schumann had for Mendelssohn. This was too much for the already sorely tried Schumann. Jumping to his feet in rage, he shouted at Liszt: 'Meyerbeer is a nonentity compared with Mendelssohn! Mendelssohn's influence has been felt over the whole world, and you would do better to hold your tongue!' With this he stormed out of the room.

Perplexed rather than offended, Liszt looked round at his fellow-guests and tried to make light of the incident, but their expressions showed him that he had stretched their tolerance to breaking-point. Taking leave of his confused and offended hostess, he said: 'Madam, tell your husband that he is the only man in the world I would allow to talk to me like that'.

Clara vowed to have nothing more to do with him. Schumann's anger eventually subsided, whilst Liszt, having suggested that Schumann's *Faust* music might appropriately be performed at the Weimar Goethe Centennial in 1849, also came to Leipzig for the première of *Genoveva* in November 1850. But a certain distrust and resentment persisted, and the old admiration and sincerity never came back.

After this unhappy episode Schumann turned his attention to the remaining acts of *Genoveva*, then, with a pause for the *Album für die Jugend*, to *Manfred*. And so, with the intervening periods of nervous exhaustion which were now an ineradicable feature of his condition, he moved into the year 1849 feeling that slowly but surely he was consolidating his reputation and extending his formal range. His domestic life was serene and settled. He had no wish, like Wagner, to hold public position in Dresden or anywhere else, and he was satisfied to live for his composition.

But there were events going on in the world outside that made him look up from his piano, political events that thrust themselves upon him not only emotionally and intellectually but physically. These events reached their climax in the Dresden Revolt of May 1849.

Throughout the year of 1848 Europe had been in the grip of revolution. The movement for liberal reform started in France, but that it travelled so fast and so far, and that leaders like Louis-Philippe and the Austrian chancellor Metternich gave in so quickly, showed how widespread was the expectation of, and resignation to, revolt. Unlike France, which was a single political unit under central metropolitan rule, Germany at this time consisted of thirty-nine self-governing units of very different size and character, some urban, some rural, some prosperous, some impoverished, some liberal and progressive to a degree, the majority inward-looking and conservative. In all of them, however, the dynastic principle prevailed, so that attempts, modelled on those in France, to establish in each state a constitution and an elected assembly brought about little substantive change, and the sources of effective power stayed in the same hands as before.

In May 1848 elected representatives from the individual German states, among them some of the most eminent intellectuals of the day, met in the Paulskirche in Frankfurt to work out a constitution for a national state that did not yet exist – a new, unified Germany. Because the only power they had was the power to talk, they failed. They had no conception, as Marx and Engels had in their Communist Manifesto published this same year, of how to broaden the base of their movement and carry the masses with them. The Frankfurt Assembly was left as a brave monument to the idealistic futility of intellectual revolution, revolution in the mind, and by the summer of the following year the last traces of projected radical reform had been swept away. When unification finally came to Germany in 1871 it was through authoritarianism, through war, the 'blood and iron' of Bismarck, not through the rose-tinted humanistic ideals of romantic liberalism.

But hopeless as the chances of the revolution were, the events and trends of thought of 1848 passed no thinking man by. The Berlin uprising in March found its way into the Schumanns' diary, and Clara recorded that her husband and Eduard Bendemann engaged each other in a discussion on the question of Prussia and Schleswig-Holstein 'which almost turned into a quarrel'. Clara herself also became involved in political arguments, upsetting many of her acquaintances with her sympathy for the new, progressive ideas. 'It is sad to see how few really liberal-minded people there are among the educated classes,' she wrote. In May, in the salon of the famous Hôtel de Saxe in Leipzig, she took part with the actor Eduard Devrient and the popular soprano Johanna Wagner, Richard Wagner's niece, in a charity concert to raise funds for the Poles in their struggle for national independence.

'Everything that goes on in the world – politics, literature, people – concerns me', Schumann once said. And, as long ago as 1827, when a schoolboy of only seventeen: 'Political freedom is what nurtures true literature and what poetry most needs for its unfolding. True literature – literature, that is, which inspires passion in the soul of the public at large – can never flourish in a land ruled by bondage and slavery'. Three years later, in his travel-diary for 1830, he copied out the text of the revolutionary song known as the 'Strasbourg Lord's Prayer' and noted the names of the towns where there had been uprisings in the wake of the Paris revolution of that year.

To be sure, he never had the intense practical involvement in politics that took his neighbour, Wagner, on to the streets in the name of the revolution and forced him into exile as a political refugee. But his sympathies, like Clara's, lay no less clearly on the side of the reformers, while being tempered, as Wagner's were not, by a fear of 'the terrible revolution that is threatening to descend upon us', as he put it. His three part-songs (without opus number and only published in 1913) to patriotic texts by Freiligrath, Ulrich and Fürst reflect these sympathies. So also do the four so-called 'Barricade' Marches (Op. 76) for piano, composed the following year, which he called 'republican' in spirit, adding: 'I knew of no better way to give vent to my feelings of excitement: the pieces were written in a moment of intense passion'. It may be passion that these marches convey, or it may be a rather strained pomposity. At all events they make the pianist wish he had more than two hands.

Out walking one day with his friend Count Wolf Baudissin, diplomat and writer, Schumann found the conversation turning towards the political situation. Baudissin, one of those well-to-do conservatives branded by Clara as lacking a liberal understanding of the *Zeitgeist*, embarked on a long justification of the constitutional monarchy as the surest guarantee of equity and stability in the state. From time to time Schumann nodded, as though carried along by the argument, but his thoughts must have long been straying elsewhere. For when Baudissin finally asked whether he had convinced him, Schumann suddenly turned to him and blurted out: 'No – a republic is the best form of government!'

On 3 April 1849 a deputation from the Frankfurt Assembly went to Berlin to ask King Friedrich Wilhelm IV of Prussia to accept the crown of a new, parliamentary German Reich as hereditary head of state. He refused. He would not, he said, 'pick up a crown from the gutter' at the request of a motley group of citizens who were offering him something that was not theirs to offer. Only crowned heads could bestow crowns. And this the rulers of Germany's separate states, still clinging hopefully to their autonomous power, declined to do. By rejecting the proposed new imperial crown, the King of Prussia rejected the proposed new parliamentary constitution. Saxony was one of the twenty-nine states that had individually agreed to the constitution, but the King of Saxony now destroyed it in his own way by dissolving the Saxon state assembly and calling on Prussia to send troops to help deal with any popular protest that might break out.

And break out it did. On 3 May the citizens of Dresden, capital of the kingdom, took to the streets and were met by the Saxon infantry. Barricades went up and arms were hastily distributed among the civilians; those who could not get hold of a weapon wrenched up paving-stones and climbed on to the barricades. A determined band of insurgents, moving from house to house in search of recruits, came to the Waisenhausstrasse and demanded that Schumann should join them. When Clara assured them that he was not there, they threatened to go out and look for him. After they had left, Schumann, Clara and their eldest daughter Marie slipped out of the back door of the house, through the garden – there was no time to collect the other children, who were left with the housekeeper – and hurried to the railway station. By train and coach they made their way to Maxen, country seat of their old friend Major Serre, where others had also sought refuge.

As news of the fighting in Dresden reached Maxen, Clara, who was seven months pregnant, feared for the safety of the children she had left behind. Had Schumann ventured back into the city, he would have found himself press-ganged into the revolutionary ranks, so two days later, despite the danger, Clara travelled back alone, passing streams of refugees and threading her way through the confusion of the fighting. Back in her house, she hastily dressed Elise, Julie and the baby Ludwig, packed a few things and within an hour had started back to Maxen.

On 9 May the army, unable to break down the barricades, began to bombard the city from the surrounding hills with their artillery, and the rebels withdrew. Clara wrote in her diary:

We heard of terrible atrocities committed by the troops. They mowed down all the insurgents they laid eyes on. Our landlady in Dresden told us later that her brother, who owned the 'Goldner Hirsch' inn in the Scheffelgasse, was made to watch while the soldiers shot twenty-six students, one after the other, that they had found there. Then we heard they had thrown dozens of people out of third- and fourth-floor windows on to the street below. It is horrible to have to live through such things. This is the way people are made to fight for their scrap of freedom. When will the time come when all men have equal rights? How was it possible for the belief that the aristocrats were somehow a different race from the rest of the people to remain so firmly entrenched for so long?

By the evening of that day the rebels gave in and the fighting stopped. The revolt had lasted a mere five days.

Clara could not understand how her father, who had lived through all these events in the city, could remain so indifferent to the political and human problems they caused, and she filled page after page of her diary with her thoughts and experiences. A walk with Schumann a few days later past the scenes of the fighting left a deep impression:

It is hardly possible to give a picture of the desolation. They have left thousands of holes in the buildings and whole walls have been blown in; the old opera house is totally gutted, so are three fine houses in the Zwingerstrasse. It is a terrible sight, and I shudder to think what the houses look like inside. The rebels broke down many of the walls between the houses in order to communicate with each other. The Frauenkirche is packed with prisoners – some 500 of them. Most of the streets have been pulled up, paving-stones are lying everywhere, and only the barricades have been cleared away. The city is swarming with Prussian soldiers, many of them lying on straw in the market square, and the place is in a state of siege.

The news that warrants had been issued for the arrest of Wagner, the architect Gottfried Semper and other rebel leaders filled Clara with dismay. Yet Schumann, in what has the character of oblivion to the tragic events around him, had tapped a vein of creativity richer than almost any he had known before and certainly than he was ever to know again. In a rare concentration of mind made possible by a state of psychological equilibrium that extended, miraculously, over almost the whole of 1849, he composed one work after another in an astonishing range of forms and for a remarkable variety of musical forces. As early as April he wrote to Hiller: 'I have been working very hard all this time – it is my most productive year, as though the conflicts in the world outside drove me in upon myself, giving me a power with which to counter the terrible events that we were made to witness'. And at the end of the year, knowing that *carpe diem* was the only motto by which he could live: 'I have been extremely busy the whole year. One has to work as long as the daylight is there'.

In the months before the rebellion forced him out of Dresden, the sight of this 'daylight' led Schumann to the completion of the *Manfred* music and to exercises with new combinations of instruments. Alongside the nine pleasant little *Waldszenen* for piano (Op. 82) and various groups of part-songs to texts by Goethe, Eichendorff, Mörike and others, he composed the three tuneful, if not particularly distinguished *Fantasiestücke* for clarinet and piano (Op. 73), the 5 *Stücke im Volkston* for cello and piano (Op. 102) and two works for horn – the Adagio and Allegro for horn and piano (Op. 70) and the *Konzertstück* for four horns and orchestra (Op. 86).

This last, virtually a three-movement concertino, is one of the most vivacious and extrovert of all Schumann's works, and he himself regarded it as one of his best. The character of the solo instruments inevitably imposes fairly firm limitations on the content that such a form will bear; it also restricts the range of sonorities, since, unlike the piano and the violin, the sounds of the horn emerge naturally from the middle register of the orchestra and thus have greater difficulty in setting themselves in individualized relief against the body of orchestral sound behind them. In the *Konzertstück*, moreover, not only do the solo instruments usually play in concert, but they are also in almost continuous action from beginning to end, so that lively – and extremely demanding – though the horn parts are, they tend to merge with the orchestra as *primi inter pares* to produce a single texture of sound. But it is cheerful and extremely attractive sound.

Each of these opus numbers was sketched in a day or two and completed equally quickly. Schumann wrote the date and place of composition on the fair copy of each manuscript as he finished it, so that we have an almost day-by-day record of his remarkable productivity.

Nor did the 'daylight', as he called it, dim when the outbreak of the rebellion forced him out of Dresden in May. First in Maxen, then in the nearby village of Kreischa, where conditions were quieter, he continued composing with hardly a break, now chiefly part-songs and choral items again. Back with Clara and their children in Dresden the following month, he composed the Three Marches for Pianoforte (Op. 76) and the three Romances for Oboe and Piano (Op. 94), set poems by Rückert, Hebbel and Byron, and sketched in a mere three days the Introduction and Allegro appassionato for Piano and Orchestra (Op. 92), a work that has only rarely emerged from the shadow of the Piano Concerto.

A song-writer's choice of poets reveals not only what attracts him as raw material, so to speak, for his musical purposes, but also the themes, emotions, attitudes of mind, even philosophies to which he responds in conceptual terms. If his values and sympathies change, so will the poetic message to which he feels most immediately drawn, and the nature of this message will have its significance for his spiritual biography.

In his great 'Liederjahr' of 1840 it had been above all the poets of romanticism – Heine, Eichendorff, Chamisso, Rückert, Burns – to whom Schumann turned. He set almost forty poems by Heine alone in that year. Yet after 1841 he never returned to him. Instead, from his Dresden years onwards he discovered the clear-cut, unsentimental, often classicistic poetry of Mörike and, even more strikingly, the psychological realism of Friedrich Hebbel. Hebbel's dramas – he specifically mentions *Judith* and *Maria Magdalene* – were among the literary works he read in the course of 1847; the starting-point for his opera *Genoveva* was Hebbel's play, while the *Nachtlied* for chorus and orchestra and the declamatory ballads *Schön Hedwig* and *Ballade vom Haidenknaben* are also settings of Hebbel. This predilection for the intense, penetrating, often gloomy poet from the northern harshness of Schleswig-Holstein, spokesman for a philosophy of inescapable fate and the tragic conflict between man and the universe, shows how far Schumann has travelled since the days when his ideal world had been bounded by the whimsical romanticism of Jean Paul, sentimental novelist of the warm, gentle south.

Perhaps in a more profound sense, however, Schumann's final

year in Dresden stood under the sign of Goethe. That Germany's greatest writer is also the poet whose verses have been most often set to music is as it should be. Schumann, for his part, returned to Goethe time and again from the moment when he set 'Der Fischer' as a schoolboy. The extraordinary range and depth of Goethe's poetry, from nature worship and erotic delight to mystery and suffering, from the rebellious exuberance of romantic youth to the mellow serenity of classical poise, elicits a response that fluctuates with the reader's mood, circumstance, age, need, yet never relinquishes a power to minister and to inspire.

At this moment it was Goethe the portrayer of grief and spiritual conflict, quietly persistent in his revelation of tragic undertones and harrowing emotions, who held Schumann's mind. During his weeks in Kreischa, away from the turmoil of political revolt, he had devoted himself to Goethe's *Wilhelm Meister* and begun to set the popular Mignon lyrics and the 'Lieder des Harfners' as solo songs. He then turned to the Requiem sung over Mignon's body near the end of the novel, and composed on this prose text a short cantata for soloists, chorus and orchestra, which Clara described, when he played it to her, as 'profoundly moving'. The nine songs and the *Requiem for Mignon* together make up Schumann's Op. 98.

These songs of 1849 and 1850 are very different from the cycles of the 'Liederjahr' – different in being declamatory, sometimes almost operatic in vocal manner, with dislocated, non-verbal rhythms; different in their degree of chromatic melody and harmony; different in their creation of thematic unity through the use of leitmotif; different above all in their creation of an atmosphere, instantly felt but difficult to describe, that seems charged with a power of disintegration, of near-incoherence, the product of a mind desperately close to losing its way and barely able to cling to its self-awareness. The *Requiem für Mignon* too, which treats Goethe's text with the same freedom, not to say licence, as Schumann claimed in his songs, leaves a strangely shadowy impression, a mixture of the conventional, sometimes even the awkward, and the innovatory, the innovation leading along a path whose course he can only imperfectly see.

From *Wilhelm Meister* Schumann returned to *Faust*, the final scene of which (Part Three of the completed work) he had composed in 1848. He now added the three scenes of Part One, which include those depicting Gretchen's anguish before the image of the Virgin Mary and later in the cathedral. Two days after he had finished these and played them to an ever-thrilled Clara, a third son was born to her, christened Ferdinand.

28 August 1849 marked the centennial of Goethe's birth. Unexpectedly a moment of public recognition came Schumann's way, all the more gratifying for its unexpectedness, when, as part of the celebrations, he was given the opportunity of having the closing scene of his *Faust* music performed in three places: Dresden, Weimar – on Liszt's suggestion – and Leipzig, at the request of the publisher Härtel. The young Hans von Bülow, who was at this time under the spell of Liszt, brought news that the performance in Weimar had been warmly received, while in Dresden too, where the Goethean programme also included Mendelssohn's *Walpurgisnacht*, Schumann's piece made a considerable impression. The part of Faust was taken by Anton Mitterwurzer, the baritone who had played Wolfram von Eschenbach in the first performance of Wagner's *Tannhäuser* four years earlier, and who sang Kurwenal in the première of *Tristan und Isolde* in 1865.

But whatever satisfaction such an occasion brought him – Clara was still more sensitive in such matters – it could not conceal the cold fact that, although he had lived and worked in Dresden for five years, he was as much an outsider in the eyes of the Saxon establishment as he had been at the beginning. When, for example, he approached Baron August von Lüttichau, director of the Royal Opera, to ask whether as well-known figures in the musical world he and Clara might be given complimentary seats, the Baron replied that such concessions were only granted to musicians who worked directly for the opera house.

In the face of a snub like this Schumann lost what little remained of his desire to become absorbed, in his own right, into the cultural life of the city. At the beginning he had looked to friends to put in a word for him with the King, and when Wagner was forced to flee the country after the rebellion in May, the post he vacated, Schumann thought, might still be one for him. But now no longer. When his old friend Ferdinand Hiller wrote unexpectedly from Düsseldorf towards the end of the year to say that he was on the point of giving up his job as orchestral director there, and would Schumann be interested in becoming his successor, the Fates seemed to have taken the decision into their own hands.

By this time, after a year of unprecedented activity during which he had completed over thirty compositions, he had again worked his musical imagination into a state of exhaustion. The register of compositions that he meticulously kept shows no entries at all for the first three months of 1850. When, in April, his powers returned, he put them to the completion of the last two (Nos 5 and 6) of his *Scenes from Goethe's Faust*. The Overture that prefaces the six scenes was not written for another three years.

Schumann's astonishing productivity during 1848 and 1849 – indeed, the frenetic intensity with which he filled every lucid, unconfused moment of his years in Dresden – is fissured with the ominous signs of a mind barely in control of itself. The sudden swings from elation to despair, from a quiet harmony with his surroundings to a suspicious withdrawal into his chosen loneliness, are companions of the manic-depressive syndrome that is an unchanging feature of his temperament from his student days onwards. And that in moments of clarity and exhilaration his creative urges, held otherwise in subjection, should burst forth with all the greater intensity is a natural concomitant of such a condition.

But that the quality of this creativity should be so uneven; that so little of it is truly original and memorable, so much, especially in the larger forms by which he set so much store, perilously close to failure; and that hardly any of its manifestations can be put alongside the inimitable works he had been writing ten, even five years earlier: all this suggests something further – a decline due to the organic damage to the brain which the post-mortem later revealed. He now misjudged the nature of his powers as a composer, seeing them as dramatic rather than lyrical, miscasting himself as a composer of opera and dramatic stage music, forcing himself in his moments of strength to do what it did not lie in his nature to do, and unable to recognize the violence he was doing to his musical personality. Or there are undistinguished pieces, like the *Adventlied* and the *Fantasiestücke* for clarinet and piano, which are so far from the inspired Schumann that one finds it hard to penetrate their *raison d'être*. Numerous moments of harmonic detail – in the Goethe songs of 1849, for instance, or the *Requiem für Mignon* – also show his lapses of concentration, the signs of an already fading power of vision and control. Finally, for him to believe that he had now acquired the technical maturity to take control of a symphony orchestra and choir, able both to inspire his musicians and to meet the demands of a public career, reveals how remote he was from reality, how distorted his vision and how powerless he was to resist the destructive power that gripped him.

In the righteous reaction against the school of biography which, from the late nineteenth century onwards, unhesitatingly and unquestioningly took Schumann's 'sickness' as the categorical, *a priori* cause of a progressive deterioration in the quality of his compositions, there has been a tendency in recent times to try and 'rescue' his late works by musical special pleading and by claiming that his entire output is a beautiful, unbroken web of creativity. Certainly, it is the individual mind that holds an *oeuvre* together, and a mechanistic application of external physical influences, however incontrovertible their presence may be, is no way to reach to the heart of that *oeuvre*. But on musical grounds alone, disregarding all awareness of impinging circumstance, one cannot blind oneself to the realization that these late works of Schumann's fail to live up to their promise and leave an uncomfortable sense of dissatisfaction and confusion which the characteristic works of his early imagination do not. The evidence – the musical evidence, that is – cannot be burked. Once it is accepted, the urge to explain it in its context soon follows. And as the mind that created it existed outside as well as inside the music, so the explanation too must embrace the totality

of that mind, both conscious and unconscious. The music may –
better, must – be where we start, but it is not where we end.

It did not take Schumann long to accept the offer from
Düsseldorf. A composer can ask for nothing more stimulating
than to have his own orchestra. And the Rhine had had its
romantic attraction for him since his youth – as it has done for
countless thousands through the ages – while Düsseldorf itself
had in its line of music directors not only Hiller but also Julius
Rietz and Mendelssohn.

Looking up the town in an encyclopedia, he discovered that
among its prominent buildings were three convents and a mental
asylum. 'As you know', he wrote to Hiller, 'I have to be careful to
avoid any experience that might cause me to become melancholy.
The former I can accept, but I found it very unpleasant to read of
the latter'. It is a remark with a chillingly prophetic ring.

The duties of the post were not onerous. He would be required
to prepare and conduct ten concerts and four programmes of
Church music each year, the choice of music to be entirely his
own. For this he would receive a salary of 700 thalers per month –
'not a great deal', Clara considered, 'but not to be despised as a
regular source of income'. They did not need him to take up
residence in Düsseldorf until the end of August but were prepared
to pay him from April, which the practically minded Clara saw
would almost cover their removal expenses.

Before he left, the kingdom of Saxony, specifically Leipzig,
had one more disappointment to offer him. He had been led to
expect that his *Genoveva* would be put into production in Leipzig
in February. Now he was told that rehearsals would have to be
postponed to make room for, of all things, *Le Prophète* by
Meyerbeer, a composer for whom he had the utmost scorn. To be
pushed aside like this by an inferior musician whose flamboyant
works were all show and no substance, symbolized, as he saw it,
the churlish treatment that had always been his lot.

It did, however, give him and Clara the chance to take up an
earlier invitation to Hamburg – she to play, he to conduct some
of his own compositions, among them the overture to *Genoveva*

and the Piano Concerto. Later they were joined there by Jenny Lind, with whom they had had the happiest of relationships for a number of years and who sang with Clara at two concerts in Altona – at that time a separate township, though now long since merged with Hamburg. They were struck by what seemed to them the cool, reserved Hamburg audiences, compared with the demonstrative enthusiasm that greeted them in Leipzig or Vienna. 'The Hamburgers do not consider it proper to clap much', said Clara, 'and when they do, it is like a shower – a patter of rain that soon passes'. However, the citizens of Hamburg rained good money into the Schumann coffers and left them with a profit of 800 thalers from their performances.

Schumann's over-sensitiveness and unpredictability often strained the goodwill of those around him. After her recital on 21 March, Clara relates, they repaired to a nearby restaurant in a mood of great conviviality with a number of friends and acquaintances, among them Karl Grädener, director of the Hamburg Singakademie. First the two guests from Saxony were toasted. Then Schumann, recalling that that date, the beginning of spring, marked the birthday of the two men he considered the greatest in the history of German culture – Johann Sebastian Bach and Jean Paul – rose to his feet and enthusiastically proposed a toast to the two geniuses. Grädener protested. He would drink to Bach, he said, but how could one possibly mention Jean Paul in the same breath – and proceeded to hold forth at length on the impropriety of such an idea. This so incensed Schumann that he jumped up and shouted at Grädener: 'You impudent fellow!' Then he stormed out of the room, followed by the embarrassed Clara. Fortunately Grädener had the graciousness to call on Schumann the next morning and apologize for his provocative behaviour. More than one contemporary observed that it seemed to be only when annoyed or angered that Schumann would break out of his silence and address a remark or two to the company.

On their way back to Dresden they stopped briefly in Berlin to pay their respects to Mendelssohn's widow and – their first duty – to visit the great man's grave. In a sentimental symbolic gesture Schumann plucked a leaf from a laurel wreath that had been laid there and took it with him 'in remembrance', as Clara put it.

The months that remained before Schumann took up his post in Düsseldorf were dominated by preparations for the first performance of *Genoveva*, now set for the end of June. He himself was to conduct. The full score had already been published, and curiosity over how the work would come across attracted musicians from as far as Bremen, Hamburg and Königsberg. The *haute volée* of Leipzig music, men like Gade and Moscheles, were present, together with Hiller; Louis Spohr, one of the Grand Old Men of German music, came especially from Kassel, and Liszt, accompanied by Joachim, from Weimar. A special pleasure for Schumann was to see Johann Gottfried Kuntzsch there, his old piano teacher from Zwickau.

The first two acts, according to Clara, went well, but a blunder in the third unsettled the singers and left an air of embarrassment and uncertainty from which the performance could not recover. In the middle scene of this third act Golo is supposed to hand over to Siegfried a letter which describes the circumstances of Genoveva's alleged adultery. But the tenor singing Golo forgot the letter when he made his entrance. So on his menacing command to Siegfried 'Lest selbst!' – 'Read for yourself!' – there was nothing for Siegfried to read. 'The two singers rushed hither and thither in desperation', wrote Clara, 'and the whole scene was completely ruined, while the singers themselves were in a state of utter confusion'.

Clara tried, characteristically, to make out that the occasion was a huge success. In reality it came close to being a flop. The singers and the composer received only two curtain calls and there was no spontaneous applause at the end of any of the individual arias or scenes. It may have been listened to with respect, but hardly with enthusiasm. According to Clara's account, two further performances – the last anywhere for the next five years – were rapturously applauded by full houses; even she, however, reluctantly and resentfully came to realize that it was not going to take its honoured place in the succession of Beethoven and Weber. Sobering too was the memory that only a few years earlier Dresden had cheered wildly at the première of another romantic opera, the work of a man who did indeed have the blood of drama in his veins – Richard Wagner's *Rienzi*.

The disharmony in Schumann's existence even carried over into the farewell dinner that his friends and associates arranged for him and Clara. The famous actor and producer Eduard Devrient, who had met Schumann a number of times in Dresden and found him disagreeable company, was among the guests. 'August 3, 1850,' he entered in his diary:

Farewell party for the Schumanns in the evening. Again he behaved quite shamelessly. A group of singers sang some of his choruses. He made them repeat what he wanted to hear again, then stood up and conducted them himself, whereupon they sang even worse than before. It had cost us a lot of money to engage them at his request. In addition he said he didn't like the wine that Bendemann had poured out for him. When Clara played, on the other hand, she was warmly received.

The last few weeks in Dresden only served to make it clearer that Schumann had nothing more to offer Saxony, nor Saxony him. Even the choral society in which he had invested so much energy was beginning to disintegrate; the male members, he complained, were very irregular in their attendance at rehearsals, and earlier in the year he had already threatened to resign if things did not improve.

On 1 September 1850 Schumann and Clara left for Düsseldorf, and never saw Dresden together again. Official circles paid as little heed to their departure as they had to their arrival.

CHAPTER ELEVEN

Disintegration and Death

The welcome they received in Düsseldorf was a wonderful contrast. Led by Ferdinand Hiller, to whose sponsorship alone Schumann owed his appointment, the concerts committee gave a reception for them on the evening of their arrival, the Concordia male voice choir sang a serenade in their honour, and handsome rooms, decorated with flowers and laurel wreaths, were awaiting them in the Breidenbacher Hof, in the centre of town. They were introduced to some of the town's artistic personalities, above all the painters and teachers of the famous Academy of Art, and a few days later were treated to a special concert of Schumann's music, hurriedly but affectionately arranged by Julius Tausch, a local pianist and teacher – the Overture to *Genoveva*, a group of songs, and Part Two of *Das Paradies und die Peri*. As they entered the hall before the concert they were greeted with a triple fanfare.

By contemporary standards the Musikverein's orchestra was a substantial body of players – 8 woodwind, 2-3 horns, 2 trumpets, 2 trombones and 27 strings, i.e. some 40 in all. The majority of the string players were amateurs, with regimental bands providing the brass and percussion sections. Schumann's first meetings with his new choir and orchestra appeared encouraging enough, while Clara, who had feared that her own activities would stagnate in this provincial Rhineland town, soon found more than enough pupils to occupy her time. So there seemed reasons for a quiet confidence in the future.

But the idyll was not undisturbed. In particular they found the housing situation depressing. 'The houses are all uncomfortable, with ugly big windows and completely flat walls,' wrote Clara, 'and with sculleries built out into the backyard, making things very inconvenient for a housewife. We were very disappointed, since, as Düsseldorf is laid out as a garden city, we could not believe it would be difficult to find somewhere near parkland and with a garden'. They eventually took an apartment on the corner of the Grabenstrasse and the Alleestrasse, the main, broad avenue in the town, but with no great enthusiasm.

Compared with Dresden or Leipzig, Düsseldorf did indeed seem almost parochial. It had acquired civic status as early as 1288, but not until the seventeenth century, when it became the seat of the Counts Palatine and the Elector Johann Wilhelm von der Pfalz, did it begin to have an influence in the field of culture. Its greatest benefactor, the man to whom it owed its subsequent reputation in the arts, was the Elector Karl Theodor, who erected a series of public buildings, added substantially to the town's art collections and founded the Academy of Art in 1767. After being in French hands for much of the later eighteenth century, it became Prussian territory after the Congress of Vienna in 1815. King Friedrich Wilhelm III revived the Academy, and under a succession of brilliant principals – Peter Cornelius, Wilhelm Schadow (son of the great sculptor Johann Gottfried Schadow) and Eduard Bendemann, whom Schumann had known in Dresden – it became the centre of an influential school of romantic painting. Schadow was its director at the time Schumann arrived, and one of his most striking works is a painting of Mignon, the sad, moving character from Goethe's *Wilhelm Meister*, whose lyrics Schumann had set to music the previous year and whose death he had portrayed in his *Requiem für Mignon*.

Among Düsseldorf's well-known sons were the philosopher Friedrich Heinrich Jacobi, friend of Goethe, the biographer and diplomat Varnhagen von Ense, and, most famous of all, the poet Heinrich Heine. In the mid nineteenth century it had a population of a mere 25,000; its development into the thriving commercial city and state capital of today only began towards the end of the century with the processes of industrial expansion. Like the

Rhineland as a whole, it was, and is, Roman Catholic: of the twenty-five churches it had in 1880, twenty-one were Catholic, only four Protestant. In this too it presented Schumann with an unaccustomed environment.

For the first of the season's ten concerts, given some six weeks after his arrival, the programme consisted of Beethoven's Overture 'The Consecration of the House', Mendelssohn's G minor Piano Concerto, Schumann's *Adventlied* for solo, chorus and orchestra, and Niels Gade's cantata *Comala*. Clara took the solo part in the concerto, 'playing from memory again', she recalled, 'for the first time in many years', and the audience's reaction suggested that they would meet a far more sympathetic response than Dresden had ever shown them. The jovial good humour and outgoing nature of the Rhinelanders also played their part.

One of Schumann's first steps in his new office was to offer the leadership of the orchestra to one Joseph von Wasielewski, a young violinist in the Gewandhaus orchestra. Wasielewski eagerly accepted, and became one of the closest observers of Schumann the man and Schumann the musician. Published a year after the composer's death, his was the first biography of Schumann, and the personal recollections in his posthumously edited memoirs give unique insights into Schumann's last years.

With his new leader installed, the goodwill of his new hosts and colleagues still intact, and above all with orchestral and choral forces that were his to command, stimulating his urge to compose, Schumann wrote cheerfully to Carl Klitsch, director of music in Zwickau: 'It does not make excessive demands on my physical strength – conducting is a very strenuous business – and I can think of no other position that I would rather hold'. From November onwards Clara, who had been keeping the family diary alone for a long while, was able to record that he was again composing with immense energy, and this 'in spite of the almost unbearable noise that goes on in the street outside this wretched house'.

And indeed, not only did the thread of song-writing, taken up again in 1849, lead on unbroken through 1850 and 1851; not only did he continue to probe into the new territory of the declamatory ballad and extend his experience of chamber-music forms; but he also completed within the space of two months, shortly before Christmas 1850, two major new orchestral works – the Cello Concerto and the Third Symphony.

The Concerto for Violoncello and Orchestra (Op. 129) is a strange piece, appreciated more, it would seem, by performers than by the public. Rostropovitch has called it the concerto he enjoys the most, while Casals said: 'It is one of the finest works one could wish to hear – sublime music from beginning to end'. Yet the earliest recorded performance only appears to date from 1860, and it has not established itself in the repertoire like the concertos of Dvořak, Saint-Saëns or Elgar. It was not published until four years after its completion, hence its late opus number.

As a solo instrument pitted against the orchestra, the cello labours under a particular disadvantage that does not afflict either the piano or the violin: its low pitch tends to submerge its voice in the body of the full orchestral sound. In lyrical moments its glowing tone can shine above its accompaniment, but in allegro movements, and especially in the virtuoso passage-work integral to a concerto, it has difficulty in making itself heard, let alone in asserting its original personality against combined orchestral forces. It is hardly by chance that the literature for cello and orchestra is so restricted.

In the list of compositions that he methodically compiled Schumann called the concerto a *Konzertstück* – the description he had given to the Introduction and Allegro appassionato for Piano and Orchestra and the piece for four horns, Op. 86. Less formally developed than a concerto so-named, less expansive and often cast in a single, sub-divided movement, 'Concert Piece' has its particular significance for Schumann, like 'Fantasie', 'Fantasy Piece' and the other terms he used. His choice of title was never idle: it conveyed, not the formal tradition to which he saw the particular work belong, but the spirit in which he had composed it. Similarly, his frequent changes of title, far from being matters of nomenclature that interest only the scholar, reflect changing attitudes towards his own creations.

Within the three linked movements of the Cello Concerto, played without a break, Schumann embeds the solo part in a texture of unified sound rather like a bas-relief, making little attempt to set up the familiar antithesis between soloist and orchestra. The cello enters eagerly at once, as in the Piano Concerto, without orchestral exposition; *vice versa* the cadenza in the Finale, traditionally the soloist's private preserve, is punctuated with an orchestral accompaniment. Schumann had played the cello on and off in his younger days, taking it up as a substitute for the piano after the injury to his right hand. He therefore had a personal knowledge of the instrument's character and wrote competently enough for it both here and in his chamber music. The orchestral forces are comparatively light for Schumann – double woodwind, two horns, two trumpets, no trombones – but the scoring still tends to sound heavier than it actually is, and the moments of introspective charm in the piece do not unite to form a memorable whole. In this it joins the company of so many of Schumann's later works.

How different from the Third Symphony – the Symphony in E flat major, Op. 97, dubbed 'The Rhenish'! On 16 November 1850 Clara wrote: 'Robert is at work on something, but he has not told me what.' By 9 December, according to Schumann's own catalogue, it was finished and fully orchestrated. He made a revealing comment to Wasielewski about this remarkable *élan*:

I cannot see that there is anything 'remarkable about composing a symphony in a month. Handel wrote a complete oratorio in that time. If one is capable of doing anything at all, one must be capable of doing it quickly – the quicker, the better, in fact. The flow of one's thoughts and ideas is more natural and more authentic than in lengthy deliberation.

Schumann knew, of course, as Wasielewski observed, that this was only part of the truth. It is palpably irrelevant, for example, to Beethoven, whose sketch-books show how interminably he could ponder, alter and refine before being satisfied with the shape of even the tiniest fragment of melody. But as a statement of an ideal vision, a commitment to the enviable values of what Schiller called the 'naïve' mode of creation, it is the counterpart of *Papillons*, of *Carnaval*, the songs of the 'Liederjahr', and the countless other moments of lyrical spontaneity in his *oeuvre*. That the naïveté could still shine through in these last years of his creative life is the exuberant message of the bouncing, extrovert tune of the last movement of the Third Symphony:

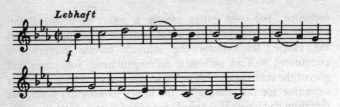

Indeed, the impetuous energy that gripped him during the four weeks that it took him to write the symphony thrusts itself to the fore in the swaying theme – also marked 'Lebhaft' – at the very beginning of the work.

Small wonder that of all Schumann's four symphonies this one alone has no slow Introduction.

As to the appellation 'Rhenish', though not, like the 'Spring' Symphony, Schumann's own, it has its origin and justification in his own experience. For firstly, as he said, it had been the sight of the unfinished Cologne Cathedral that inspired him. Then, already embarked upon the composition, he learned of the celebrations planned to accompany the elevation of Archbishop Ceissel of Cologne to the College of Cardinals. His response to this occasion was to interpolate an extra movement in the symphony, headed 'To accompany a solemn ceremony'. Not only is this unusual in itself, but the movement in question – the fourth of the five – with its grave polyphony and its introduction of trombones into the scoring for the first time in the work, thereby acquires a romantic, semi-programmatic character that sets it apart from Schumann's other symphonies yet remains entirely true to his nature.

Equally true to his nature is that he removed the explanatory heading from the score when it was published the following year, saying: 'There is no need to reveal one's heart to the world. It is better for people to be given a general impression of the work; then they won't make any false comparisons'. He had spoken in the same tone years earlier when describing the relationship between the music of works like *Papillons* and *Carnaval* and the literary-cum-pictorial programme behind them. As then he had protested against the view that his pieces were depictions in music of extra-musical scenes or objects, insisting that the music came first and the descriptive titles were merely imaginative after-thoughts, so now he continued to argue for the primacy of the musical experience. In so doing, he was re-stating the principle central to the whole question of so-called programme music, viz., that in the last analysis the work can only be received qua music, without reference to the nature, the interest, the quality or any other consideration proper to the non-musical background. At the same time one must accept that the Third Symphony only acquired its fourth movement because of Cologne Cathedral and a specific ecclestiastical occasion that was celebrated there, and if the polyphonic solemnity of the music makes one think in terms of a pontifical procession down a lofty, echoing nave, the association must be allowed to stay. Clara, strangely, had difficulty in fully understanding this movement, 'whereas there is hardly a single bar in the other movements that is not clear to me'.

As to his own view of the other movements, Schumann said: 'I wanted elements of popular music to predominate, and I think I have succeeded'. The realistic, Ländler-like charm of the second movement and the fresh, open-air gaiety of the Finale show what he meant. But never again did he achieve the relaxed happiness, the appealing, uncomplicated directness that comes from the heart of his music. It stands like an erratic block, dominant and proud, in the generally triste landscape of Schumann's last years.

Outwardly life passed serenely enough. Schadow, the sculptor Adolf von Hildebrandt, the painter Karl Sohn and other members of the Academy of Art offered stimulating intellectual company, and continuing the custom that they had followed wherever they lived, Schumann and Clara arranged regular evenings of chamber music in their house with Wasielewski and young Ruppert Becker, son of Schumann's old Freiberg friend Carl Becker, as violinists, the cellist Christian Reimers and others. In the centre, directing the performance, stood Clara.

Schumann himself, as Wasielewski came to know him during these years, showed the same uncommunicativeness, the same lapses into anti-social silence as people had found in him for a long while. His years spent with the *Neue Zeitschrift* had shown his deep concern with the affairs of the outside world – social and moral as well as musical – but he never sought the company of others with whom to discuss these affairs. And since leaving Leipzig he had withdrawn even further into the recesses of his own mind, the lives of his wife and children setting the outer limits of his real emotional involvement.

He knew full well what he was like and what impression he made. Back in 1837, when Zuccalmaglio wrote to ask whether he might pay him a visit, he had replied: 'I would be delighted to see you here, but you would not get much out of me. I scarcely speak a word – rather more in the evening perhaps, and most of all at the piano'. 'Generally', Wasielewski confirmed fifteen years later, 'he spoke in short, unfinished sentences in a soft and muffled voice, as though he were talking to himself'. As a result of his shortsightedness he screwed up his eyes a lot. Wasielewski described his general appearance thus:

His full, rounded features, ruddy in complexion, wore a benevolent expression but one of no particular interest. His lips were pursed and he often brushed his thick, dark brown hair to one side with his right hand. He had a heavy gait, dragging his feet somewhat. He would sometimes walk softly up and down in his room on tiptoe, as though concerned not to disturb the tranquility of the place. This peculiarity fitted in with his tendency to a certain secretiveness.

He always wore black during his later years, and usually a top-hat as well. This garb, taken in conjunction with his quiet, unhurried manner, could have led people to think he was a clergyman.

The turn of 1850–1 found his health still good and his creativity undiminished. He was considering, among other things, an oratorio on the subject of Martin Luther. 'It would have to have broad popular appeal', he considered, 'a work intelligible to townsman and peasant alike, in keeping with the nature of the hero himself, who was a great man of the people'. The appropriate musical style 'would not be sophisticated, involved or contrapuntal but simple, vigorous, relying for its effect chiefly on melody and rhythm'. The plan came to nothing, but at this moment a young student called Richard Pohl, who was to initiate a brief episode in the story of Schumann's final years, approached him with a libretto for an opera on Schiller's classical tragedy *Die Braut von Messina*. No opera appeared, but in its place came the first of three concert overtures in which Schumann sought to crystallize the dramatic content of a group of literary works.

What emerges in his *Braut von Messina* (Op. 100), as he concentrates his gaze on the theme of the fatal curse that wreaks its havoc on the house of Messina, is a compact movement in sonata form, the curse eliciting a Leitmotif that dominates the piece. It is Schumann the symphonist at work, borrowing the accoutrements of the grand manner as he essayed the, to him, alien task of expressing dramatic conflict and tragic fate. It met with a lukewarm reception when he conducted it a few months afterwards. 'I am accustomed to finding that the majority of the public fail to understand my works on a first hearing, especially the best and profoundest of them', he wrote to Pohl. 'But this overture, which is so clear and straightforward, I had expected them to grasp more quickly'. Maybe they found that there was not all that much to grasp.

The musical substance of the other two orchestral overtures – *Julius Caesar* (Op. 128), written a few weeks after *Die Braut von Messina*, and *Hermann und Dorothea* (Op. 136), sketched in the space of five hours one day in December 1851 – conveys even less of the vital spirit of their literary sources. The former reduces Shakespeare's play to a pattern of heavily-scored marches and jerky rhythmic sequences; the latter, drawing on Goethe's epic poem of the vicissitudes that attended the love of two young people at the time of the French Revolution, consists of little more than phrases of the 'Marseillaise' bandied about from one group of instruments to another. He had, incidentally, worked the Marseillaise into his music on three earlier occasions – in his setting of Heine's 'Die zwei Grenadiere', in the *Faschingsschwank aus Wien* and in the Four Marches for Piano Op. 76, written at the time of the Dresden Revolt, which he dubbed 'republican' in spirit.

As, in these early Düsseldorf years, he explored the new area of the concert overture, so also, with a resident orchestra and choir at his disposal, he turned his thoughts to the composition of extended works for chorus and orchestra. This medium, indeed, now became his main preoccupation, opening his imagination to a variety of literary stimuli, and with memories of *Das Paradies und die Peri*, of *Genoveva*, and of *Manfred* in his mind, he sought again to realize the dramatic substance of the romantic poetry to which he felt drawn.

Thus in May 1851 he set a rhymed fairy-tale, *Der Rose Pilgerfahrt (The Pilgrimage of the Rose)*, Op. 112, by a young, little-known Saxon poet called Moritz Horn, for soloists, chorus and piano, later scoring the piano accompaniment for full orchestra. In form and content it belongs to the lineage of *Das Paradies und die Peri* but has 'a more rustic, more German character', he observed, in its twenty-four numbers. A few weeks later came *Der Königssohn (The King's Son)*, Op. 116, also for soloists, chorus and large orchestra (including three trombones and tuba), a setting of the ballad by the most famous of German ballad-poets, Ludwig Uhland, and likewise divided into separate numbers. The following year, helped by young Richard Pohl, who adapted the text, he set the best-known of Uhland's ballads, 'Des Sängers Fluch' ('The Minstrel's Curse'), Op. 139, and the four ballads by Emanuel Geibel 'Vom Pagen und der Königstochter'. ('The Page and the King's Daughter'), Op. 140. Both these opus numbers were published posthumously. The Mass (Op. 147) and the Requiem (Op. 148), also composed in 1852, form part of the same context.

Time and again, when talking of Schumann's essays in larger forms, whether of absolute or, in the broadest sense, programme music, one finds oneself acknowledging individual moments of beauty and power while being forced to concede that the work as a whole does not grip the listener's mind in the way that great art must. These ballad cantatas, products of a creative consciousness that has lost the cutting edge of its concentration, belong to this company. The very choice of this form, indeed, implies an unawareness – unawareness of the discrepancy between what the form demanded, or admitted, and what he was able to bring to it.

The dramatic tension created, for instance, in a classic ballad like Schubert's 'Erlkönig' or Loewe's 'Edward' lies beyond Schumann's reach. To a large extent this rests on his characteristic tendency to dwell on the part rather than on the whole, to repeat individual words or phrases as the spirit willed him, without regard for the forward movement of the whole and thus for the format of the action as the poet conceived it. The sense of urgency and purpose is lost. In a lyrical context, as he allows his musical fantasy to muse on a scene, an image, an emotion, there is no conflict of interest between poetic meaning and musical meaning, poetic ethos and musical ethos. His songs are the triumphant proof of this. But in the narrative world of the ballad, where the epic and the dramatic demand their rights, the triumph of the lyrical is a sad irrelevance, and the works so created bear a fatal flaw.

To this inner contradiction was now added, in these word-settings of Schumann's last creative years, a feature disturbing in another, not unrelated way: a concern with the poetry of second- and third-rate writers. Geibel is no Eichendorff, Uhland no Heine. But Schumann did not stop here. In May 1850 he composed a group of six songs (Op. 89) to poor, tasteless verses by the poet who called himself Wilfried von der Neun. For three continuous weeks before this he had been living in the world of Goethe, working on the scene 'Fausts Tod' from his *Faust*. From the von der Neun poems he then went back to Goethe to set 'Wandrers Nachtlied', returned to von der Neun for two more songs, set, in random succession, verses by important poets like Mörike and Platen and by poetasters such as Moritz von Strachwitz and Ferdinand Braun, and finally rounded off the burst of activity with six settings of Lenau (Op. 90).

These darting inconsistencies of level are strangely incongruous in a composer who at the height of his powers had lived only in select company. Schumann had a fastidious awareness of literary values, which is a statement about a feature of his intellectual personality that he could as little change at will as he could change his close-tongued, uncommunicative manner. If the sureness of this acquired instinct for quality falters, the cause can only lie in forces beyond his control – in his medical condition, the condition that governed his unpredictable bouts of frenzied activity on the one side and his lapses of concentration both in his creative musical thought and in his dealings with the singers and players for whom he was responsible, on the other. In his music it reveals itself in the dichotomy between a strangely jumbled chromaticism, like that of the late Goethe settings, and the flat, diatonic style of 'Die Meerfee' or 'Husarenabzug' (both from Op. 125).

When he was a student in Leipzig, Schumann had hung on the walls of his room portraits of Bach, Jean Paul and the liberal writer Gottfried Seume. When Richard Pohl visited him in Düsseldorf, he noticed that above the desk there was a picture of the sentimental minor poetess Elisabeth Kulmann, whose poems he also set. The scene has a melancholy symbolism.

In the summer of 1851 Schumann and Clara moved to a splendid new apartment on the first floor of a large house in the chestnut-lined Königsallee, in the middle of the town. Here their special joy was a large salon that would hold some sixty or seventy people. Two grand pianos stood in the room, and many of the choral and instrumental works he wrote in the course of this year were first heard here. A holiday to South Germany and Switzerland took them past places Schumann had last seen in his student days twenty years before – Assmannshausen on the Rhine, Heidelberg, Baden-Baden, down to Basle and eventually to Geneva, 'an attractive, elegant city with remarkably cheap champagne – only 1½ francs a bottle,' he noted approvingly.

Soon after their return he was summoned to Antwerp to help adjudicate at an international male voice choir competition which lasted from 11 in the morning until 11 at night, with only an hour's break. Fortunately the warmth of their reception and the beauty of the old town, with its wonderful collection of Rubens' paintings, helped him to recover from the experience, which had been made more agonizing by the lamentable quality of much of the music. Scarcely were they back in Düsseldorf than Liszt unexpectedly arrived, accompanied by his consort Princess Carolyne von Sayn-Wittgenstein, her fourteen-year-old daughter and a governess. Clara was in the midst of preparations for Marie's tenth birthday the following day – 'but when Liszt comes on the scene, all one's domestic arrangements are upset, and he keeps one in a permanent state of agitation'. Of the Princess, who had been living with Liszt in Weimar since 1848 but who never married him, Clara wrote: 'We were surprised to find her a somewhat matronly woman, whose hold over him rests on her charm, her intelligence and her education, all of which she possesses in full measure. She adores and worships him, and he told Robert that her devotion was beyond description'. In the evening they performed Schumann's Second Symphony – two pianos, eight hands – then Liszt played a number of his *Harmonies poétiques et religieuses*, to their considerable displeasure:

He played with a demonic brilliance, as always, with a mastery like that of the devil himself (I can think of no other way of putting it). But oh, what terrible compositions! If a youngster were to write such stuff, one could forgive him on account of his age, but what can one say when a full-grown man is so deluded? We both felt very sad – it is so depressing. Liszt himself seemed offended that we did not say anything, but how can one, when one feels so angry?

It was not the first time they had been made to realize how wide was the gulf that separated Liszt's personal and musical world from theirs.

A more congenial, less strenuous visitor who presented himself with great deference, was the young philosophy student Richard Pohl from Dresden. Pohl had written to Schumann the previous year with a proposal that they should collaborate in an opera on Schiller's *Die Braut von Messina*, and this contact developed into an attractive friendship. Pohl now arrived bearing a libretto for Schumann's projected oratorio *Luther* and an adaptation, at Schumann's request, of Uhland's ballad 'Das Sängers Fluch'. He found Schumann in his study at the back of the house, overlooking the courtyard. He was working on the stage version of *Manfred* which Liszt had asked him to prepare for performance in Weimar:

By the window there was a standing-desk with manuscripts lying on it, and as well as a large writing-desk the room contained an elegant bookcase full of books and music, all beautifully bound and perfectly arranged. Quickly casting my eye over them, I noticed scores of Bach, Handel and Beethoven. The walls were adorned with portraits of famous composers . . .

Pohl had been warned about Schumann's silent manner, and was not put out to find that Schumann just let him talk, nodding from time to time or putting in the odd word of query or concurrence. But a few days later he was invited to join the family on a country picnic, where he found a quite different Schumann:

Here I came to know him in a social setting, as paterfamilias. He was very cheerful and talked a great deal. Indeed, from our first meeting I would never have believed that he could be like this.

Few outsiders, indeed, were ever permitted to glimpse into the private life of the family. Sincere as Schumann's affection for his children was, and above all for Clara, the withdrawn, introspective manner familiar to the outside world found its way into the family circle also. There was a story that he once even failed to recognize his own children when he passed them in the street. Seeing a group of young people approaching him, among them his daughters, he took out his lorgnette, regarded them for a moment and said in a friendly tone: 'Well, children?' Then, resuming his former absentminded expression, he went on his way, as though nothing had happened. Marie, the eldest daughter, later recalled that although the children always felt secure and well cared for, their father tended to live in his private world, which they grew to accept as a manifestation of his artistic preoccupations. He took breakfast alone with Clara. At the midday family meal, said Marie, he occasionally spoke to them but was often silent or talked only with their mother, and they would not have dared to speak out of turn. In the evenings he was more relaxed, playing little games with them, sometimes playing a piece on the piano or reading out loud – Marie remembered in particular hearing *Uncle Tom's Cabin* and Jeremias Gotthelf's *Uli der Knecht*.

As well as occupying himself with *Manfred*, composing the occasional song and returning, for the first time in over two years, to the solo pianoforte (the three *Fantasiestücke*, Op. 111), Schumann produced in the latter half of 1851 the last of his three Piano Trios (in G minor, Op. 110) and essayed a new genre with two sonatas for violin and piano – No. 1 in A minor (Op. 105) and No. 2 in D minor (Op. 121).

Whether this concentration on minor keys should be given any particular significance – at the end of the year he also revised his D minor Symphony – may be a matter for argument. Certainly the cumulative effect of these works, with the sense of uncertainty and tension innate in minor keys, is of a grave, sombre disharmony, a disquieting state of unresolved strain. Equally unmistakable is their introspective, subdued, almost fatalistic tone. The stringed instruments have few moments of virtuosity, there is little pizzicato, tremolo or other characteristic string writing, the dull cello part in the Piano Trio spends much of its time doubling the bass line of the piano, which itself spins a web of thick, almost unbroken sound. In the violin sonatas the violin speaks almost entirely from the middle register, denying the player access to the soaring lyricism that awaits him in the higher positions, and merely consolidating the already heavy texture of the piano part. The analogy will scarcely hold, but one is put in mind of the singer or the brass player who, as his physical powers decline, finds himself losing his upper notes and living involuntarily in the middle and lower registers. It is with mixed feelings that one recalls Schumann's remark a few weeks after he had finished the D minor Sonata: 'I didn't like the first violin sonata, so I wrote a second, which I hope turned out better'.

He in fact started a third a few months later, completing an undistinguished slow movement and an equally undistinguished Finale. These were later incorporated into the so-called F.A.E. sonata dedicated to Joachim (whose personal motto was *'Frei Aber Einsam'*, 'Free but lonely'), for which Albert Dietrich and Brahms wrote the other two movements.

On 1 December the Schumanns' seventh child was born – a girl, christened Eugenie. Like her eldest sister Marie, Eugenie never married, and also like Marie, later settled as a piano teacher in Interlaken, where she died in 1938, the longest surviving child of the family. In 1931 she published a biography of her father, based on letters and other family documents, as well as on the memories of Marie and others, and on printed sources like Wasielewski's book. She was only two years old when her father was removed to the mental asylum.

As Schumann could look back with satisfaction on his remarkable productivity in 1851, so also in his own eyes he was proving an undoubted success in his official position. Unhappily he was deceiving himself, both over the public recognition of this success and, indeed, over the reality of the success itself, and a sad chronicle of events was to be unravelled in the year that followed.

Cracks in the smooth, smiling surface of his public position already began to show towards the end of the first season of subscription concerts. In particular the singing of the choir deteriorated, as both audience and singers themselves could not fail to recognize. The atmosphere at rehearsals became tense, singers turned up late or not at all, while the orchestral players, who had a 'nine-to-five' attitude towards their art, merely went through the motions. In particular Schumann complained of their sullen unwillingness to learn anything new, such as his own pieces, or even to put their minds to studying classical works that demanded serious concentration, like those of Bach.

The choir and orchestra, on their side, grumbled at what they felt to be wavering and indecisive leadership on their new director's part. They were used to being driven, not coaxed, and they thought back sulkily to the days when Mendelssohn, who knew exactly what he wanted, had instilled an enthusiastic sense of purpose into them. Now, by unhappy contrast, they found themselves confronted with a diffident conductor, a man of few words who laboriously, even painfully, struggled to communicate his musical intentions to them.

In his memoirs Tchaikovsky recalled being told by his friend Carl Reinecke, conductor of the Leipzig Gewandhaus orchestra in the 1880s, that every word Schumann spoke seemed to cost him enormous effort. Reinecke also quoted a number of episodes, Tchaikovsky went on,

which showed that Schumann was not even able to distinguish properly the sounds of the different instruments in the orchestra, and that the innate sense of rhythm so indispensable for a conductor was very inadequately developed in him. How strange to find such an anomaly in a musician who, judged by his own compositions, was so highly inventive precisely in matters of rhythm. He also became increasingly unable to cope with quick tempi. This showed itself in the measured, not to say sluggish tempi that he adopted with his orchestra. It also had a related effect, psychologically, on the nature of his own compositions – in such features as a preference for more sombre texts in his vocal works, for contrapuntal techniques, which inevitably slow down the pace of the music, and a more marked tendency towards minor keys.

Schumann had, in truth, as little aptitude for conducting as he had for teaching. During his few months at the Leipzig Conservatoire he had done hardly anything for the young people who came to him, seemingly unable to identify the shortcomings of what they played or wrote, or to help them overcome their mistakes, and the experience had been as unrewarding for him as for them. In that situation he had been confronted with one student at a time, or perhaps a few. Now, standing in front of an orchestra or a choir, or both, he was still more exposed. Because he barely spoke, and then so softly, almost privately, that few could understand what he meant, he developed no rapport with the performers. On occasion it would even be Clara, who accompanied at choir rehearsals, that passed his directions on to the singers, Schumann nodding in agreement while she spoke, as though he too were receiving his instructions. He conducted with his head in the score, as though unsure of what came next, and thus gave the impression of having no overall view of the work in hand.

This air of insecurity – though it may not necessarily have been that – quickly communicated itself to performers and public alike. One cannot willingly believe that when conducting his own works, for instance, he did not know how they sounded. The problem he never overcame was how to make others aware of how he wanted his or any other composer's music to sound. The sheer physical exertion of conducting, moreover, took its toll of his strength, and Wasielewski remembered that he frequently had to sit down and rest in the course of rehearsals.

And these rehearsals became more and more chaotic. After an evening devoted to work on the St Matthew Passion in March 1852, Clara wrote:

There is absolutely no trace of enthusiasm left in the choral society. The ladies hardly open their mouths, and apart from a few who know better, they behave disgracefully, sit down while they are singing, fidget and shuffle about like ill-bred children, making me thoroughly angry. I should like nothing better than for Robert to give up the society – it is not a fit position for a man of his standing.

Clara was not the only one who wanted him to give up the choral society. The concerts committee which had invited Schumann to Düsseldorf in the first place had become uneasy at the friction that had developed, and was beginning to look for a discreet way of relieving him of his duties. To be sure, he had his supporters, few of whom, however, could have suspected the physical cause of his psychological state. But at the same time they could not fail to see that the musical life of the town, with its splendid recent tradition, was in danger of crumbling under the strain of the embarrassing incompatibility between the musicians and their director. One particular area of criticism concerned his concert programmes, which were indeed strangely idiosyncratic. Bach, Mendelssohn and his own works figured prominently, but he ignored Mozart almost completely, while for the 'moderns' Liszt and Wagner he could have no sympathy. French composers found no place in his repertoire, and only a few Italians. It was hardly what could fairly be expected of the director of an important civic orchestra.

For the present things were left as they stood, since neither side was quite sure of itself. An invitation to Leipzig for a concert that

included the *Manfred* overture and *Der Rose Pilgerfahrt* helped
to relieve the tension of the moment and restore something of
Schumann's confidence. He had not been in the Gewandhaus for
two years, and in the company of those who appreciated his
music – Moscheles was there, together with long-standing Leipzig
friends like Dr Moritz Reuter, Pohl came from Dresden, Liszt and
Joachim from Weimar – he and Clara spent a happy two weeks
among cherished old surroundings. He was never to see them
again.

From the moment he got back to Düsseldorf his productivity of
the last twelve months began to flag. The last of his ballad settings –
an adaptation of Uhland's *Das Glück von Edenhall* ('The Fortune
of Edenhall') for male voice choir and orchestra (Op. 143) – came
in March. At the end of that month he finished his Mass (Op. 147)
and in April composed the Requiem (Op. 148), both works
stimulated by that side of his duties which obliged him to arrange
periodical concerts of church music. He worked on *Vom Pagen
und der Königstochter* between June and August and set 'Die
Flüchtlinge', based on Shelley's 'Fugitives', as a brief melodrama,
but then produced nothing until the five settings of short poems
attributed to Mary Queen of Scots (Op. 135), which he gave Clara
as a Christmas present in 1852 – the last songs he wrote. The
words of these songs – or, more accurately, the words of the
German translations to which Schumann responded – have a
melancholy, at times maudlin quality which again makes one feel
that one is in the presence of a mind under physical and psychological stress.

The Mass and the Requiem, both scored for soloists, chorus
and orchestra, offer a prospect of conventional, harmonically
unexciting homophony interspersed with somewhat half-hearted
fragments of unsustained polyphonic writing. Indeed, the
prevailing pattern within the successive movements is that of a
contrapuntal opening which, after the voices have made their
individual entries, peters out in a four-square, rhythmically
repetitive chordal manner. The uneasy, because non-integrated
juxtaposition of polyphonic and harmonic material shows itself
again the following year – the last of his creative life – in the five
piano pieces *Gesänge der Frühe* ('Songs of the Morning').

In the summer of 1852, after only a year there, the big house in which Schumann and Clara had been so comfortably settled was sold, and they had to move out. Needing two music rooms and a study, as well as living rooms for a family of eight, they only managed to find quarters in the Herzogstrasse, some way from the centre of the town.

Here they discovered that their neighbours on one side were an English family whose children hammered away incessantly on the piano, while on the other side a new house was being built, to the accompaniment of the banging and shouting of the workmen. To complete the nightmare, the street in front of the house was being cobbled. They were forced to put up with these conditions for over six months before taking rooms that finally met their needs on two floors of a house on the Bilkerstrasse, off the Karlsplatz. The house is still standing (No. 15).

Shortly after they moved to the Herzogstrasse, and scarcely unconnected with the intolerable conditions there, Schumann's health deteriorated alarmingly. His powers of concentration faltered and occasional difficulties of speech made themselves noticeable. What he took to be rheumatic pains disturbed his sleep – they were more likely part of the *tabes dorsalis* syndrome, one of the manifestations of tertiary syphilis – and he felt too ill to travel to Weimar in June for the first dramatic performance of the complete *Manfred* under Liszt (though to find that Liszt interpolated Wagner's *Faust Overture* as an entr'acte would hardly have pleased him). A few weeks later, seeking relief on a short holiday in the countryside of the Rhineland, he suddenly collapsed in spasms while walking with Clara by the river, and had to be taken back at once to Düsseldorf. A similar convulsive attack a year later was diagnosed as springing from what was called at that time 'softening of the brain', i.e. a cerebral vascular stroke of the kind common in the early stages of general paresis, and this early attack bore the same symptoms. His latent hypochondria took hold of him, and suffering of the mind fed upon suffering of the body.

The dramatic lapses of concentration to which he became more and more prone disconcerted many people, for having exchanged an initial greeting with them, he would apparently at once forget who they were and why they were there. There was, for example, an occasion when one Carl Witting came from Paris on behalf of the Société Sainte-Cécile, a body devoted to promoting new music. The Society was in doubt over the tempi and other points of interpretation in the Overture to *Manfred*, which they intended to perform, and Witting was sent to sound out the composer's intentions. He was received by Schumann, who was smoking his eternal cigar, explained the purpose of his visit, and expected that Schumann would give him the definitive answers he was looking for. Instead Schumann asked: 'Do you smoke?' 'Yes,' replied Witting, taken aback. Silence followed. Since Schumann neither offered him a cigar nor showed any inclination to answer the questions, Witting hesitantly put them again – with exactly the same result: 'Do you smoke?' asked Schumann. After a third fruitless attempt Witting rose and left the room, unnerved by what he had experienced.

In any biographical exercise one must beware of imposing a pattern, linear or cyclical, on a sequence of events in response to a speculation that the facts could be made to fit such a pattern – a wish to see an underlying plan, physically or psychologically motivated, where no such plan exists. At the same time, the continuity of personality invites one to believe that certain features will indeed recur in the life of an individual when that individual is exposed to physical or psychological pressures of a recurrent type. Conversely, the presence and application of such pressures may allow one to draw conclusions about the character of the individual whose mind and body are subjected to them.

Against this background one cannot but be struck by Schumann's periodic return, from the summer of 1852, to the world of literature in which he had lived as a youth. First he began to assemble his many critiques, chiefly from the *Neue Zeitschrift für Musik*, for publication in book form. Then he began to read a great deal in search of items for his *Dichtergarten*, an anthology of writings about music drawn from the poets of the ancient and modern worlds. Particularly noticeable is the number of times the name Jean Paul recurs in his 'Haushaltsbuch' – *Flegeljahre, Titan, Hesperus* and all the other novels that had swept him off his feet as a schoolboy and a young man. Then, under the date 28

October 1852, stands one word – *Resignationszeit*, 'time of resignation', as though, wrote Eugenie Schumann in her book on her father, 'he sensed that the end was near'. And the following year, survivors of a seemingly forgotten and irrecoverable past, the associative names Clara and Eusebius, linked by Aurora, reappear on their appointed saints' days of 12, 13 and 14 August.

'In my end is my beginning', runs T.S. Eliot's line. 'Is it not as though beginning and end stretched out their hands to each other?' mused Eugenie, as she looked at her father's diary for his last years. The panache of Florestan, spokesman for the extrovert enthusiasm of youth, had long since vanished, leaving the stage to the withdrawn, inward-looking Eusebius – Schumann as he inexorably became, the Schumann the world knew, living with his Clara under the sign of Aurora, a new dawn.

Although he improved for a while after a course of saline baths, Schumann was in no state to take up his duties at the beginning of the 1852–3 season that autumn, and the first two concerts had to be conducted by his deputy, Julius Tausch. When he reappeared for the third concert in December, having partially regained his strength, the audience received him with little enthusiasm. Certain members of the committee had gleefully seized on his absence to start a campaign to have him relieved of his post and permanently replaced by Tausch. '11th December: Stormy meeting. 14th: Impertinent letter from Herr W. and others. 15th: Great agitation as a result of this letter – visit from Hasenclever, Euler and Dietrich. 16th: Stormy meeting.' Such jottings in Schumann's *Haushaltsbuch* give a glimpse of the plotting and counter-plotting that surrounded him.

For the time being the pro-Schumann faction, led by Dr Richard Hasenclever, son-in-law of Schadow and the Schumanns' family physician, a lawyer named Euler, who concerned himself with the legal aspects of Schumann's position, and the young composer and admirer Albert Dietrich, managed to stave off disaster. Düsseldorf held an annual Rhine Music Festival each Whitsun, and preparations for the thirty-first such Festival in May 1853 could not possibly exclude the participation of the current music director in the four concerts. So an uneasy truce was agreed upon, leaving Schumann with the indignant but unmistakable awareness that many people in the town would like to see him go – many in the choir and orchestra too, one must add.

Mammoth musical forces were assembled for the occasion – an orchestra of 160 (65 violins, 27 violas, 25 violoncellos, 12 double-basses and 31 wind and brass) and a choir of 490 (121 sopranos, 77 contraltos, 133 tenors and 159 basses). There were excerpts from Handel's *Messiah*, from Mendelssohn's *Elijah* and *St Paul* and from Gluck's *Alceste*. Pieces by Hiller, who led the orchestra, and by Julius Tausch, who shared in the conducting, were added to those of Mendelssohn to represent the work of other 'local' musicians, but there was no Bach. Among the soloists Clara Novello, whose singing had so enthralled Schumann in Leipzig fifteen years ago, was specially invited from London to perform at two of the concerts.

The highlights, however, were Joachim's appearance in Beethoven's Violin Concerto and Hiller's conducting of the Ninth Symphony. The day after his performance, Joachim came to the house in the Bilkerstrasse and played Schumann's A minor Sonata with Clara to a small company of friends, and from this time onwards became an unfailing source of sympathy and encouragement to them both.

Schumann's own contribution to the Festival met with far more modest success. Clara played his Piano Concerto at the third concert. The D minor Symphony, newly orchestrated since its original appearance in 1841, and the opening work of the Festival, went down surprisingly well, better, probably, than anything else of his that had been given in Düsseldorf. But the work he had specially composed for the occasion and given, as he thought, an appropriately Rhenish flavour – the *Festouvertüre über das Rheinweinlied* for orchestra with choral finale (Op. 123) which brought the three days music to a close – made no impression. The festivities thus ended rather limply, and the patrons left with less than complete pleasure in the achievement of their director.

Clara, helpless witness both of her husband's fluctuating health and of the tension between him and those – the Musikverein committee, the performers, the public – in whose midst he worked, displayed a loyalty as blind to the true nature of the former as to the objective realities of the latter. She seemed to have been less aware than outsiders of increasingly disturbing symptoms such as a declining articulacy and a susceptibility to sensory delusions. Since he still found the energy to conduct and compose, she reasoned, these could only be passing ripples on the surface. Equally self-deceiving was she over the quality of the works he was writing and the reception they were given. She found glowing words to say about piece after piece, performance after performance, where a clearer judgement would have discerned shortcomings and signs of failing powers. When she writes that one of his works was enthusiastically received we are almost forced to transpose her words to mean that it was met with polite applause. And if she indignantly records that the audience gave only a lukewarm response to his efforts, it is tantamount to admitting that the occasion was a flop.

Particularly alarming was his preoccupation at this time with the more dubious aspects of spiritualism, specifically with the 'mystical' way in which, in séance-like scenes, the table would begin to rock to and fro under the influence of occult forces. Of his first exciting experience he wrote in April to Hiller:

Yesterday we felt the table rock for the first time. A miraculous force! Just imagine – I asked it what the rhythm was of the first two bars of Beethoven's Fifth Symphony. It hesitated longer than usual before replying. Then it began: ♪ ♪ ♪ ♪ | ♩ | — but very slowly. When I said, 'But the tempo is faster, dear table,' it quickly struck up the correct tempo. Then I asked it to guess the number I was thinking of, and it answered correctly 'Three'. It was as though we were surrounded by miracles.

Visitors to the house were disturbed by the extent to which these 'miracles' had taken hold of his mind. Wasielewski arrived one afternoon and found him lying on a sofa absorbed in a book on the subject. 'Do you know anything about table-rocking?' he asked. 'Of course,' replied Wasielewski, jokingly. Schumann's eyes were usually half-closed, as if he were dreaming to himself. But now he opened them wide, stared at his visitor with a strange, unnerving expression on his face and said: 'Tables know everything!' So emphatically, even threateningly, did Schumann deliver this dictum that Wasielewski was fearful of becoming involved in a painful argument, and merely made an embarrassed pretence of agreeing with him. His uneasiness became even greater when Schumann fetched his daughter Elise, sat down with her at a little table and began to make it give out the same opening motif of Beethoven's Fifth Symphony.

Clara, for her part, could not, or would not, allow herself any scepticism, even gentle misgiving. 'Robert is enchanted with these magic powers,' she wrote gravely, 'and has grown very fond of his little table. He has even promised to buy it a new dress – that is to say, a new tablecloth.'

By Schumann's forty-third birthday on June 8 – the last that he was to celebrate in the company of the family – Clara had regained sufficient of her independence to start composing again. 'The first songs I have written for seven years,' she recorded happily in her diary, 'and three piano pieces. Robert was pleased with them.' Schumann had always been a lover of nature, especially of bird-song, and on the afternoon of his birthday he took his family by coach to the nearby village of Benrath and walked with them through the woods in a rare moment of idyllic happiness. Only a few weeks later Clara noticed that 'his voice became strangely weak', and in July he suffered what seems to have been another mild stroke, with the same symptoms as in the attack of the previous summer. The artist J.-J.-B. Laurens, who made a chalk drawing of Schumann in 1853, showing him with unpleasantly fat, almost bloated features, was struck by the abnormally enlarged pupils of his eyes.

But the same happiness overflowed at their wedding anniversary on 12 September and on Clara's thirty-fourth birthday the following day. Again they went for a walk in the country. When they got back to the Bilkerstrasse around five o'clock, Clara wrote,

I found a new grand piano in the middle of the room, covered with flowers. Behind it stood two ladies and two men, with Fraülein Thon [a pupil of Clara's] sitting at the piano. As I came in they started to sing – and what was it they sang? The words of the poem which Robert had written thirteen years ago when he gave me the Härtel grand, and which he had now set to music. And the last thing that I expected was that the piano was his real present to me – I thought it had just been brought in for the singing. It was far too expensive for people in our position . . .

But then, when I saw what was lying on the piano, I felt my heart begin to ache, for my joy was so great. It was the result of all his ceaseless work – a Concert Allegro with orchestral accompaniment, written for me, a Fantasie for Violin and Orchestra, and his *Faust* Overture, in full score, together with arrangements for piano solo and piano duet. I cannot put my feelings into words. It may sound boastful, but is it not true that I must be the happiest woman in the world?

The 'ceaseless work' of August and September 1853 was Schumann's last spasm of creative activity. As well as the pieces that Clara mentions, it produced the Violin Concerto and a group of six little piano duets for children called *Kinderball* (Op. 130). But it is the music of a tired mind, a mind almost bereft of original thought, expressing itself in forms at times awkward, at times conventional to the point of cliché. The Introduction and Allegro (Op. 134), also known as the Concert Allegro, is a single sonata movement with a short introduction, in the ubiquitous D minor of Schumann's late works. From the formal point of view, as from that of the relationship between soloist and orchestra, the *Fantasie* for violin and orchestra (Op. 131) belongs to the same world and speaks the same somewhat pallid language, lacking incisiveness. It was written for the twenty-two-year-old Joachim and is Schumann's gesture of thanks for their new-found friendship.

In his own way, Schumann lived with his *Faust* as Goethe had lived with his. Goethe started at the beginning and had told the familiar Faust-Mephistopheles-Gretchen story by 1775: he did not finish Part Two until just before his death almost sixty years later. Schumann, like Wagner with *Der Ring des Nibelungen*, started at the end with 'The Apotheosis of Faust' and now, nine years on, completed his setting with the Overture. One of the exercises to which he had subjected himself earlier in the year was to write piano 'accompaniments' to unaccompanied violin and cello works by Bach, and as in the pianoforte Fughettas of June, so in the *Faust* Overture that he laid on Clara's new grand piano in September, the contrapuntal and figurational spirit of the baroque age shows through the romantic harmonic idiom.

The Violin Concerto, which Schumann records in his 'Haushaltsbuch' as having been finished on 1 October 1853, a mere ten days after starting it, was his last major work. It has had a strange history. Shortly after completing it Schumann sent it to Joachim, with a request that he point out whether there were any passages that 'savoured of being unplayable' (a strange insecurity from one who had written a great deal of orchestral music, string quartets, violin sonatas and so on). Joachim welcomed the work but neither performed it nor returned the score, and Schumann never heard it played. After Schumann's death Joachim seems to have persuaded Clara that it was too unsatisfactory to be published or performed as it stood, and it disappeared from view. Asked in 1898 what had become of it, Joachim replied that it had been withdrawn because it was unworthy of the composer. Forty years later Eugenie Schumann wrote an article in *The Times* (15 January 1938), recalling how her mother had come into the room one day and said: 'I have just settled with Joachim and Johannes [i.e. Brahms] that the Concerto is not to be published, not now or at any time. We are quite agreed on the subject.'

The decisive voice was probably that of Brahms, who objected on principle to the posthumous publication of works that might detract from an artist's reputation, and who destroyed large numbers of his own compositions for fear that such a fate might also be his. Hence his further decision not to include the Violin Concerto in the supplementary volume of Schumann's posthumous works in the complete edition.

After Joachim's death in 1907 the manuscript found its way to the Staatsbibliothek in Berlin where, in 1937, the then head of the music department, Georg Schünemann, edited and published it. Faithful to her memory of what her mother had said, Eugenie had tried to prevent its publication and now objected to its performance, but her will could not prevail. The concerto was first played by Georg Kulenkampff in Berlin in December 1937 and by Jelly d'Aranyi – a great-niece of Joachim – in London two months later.

It is a work that has divided modern opinion along predictable lines. Some, probably the majority, claim that it really is inferior, and that Joachim and Brahms were right. Certainly it is a rarity in concert programmes and has not found soloists to champion it, as has the Cello Concerto. Others, particularly those, like Tovey, who denied that Schumann's late works showed alarming signs of declining powers, draw attention to the moments of great beauty, like the theme of the slow movement, hoping that at least a few swallows will make a summer. As so often in his large-scale works, movements towards a build-up of dramatic tension quickly subside into the lyricism of his truest and deepest nature, but it is a static lyricism, harmonically often sluggish and with extended passages stretched over a pedal-point. Even in the Finale, a Polonaise, there is a good deal of repetition, and one is left with the feeling that not very much has been said.

A series of short entries in the 'Haushaltsbuch' for the end of September and the beginning of October 1853 heralds the last great friendship of Schumann's life and a famous encounter in the history of music:

30 Sept: Herr Brahms from Hamburg.
1 Oct: Finished the Violin Concerto. Visit from Brahms (a genius).
2 Oct: A great deal with Brahms. Sonata in F sharp minor.
4 Oct: Music at home at 5. Brahms' *Phantasie*.

Clara, true to her outgoing nature, showed far more excitement:

This month brought us the wonderful arrival of the twenty-year-old composer Brahms from Hamburg. It is as though he had been sent by God himself! He played sonatas, scherzos and so on that he had written, everything brimming over with imagination and emotional intensity, and consummate in form. It is really moving to watch this young man, with his fascinating features, sitting at the piano with an expression of ecstasy on his face. He has very attractive hands, which master the greatest of difficulties with the greatest of ease – his works are very hard. Robert says one can only hope that Heaven will grant him health.

Schumann, Clara, Joachim, Brahms all spent hours together

playing and listening to music, their own and others', and
Schumann knew that he had found in his new young friend a
great composer of the future. A few weeks later he sent to the
Neue Zeitschrift für Musik an article called 'Neue Bahnen', 'New
Paths', the first piece of criticism he had written for years – and
his last. As such, it parallels that article at the very beginning of
his journalistic career in which, with precocious prescience, he
had divined the greatness of the young Chopin:

I have felt in recent years that a new force was entering music, and that
from out of the ranks of those pursuing these new paths one man would
suddenly emerge to epitomize the new age, as Athena sprang fully armed
from the head of Zeus. That man has now appeared. His name is
Johannes Brahms.

As his salute to Chopin was inspired only by the early 'Là ci
darem' Variations, so all he knew of Brahms – virtually all,
indeed, that there was to know – consisted of a handful of as yet
unpublished piano pieces and songs. Six months before coming to
Düsseldorf, Brahms had sent Schumann two compositions
whimsically signed, under the persistent spell of E.T.A.
Hoffmann, 'Der junge Kreisler'. Schumann returned the parcel
unopened. But now it was a different story. Scarcely had
'Beethoven's successor', as Joachim introduced him, sat down at
the piano and started to play one of his own pieces than
Schumann interrupted him with: 'Clara must hear this too'.
Fetching her into the room, he said: 'Clara, you're now going to
hear music such as you've never heard before. Start that piece
again from the beginning, young man'.

From this moment on the 'young man' became an inseparable
part of the Schumann household. It had been the music of Robert
Schumann that led him to Düsseldorf, and Schumann
immediately took it upon himself to attend to his young admirer's
development, both as man and musician. But it was to be the
person of Clara Schumann who, over the next forty years, held
him in intimate loyalty to herself, her children and her husband's
music, in a relationship that has never ceased to fascinate and
intrigue.

Brahms came from a poor family and as a boy had had to make his own contribution to the family income by playing the piano in sailors' bars in Hamburg. He had a precocious musical talent but a scant general education and few intellectual pretensions. So when, after a rough-and-ready period travelling through Germany with a Hungarian violinist called Remenyi as a violin and piano duo, he found himself invited into a real family circle, comfortable in its middle-class security and taking the enjoyment of a general culture for granted, it seemed very new to him. The afternoon family promenades in the surrounding countryside were totally strange to any mode of life he had known. So too was a household full of books. Here he began to study the works of Jean Paul, E.T.A. Hoffmann and Schumann's other literary heroes, becoming a willing captive of this romantic world, as his host had done before him. When Hanslick first saw him in Düsseldorf in 1855, he wrote: 'With his long blonde hair, his forget-me-not eyes and his complexion half-milk, half-blood, he looked like one of those idealized young men from the pages of Jean Paul'.

For the Schumann children he was from the beginning like a lionized older brother, playing games with them, learning chess from their father and joining with their mother in piano duets. After Schumann's committal to the mental asylum, and as Brahms' relationship to Clara grew more and more intimate, he also slipped into the role of surrogate head of the household, as well as that of joint custodian of the Schumann musical heritage.

Eugenie Schumann recalls in her memoirs an episode from these days:

I can still see, as though I were looking at a picture, a hall in a house in Düsseldorf, with a group of children gazing up in amazement at the banisters on the landing above. There a young man with long, fair hair was performing the most hair-raising gymnastic exercises, hanging by his arms and swinging backwards and forwards, from one side to the other. Finally he swung himself up until he was balancing on his hands, stretched out his legs and leapt down into the hall below, landing in the midst of the admiring children. The young man was Johannes Brahms; the children were the Schumann family.

Schumann set out to promote Brahms' education, sending him to

Leipzig to get to know the musical world there, giving him an introduction to the publishers Breitkopf and Härtel and widening his general cultural horizons. Schumann's own compositions during the last part of 1853, all in smaller forms, range from the five strangely diffuse and insubstantial piano pieces of *Gesänge der Frühe* (Op. 133) inspired by his reading of the poet Hölderlin, through exercises in counterpoint (*7 Pieces in Fughetta Form,* Op. 126) to the last of his three strange melodramas, or dramatic ballads – Hebbel's *Ballade vom Haidenknaben* ('Ballad of the Pagan Boy') (Op. 122, No. 2).

But his official career in Düsseldorf was facing its final crisis. Relations with the choir and the orchestra had become unbearable for all parties. During a rehearsal of Joachim's *Hamlet* Overture at the end of October, wrote Clara, 'the cellist Forberg just got up and walked out, then returned later, yet nobody said a word to him. He should have been sent away and told not to come back. There is no discipline here at all'. Everyone knew why. Everyone except Clara, that is.

There were other episodes, almost comical in their tragic context. Once, during Mass in the Maximilianskirche, Schumann went on conducting after the choir had finished singing and the priest had started to intone, as though he had completely lost track of the music. More than once he dropped his baton during a performance. Frederick Niecks' father, a violinist in the Düsseldorf orchestra, remembered him doing so at a rehearsal. He left the rostrum, then came back with the baton tied to his wrist with a piece of string, saying, 'with childlike simplicity and a gratified expression on his face and in his voice,' wrote Niecks: '"Look, now it can't happen again".' This inability to grip the baton, like the execrable handwriting in his diaries, and the often illegible notes he later made in the asylum at Endenich, can hardly have been unconnected with the damage to his right hand.

Before matters could get any worse, the Musikverein Committee took action. They decided to ask Schumann to hand over to his deputy, Josef Tausch, the responsibility for conducting all works save his own. Aware both of Schumann's eminence and of his touchiness, they sent two of their members to Clara to ask her to put the idea before her husband. Clara indignantly retorted that he would never consider such an insulting proposal. 'What impertinence!' she put in her diary. 'I would have given anything if Robert and I could have left on the spot, but with six children that's not so easy'. Schumann was more curt. 'A despicable lot', he said.

Two days later he wrote to the committee, rejecting their suggestion as a breach of the terms of his employment but announcing his intention to resign from October 1854. What the committee, in its difficult position, regarded only as a diffident suggestion for resolving the embarrassing discord, the hypersensitive Schumann took as an attack on his legitimate responsibilities, a virtual 'lock-out'. So the next day, when he was expected to conduct a rehearsal for the coming subscription concert, he stayed at home. The musicians waited half-an-hour. When it was clear he would not turn up, Tausch took his place, conducting both the rehearsal and, at the committee's bidding, the concert itself. In this unhappy manner Schumann's career as a conductor came to an ignominious end.

That this end could not he far away had been clear for some time. The style of its coming, too, though unpleasant, had a characteristic inevitability about it. For on the one hand Schumann certainly and knowingly broke his contract by not taking the rehearsal or conducting the subsequent concert. On the other hand the committee of the Musikverein, however tactfully they thought they were behaving, had negotiated with Tausch behind Schumann's back against such a contingency, so that their proposal came virtually as an ultimatum, with the connivance of a far from disinterested third party. Indignation, suspicions of bad faith, spurned responsibilities and the like corroded minds on all sides – though the members of the committee, it must be said, caught between their concern for the musical life of the town and their respect for the sick, manifestly ill-suited composer they had called upon to organize it, preserved an admirable decorum and sympathy.

But nothing could now prevent the final break. In the middle of November, less than a week after receiving Schumann's letter, the committee wrote to him respectfully, almost deferentially, accepting his resignation. At the same time they invited Tausch to complete the 1853-4 season and appointed him Schumann's official successor for 1854-5. At the end of the month, as though in a demonstrative gesture that they too saw little point in pretending that Düsseldorf had anything more to offer them, Schumann and Clara left for Holland, where they had been jointly invited to perform. The Düsseldorf town council was not too happy at losing the services of such a distinguished musician, but the break with the Musikverein was beyond healing. When they got back from Holland, they decided, they would finally move to Vienna.

Like his decision to leave Leipzig for Dresden, then Dresden for Düsseldorf, Schumann's break with the Rhineland capital was played out in a minor key – in a negative frame of mind embittered by disappointment and disillusion. Hopes had been frustrated, opportunities denied, efforts unrewarded, sympathy and recognition withheld. The *élan* of the days of *Papillons* and *Carnaval*, the purposiveness of his years with the *Neue Zeitschrift*, the lyrical wonder of the 'Liederjahr' – nothing had come to take the place of these great moments of the past. Activity there had been in plenty, but little of it, sadly – or, at any rate, disproportionately little of it – had left its unique mark on the memory. And gradually, inevitably, he had been losing his grip on his creative processes, as his concentration wavered and his inspiration flagged. Yet no one could know his utter disintegration was so close.

The trip to Holland, which took them to Utrecht, the Hague, Rotterdam and Amsterdam, was like a triumphal procession. Schumann conducted his Second and Third Symphonies, and Clara played the Piano Concerto and the Concert Allegro, together with works by Beethoven and Mendelssohn. Not only did audiences rise to them at their concerts but important members of the local communities went out of their way to pay their individual tributes, among them Schumann's old Dutch friend of Leipzig days, Johann Verhulst, who had since become a well-known conductor in his native country. The beginning of 1854 took them on an equally profitable trip to Frankfurt, where Brahms and Joachim were also present and where they made the acquaintance of the poet Platen.

Schumann had started the previous year to put together his writings on music for publication in book form. At that time, strangely, Breitkopf and Härtel showed no interest in the idea, so now he offered the collection to the firm of Georg Wigand in Leipzig, who bought it for 300 marks and published it later in the year. 'I was delighted to discover,' wrote Schumann to August Strackerjan, one of his loyal supporters in Düsseldorf, 'that over the long period of twenty years or more since I wrote the first of these pieces, I have scarcely departed from my original opinions'. He also took up his *Dichtergarten* again, turning his attention to the Bible and to classical authors. 'I have found some wonderful passages, especially in Plato,' he wrote in what was to be his last letter to Joachim. It was dated 6 February 1854. He had composed nothing since the previous November. But although he complained of an occasional recurrence of the disturbing tinnitus in his ears, his condition seemed quietly stable.

Four days later, on February 10, Clara's diary reads:

Throughout the night Robert had such terrible sounds in his ears that he couldn't sleep for a single minute. First there was a continuous drone on one note, then an occasional second note as well. During the day it eased off. The next night was just as bad, and the following day as well – he had a mere two hours respite in the early morning, and at ten it all came back afresh. He is in terrible agony. Every sound he hears turns to music – music played on glorious-sounding instruments, he says, more beautiful than any music ever heard on earth. It utterly exhausts him. The doctor says there is nothing he can do.

His symptoms worsened from one day to the next. February 17:

In the night, not long after we had gone to bed, Robert got up and wrote down a melody which, he said, the angels had sung to him. Then he lay down again and talked deliriously the whole night, staring at the ceiling all the time. When morning came, the angels transformed themselves into devils and sang horrible music, telling him he was a sinner and that they were going to cast him into hell. He became hysterical, screaming in agony that they were pouncing on him like tigers and hyaenas, and seizing him in their claws. The two doctors who luckily came only just managed to control him.

This melody – it is apparently that which, according to Wasielewski, Schumann said was dictated to him by Mendelssohn and Schubert, though Clara says nothing of this – has survived in Schumann's own handwriting in piano score. It is a modification of the theme of the slow movement of his Violin Concerto – as though this motif were still running through his head without his realizing he had already used it. In the days that followed he wrote five variations on the theme.* He frequently told Clara to go away and leave him alone, for he was afraid lest he might act violently towards her. Then he would say it would soon be all over with him, said goodbye to her and proceeded to make arrangements about the custody of his musical compositions, his money and so on.

There were, nevertheless, interludes of fleeting lucidity when the chance visitor did not suspect that anything was dramatically amiss, let alone that tragedy was but one step away. The violinist Ruppert Becker, who had heard that he was going out of his mind, accompanied him for an hour's walk on 24 February and found nothing particular to wonder at, 'save that he told me the figure of Franz Schubert had sent him a glorious melody which he had written down and on which he had composed a set of variations'. It was Clara, rather than her husband, whose condition alarmed Becker. 'Never have I seen Frau Schumann look so ailing, so full of suffering', he wrote in his diary. 'At night she just sits on the bed and listens for his every movement'. She was also carrying their eighth child, who was born four months later.

On 26 February, Palm Sunday, he seemed better. Young Albert Dietrich called in the evening, and in a mood of wild enthusiasm Schumann played him a sonata by a young composer called Martin Cohn. He ate supper in a feverish haste, then, at half-past nine, suddenly got up from the sofa, asked for his outdoor clothes and said he had to go to the mental asylum because he was no longer in control of himself and did not know what he might do in such a state. He calmly laid out everything he wanted to take with him – his watch, money, music paper, pens, cigars. 'But Robert',

---

*Brahms' Variations Op. 23 (piano, four hands) is also based on it.

said Clara, 'do you want to leave your wife and your children alone?' 'It won't be for long', he replied. 'Soon I shall come back, fully recovered.' Dr Böger, his regular physician, was called and persuaded him to lie down again, but he would not allow Clara to stay in the room, and a male nurse had to watch over him throughout the night.

The next day, Monday 27th, the carnival celebrations of *Fasching* were in full swing – the great Rhineland festivities that precede the arrival of Lent. Accounts differ over exactly what happened. Certain is that soon after lunch, at which Albert Dietrich and Dr Hasenclever, physician and friend, were also present, Schumann slipped out of the house unnoticed. The others assumed he was in his study, working on the variations. It was pouring with rain, but he put on neither his coat nor his boots. When they discovered he was missing, Dietrich and Hasenclever, together with Clara, her daughter Marie and the maid Bertha, ran out to try and find him, but he was nowhere to be seen.

An hour later two strangers brought him back to the house, cold and wet. He had thrown himself into the Rhine from the bridge. The two men, fishermen, had seen it happen and quickly rowed after him as the current bore him downstream. Lifting him into their boat, they made for the shore; according to the account in Ruppert Becker's diary, written three weeks after the event, he apparently tried to throw himself back into the water from the boat but the men managed to restrain him. They then made their laborious way back with him to the house through the crowds of carnival revellers. Clara was told nothing about how or where they had found him, and Dr Hasenclever would not allow her to see him for fear of the effect it might have on him. She went to stay with Fräulein Rosalie Leser, an elderly, well-to-do blind woman who had been a faithful friend throughout these years in Düsseldorf. 'To stay in the house and not be allowed to see him would have been too much for me,' she wrote.

It was two-and-a-half years before she saw him again – two days before he died.

One thing that attracted the attention of Dr Hasenclever and the others who tended him was that he no longer had his wedding ring. After his death Clara found among his papers a note that read:

Dear Clara,
I am going to throw my ring into the Rhine. Please do the same – then the two rings will be united.

Only after learning the full story, and that he had no longer been wearing his ring when the fishermen brought him back to the house, did she realize what the note meant.

For the next three days, frequently visited by his doctors and watched over by two male nurses, Schumann stayed in his room, insistently, even obsessionally requesting to be taken to an asylum. A message to Clara assured her that he felt well. He also made a fair copy of the variations and sent it to her.

The doctors realized they could do nothing for him. Hasenclever knew of a private mental institution run by a Dr Franz Richarz in Endenich, near Bonn, some forty miles up the river from Düsseldorf, and arranged for him to be transferred there. Joachim, who had heard the news, came quickly from Hanover to offer what help he could. So did Brahms, who took a small room in the town, just to be on hand 'to cheer me up with his music-making whenever I felt like it', as Clara put it. Clara's mother had also hurried to Düsseldorf from Berlin the moment she learned of her son-in-law's attempted suicide.

Finally, on the morning of 4 March, as the sun shone out of a cloudless sky, Schumann's last day in Düsseldorf came. 'The coach drew up in front of our door', wrote Clara. 'Robert hastily dressed himself and got in together with Hasenclever and the two attendants, without asking after me or his children. I sat there with Fräulein Leser, numb and lifeless'. When the coach reached Endenich, he was given two pleasant rooms on the ground floor of one of the asylum buildings, facing the Siebengebirge on the other side of the Rhine. A week or so later Clara's mother went to consult the doctors there. She was not allowed to see Schumann but she brought the comforting news that the medical staff were very kind and understanding, and that the asylum itself, far from being an impersonal, clinical institution, stood in a large garden abounding in trees, in an atmosphere of utter peace and serenity. The house, still standing, is now a Schumann museum.

Schumann's condition improved through the summer, and he was able to take walks outside the grounds, accompanied by male nurses. But he was not permitted to receive visitors. He did not enquire after his friends, nor even, to her bitter sadness, after Clara and their children. To her old friend Hedwig Salomon, who visited her from Leipzig, she said: 'If I did not cherish the firm hope that my husband would get better, I would not wish to live any longer – I cannot live without him. The terrible thing is that I am not allowed to be with him, and that the whole time he has not asked after me even once.' She still knew nothing of his attempt to drown himself.

On 11 June she gave birth to their last child, a boy, for whom, in honour of Mendelssohn, she chose the name Felix. His father never saw him.

In August a young friend and musician called Otto Grimm wrote to Albert Dietrich that he and Brahms had been given permission by Dr Peters, Richarz's deputy at Endenich, to hide beneath a window in order to watch and listen to Schumann:

I could hardly control the trembling that seized me – Brahms was similarly affected. However, I must say that Schumann looked very well: he has become somewhat stouter, otherwise there is no change in his appearance. There is nothing insane in his eyes, and his whole manner is the same as of old, so mild and gentle.

In his account of the same occasion to Clara, Grimm confirmed these encouraging symptoms but also told of disturbing moments:

Yesterday evening as he was drinking his wine he suddenly stopped before draining the glass and said there was poison in it. Then he poured the rest on to the floor.

Among the often illegible jottings he made during these days was one that his doctor deciphered as: 'Robert Schumann, honorary member of Heaven'.

On his wedding anniversary, 12 September, he suddenly thought of his family and said to Dr Richarz that since he had not heard anything for so long, he thought they must have died. Richarz at once told Clara. Overjoyed yet apprehensive, even afraid of what the last seven months might have done to him, she sent him a letter to which he replied affectionately, wistfully, lucidly, the moment he received it:

Endenich, 14 September 1854

How glad I was, my beloved Clara, to see your handwriting, and to learn that you and the children still think of me with affection. Embrace them for me. Would that I could see and speak to you all, but it is too long a journey. There is so much I want to know – how you are, where you all live, whether you still play so wonderfully, whether Marie and Elise are making good progress, where my scores, manuscripts, correspondence, the *Neue Zeitschrift* and so on have got to . . . I need some music paper, because I occasionally want to write something down. I lead a very simple life and take great delight in the beautiful view over Bonn or in visiting Bad Godesberg and the Siebengebirge . . .

Tell me too whether you have been attending to my clothes and sometimes sending me cigars – I very much want to know this . . .

I have so much to ask and so many requests to make – if only I could come to you and talk at length. But if you want to draw a veil over one or other of the things I have asked, then do so.

With that I bid you farewell, my beloved Clara – you and the dear children. Write to me soon.

Your old and faithful
Robert

Simple, direct, sincere – but it is the letter of a man no longer part of the world of which he writes, the world to which his unhappy existence is tied. His voice is that of one who, as Berthold Litzmann, biographer of Clara Schumann, put it, 'does not know that he is dead'. 'Touching, as gentle as a child, but without a breath of life: his weary imagination is completely shrouded in the past – the future is dead'.

A few further letters passed between them in the following months, but after May 1855 he wrote nothing more to her, though he still had over a year to live. He also sent letters to Joachim and to Brahms, expressing to the latter his admiration for the Variations (Op. 9) on a theme from the *Bunte Blätter*, thanking him for his attentiveness to Clara and the children, then slipping back into the obsessional commonplaces about which he kept talking to his doctors – the charm of the landscape, the Beethoven monument in Bonn, the views of the Siebengebirge and so on. He lived on his memories and on the sense impressions of the moment. There is no thought for the morrow, no hint of a creativity that might survive the serene inertia into which he had fallen.

Unsettled in mind though she felt and anxious to be on hand if unexpectedly called to Endenich, Clara now found herself in financial difficulties which made her think of returning to her concert career. Schumann's salary had come to an end when he broke with the Musikverein, some three months before his collapse. She had the responsibility of the seven children and in addition the costs of the mental clinic to bear. 'There is no money left,' she wrote in her diary at the end of September 1854, 'yet I cannot bring myself to sell even one of Robert's manuscripts'.

The following month she set out on a strenuous tour that lasted until just before Christmas – Leipzig, Weimar, Frankfurt, Hamburg, Berlin, Breslau and other places – playing works from the classical repertoire but also, on every occasion, compositions by her husband and sometimes also by Brahms. Shortly after his death she was able to tell her children that she had added 5,000 thalers to their father's capital during his final illness. But it was money earned at the price of much loneliness. Liszt treated her with great tact and sympathy in Weimar, and Brahms travelled especially to his native Hamburg to be on hand for her recital there, but a letter from Dr Peters in Endenich that reached her in Berlin, saying it would be months before she could visit her husband, plunged her back into a state of depression. 'Where can I find the courage to go on working? I am so lonely here. But my faithful friend Johannes [i.e. Brahms] has raised my spirits a little in a kind letter I have just received'. It was Brahms, together with Joachim, who went to Hanover to travel with her on the last stage of her journey back to Düsseldorf. And it was in the company of Brahms, alone, that she celebrated – though that is hardly the appropriate word – the arrival of the New Year. Later on New Year's Day little Felix Schumann was christened, and Brahms was present as his godfather.

In the last days of the old year Joachim went to Endenich and was allowed to see Schumann for a short while – his first visitor in the ten months he had been there – returning with deceptively encouraging news of his progress. A few months later Brahms also visited him. He played him a few of his own pieces, then he and Schumann together played the *Julius Caesar* Overture.

'When Brahms wanted to leave, after being there for four hours, Schumann could not bear to part from him,' wrote old Fräulein Leser, Clara's friend, to Dietrich. 'He accompanied him to Bonn, showed him the minster and Beethoven's monument, and only left him when Brahms had to hurry to the station to catch the train.'

'It was Johannes alone who sustained me', wrote Clara in her diary, which had now become a collection of private memoirs through which her children could later re-live these harrowing times. 'Never forget this, dear children, and never lose your gratitude to the friend who will surely remain a friend to you too'. Clara was thirty-five, Brahms twenty-one. She knew that tongues were wagging. They have been wagging ever since. That she later destroyed almost all her letters to him from these early years of their friendship has helped to keep them so. The 100 or so letters from him to her during the same period show in the manner of their address alone his growing affection. From *'Geehrte Frau'* he moved to *'Teuerste Freundin'* and eventually to *'Herzliebe Clara'*, crying almost in despair, 'What have you done to me? Can't you lift the spell you have cast over me?' When Clara left the Bilkerstrasse after Schumann's death, the house in the Poststrasse into which she moved had a room in it for Brahms.

A struggling music teacher, young in years yet mature in instinct, Brahms realized that if Clara were to survive her trial she needed, not condolences and well-meant gestures but the stimulation of her own creative impulses, a kind of self-generated music therapy. Whatever it may or may not have later become, the relationship rested on a communion in music, music not as a mere solace but as a fount of spiritual strength and renewal. Brahms' very youthfulness, moreover, brought Clara an experience of which, largely because of her own fame and success, she had known little. Since the childhood days when Friedrich Wieck had begun to groom her as a virtuoso pianist, she had known none of the relaxed, carefree pleasures that come the way of most young people – in fact, she had hardly had a youth at all. Twenty-one when she married Schumann, she bore her first child the following year and had been from then on totally committed to the claims of her family and her career. Brahms now offered her a freshness of personal and musical experience – on the one hand a requital for what she had lost, or never had, on the other a revived confidence in her own future.

In April they went together to Cologne to hear a performance of Beethoven's Missa Solemnis, and from there Brahms went on to Endenich. Schumann, it seems, had lost his initial sense of contentment, was sleeping badly, felt lonely and was agitating to leave the asylum. This was a worrying turn of events both for his doctors and for Clara, who could not contemplate looking after him in this distressed condition. He also showed a feverish desire to work – a development which the doctors found the very opposite of encouraging.

On 5 May he wrote:

Dear Clara,

On May Day I sent you a herald of spring, but the days that followed were restless. I will tell you more in a letter that will reach you by the day after tomorrow – a shadow hangs over it, but the rest of its contents, my dearest, will delight you [it was never written].

I overlooked the date of our beloved friend's birthday [Brahms' birthday was May 7], so I shall have to don wings if this and the score are to arrive tomorrow [we know nothing of any score].

I enclose the drawing of Mendelssohn for you to put in our album – a treasured memory.

Farewell, my love.

Your

Robert

It was his last letter to her.

Later that month the poetess Bettina von Arnim, who had become a friend of Clara's in Berlin in the late 1830s, took it upon herself to visit Schumann on her own account, accompanied by her daughter Gisela. Her description of what she saw, and in particular her insinuation that the doctors treating him were incompetent, horrified Clara. 'We passed through a deserted courtyard', wrote Bettina,

into an equally deserted house and were taken to an empty room, where we waited for the doctor. When he finally arrived, I insisted on being allowed to see your husband. He led us through bare corridors into a second house, where it was so quiet that you could have heard a mouse run across the floor. The doctor left us alone for a considerable time . . . At last Schumann appeared. I hurried towards him, and his face flushed with pleasure at the sight of us . . . He found it more and more difficult to talk, he said, since he had so rarely spoken to anyone for over a year. He talked about the interesting moments in his past life, about Brahms, Woldemar Bargiel and Joachim, in short, about anything that he remembered with pleasure . . . Kind and just, he was full of enthusiasm for his former pupils . . .

It is obvious that his unexpected illness was merely a nervous attack which could have been cured more quickly if people had understood him better and realized what was going through his innermost mind. But Dr Richarz, who is himself a hypochondriac, failed to do so, seeing in Schumann's nobility of spirit rather a symptom of his sickness.

Bettina must have meant well. But as her account of the dismal atmosphere in the asylum made Clara's heart sink, so her amateur diagnosis of Schumann's condition as a temporary indisposition raised false hopes of an early recovery. Joachim hastened to Endenich to see for himself whether the situation had suddenly deteriorated, and was able to reassure Clara that nothing had changed, yet he could not completely undo the harm that Bettina had unwittingly done. A performance of *Das Paradies und die Peri* at the annual Musikfest in June brought old friends back to Düsseldorf – Otto Grimm, Karl Grädener, Liszt, Jenny Lind, who sang the role of the Peri. Stephen Heller came from Paris, Hanslick from Vienna, and the critic Henry Chorley from London. But thoughts turned repeatedly to the man to whom the occasion most profoundly belonged.

When Josef von Wasielewski, like Grimm the previous year, was admitted to Endenich that summer and allowed to watch Schumann unobserved, he saw the patient sitting at the piano that stood in his room. 'He was improvising', wrote Wasielewski:

we were able to observe him unnoticed through an opening in the door for a long time. It was a heartbreaking sight, this noble man, his physical and mental powers shattered, this great master who has given us so much beautiful music and ceaselessly devoted his quiet yet active life to the achievement of the highest goals. For his playing was unbearable. It was as though the mind from which it issued were completely paralysed.

The instrument in Schumann's room was a square piano built by Richard Lipp of Stuttgart in 1843. It had been used by Liszt at the first concert to commemorate the dedication of the Beethoven monument in Bonn in 1845. When Schumann asked for the use of a piano, this was the instrument offered to him and that at which he wrote the chorale to the words 'Wenn mein Stündlein vorhanden ist.' It stands today in the Endenich museum.

The summer slipped away. On 10 September Dr Richarz wrote to Clara that there was now no hope that Schumann would ever completely recover. Two days later, in the subdued company of Brahms and of her children, she commemorated in silent suffering her fifteenth wedding anniversary.

Autumn passed into winter, and his condition remained unchanged. Clara was invited to Detmold, Göttingen, Berlin and elsewhere, generally for public performances but also to give lessons to the children of aristocratic families. At the end of the year she returned to Vienna for the third time to give a series of five concerts, playing above all works by Schumann and Beethoven. Public taste in that city had progressed since her last visit nine years before when the pieces by Schumann that she played had met with a frosty, largely uncomprehending reception. Now it was a different story, and from her first concert onwards success followed success.

Scarcely was she back in Düsseldorf than she set out on yet another round of concerts, this time in England. The prospect of playing in London, where a line of German musicians from Handel to Mendelssohn had found a welcome at court under a succession of royal hosts, had appealed to her for some time, and an invitation from Sterndale Bennett to play at two New Philharmonic Society concerts now gave her a specific incentive. Taking leave of Brahms with a heavy heart, she arrived early in April and stayed some two and a half months, playing in London, Manchester, Liverpool and Dublin.

She found musical life in England, and the English in general, almost as insufferable as Wagner had done when he conducted there the previous year, also at the invitation of the Philharmonic Society. To Wagner the English were a people totally impervious to culture, interested only in balance sheets and profit-and-loss accounts. 'I can conceive of no one more objectionable than the authentic Englishman', he wrote to Otto Wesendonk. 'He is like a sheep, with the sheep's practical instinct for sniffing out its food in the field. But the beauty of the field and the sky above is beyond his perception'. Clara too was struck by the air of commercialism that hung over English musical life, together with a conservatism that bordered on backwardness. 'They are terribly behind the times,' she wrote in her diary. ' – or you might call it one-sided: the only modern composer who counts, as far as they are concerned, is Mendelssohn, whom they revere like a god'. Nor, despite Schumann's liking for him, had she ever thought much of Sterndale Bennett.

Nevertheless she stayed for almost three months and gave twenty-six public performances, concentrating, as in Vienna, on Schumann and Beethoven, but including pieces by Bach, Mendelssohn, Chopin and Brahms as well. She also played privately before Queen Victoria, at the royal request, and by the end of her stay had come to discover in the English character some endearing traits lurking beneath a substantial veneer of coolness and reserve. Such was the respect she earned that towards the end of her stay she was presented with an Erard grand – the piano preferred by most concert performers of the day. At the beginning of July she took the boat for Antwerp, where Brahms, who had been helping Fräulein Bertha to look after the children, came to meet her.

News of Schumann's gradually deteriorating condition had reached her in England through Brahms' many letters. Barely a week after her arrival he had written that Dr Richarz had given up all hope of Schumann's recovery, and that he was too unwell to be moved to another clinic. In a letter written on his twenty-third birthday, 7 May, Brahms said that on a recent visit to Endenich Schumann had hardly taken any notice of him but pored for hours over an atlas – it had been his main occupation for weeks – and picked out names that he interchanged at random. He had subsequently become very weak and was spending more and more time in bed, suffering in particular from swollen feet. On 14 July, a week after getting back to Düsseldorf, she hurried to the asylum to ask to be allowed to see him at last. Richarz refused. It was not callousness or authoritarianism on his part but a principle of his therapy. A man deeply concerned with the agonies of mental suffering, Richarz had founded his institution in 1844, when he was thirty-two, with the aim of putting into practice the progressive theories of psychiatric treatment that he had evolved on the basis of the so-called 'romantic medicine' of Carl Gustav Carus and others. One of his principles was that a patient should be isolated from everything that reminded him of the deep-rooted past, source of his disturbed condition, and this often involved denying those closest to him the access that outsiders would have thought the most natural.

The one most painfully affected by this reglement was, of course, Clara. Yet whatever view one may take of Richarz's methods of treatment – and modern psychiatrists have suggested that he may have done more harm than good – it is hard to resist the conclusion that she was actually far from anxious to see her husband, whether out of embarrassment, fear of what she might find, or even shame at his fate. Mental illness has still not entirely lost its stigma, the lingering suspicion of a measure of culpability, individual or inherited, for an anti-social condition, and the nineteenth century judged the matter far more radically. That Clara was a person of European fame made her sensitivity and vulnerability all the greater. And might even the presence of Brahms have affected her behaviour?

On 23 July she received a telegram from Richarz, saying that if she wanted to see her husband again before he died, she should come at once. She left immediately with Brahms and Fräulein Jungè, a travelling companion. When they arrived, they found that the immediate danger had passed, and although Brahms visited him, he persuaded Clara that it would only upset her to do so too. So they went back to Düsseldorf without her having seen him.

The worry and uncertainty, however, gave her no rest. On the 27th, a Sunday, she went back to Endenich with Brahms and met her husband that evening for the first time in two-and-a-half years:

He smiled at me, and with great effort – he could no longer control his limbs – put his arm round me. I shall never forget that moment, and I would not surrender that embrace for all the treasures in the world . . . Everything around the noble man, the air that he breathed, was holy to me.

Apparently he still conversed a great deal with the spirits, and could stand company only for a short period, after which he became restless. One could hardly understand anything he said.

The next day they went to see him from time to time and also watched his behaviour through a little window in the wall. The doctor did not think he was suffering, but his limbs were constantly jerking to and fro in spasms, and he began to talk loudly and violently. For weeks the only sustenance he had been willing to take had been some fruit jelly and a little wine. Clara now brought it to him and he devoured it feverishly, licking the wine from her fingers when some was accidentally spilt. He may or may not have recognized her. She desperately persuaded herself that he did.

At four o'clock the following afternoon, Tuesday July 29 1856 he died quietly. No one was in the room at that moment. Clara had gone into the town to meet Joachim, who had hurried to Düsseldorf from Heidelberg in response to her telegram. When she got back half an hour later, she found him at peace, relieved at last of his earthly burden. His two male nurses, who occupied the room next door, had already reported his death.

The autopsy carried out by Dr Richarz showed the alarming extent of the damage to his brain. The blood vessels were dilated, especially at the base of the brain, there was ossification at the base of the skull, and a considerable atrophy of the brain as a whole, which weighed almost seven ounces less than it should have done in a man of Schumann's age. The serious disease that these features betray had its roots, Richarz continued, in his early life, gradually infected his entire being and ultimately brought about his madness. His intense mental activity during the periods when his state of health permitted it had increased the strain and accelerated the progress of his disintegration.

This organic disease of the brain, plausibly seen as the manifestation of tertiary syphilis, that is, general paresis, was superimposed on the manic-depressive disposition – Richarz calls it chronic melancholia – central to his personality. On the one hand this disposition induced in him a more intense self-awareness, including an awareness of his sickness; on the other it bore a causal responsibility for the hallucinations that began in the auditory realm, then spread to the organs of taste and smell as his general weakness spread. Richarz concluded his report:

His mental faculties, together with the instincts, inclinations and habits associated with them, retained their power to a relatively high degree, though slowly waning. On the other hand the influence of his melancholia on the nervous system meant that his physical survival could only be prolonged for a brief period and with great effort. He frequently refused all sustenance, so that he became progressively weaker and died in a state of extreme emaciation.

He was buried in the Alter Friedhof in Bonn two days later, at seven in the evening, without great ceremony. Clara wished it that way and told only a few close friends. In front of the coffin, borne by young men from the Concordia male voice choir, walked Brahms, Joachim and Albert Dietrich – all three, deeply committed to Schumann and his music, only in their early or mid-twenties. Behind walked Clara, the pastor, the Bürgermeister of Bonn and a few civic dignitaries from Düsseldorf, and Ferdinand Hiller, now director of the Conservatoire in Cologne. A brass ensemble played hymns and chorales as the cortège passed through the streets on its way to the cemetery.

A little less than a year later, on 8 June 1857, a simple headstone, for which Brahms had made the arrangements, was erected on the grave. Not for a further sixteen years, and only then on the private initiative of Clara and her friends, not of any public body, was the idea broached for a more lavish memorial. 4,000 thalers were raised from a festival of his music in August 1873 and an elaborate, figured monument erected in May 1880 to replace the original stone. 'We cannot warm to it,' wrote Clara in her diary. 'The relief is not without a certain resemblance to him, but as to the spirit it exudes . . .' Its formal, classicistic, slightly heavy spirit is that of Schumann the forced symphonist rather than of Schumann the natural lyricist. Perhaps Clara's doubts, sensed rather than expressed, had their own spiritual justification.

Clara was thirty-seven when her husband died, and had shared his life for only sixteen years. She never remarried. On 24 May 1896, forty years later – and less than a year before Brahms – she was laid to rest beside him.

Postscript

The contours of artistic originality soften with the passage of time. Today's novelty is tomorrow's commonplace, and what may meet with incomprehension or consternation at the moment of its creation becomes irresistibly absorbed into the experience of those of whose heritage it forms part. There is not a linear progress in art as there is in science: art does not get 'better' in the sense in which science becomes more accurate or more efficient. Indeed, it is not difficult to sustain the thesis that art – European art, that is – has been in a state of irreversible decline since the Renaissance, or at least since the middle of the nineteenth century, whereas science, measured by the criteria proper to its nature and function, has been remorselessly in the ascendant.

Be this as it may, the artist who breaks new ground has always had to contend with the bafflement or the hostility of the conservative majority of his contemporaries, and the history of the reception of his work, in his own and later ages, is to a large degree the history of the way in which the bafflement and the hostility give way to understanding and admiration – or do not.

An artist with strikingly original things to say, Schumann was made aware throughout his life of the price of his originality. The reviews of his earliest published works show the difficulties that critics had in coming to terms with these fleeting moments of fantasy, and even Clara, whom a determined loyalty blinded to such things, was often forced to record, with indignation rather than sadness, that audiences showed little enthusiasm when she played her husband's music. Under the weight of his inescapable disillusionment, he later declared that his career as a composer had really begun only with the songs of the 'Liederjahr', 1840, and the First Symphony the year after.

True, by the 1850s performances were becoming more frequent, and towards the end of his life critics were calling him a leading composer of the age. But their notices showed a remarkable reluctance to penetrate the spirit of his music or do much more than describe its external features. The long reviews of his first Symphony in the *Allgemeine musikalische Zeitung* in 1842, and of his Second Symphony in 1844, are little more than movement-by-movement theme-detecting exercises of the kind extracted from helpless junior students of form and analysis. Even his first biographer, Joseph Wilhelm von Wasielewski, who had a uniquely privileged position for his task, rarely came close to the heart of his subject.

The earliest notices already made clear the dichotomy which worried Schumann's contemporaries and which, in the generalized historical form of the antithesis of classic and romantic, still provides a framework for a characterization of his achievement today. The *Allgemeine musikalische Zeitung* described the *Papillons* and the *Impromptus* in 1833 as 'fresh and imaginative' but deplored their 'exaggerations and excesses', which, the reviewer maintained, should have been eradicated. Over ten years later, in 1844, writing in the same journal, Kossmaly still called his music, including these early piano pieces, 'immature and unrefined'. Original, yes, despite reminiscences of Schubert, Mendelssohn and Chopin, but still little known outside a close inner circle; indeed, very little, said Kossmaly, was written about Schumann in general.

Likewise his songs, according to a general review of his vocal works in 1842, seemed unsettling, fidgety, over-hastily written, with too much weight laid on the accompaniment: 'Weird and wonderful visions are conjured up by this music but one misses what is essential to any work of art, viz. an immanent sense of felicity permeating the work as a whole.' The general tone of the *Allgemeine musikalische Zeitung* was bland, even characterless, as though reviewers wanted to avoid searching criticism or pejorative judgement. The positive features of Schumann's music were described in the same smug, non-committal style as those of long-forgotten minor composers such as J. Dürmer and J. Hoven. On the few occasions, therefore, when a harsh critical word was spoken, it expressed a deep dissatisfaction and unease, and these strange pieces by a new young composer clearly disturbed most reviewers' critical balance.

The review of Schumann's First Symphony in 1842 expressed a guarded view that here was a promising composer who might well achieve fame, but also stated categorically that at that time he was better known, both in Germany and abroad, as a journalist than as a composer. A performance of his Second Symphony in 1848 led to a detailed analysis of the work movement by movement but evoked a renewal of the complaint, in critical conclusion, that his works were somehow lacking in 'rounded artistic perfection'.

Yet although his music was not praised and welcomed like that of, say, Mendelssohn, neither did Schumann have to contend with a concerted opposition, as did Wagner and, later, Brahms. He did not divide the musical world, like Wagner, nor could his music be pressed into service by the anti-Wagner faction, as was Brahms'. Since Schumann was a withdrawn, almost negative personality, one cannot imagine opprobrium being heaped upon him as it was upon Wagner the man and Wagner the musician; nor, on the other hand, would his music have provoked a snide remark such as that of a French critic quoted by Felix Weingartner: 'Brahms works exceedingly well with ideas he does not have'. So, as the nineteenth century progressed, his works, with a great number of silent exceptions which have remained silent to this day, gradually took root in the minds of performers and audiences, as did Brahms' a little later and Wagner's later still.

Not that the earlier scepticism disappeared overnight. The famous actor Eduard Devrient, for example, friend of Mendelssohn's and a man of culture, went to a concert given by Clara two years after Schumann's death. '*Carnaval*, composed by her husband and accompanied with a high-flown programme,' he wrote disparagingly in his diary, is in general banal stuff, not particularly imaginative – as though a skilful musician were improvising without being properly in the mood. These modern composers reckon they have done their job if they provide their products with an explanatory text, rather like those poor old fellows in medieval wood-cuts with a string of words coming out of their mouths, so that we can tell what they're supposed to represent.

The critic Eduard Hanslick, for whom music 'reached its climax in Beethoven, Schumann and Brahms', as he put it, had many uncomplimentary things to say in the 1870s about Schumann's later compositions, which had a weariness and pallidity about them that he ascribed to Schumann's medical condition. 'It is painful,' he wrote in 1873, 'to see this once so lavishly endowed heart so cold, so sullen, as though the chill hand of old age lay upon it.'

Tchaikovsky, on the other hand, who played piano reductions of Schumann's symphonies and overtures over and over during the 1860s, and translated the *Instructions to Young Musicians* into Russian, looked beyond the many unhappy miscalculations and infelicities in Schumann's work to the incomparable richness and originality of his imagination, while still conscious of the faults, the decline and above all the unevenness of his music. 'Schumann's greatness,' wrote Tchaikovsky in 1872,

lies on the one hand in his wealth of emotion, on the other in the depth of his spiritual experience and his striking originality. His actual expression of this experience, however, leaves a great deal to be desired, and it is probably only in those moments when he is at his best that he achieves a real clarity and plasticity . . . With the shadow of his insanity already hanging over him [Tchaikovsky has the 'Rhenish' Symphony of 1850 in mind], this inspired poet of human suffering seemed incapable of finding those moments of tranquillity in which he could establish an objective relationship to his music.

This last shortcoming, for Tchaikovsky, was the source of such aesthetically disturbing features in Schumann's music as the poor instrumentation of his orchestral works.

The most indefatigable champion of Schumann's music, right down to her death in 1896, remained Clara. Hardly a concert went by in which she failed to include at least one of his works, and together with Brahms, who grew more and more attached to her after her husband's death, she edited between 1881 and 1893 a complete edition of his published works in 31 volumes. With these texts available, and *pace* the corrections that later scholars have seen fit to make, the way lay open at the turn of the century for detailed studies of his music in all genres. Parallel to this were the various published collections of letters that appeared between the 1880s and the early 1900s, together with his articles from the *Neue Zeitschrift für Musik*. By this time his symphonies, songs, much of the piano music and the Piano Concerto had become part of the general musical scene, both in Germany and abroad. Then, particularly in the 1920s, with the growth of interest in psychiatry, attention switched back to the biographical and to the investigation of what lay behind his attempted suicide and his mental sickness.

Opinions on his significance and rank, however, continued to fluctuate – more so than with Mendelssohn, for example, though less than with Chopin or Liszt. These fluctuations derive to a large extent from the direction in which people have chosen to look. That *Papillons, Carnaval,* the *Kreisleriana* and much of his other early piano music shows a remarkably original mind at work, and that the songs of the 'Liederjahr' belong to the most beautiful in the whole repertoire of European lyricism, are judgements from which there is today no dissent. The unique historical significance is a matter of critical awareness and admiration; the beauty, an experienced reality of emotional enrichment and aesthetic joy. Further comment is superfluous – and has long been so.

If one looks at the symphonies, on the other hand, the chamber music, or the choral and dramatic works, one hesitates, expresses reservations which turn to criticisms, to the inescapable recognition of flaws from which the music cannot be delivered. There is in these works a fatal dichotomy between impulse and expression, between the nature of Schumann's inner creative self and the utterances he was forcing this self to make. The lyrical, the impulsive, the uninhibitedly romantic within him is shackled, all but suffocated, in an unnatural quest for the grand, measured, intellectually consolidated classical manner.

To be sure, he did at times, and for fleeting moments, find it. But the price he paid was one that he should not have compelled himself to pay. Compared with Brahms, who, also above all in songs and piano music, has the same lyrical freshness, the same natural, naïve perfection in miniature forms, Schumann lacked an architectonic sense, the sustained drive that powers a symphony along its relentless course, through heroism and gentleness, gaiety and serenity, towards triumphant fulfilment, towards dramatic resolution. A large-scale work is not a small-scale work magnified. It is qualitatively different, and demands qualitatively different virtues and energies. As the natural milieu of, say, Wordsworth or Keats is not the expansively epic, like Milton's, or the pulsatingly dramatic, like Byron's, but the lyrical, now spontaneous, now reflective, so also is Schumann's. The drama and the epic sweep of Beethoven's symphonies on the one hand or of Wagner's operas on the other were not part of his true world.

But it remains a very special world – special in its originality, special in the quality of its imagination. Special, above all, in its characteristic, precious, inescapable beauty.

A Note on Sources

For the biographical and circumstantial evidence used in the book I have as far as possible gone back to original, or at least contemporary sources. To assign a footnote to each reference would have been, I think, wearisome and disturbingly cumbersome, but readers may still like to know what the sources are. To have listed them chapter by chapter would have been tedious and repetitive. The following information, however, arranged as a kind of chronological catalogue raisonné, will indicate where the evidence can be found. The Bibliography supplements these sources.

Schumann's family background, childhood and student days, 1810–30 (Chapters I and II)

Emil Herzog, *Chronik der Kreisstadt Zwickau* (Zwickau, 1839–45): a record of life in Schumann's birthplace over the centuries, giving interesting cameos of the historical scene during the lifetime of his parents and his own childhood there; Robert Schumann, *Jugendbriefe*, ed. Clara Schumann (Leipzig, 1886): chiefly letters to his mother, other members of his family and Clara herself; *Robert Schumanns Briefe: Neue Folge*, ed. F. Gustav Jansen (Leipzig, 1886, 2nd enlarged ed. 1904): a standard collection, excluding the contents of the *Jugendbriefe*. Further assemblages from Schumann's letters and diaries are given in the

Bibliography below; C.E. Richter, *August Schumann* (Zwickau, 1820): on Schumann's father; Robert Schumann, *Tagebücher I* (Leipzig, 1971): diaries covering the years 1827-38, the first of three planned volumes; Kurt Wagner, 'Robert Schumann als Schüler und Abiturient' (*Veröffentlichungen der Robert-Schumann-Gesellschaft* II, Zwickau, 1928): interesting information on school life in Schumann's day and on his school record; Emil Flechsig, 'Erinnerungen an Robert Schumann' (*Neue Zeitschrift für Musik* CXVII, 1956): the memories of a school friend; Carl Grosse, *Geschichte der Stadt Leipzig* (3 vols, Leipzig, 1897–9): background information on the city where Schumann studied and began his career as composer and journalist; *Allgemeine musikalische Zeitung*: the house journal of the publishers Breitkopf and Härtel in Leipzig, and the leading music periodical of the day founded in 1798; A.F.J. Thibaut, *Über Reinheit der Tonkunst* (Leipzig, 1825): the aesthetics of Thibaut, professor of jurisprudence at the University of Heidelberg, made a deep impression on the young Schumann; Joseph Wilhelm von Wasielewski, *Robert Schumann: Eine Biographie* (Leipzig, 1858: trans. A.L. Alger as *Life of Robert Schumann,* Boston 1871): Wasielewski, who played under Schumann in the Düsseldorf orchestra and was his first biographer, had unique access to primary source material.

Leipzig 1831–44 (Chapters III to IX)

Jugendbriefe, op.cit; *Briefe: Neue Folge,* ed.cit; *Tagebücher I,* ed.cit; B. Litzmann, *Clara Schumann: Ein Künstlerleben* (3 vols, Leipzig, 1902): still the best-documented and most informative work on both Schumann and Clara, drawn largely from their letters and diaries. Volumes I and II cover their years together, while Volume III deals with Clara's life from 1856 to her death in 1896; Friedrich Wieck, *Clavier und Gesang* (Leipzig, 1853): a statement of the musical principles that Wieck implanted in his pupils, including Schumann; Marie Wieck, *Aus dem Kreise Wieck-Schumann* (Dresden, 1912): memoirs of Clara's half-sister, Wieck's daughter by his second wife; A. Meichsner,

Friedrich Wieck und seine beiden Töchter (Leipzig, 1875); V. Joss, *Der Musikpädagoge Friedrich Wieck und seine Familie* (Leipzig, 1902); Heinrich Dorn, *Aus meinem Leben* (3 vols, Berlin, 1870–2): reminiscences of one of Schumann's music teachers; F. Gustav Jansen, *Die Davidsbündler: Aus Robert Schumanns Sturm-und-Drang Periode* (Leipzig, 1883): in essence an account of Schumann's life and activity in Leipzig but beyond this an invaluable source of documented information on his friends and associates, on the *Neue Zeitschrift für Musik* and many related matters; the *Neue Zeitschrift für Musik* itself, with numerous articles by Schumann which reveal his attitudes not only to composers of his own and earlier ages but also to the social role of art; James R.S. Bennett, *The Life of William Sterndale Bennett* (Cambridge, 1907): the English composer's recollections of Schumann in Leipzig; Felix Mendelssohn-Bartholdy, *Reisebriefe* and *Briefe aus den Jahren 1830-1847* ed. Paul Mendelssohn (Leipzig, 1899; English trans. *Letters,* ed. G. Selden-Goth, London, 1946): references to Schumann; A. Dörffler, *Geschichte der Gewandhaus-Konzerte* (Leipzig, 1884) and E. Creuzberg, *Die Gewandhauskonzerte zu Leipzig* (Leipzig, 1981): accounts of the institution that dominated the musical life of Leipzig at this time; *Das Königliche Conservatorium der Musik* (Leipzig, 1893): the foundation and history of the academy at which Schumann, Mendelssohn and others taught; W. Boetticher (ed.), *Briefe und Gedichte aus dem Album Clara und Robert Schumanns* (Leipzig, 1978): contains tributes and comments by many of Schumann's friends, with editorial notes; Joseph Wilhelm von Wasielewski, *Schumanniana* (Bonn, 1883) and *Aus siebzig Jahren. Lebenserinnerungen* (Stuttgart/Leipzig, 1897): personal memories of one of Schumann's students at the Leipzig Conservatoire who later became leader of his orchestra in Düsseldorf.

The Dresden Years 1845–50 (Chapter X)

Briefe; Neue Folge, ed.cit; B. Litzmann, op.cit; Ferdinand Hiller, *Briefe an eine Unbekannte* (Leipzig, 1877): the composer and conductor Hiller was one of Schumann's closest friends in Dresden; Eduard Devrient, *Aus seinen Tagebüchern*, ed. R. Kabel (Weimar, 1964): the famous actor had several encounters with Schumann. His *Meine Erinnerungen an Mendelssohn* are also of interest; Friedrich Hebbel, *Briefe* ed. R.M. Werner (2 vols, Berlin, 1900): contains a number of references to Schumann; Richard Wagner, *Mein Leben* (complete text by Martin Gregor-Dellin, Munich, 1963): Wagner was also living in Dresden during these years, and the two men met on occasion; Max von Weber, *Carl Maria von Weber, Ein Lebensbild* (Leipzig, 1864–66) contains memories of Schumann by the son of Carl Maria von Weber; Eduard Hanslick, *Aus meinem Leben* (2 vols, Berlin, 1894): the autobiography of the famous Viennese critic who had a good deal to say, here and elsewhere, about Schumann the man and the composer; Frederick Niecks, *Robert Schumann: A Supplementary and Corrective Biography* (London, 1925): contains documentary evidence which supplements that given in Wasielewski's biography.

The Düsseldorf Years 1850–6 (Chapter XI)

Briefe; Neue Folge, ed.cit; B. Litzmann, op.cit; J.W. von Wasielewski, op.cit; Richard Pohl, 'Erinnerungen an Robert Schumann' (*Deutsche Revue* II, 1878): Pohl was a young student who approached Schumann with offers to provide him with dramatic texts to set to music; Julius Huebner, *Schadow und seine Schule* (Berlin, 1869): an account of the famous Düsseldorf School of painters in whose company Schumann moved; Andreas Moser, *Briefe an und von Joachim* (3 vols, Berlin, 1911–3) and *Briefwechsel Joachims mit Johannes Brahms* (Berlin, 1908): the violinist Joachim was a frequent visitor in the Schumann household during these final years and one of the few people allowed to see him in the mental asylum; *Clara Schumann – Johannes Brahms: Briefe* (2 vols, 1927) and L. Henning, *Die Freundschaft Clara Schumanns und Johannes Brahms'* (1952): Brahms, together with Joachim, was constantly with Schumann and Clara from 1853 to 1856, and his attachment to Clara became increasingly intense after Schumann's death; Bettina von Arnim, *Werke und Briefe* ed. Gustav Konrad (Frechen, 1959–63): Bettina visited Schumann in Endenich a year before he died; Josef Neyses, 'Robert Schumann als Musikdirektor in Düsseldorf' (*Düsseldorfer Heimatblätter V*, 1936).

Bibliography

Consonant with the nature and purpose of the book, the bibliography is in general confined to works that deal with Schumann's life, personality and work as a whole, or with specific biographical and psychological questions. I have not tried to select from the immense literature on his music either in general or in particular except where such studies may have a bearing on the creative processes of his mind. The most comprehensive bibliography of works covering both the biographical and musical spheres is that given at the end of the article on Schumann in the latest edition (1980) of *Grove's Dictionary of Music and Musicians*, which also includes a complete list of Schumann's compositions.

Albert, H., *Robert Schumann* (Berlin, 1920)

Abraham, G. (ed.), *Schumann: A Symposium* (Oxford, 1952)

——'Recent Research on Schumann' (*proceedings of the Royal Musical Association*, 1948-9)

Alf, J., *'Der Kritiker Robert Schumann'* (Niederrheinisches Musikfest, Düsseldorf, 1956)

Ambros, A.W., 'Robert Schumanns Tage und Werke' (in Ambros, *Culturhistorische Bilder aus dem Musikleben der Gegenwart*, Leipzig, 1860)

Basch, V., *Schumann* (Paris, 1926)

—— *La vie douloureuse de Schumann* (Paris, 1928)

—— 'L'esthétique de Schumann' (*La Revue Musicale XV*, 1935)

Beaufils, M., *Schumann* (Paris, 1932)

Bedford, H., *Schumann* (London, 1933)

—— 'Robert Schumann in seinen Beziehungen zu Johannes Brahms' (*Die Musik* XXIX, 1937)

Bennett, J.R.S., *The Life of William Sterndale Bennett* (Cambridge 1907)

Bötticher, W., *Robert Schumann in seinen Schriften und Briefen* (Berlin, 1942)

—— *Robert Schumann, Einführung in Persönlichkeit und Werk* (Berlin, 1941)

—— (ed.) *Briefe und Gedichte aus dem Album Clarà und Robert Schumanns* (Leipzig, 1978)

Boucourechliev, A., *Robert Schumann* (Paris, 1956; tr. A. Boyars, New York, 1959)

Brion, Marcel, *Schumann and the Romantic Age* (tr. G. Sainsbury, London, 1956)

Brown, T.A., *The Aesthetics of Robert Schumann* (New York, 1968)

Bücken, E., *Robert Schumann* (Cologne, 1940)

Burk, J.N., *Clara Schumann: A Romantic Biography* (New York, 1940)

Calvocoressi, M.D., *Schumann* (Paris, 1912)

Chantavoine, J., *La jeunesse de Schumann* (Paris, 1912)

Chissell, J., *Schumann* (London, 1962; 4th ed. 1977)

Coeuroy, A., *Robert Schumann* (Paris, 1950)

Creuzburg, E., *Die Gewandhauskonzerte zu Leipzig* (Leipzig, 1931)

Dahms, W., *Schumann* (Stuttgart, 1916)

Dörffer, A., *Geschichte der Gewandhauskonzerte* (Leipzig, 1884)

Dorn, H., *Aus meinem Leben* (3 vols, Berlin, 1870-2)

Eismann, G., *Robert Schumann: Ein Quellenwerk über sein Werk und Schaffen* (2 vols, Leipzig, 1956)

Erler, H., *Robert Schumann: Aus seinen Briefen geschildert* (2 vols, Berlin, 1887)

Felber, R., 'Schumann's Place in German Song' (*Musical Quarterly* XXVI, 1940)

Fischer-Dieskau, D., *Robert Schumann: Wort und Musik* (Stuttgart, 1981)

Flechsig, E., 'Erinnerungen an Robert Schumann' (*Neue Zeitschrift für Musik* CXVII, 1956)

Fuller-Maitland, J.A., *Robert Schumann* (London, 1884)

Garrison, F.H., 'The Medical History of Robert Schumann and his Family' (*Bulletin of the New York Academy of Medicine,* 1934)

Gensel, J., *Robert Schumanns Briefwechsel mit Henriette Voigt* (Leipzig, 1892)

Gertler, W., *Robert Schumann in seinen frühen Klavierwerken* (Wolfenbüttel, 1931)

Hanslick, E., 'Robert Schumann in Endenich' (in Hanslick, *Am Ende des Jahrhunderts,* Berlin, 1899)

——*Aus dem Tagebuch eines Musikers* (Berlin, 1892)

——*Aus meinem Leben* (Berlin, 1894)

Henning, L., *Die Freundschaft Clara Schumanns und Johannes Brahms* (Zurich, 1952)

Hiller, F., *Briefe an eine Unbekannte* (Leipzig, 1877)

Homeyer, H., *Grundbegriffe der Musikanschauung Robert Schumanns* (Münster, 1956)

Hueffer, F., *Die Poesie in der Musik* (Leipzig, 1874)

Jacobs, R.L., 'Schumann and Jean Paul' (*Music and Letters* XXX, 1949)

Jansen, F.G., *Die Davidsbündler: Aus Robert Schumanns Sturm-und-Drang Periode* (Leipzig, 1883)

——'Briefwechsel zwischen Robert Schumann und Robert Franz' (*Die Musik* VIII, 1908-9)

Joss, V., *Friedrich Wieck und sein Verhältnis zu Robert Schumann* (Dresden, 1888)

——*Der Musikpädagoge Friedrich Wieck und seine Familie* (Leipzig, 1902)

Kalbeck, M., 'Aus Robert Schumanns Jugendzeit' (*Oesterreichische Rundschau,* 1883)

Kerner, D., *Krankheiten grosser Musiker* (Stuttgart, 1963)

Kleinebreil, H., *Der kranke Schumann* (Jena, 1943)

Das Konigliche Conservatorium der Musik in Leipzig (Leipzig, 1893)

Korte, W., *Robert Schumann* (Potsdam, 1927)

Kötz, H., *Der Einfluss Jean Pauls auf Robert Schumann* (Weimar, 1933)

La Mara, *Robert Schumann* (Leipzig, 1911)

Laux, K., *Robert Schumann* (Leipzig, 1972)

Legge, R.H., 'Letters from Brahms to Schumann' (*Studies in Music* ed. R. Grey, London, 1901)

Linder, M. *Die Psychose Robert Schumanns* (Basel, 1959)

Litzmann, B. *Clara Schumann: Ein Künstlerleben* (3 vols, Leipzig, 1902)

—— *Letters of Clara Schumann and Johannes Brahms 1853-1896* (London, 1927)

Macmaster, H., *La folie de Robert Schumann* (Paris, 1928)

Meichsner, F., *Friedrich Wieck und seine beiden Töchter* (Leipzig, 1875)

Möbius, P.J., *Über Robert Schumanns Krankheit* (Halle, 1906)

Moser, H.J. and Rebling E. (eds.) *Robert Schumann. Aus Anlass seines 100. Todestages* (Leipzig, 1956)

Mendelssohn-Bartholdy, F., *Briefe aus den Jahren 1830-1847* (Leipzig, 1863)

Munte, F., *Verzeichnis des deutschsprachigen Schrifttums über Robert Schumann* (Hamburg, 1972)

Niecks, F., *Robert Schumann. A Supplementary and Corrective Biography* (London, 1925)

Ninck, M., *Schumann und die Romantik in der Musik* (Heidelberg, 1929)

Nussbaum, F., *Der Streit über Robert Schumanns Krankheit* (Cologne, 1923)

Petzoldt, R., *Robert Schumann, sein Leben in Bildern* (Leipzig, 1956)

—— *Robert Schumann, Leben und Werk* (Leipzig, 1941)

Peyser, H.F., *Robert Schumann: Tone-Poet, Prophet and Critic* (New York, 1948)

Pitrou, R., *La vie intérieure de Robert Schumann* (Paris, 1925)

Plantinga, L.B., *Schumann as Critic* (Yale, 1967)

Pohl, R., 'Erinnerungen an Robert Schumann' (*Deutsche Revue* II, 1878)

Rehberg, P. and W., *Robert Schumann, sein Leben und Werk* (Zurich and Stuttgart, 1954)

Reinmann, H., *Robert Schumanns Leben und Werke* (Leipzig, 1887)

Rochefort, R., *Robert Schumann* (Paris, 1968)

Sammelbände der Robert-Schumann-Gesellschaft, Sitz Zwickau, Vols 1-2 (Leipzig, 1961, 1966)

Sams, E., 'Did Schumann use Ciphers?' (*Musical Times,* August 1965)

—— 'The Schumann Ciphers' (*Musical Times*, May 1966)

—— 'The Schumann Ciphers: A Coda' (*Musical Times*, December 1966)

—— *The Songs of Robert Schumann* (London, 1969; rev. ed. 1975)

—— 'A Schumann Primer?' (*Musical Times*, November 1970)

—— 'Schumann's Hand Injury' (*Musical Times*, December 1971)

Schauffler, R.H., *Florestan: The Life and Work of Robert Schumann* (New York, 1945)

Schnapp, F., *Heinrich Heine und Robert Schumann* (Hamburg and Berlin, 1924)

Schneider, L. and Maraschel, M., *Schumann, sa vie et ses oeuvres* (Paris, 1905)

Schoppe, M. and Neuhaus, G., *Das Robert-Schumann-Haus* in *Zwickau* (Zwickau, 1973)

Schumann, Clara, *Clara Schumann – Johannes Brahms. Briefe 1853-1896* (2 vols, Leipzig, 1927; tr. M. Savill as *A Passionate Friendship: Clara Schumann and Johannes Brahms,* London, 1956)

Schumann, Eugenie, *Erinnerungen* (Stuttgart 1925; tr. M. Busch, London, 1930) (*Memoirs of Eugenie Schumann,* tr. M. Busch [London, 1927])

—— *The Schumanns and Johannes Brahms* (New York, 1927)

—— *Robert Schumann: Ein Lebensbild meines Vaters* (Leipzig, 1931)

Schumann, Robert, *Jugendbriefe Robert Schumanns,* ed. Clara Schumann (Leipzig, 1885; tr. M. Herbert as *Early Letters*, London, 1888)

—— *Briefe: Neue Folge*, ed. F.G. Jansen (Leipzig, 1886; 3rd enlarged ed. 1904)

—— *Schumanns Briefe in Auswahl*, ed. K. Storck (Leipzig, 1910; tr. H. Bryant as *The Letters of Robert Schumann* London, 1907; reissued New York, 1979)

—— *Gesammelte Schriften über Musik und Musiker* ed. F.G. Jansen (Leipzig, 1891; 5th ed. ed by M. Kreisig, 1914)

—— *Tagebücher I* (Leipzig, 1971; 2 more volumes are planned)

—— *Der junge Schumann. Dichtungen und Briefe* ed. A. Schumann (Leipzig, 1910)

—— *Aus Robert Schumanns Briefen und Schriften* ed. R. Münnich (Weimar, 1956)

—— *The Musical World of Robert Schumann* ed. H. Pleasants (New York and London, 1865)

—— *Robert Schumann im eignen Wort* ed. W. Schuh (Zurich, 1967)

—— *Briefe und Notizen Robert und Clara Schumanns* ed. S. Kross (Bonn, 1978)

Robert Schumanns Düsseldorfer Jahre (Catalogue of an exhibition in the Heinrich-Heine-Institut, Düsseldorf, 1981)

Slater, E. and Meyer, A. 'Contributions to a Pathography of the Musicians: I. Robert Schumann' (*Confinia Psychiatrica* II, 1959)

Spitta, P., *Robert Schumann: Eine Lebensbild* (Leipzig, 1882)

—— 'Über Robert Schumanns Schriften' (in Spitta, *Musikge-schichtliche Aufsätze*, Berlin, 1894)

Springer, B., *Die genialen Syphilitiker* (Berlin, 1933)

Sutermeister, P., *Robert Schumann: Sein Leben nach Briefen, Tagebüchern und Erinnerungen* (Zurich, 1949)

Tessmer, H. *Der klingende Weg* (Regensburg, 1923)

—— *Robert Schumann* (Stuttgart, 1930)

Wagner, K. 'Robert Schumann als Schüler und Abiturient' (*Veröffentlichungen der Robert-Schumann-Gesellschaft* II, Zwickau, 1928)

Walker, A. (ed.), *Schumann: The Man and his Music* (London, 1972; rev. ed. 1976)

Wasielewski, J.W. von, *Robert Schumann: Eine Biographie* (Leipzig, 1858; 4th ed. 1906) (*Life of Robert Schumann with letters 1833-1852* tr. A.L. Alger [London, 1878])

—— *Schumanniana* (Bonn, 1883)

—— *Aus siebzig Jahren, Lebenserinnerungen* (Stuttgart/Leipzig, 1897)

—— 'Felix Mendelssohn-Bartholdy und Robert Schumann' (*Deutsche Revue* XIX, 1894)

Wieck, F., *Clavier und Gesang* (Leipzig, 1853)

Wieck, M., *Aus dem Kreise Wieck-Schumann* (Dresden, 1912)

Wolff, V.E., *Robert Schumanns Lieder in ersten und späteren Fassungen* (Leipzig, 1914)

Wörner, K., *Robert Schumann* (Zurich, 1949)

Young, P.M., *Tragic Muse: The Life and Works of Robert Schumann* (London, 1957)

General Index

Alexis, Willibald 52-4, 104
Allgemeine musikalische Zeit?urg 90-1,
101, 102, 259, 331
Allgemeiner musikalischer Anzeiger 75,
76, 77-8, 90, 163
Andersen, Hans Christian 187, 215, 232
Arnim, A. von 147
Arnim, Bettina von 252, 322-3
Arnold, J.K. 230
artist in society 106-7

Bach, Johann Sebastian 42, 278
  Art of Fugue 72
  Schumann on 71, 105
  Well-tempered Clavier 71, 82, 185,
  263
Banck, Carl 91, 111, 138, 146, 178
Bargiel, Adolf 49, 146
Baudissin, Count Wolf 268
Becker, Alfred Julius 175
Becker, Carl Ferdinand 174, 221-2
Becker, Ernst 146, 148-9, 183
Becker, Ruppert 288, 315, 316
Beethoven Ludwig van 105, 144, 147,
  166, 177, 194, 204, 216, 250
Behrens, Stadtrat 176
Bendemann, Eduard 243, 264, 267, 280,
  282
Bennett, William Sterndale 76, 140-2,
  146, 324-5
Berger, Ludwig 109
Berlioz, Hector 89, 105, 126, 212, 224
Böttger, Adolph 208
Brahms, Johannes 76, 195, 296, 313,
  317, 320-1, 328

and Schumann's Violin Concerto 307
appearance 310
on *Faust* 239
relationship with Clara 321-2, 326
visits Schumann 308-11, 318, 321, 322
Braun, Ferdinand 291
Breitkopf and Härtel 90, 114
Brendel, Franz 93, 259
Bruch, Max 253
Bülow, Hans von 274
Burgmüller, Norbert 76
Burns, Robert 186, 272
Byron, George Gordon 255, 257, 259-60

Carus, Agnes 32-3, 35, 47
Casals, Pablo 284
chamber music 71, 216-20, 283, 333
Chamisso, Adalbert von 39, 187, 189,
  198, 199
Cherubini, Luigi 105
Chopin, Frédéric François 17, 83-4, 101,
  158
  and *Carnaval* 115
  in Leipzig 122-3
  Schumann on 75-8, 105-6, 193, 217
Chorley, Henry 323
Cimarosa, Domenico 241
Classicism 14, 72, 127-8, 272ß
  and Schumann's orchestral music
  207, 246-7
  v. Romanticism 205-6
Cohn, Martin 315
Cologne cathedral 286-7
concert overtures 207, 289
'correspondances' 110

d'Aranyi, Jelly 307
David, Félicien 94, 225
David, Ferdinand 140, 222, 254, 264
'Davidsbündler' 31, 78, 82-3, 93, 95-6,
    102-4, 113, 118, 174
Debussy, Claude 89
Devrient, Eduard 124, 267, 280, 332
Devrient, Johanne 170, 172, 178, 224
Dietrich, Albert 296, 302, 315, 316, 318,
    328
Döhner, Archidiaconus Hermann 24-6
Doppelgänger device 39, 74
Dorn, Heinrich 70-1, 79-80, 96, 123
Dresden 21, 234-5, 263-4, 266, 269-70,
    280, 290
Droste-Hülshoff, Annette von 247
Düsseldorf 277, 281-3
    Musikverein 281, 296-8, 302, 311-13
Dvořak, Antonin 284

Ehlert, Louis 223
Eichendorff, Joseph von 186-7, 198-9,
    251, 272, 291
Elgar, Edward 284

Field, John 76
Fink, Gottfried Wilhelm 77, 90
Flechsig, Emil 20, 28, 31-2, 35-8, 39,
    45-8, 51, 60, 226
Florestan and Eusebius 77-9, 82, 95-8,
    115, 118-20, 123, 128-31, 144, 153,
    208, 302
    see also 'Davidsbündler'
Frege, Livia 227, 232
Freiligrath, Hermann Ferdinand 268
Fricken, Baron Ignaz von 111-12, 118
Fricken, Ernestine von 110-13, 114, 132,
    133, 138, 178
Friedrich, Caspar David 13, 89
Friedrich August, King of Saxony 21,
    221
Friedrich Wilhelm IV, King of Prussia
    268

Gade, Niels 232, 253, 279, 283
Geibel, Emanual von 198, 252, 290, 291
Gluck, Christoph Willibald 194
Goethe, Johann Wolfgang von 38, 42,
    52-3, 61, 63, 92, 199, 272-4
    and bettina von Arnim 147
    and *Faust* 237-40, 274, 291
    and *Myrthen* 186

concept of songwriters 194
    Wilhelm Meister 82, 273
'Göttinger Hainbund' 31
Grädener, Karl 278, 323
Grieg, Edvard 192
Grillparzer, Franz 74, 151, 251
Grimm, Otto 318, 323

Hallé, Charles 165
Handel, George Frederick 55, 264
Hanslick, Eduard 15, 130, 250, 258-9,
    310, 323, 333
Häring, Wilhelm *see* Alexis, Willibald
Härtel, Wilhelm 156, 180
Hartmann, Johannes 93n
Hasenclever, Dr Richard 302, 316-7
Hauptmann, Moritz 221, 254
Haydn, Joseph 105, 216
Hebbel, Friedrich 256-7, 272, 311
Heidelberg 43, 51-2, 54, 56, 57, 60
Heine, Heinrich 13, 43, 165
    and Doppelgänger device 39, 74
    Buch der Lieder 43, 189, 196-8
    Schumann on 44
    songs 186-7, 188-9, 195, 200, 272
Helbig, Dr 235-6
Heller, Stephen 165, 323
Hempel, Liddy 35, 39, 111
Hensel, Fanny 252, 254
Henselt, Adolph 230
Herz, Henri 64, 87, 146
Hiller, Ferdinand 94, 232, 243-4, 253,
    275, 279, 281, 303, 304
Hirschbach, Hermann 76, 143, 157, 193
Hoffmann, E.T.A. 13, 39, 47, 74, 78,
    90, 309
    and *Faschingsschwank* 168
    and Nachtstücke 167
    Doge und Dogaresse 187, 255
    Fantasiestücke in Callots Manier 154
    Kreisler *alter ego* 110, 158, 188
    on music as romantic art 117
    review of Beethoven's Fifth
        Symphony 98
    'Serapion Brotherhood' 31, 95-6
Hofmeister, Friedrich 91, 98-9, 102
Hölderlin, Johann Christian Friedrich
    311
Horn, Moritz 290
Hübner, Julius 243, 264
Hummel, Johann Nepomuk 63, 65, 75
Humperdinck, Engelbert 253

Jansen, F. Gustav 12
Jean Paul *see* Richter, Jean Paul
    Friedrich
Joachim, Joseph 221, 303, 317, 323,
    327, 328
    and Brahms 309, 313, 320
    and F.A.E. Sonata 296
    and *Fantasie* (Op. 131) 306
    and Liszt 279, 299
    and Mendelssohn 127, 243
    and Schumann's Violin Concerto 307
    visits Schumann 321
July Revolution 60

Kalkbrenner, Friedrich 64, 87
Keferstein, Gustav Adolph 179, 182,
    240
Kerner, Justinus 47, 129, 198
Kirchner, Theodor 76, 192
Klitsch, Carl 283
Knorr, Julius 91-2, 99, 174
Komet 95, 108
Krüger, Eduard 225, 236-7
Kulenkampff, Georg 307
Kulmann, Elisabeth 292
Kuntzsch, Johann Gottfried 25-6, 70,
    279
Kurrer, Dr Heinrich von 44

large-scale works 210, 239, 245, 276,
    285, 290-1, 335
late works 276
Laurens, J.J. 305
Leipzig 18, 41-3, 45-7, 48 *et passim*
    Conservatoire 221-3
    Gewandhaus 42-3, 82, 83 *et passim*
    provincial 162
    Schumann on 233
    Thomaskirche 42, 64, 109, 222
Leser, Rosalie 316-17, 321
Lind, Jenny 249-51, 278, 323
Lipinski, Carl 241
List, Emilie and Elise 164, 183, 209, 224
Liszt, Franz 50, 83, 89, 92, 101, 116,
    264-5, 274, 279, 299, 323
    and Clara 151, 211-12
    and managers 151-2
    and *Manfred* 261, 300
    dedicatee of *Fantasie* 144-6
    in Leipzig 179-82 *et passim*
    on *Carnaval* 115, 151, 180
    on Schubert 205

on Schumann 180, 206
on Sonata No. 3 139
repertoire 180-1
Schumann on 76, 105, 180
technique 180
visits Düsseldorf 293
Litzmann, Berthold 12, 319
Lobe, Johann Christian 259
Lorenz, Oswald 163, 172
Luther, Martin 289, 293
Lvov, Alexis 230
Lyser, Johann Peter 87, 91, 102, 109

Marbach, Oswald, 247, 255
'Marriage Book' 184-5
Marseillaise 289-90
Mendelssohn-Bartholdy, Felix 17, 76,
    83-4, 175, 224, 232, 244, 245, 248,
    278-9
    and Bach 55, 105, 124
    and Bennett 140-1
    conducts Schubert 167
    death 253-5
    duet with Clara 202-3
    'F. Meritis' 103, 126
    in Leipzig 123-7 *et passim*
    meets Chopin 123
    on managers 151-2
    on Schumann 127
    plays Beethoven 173
    Royal Saxon Kapellmeister 221-2
    Schumann on 254, 265, 278-9
Meyerbeer, Giacomo 164, 251, 265, 277
Mitterwurzer, Anton 274
Moore, Gerald 194
Moore, Thomas 211, 225-6
Mörike, Eduard Friedrich 271, 272, 291
Moscheles, Ignaz 57, 58, 113-14, 152,
    254, 279, 299
    on Sonatas 128-9, 139
Mozart, Wolfgang Amadeus 104, 194,
    204, 216, 225
Müller, Christian Gottlieb 203

Neue Zeitschrift für Musik 83, 88, 93-4,
    98-107, 108-9, 123, 125-6, 128-9,
    161, 163, 166-7, 176, 211-12
    et passim
Neun, Wilfried von der 291
Nicholas, Tsar 230
Niecks, Frederick 67, 138, 252
Novalis 47, 89, 97
Novello, Clara 157, 303

Ortlepp, Ernst 91, 175

Paganini, Niccolò 58, 63, 101, 115
Palestrina 55, 264
Platen-Hallermünde, August von 291,
    313
Pohl, Richard 260, 289, 290, 293-4, 299
Pohlenz, Christian August 109, 125, 222
Portius, Karl 84-5
'programme' music 73-4, 116, 205, 287,
    290-1

Ravel, Maurice 206
Redern, Count 252
Reichardt, Johann Friedrich 194
Reimers, Christian 288
Reinecke, Carl 297
Reinick, Robert 187, 256-7
Rellstab, Ludwig 73, 90
Reuter, Dr Moritz 67, 174, 175, 176,
    183, 299
Richarz, Dr Franz 249, 317, 318-19,
    324-7
Richter, Carl Ernst 27, 33, 34
Richter, Jean Paul Friedrich 13, 38-9,
    43-4, 46, 47, 53, 71, 77-8, 120, 124,
    278, 301
    Flegeljahre 73-4, 117-18, 129, 188
Rieffel, Amalie 182-3
Ries, Mme Ferdinand 53
Rietschel, Ernst 243
Robert-Schumann-Haus, Zwickau
    11-12, 15-16, 20, 185
Rochlitz, Friedrich 90
Röller, Eduard 60
Romanticism 13, 14, 29, 37, 72, 89, 96,
    116, 120, 127-8
    and Schumann's piano music 207
    v. Classicism 205-6, 334
    and *Genoveva* 258
    and song writing 272
Rosen, Gisbert 43, 48, 59
Rossini, Gioacchimo 105, 248
Rostropovitch, Mstislav 284
Rubinstein, Anton 130, 180, 214, 250
Rückert, Friedrich 186, 199-200, 264
Rudel, Gottlob 34, 41, 55
Ruppius, Frau 24

Saint-Saëns, Camille 284
Saloman, Hedwig 318
Sams, Eric 14, 69

Sayn-Wittgenstein, Carolyne von 293
Schadow, Johann Gottfried 252, 282
Schadow, Willhelm 282, 287
Schiller, Johann Christoph Friedrich
    von 31, 33, 38, 120, 289
Schlegel, August Wilhelm 89
Schlegel, Friedrich 89, 144, 145
Schnabel, Abraham Gottlieb 17-18
Schnabel, Karl Gottlob 230
Schoenberg, Arnold 90
Schröder-Devrient, Wilhelmine 179, 198
Schubart, Christian Friedrich Daniel 30
Schubert, Ferdinand 166
Schubert, Franz (violinist) 94
Schubert, Franz Theodor 17, 32-3, 47,
    56, 105, 166-7, 194-5, 315
Schumann, August (father) 17-20, 21,
    23, 27, 30, 32-4, 43-4, 46, 58, 71,
    234
Schumann, Christiane (mother) 13, 17-
    18, 19, 23-4, 30, 32, 34, 41, 45, 48,
    55, 58, 74, 86, 134-7
Schumann, Clara Josephine (wife) 39,
    104
    and Brahms 309-11, 321-2
    and Ernestine von Fricken 113, 121
    and Liszt 211-12, 264-5, 293
    as a child 49-50, 51, 59, 63-4
    'Cecilia' 82
    character 134
    'Chiara' 126
    children born 202, 213, 240, 248-9,
        261, 318
    concert tours 63-4, 122, 133-4, 147,
        151-2, 155, 161, 164, 173, 182, 214-
        15, 223, 229, 249-52, 277-8, 313,
        320, 324-5
    courtship 133-7, 147-50
    diaries 11, 12, 64, 202, *et passim*
    distress at separation 150-1
    education 184, 185
    engagement 149
    feast day 103-4
    first kiss 122, 133
    Kaiserlich Königliche Kammer-
        virtuosin 151, 178
    last visit to Schumann 326-7
    letters 11, 83 *et passim*
    loneliness 122, 134, 151, 165, 173,
        215, 320
    marriage 67, 69-70, 134, 177-9, 184-5,
        186, 201-2

on Bettina von Arnim 147
on citizens of Hamburg 278
on Dresden Revolt 269-70
on Hans Christian Andersen 215
on her father 176
on Kuntzsch 25
on orchestral composition 204, 246
on Wagner 83
piano playing 63-4, 283
Piano Concerto 146
plays to Chopin 123
plays with Mendelssohn 203, 244
repertoire 177, 202-3, 214, 250, 325, 333-4
Schumann's champion 333-4
Schumann's inspiration 186-8, 200
Schumann, Eduard (brother) 17, 33, 41, 74, 85, 99, 171
Schumann, Elise (daughter) 223-4, 229, 262, 269, 305
Schumann, Emilie (sister) 17, 33-4, 73-4
Schumann, Emil (son) 248, 252
Schumann, Eugenie (daughter) 213, 296, 302, 307, 310
Schumann, Felix (son) 318, 320
Schumann, Julie (daughter) 240, 252, 262, 269
Schumann, Julius and Karl (brothers) 17, 30, 33, 41, 52, 74, 82, 85-6, 99, 175, 229
Schumann, Laura (sister) 17
Schumann, Ludwig (son) 262, 269
Schumann, Marie (daughter) 213-14, 262, 269, 293, 294-5, 316
Schumann, Robert Alexander
    and 'daylight' 271
    and Leipzig Conservatoire 187, 222-3
    and politics 46, 187, 267-8
    and quotations 99
    and spiritualism 84-5, 304-5
    and von Fricken's theme 118
    and women 48, 57-8, 81-2
    appearance 71, 93-4, 182-3, 230-1, 288, 305
    assessed 334-5
    attempts suicide 316
        autopsy 327
    awarded Ph.D 179
    ballads 290-1, 299, 311
    'Briefbuch' 12, 185
    born 17
    childhood 24-6

comes of age 71
compared to Bach 207
compared to Chopin and Mendelssohn 83-4
composition 47-8, 172, 186-7, 191, 208, 283
conductor 12, 213, 223, 250, 279, 283, 296-8, 311-13
death 327-8
diaries 11, 35-6, 39, 48, 56-7 *et passim*
diffidence 94, 222-3, 227, 230-3, 278, 288, 294, 296-7, 332
drunkenness 178
extravagance 46, 52, 55, 60, 65, 138
family man 294-5
fondness for champagne and cigars 36, 47-8, 84, 93-4, 237, 301, 319
founds *New Zeitschrift* 93, 99-107
fragmentation 210
habit of revision 119-21, 128-9
hallucinations 236, 248, 314, 327
Haushaltsbücker 12, 301, 302, 307, 308
health 235-7, 240, 266, 300
homesick 45ß
hypochondria 80-1, 85, 106, 248
improvisation 172, 324
income 109, 220
inconsistency 291-2
in Berlin 176
in Russia 229-32
in Vienna 162-4, 166-71, 249-50
individualism 207
injured hand 65-9
letters 11, 12-13, 27 *et passim*
literary bent 29-32, 36-9, 161, 188, 195, 199, 292, 301, 314
manic depression 60-1, 80, 86-7, 92-3, 134-5, 231, 235-6, 275, 277, 327
on indivisibility of arts 97-8
on keyboard gymnasts 101-2
on Law 45
on Lieder 182, 192, 193-4, 255
on piano composition 204, 206
opera, ideas for 255-6
orchestration 206-7, 209, 213
originality 79, 330-31
pattern of work 252-3
personality 13, 24, 39-40
pianist 25, 29, 46-7, 49, 53, 56-7, 65-70
'Project Book' 223, 255

rudeness 241, 280
schooling 24-8, 31-2, 36-8
self portrait 62
shortsightedness 67, 288
student 49-60
studies counterpoint 240, 244, 247
syphilis 57-8, 68-70, 139, 275-6, 300.
   327-8
terminal illness 249, 300, 314, 316-28
vertigo 67, 248
see *also* Florestan *and* index of
   individual works
Schumann, Rosalie (sister-in-law) 73, 85
Schumann, Therese (sister-in-law) 48,
   56, 73-4, 145, 171
Schünemann, Georg 307
Schunke, Ludwig 87-8, 92, 99, 108
Scott, Sir Walter 19-20, 21, 52
Semmel, Moritz 48, 67
Semper, Gottfried 243, 270
'Serapion Brotherhood' 31, 95-6
Serre, Major 248, 269
Seume, Johann Gottfried 27, 292
Sire, Simonin de 66-7, 159
Spohr, Louis 180, 208, 279
Steffen, Emilie 252-3
Stifter, Adalbert 251
Strackerjan, August 314
Strachwitz, Moritz von 291
Strauss, Richard 116, 195
Stravinsky, Igor 89
Strelizki, Anton 180
Suckow, Karl von 260
symphonic poem 116, 205
synaesthesia 110

Tausch, Julius 281, 302, 303, 311-13
Tchaikovsky, Piotr Ilyich 13, 297, 333
Thibaut, Prof. Anton 54, 58
Tieck, Ludwig 89, 90, 97, 256, 257
Töpken, Theodor 56, 58, 66, 67-8, 182
Tovey, Donald Francis 308

Uhland, Ludwig 290, 291, 293, 299

Verhulst, Johannes 213, 237, 313
Viardot-Garcia, Pauline 164, 252
Voigt, Carl and Henriette 88, 103,
   109-10, 112-13, 125, 129, 141, 224

Wackenroder, Wilhelm 97
Wagner, Johanna 267
Wagner, Minna 242, 264
Wagner, Richard 13, 36, 45, 76, 79, 83,
   89, 105, 124, 126, 203, 264, 270
   and *Genoveva* 256
   in Dresden 242-3 *et passim*
   Mein Leben 242
   Musician in Paris 98
   on the English 325
   visits Schumann 215-16
Walt and Vult *see* Richter, Jean Paul:
   Flegeljahre
Wasielewski, Josef von 67, 112, 213,
   222-3, 260, 283, 285, 288, 304-5,
   323-4, 331
Weber, Carl Maria von 29, 31, 34, 89,
   105, 243
Weber, Max von 240-1
Weingartner, Felix 209
Weinlig, Theodor 64
Wieck, Clementine 63, 111, 138, 174
Wieck, Friedrich 49-51, 56, 59, 60, 79,
   88, 92, 99, 110-13, 241-2
   as a teacher 50-1, 59, 63-8
   Clara's manager 151
   Clavier und Gesang 51, 68
   makes peace 201-2, 227-8
   Marie's manager 242
   'Meister Raro' 82, 154
   on Schumann's character 112
   opposes Schumann's suit 68-70, 104,
      133-9, 149-50, 155, 173-4, 176-9
Wieck, Marianne 49, 63, 146, 175-6,
   183, 317
Wieck, Marie 242
Wiedebein, Wilhelm 47
Wittgenstein, Princess Marie 256
Wolf, Hugo 194, 198, 205
Wordsworth, William 89

Zedtwitz, Christiane 112
Zedtwitz, Wilhelm 113
Zelter Carl Friedrich 124, 193-4
Zuccalmaglio, A.W.F. von 174-5,
   211-12, 288
Zwickau 11-12, 15-16, 17, 19, 20-8,
   31-9, 44-5 *et passim*

Index of Works

'Abegg' Variations (Op. 1) 57, 71-3, 115
Adagio and Allegro (Op. 70) 207, 271
Adventlied (Op. 71) 200, 264, 276, 283
Album für die Jugend (Op. 68) 106,
    156, 261-3
Albumblätter (Op. 124) 211
Allegro (Op. 8) 129, 203
Allerley ... 30
Arabeske (Op. 18) 169

Ballade vom Haidenknaben (Op. 122,
    No. 2) 311
'Barricade Marches' (Op. 76) 268
Beim Abschied zu Singen (Op. 84) 252,
    253
Blätter und Blümchen ... 30
Blumenstücke (Op. 19) 169
Braut von Messina (Op. 100) 207, 289,
    293
Briefe 12

Carnaval (Op. 9) 36, 72-3, 77, 103, 104,
    113-16, 127-8, 151, 153, 167, 180,
    332-4
Cello Concerto (Op. 129) 284-5, 308
Concert Allegro ... (Op. 134) 245
Corsair 255

Davidsbündlertänze (Op. 6) 104, 152-4
Dichtergarten 301, 314
Dichterliebe (Op. 48) 71, 187, 189, 192,
    196-8, 200

Etudes symphoniques (Op. 13) 104,
    118-21, 127-8, 141, 147, 180

F.A.E. Sonata 296
Fantasie in C major (Op. 17) 142-6
Fantasie for Violin and Orchestra
    (Op. 131) 306
Fantasiestücke
    (Op. 12) 152, 154-5, 189, 191
    (Op. 73) 192, 271, 276
    (Op. 88) 207
    (Op. 111) 295
Faschingsschwank aus Wien (Op. 26)
    167-8, 188, 290
Festouverture (Op. 123) 303
'Flüchtlinge' 299
Frauenliebe ... (Op. 42) 71, 187, 189-90,
    192

Genoveva 253, 256-9, 264, 265, 277,
    279, 281
Gesänge der Fruhe (Op. 133) 299, 311
Glück von Edenhall (Op. 143) 299

Hermann und Dorothea (Op. 136) 289
'Hottentottiana' 36, 39
Humoreske (Op. 20) 169-70

Impromptus (Op. 5) 73, 85, 331
Instructions to Young Musicians 106,
    262-3, 333
Intermezzi (Op. 4) 73, 74-5, 208
Introduction and Allegro (Op. 143) 306
Introduction and Allegro appassionato
    ... (Op. 92) 245, 272, 284

Julius Caesar (Op. 128) 289, 321
Juniusabende und Julitage 31

Kinderball (Op. 130) 306
Kinderszenen (Op. 15) 116, 152, 156-8,
    165, 191
Klavierstücke (Op. 32) 167
Königssohn (Op. 116) 290
Konzertstück (Op. 86) 271, 284
Kreisleriana (Op. 16) 36, 98, 127, 152,
    157-60, 188, 231, 334 *see also*
    Hoffmann, E.T.A.

'Leben des Dichters' 37
Liederalbum für die Jugend (Op. 79)
    262
Liederkreis (Ops 24 and 39) 186, 188-9,
    198-9

Manfred (Op. 115) 261, 271, 294-5, 299,
    300, 301
Märchenbilder (Op. 113) 192
Marches for Piano (Op. 76) 272, 290
Mass (Op. 147) 290, 299, 311
Myrthen (Op. 25) 186, 199

Nachtstücke (Op. 23) 167, 189
Novelletten (Op. 21) 152, 156-7

(Ops 34, 36, 43) 187
(Op. 46) 224
(Ops 55 and 59) 248
(Op. 89) 291
(Op. 125) 292
Overture, Scherzo and Finale (Op. 52)
    210, 211

Vom Pagen und der Königstochter
    (Op. 140) 299
Papillons (Op. 2) 25, 36, 57, 73-5, 83,
    85, 103, 113, 117, 127, 153, 167,
    188, 331, 334
Paradies und die Peri (Op. 50) 224-7,
    252, 281, 323
Piano Concerto (Op. 54) 127, 191, 206,
    210, 244-5, 249, 250, 252, 255, 278,
    303, 313, 334
Piano Quartet (Op. 47) 71, 203, 217-20,
    252
Piano Quintet (Op. 44) 71, 203, 217-18,
    231, 252, 265

Piano Sonatas 204
    (No. 1, Op. 11) 104, 123, 128-9
    (No. 2, Op. 22) 129-31, 167, 207
    (No. 3, Op. 14) 139-40
    für die Jugend (Op. 118) 262
Piano Trios
    (No. 1, Op. 63) 253, 264-5
    (No. 2, Op. 88) 217
    (No. 3, Op. 110) 295

Requiem (Op. 148) 290, 299
Requiem für Mignon (Op. 98) 273-4,
    276
Romances for Oboe and Piano (Op. 74)
    272
Romanzen (Op. 84) 192
Romanzen und Balladen (Op. 64) 211
Rose Pilgerfahrt (Op. 112) 290, 299

7 Pieces in Fughetta Form (Op. 126) 311
Six Fugues on BACH (Op. 60) 72, 240
Six Studies after Caprices by Paganini
    (Ops 3 and 10) 83
Sonatas for Violin and Piano (Ops 105
    and 121) 295, 303
String Quartets (Op. 41) 71, 203, 207,
    216-17
Stücke im Volkston (Op. 102) 271
Studies and Sketches for Pedal Piano
    (Ops 56 and 58) 25, 240
Symphonies 33
    (No. 1) 71, 167, 203, 207-9, 214, 250,
        255, 331-2
    (No. 2) 211, 244, 246-8, 252, 293, 313
    (No. 3) 211, 284, 285-7, 313, 333
    (No. 4) 71, 206, 211, 212-13, 295, 303,
        331-2
    unfinished in G minor 83
Szenen aus Goethes Faust 232, 237-40,
    253, 274, 275, 291, 306

Three Romances (Op. 28) 173
Toccata (Op. 7) 73, 88
trios for female voices (Op. 114) 200

Violin Concerto 306, 307-8, 315, 317

Waldszenen (Op. 82) 271